Snow White with the Red Hair

Sorata Akiduki

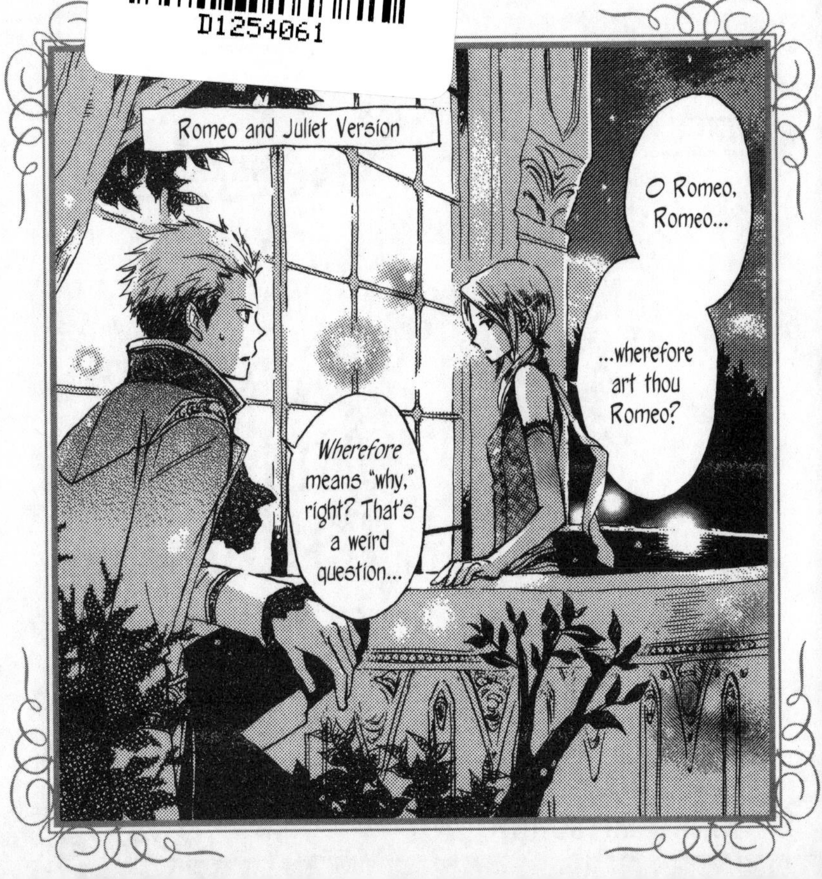
Romeo and Juliet Version
O Romeo, Romeo...
...wherefore art thou Romeo?
Wherefore means "why," right? That's a weird question...

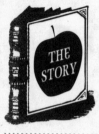

THE STORY

Shirayuki was born with beautiful hair as red as apples, but when her rare hair earns her unwanted attention from the notorious prince Raj, she's forced to flee her home. A young man named Zen helps her in the forest of the neighboring kingdom, Clarines, and it turns out he is that kingdom's second prince! Shirayuki decides to accompany Zen back to Wistal, the capital city of Clarines. In order to earn palace access and help out her new friends, Shirayuki takes the court herbalist exam.

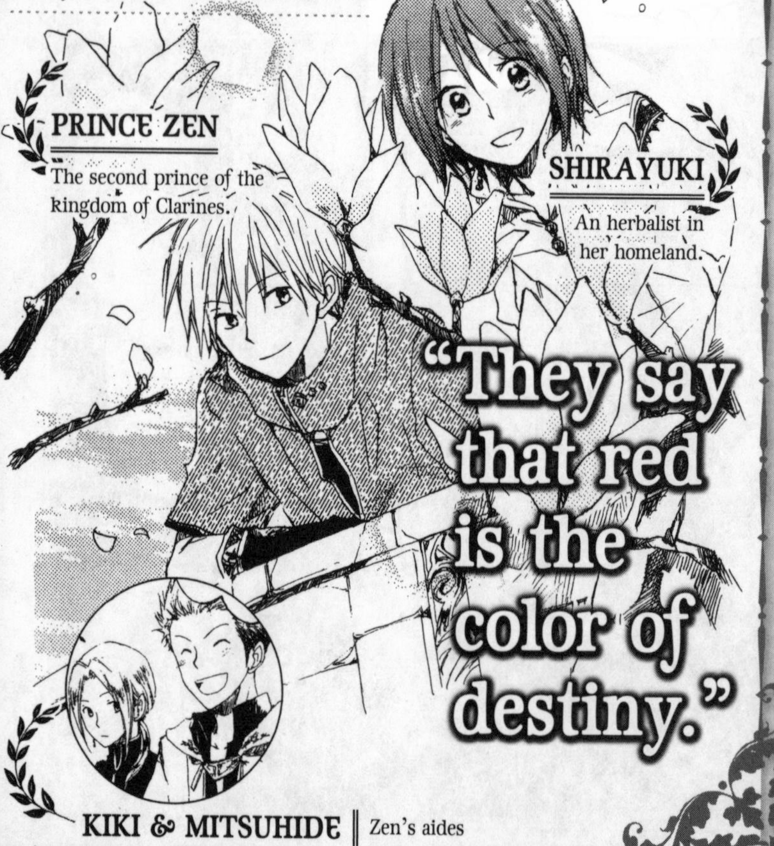
PRINCE ZEN
The second prince of the kingdom of Clarines.
SHIRAYUKI
An herbalist in her homeland.
"They say that red is the color of destiny."
KIKI & MITSUHIDE | Zen's aides

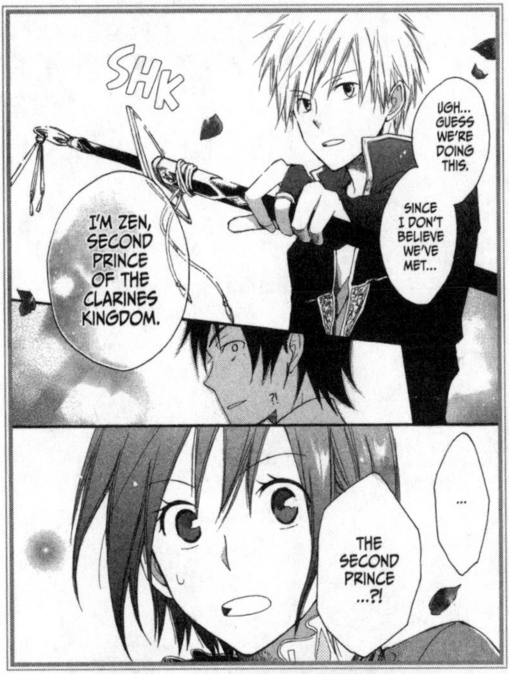
SHK
UGH... GUESS WE'RE DOING THIS.
SINCE I DON'T BELIEVE WE'VE MET...
I'M ZEN, SECOND PRINCE OF THE CLARINES KINGDOM.
...
THE SECOND PRINCE ...?!

If the selfish prince Raj had his way, Shirayuki would've become his concubine. Her savior? None other than the second prince of Clarines, Zen!

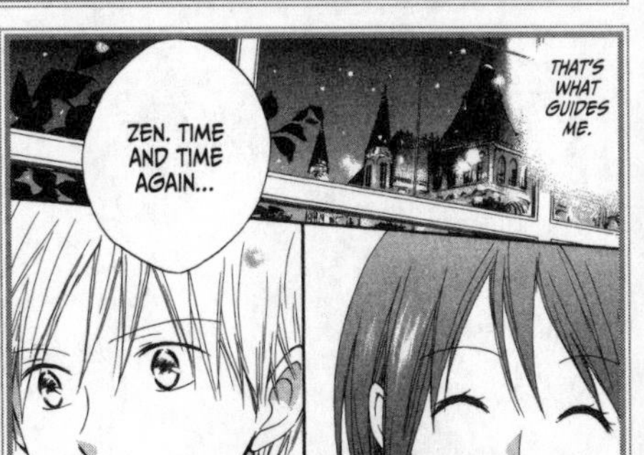
THAT'S WHAT GUIDES ME.
ZEN. TIME AND TIME AGAIN...
...YOU'VE GIVEN ME THE STRENGTH...
...TO KEEP MY CHIN UP.

Their hearts grow closer by the day, and now Shirayuki awaits the results of her court herbalist exam!

Snow White with the Red Hair

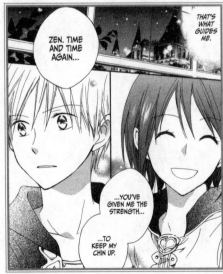

VOLUME 2
TABLE *of* CONTENTS

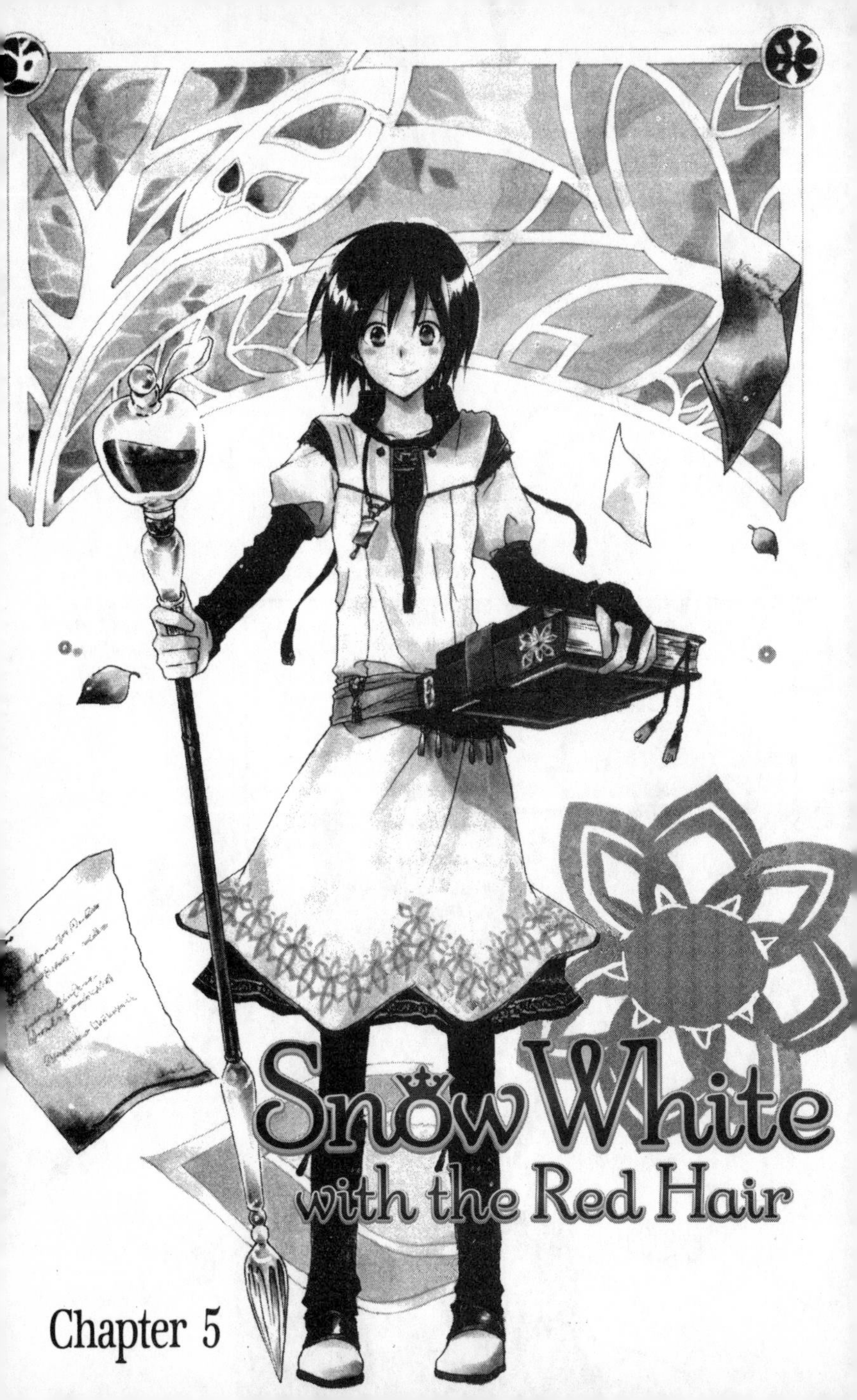
Snow White
with the Red Hair

Chapter 5

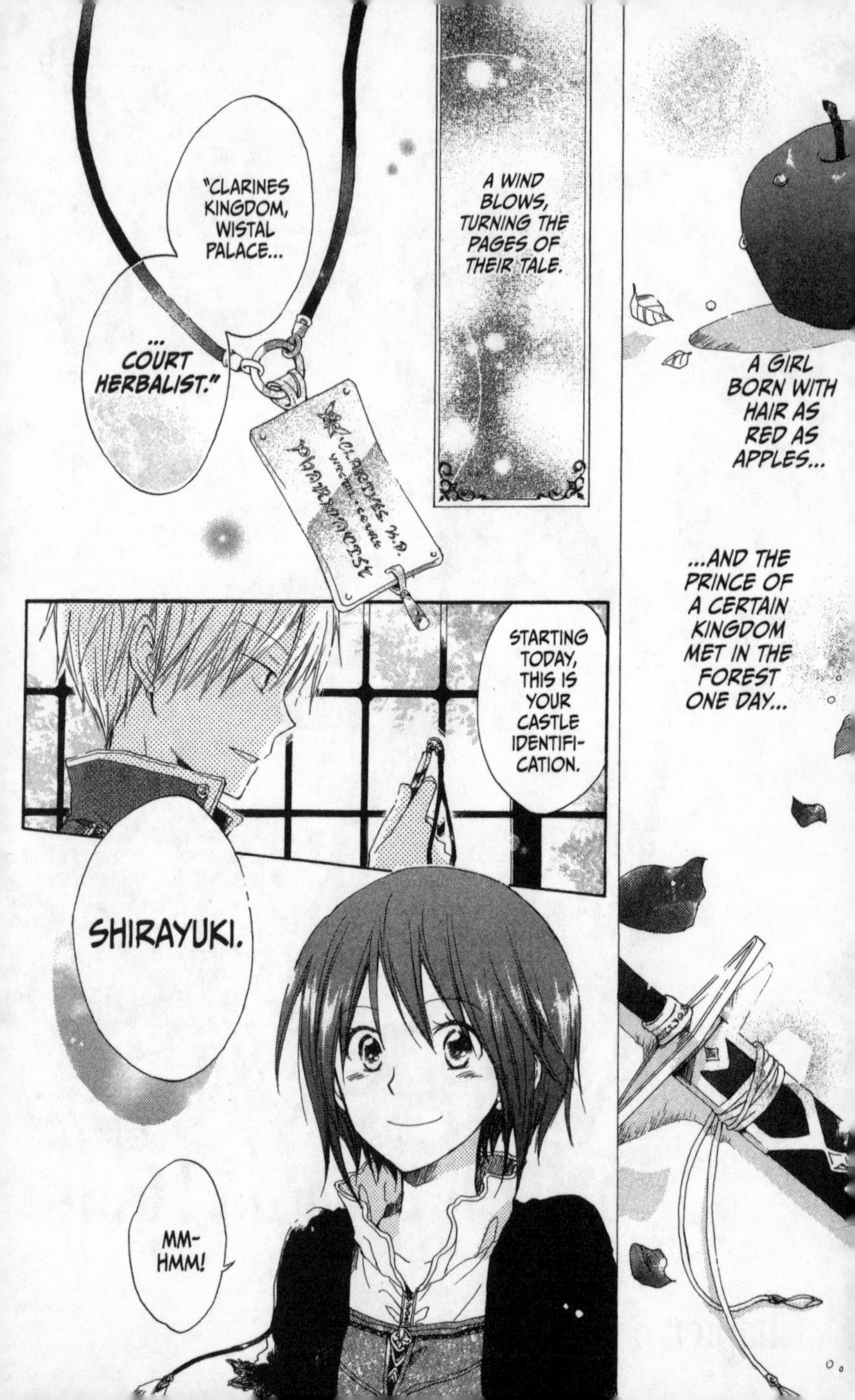
A GIRL BORN WITH HAIR AS RED AS APPLES...
...AND THE PRINCE OF A CERTAIN KINGDOM MET IN THE FOREST ONE DAY...
A WIND BLOWS, TURNING THE PAGES OF THEIR TALE.
"CLARINES KINGDOM, WISTAL PALACE...
...COURT HERBALIST."
STARTING TODAY, THIS IS YOUR CASTLE IDENTIFICATION.
SHIRAYUKI.
MM-HMM!

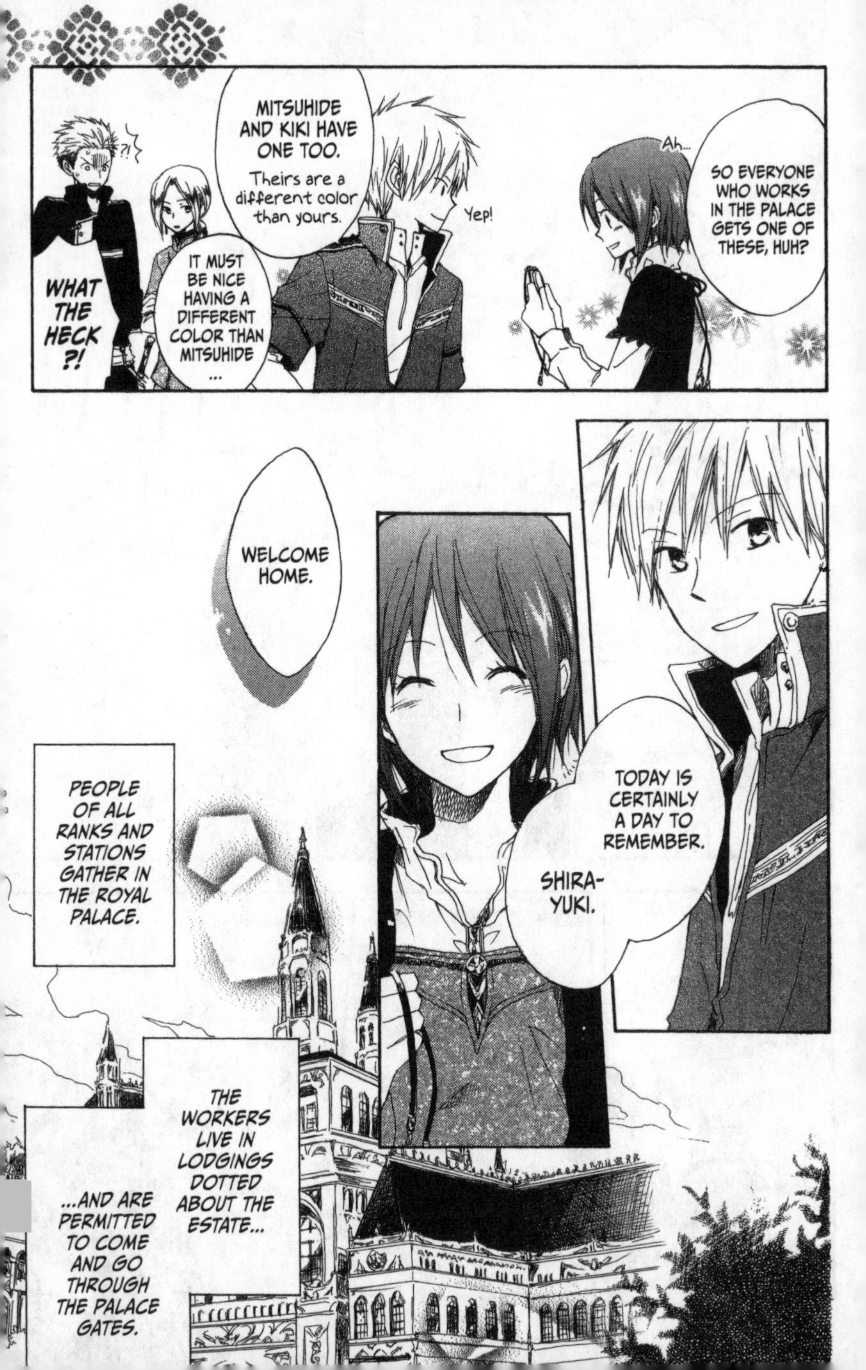
Ah...
SO EVERYONE WHO WORKS IN THE PALACE GETS ONE OF THESE, HUH?
Yep!
MITSUHIDE AND KIKI HAVE ONE TOO.
Theirs are a different color than yours.
IT MUST BE NICE HAVING A DIFFERENT COLOR THAN MITSUHIDE...
?!
WHAT THE HECK?!
TODAY IS CERTAINLY A DAY TO REMEMBER.
SHIRAYUKI.
WELCOME HOME.
PEOPLE OF ALL RANKS AND STATIONS GATHER IN THE ROYAL PALACE.
THE WORKERS LIVE IN LODGINGS DOTTED ABOUT THE ESTATE...
...AND ARE PERMITTED TO COME AND GO THROUGH THE PALACE GATES.

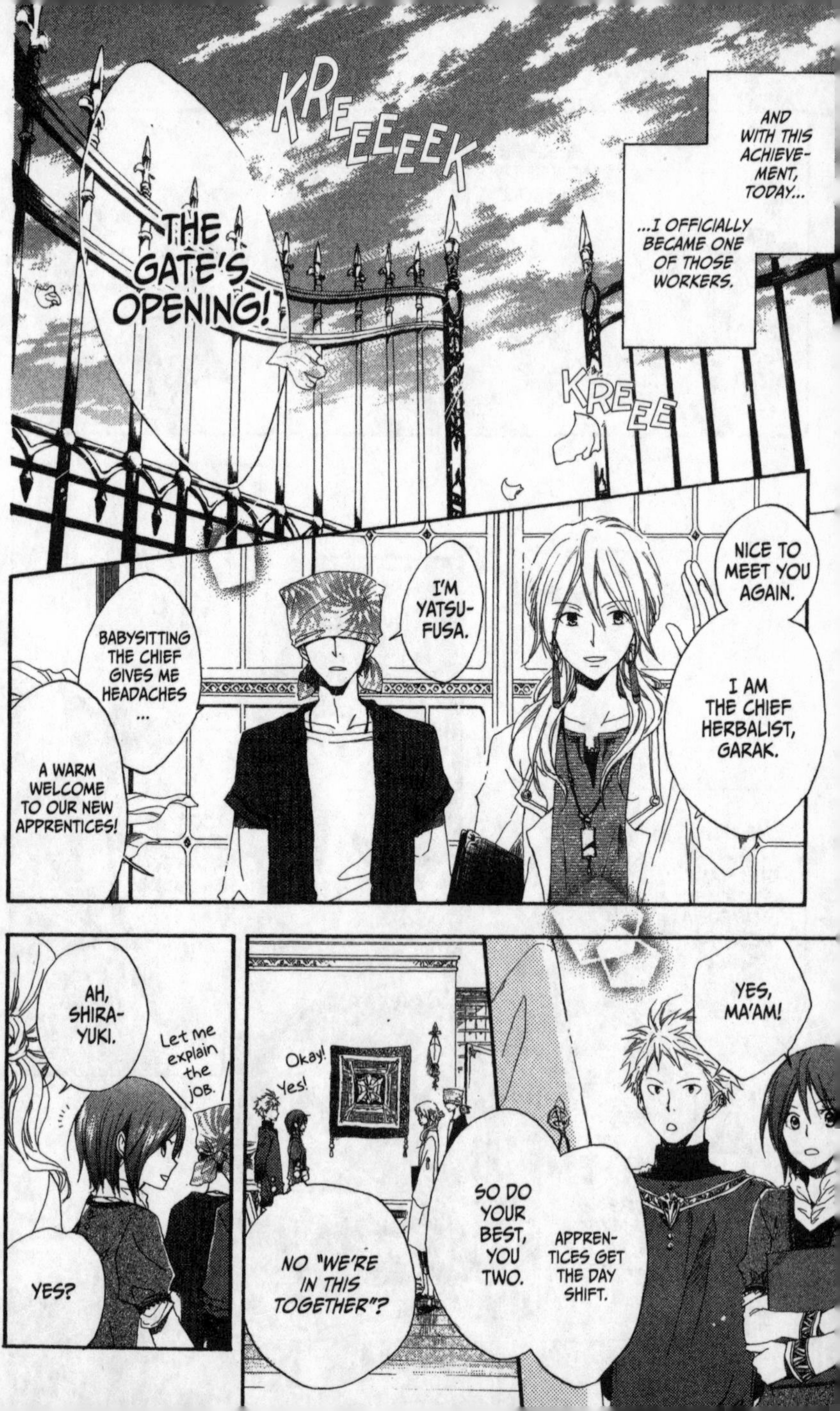
AND WITH THIS ACHIEVEMENT, TODAY...
...I OFFICIALLY BECAME ONE OF THOSE WORKERS.
KREEEEEK
THE GATE'S OPENING!
KREEE
NICE TO MEET YOU AGAIN.
I AM THE CHIEF HERBALIST, GARAK.
I'M YATSUFUSA.
BABYSITTING THE CHIEF GIVES ME HEADACHES...
A WARM WELCOME TO OUR NEW APPRENTICES!
YES, MA'AM!
APPRENTICES GET THE DAY SHIFT.
SO DO YOUR BEST, YOU TWO.
NO "WE'RE IN THIS TOGETHER"?
Okay!
Yes!
AH, SHIRAYUKI.
Let me explain the job.
YES?

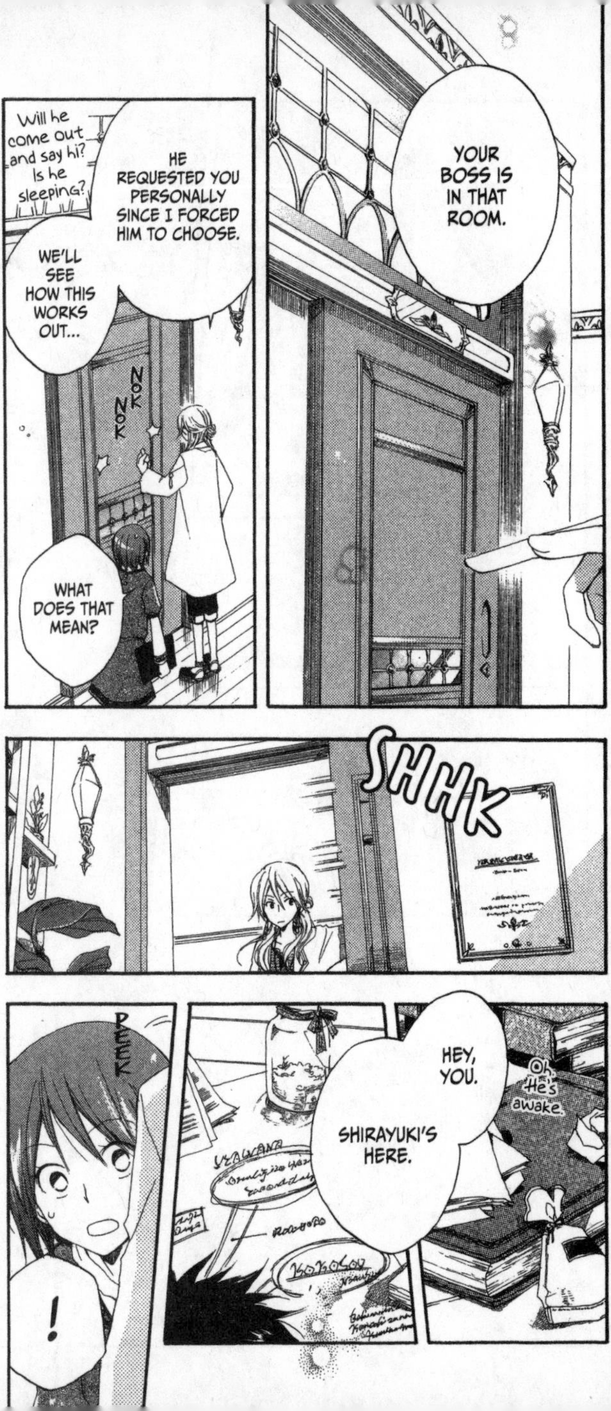
YOUR BOSS IS IN THAT ROOM.
HE REQUESTED YOU PERSONALLY SINCE I FORCED HIM TO CHOOSE.
Will he come out and say hi? Is he sleeping?
WE'LL SEE HOW THIS WORKS OUT...
NOK NOK
WHAT DOES THAT MEAN?
SHHK
Oh. He's awake.
HEY, YOU.
SHIRAYUKI'S HERE.
PEEK
!

Greetings!

Hello. I'm Sorata Akiduki. Thanks for purchasing volume 2 of *Snow White with the Red Hair*!

It's volume 2...

I'm already sentimental. I hope you enjoy it.

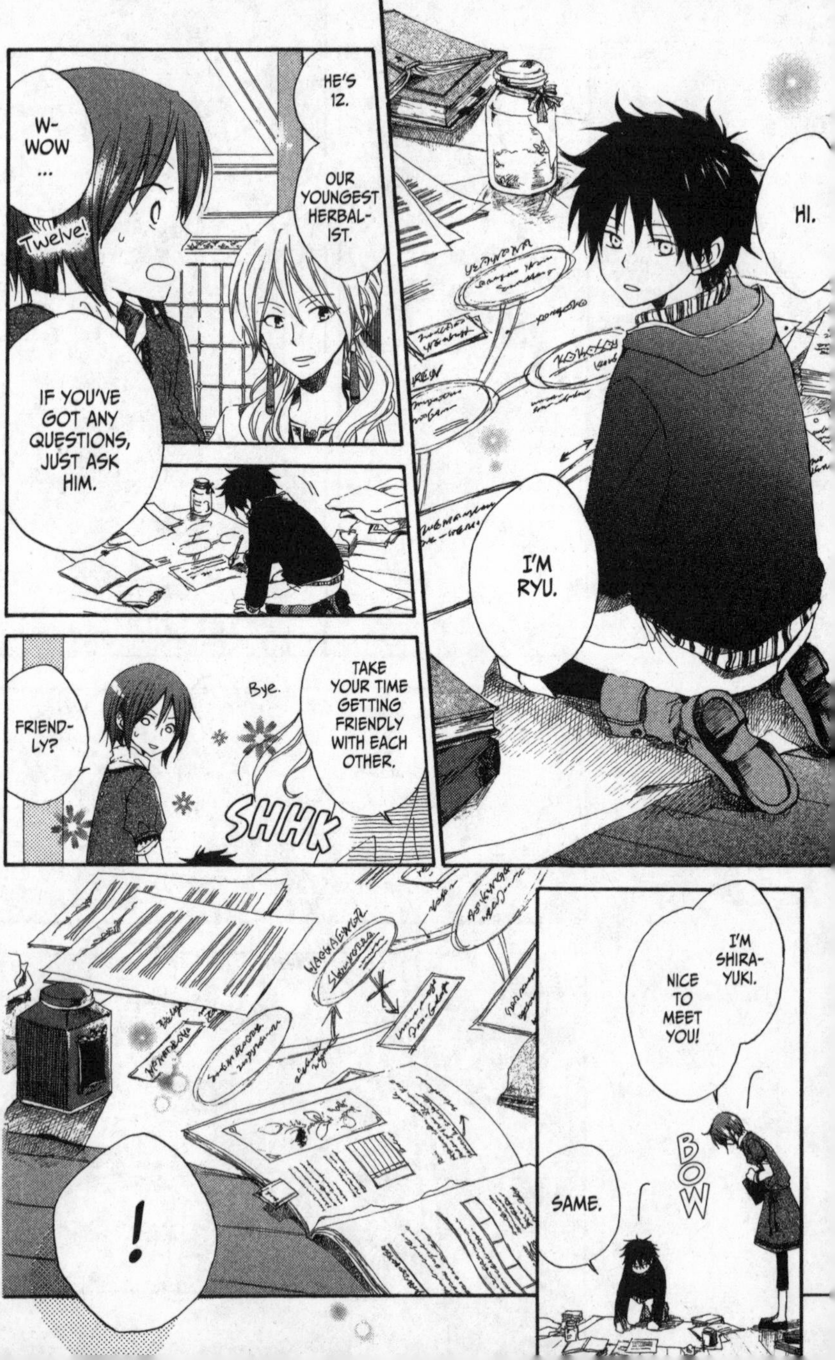
HI.
I'M RYU.
HE'S 12.
OUR YOUNGEST HERBAL-IST.
W-WOW ...
Twelve!
IF YOU'VE GOT ANY QUESTIONS, JUST ASK HIM.
TAKE YOUR TIME GETTING FRIENDLY WITH EACH OTHER.
Bye.
FRIEND-LY?
SHHK
I'M SHIRA-YUKI.
NICE TO MEET YOU!
BOW
SAME.
!

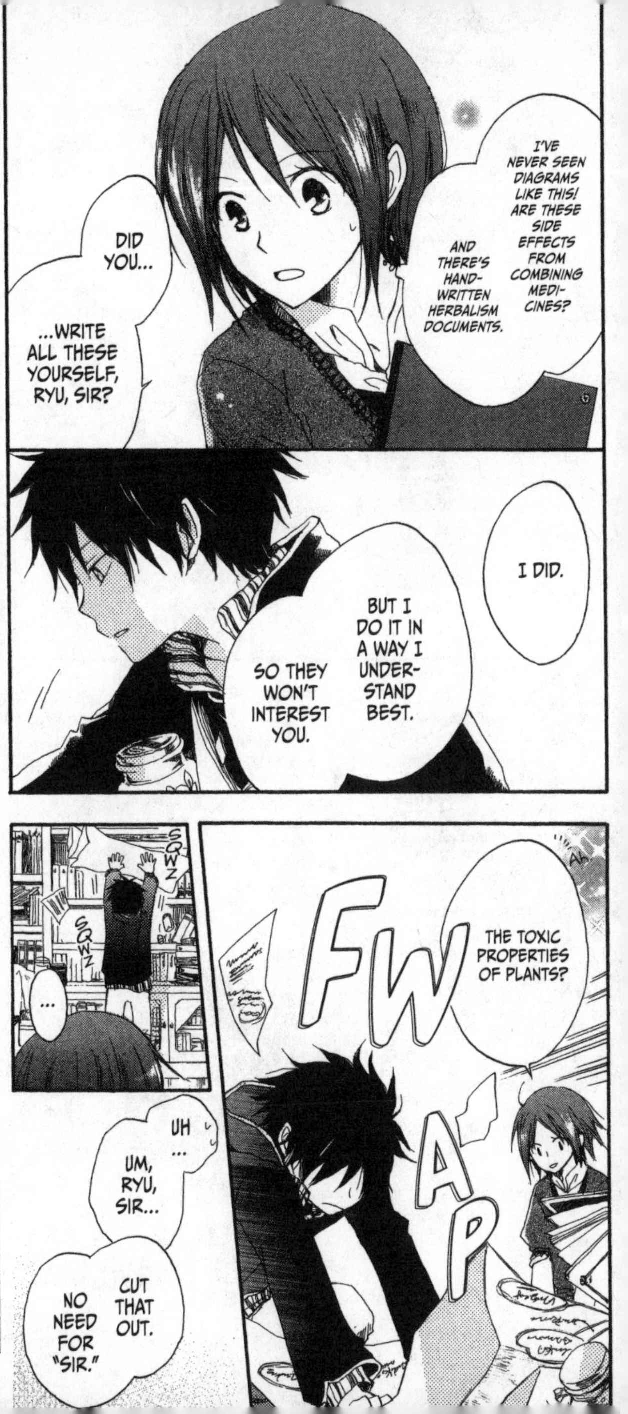
I'VE NEVER SEEN DIAGRAMS LIKE THIS! ARE THESE SIDE EFFECTS FROM COMBINING MEDICINES?
AND THERE'S HAND-WRITTEN HERBALISM DOCUMENTS.
DID YOU...
...WRITE ALL THESE YOURSELF, RYU, SIR?
I DID.
BUT I DO IT IN A WAY I UNDERSTAND BEST.
SO THEY WON'T INTEREST YOU.
AH
THE TOXIC PROPERTIES OF PLANTS?
FWAP
UH ...
UM, RYU, SIR...
CUT THAT OUT.
NO NEED FOR "SIR."
SQWZ
SQWZ
...

Chapter 5

Shirayuki is now a court herbalist in training, and she's got a mentor.

When I think about herbalists in the fantasy genre, I picture wizened, grumpy old men, surrounded by tools and vials, who're always fiddling with something or other (medicine, I guess) and being rude to patients.

But having a character like that in this series (in the royal palace's pharmacy no less) would trigger a flood of people questioning what sort of manga this actually is, so I didn't go that route.

Which is how I wound up with little Ryu.

And it's why he's only 12.

I love drawing kids!

2

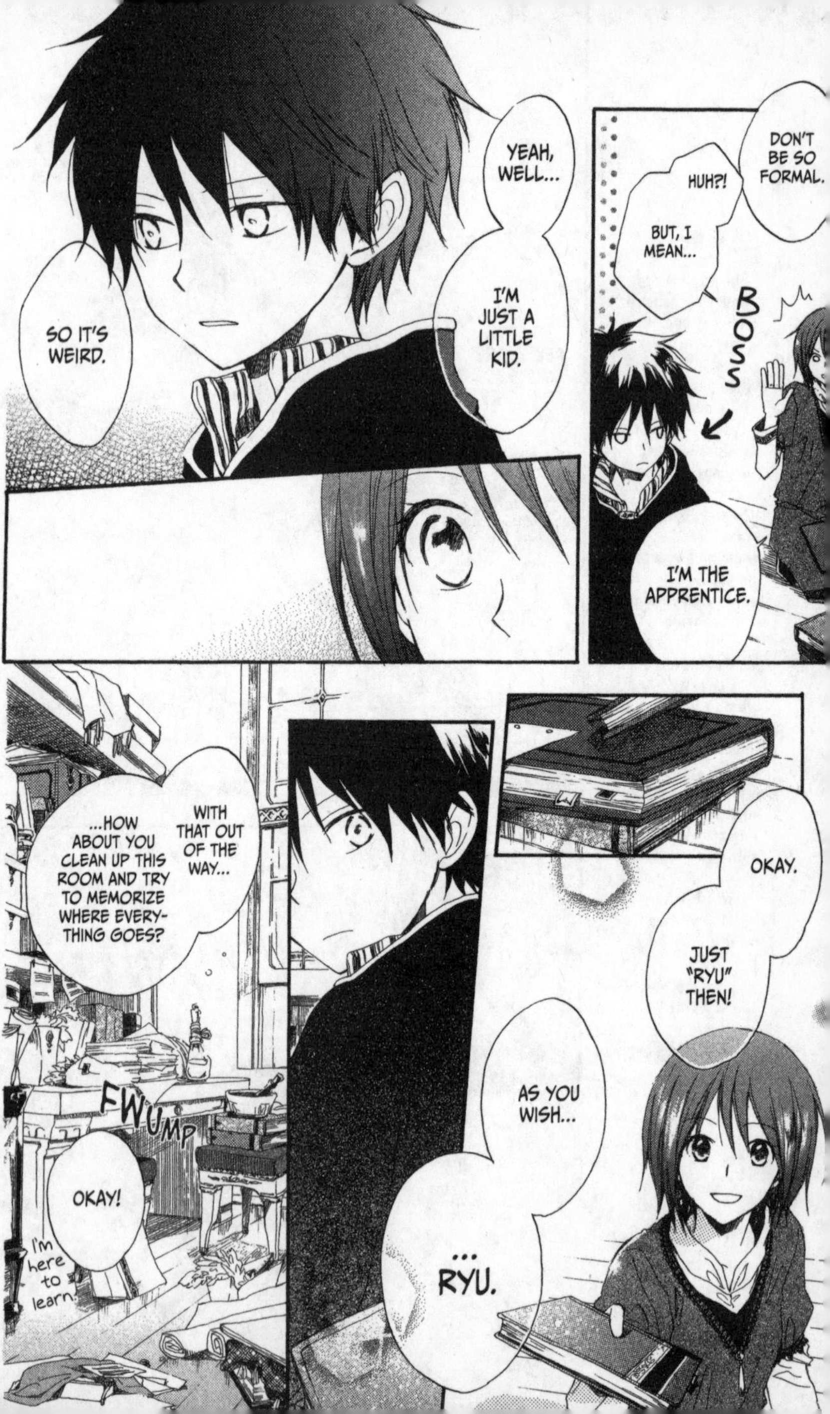
DON'T BE SO FORMAL.
HUH?!
BUT, I MEAN...
BOSS
I'M THE APPRENTICE.
YEAH, WELL...
I'M JUST A LITTLE KID.
SO IT'S WEIRD.
OKAY.
JUST "RYU" THEN!
AS YOU WISH...
...RYU.
WITH THAT OUT OF THE WAY...
...HOW ABOUT YOU CLEAN UP THIS ROOM AND TRY TO MEMORIZE WHERE EVERYTHING GOES?
FWUMP
OKAY!
I'm here to learn.

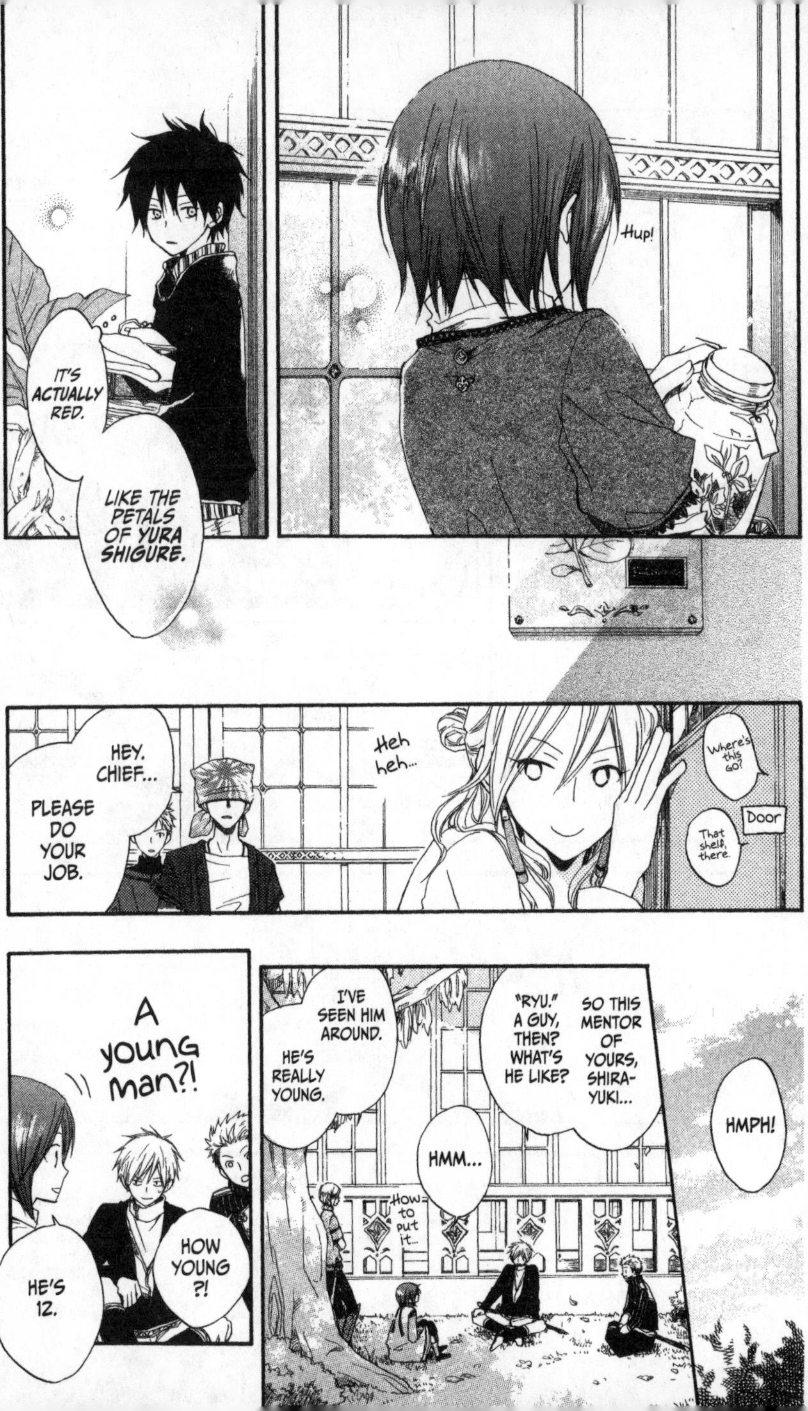
Hup!
IT'S ACTUALLY RED.
LIKE THE PETALS OF YURA SHIGURE.
Where's this go?
Door
That shelf, there.
Heh heh...
HEY. CHIEF... PLEASE DO YOUR JOB.
HMPH!
SO THIS MENTOR OF YOURS, SHIRA-YUKI...
"RYU." A GUY, THEN? WHAT'S HE LIKE?
HMM...
How to put it...
I'VE SEEN HIM AROUND.
HE'S REALLY YOUNG.
A young man?!
HOW YOUNG?!
HE'S 12.

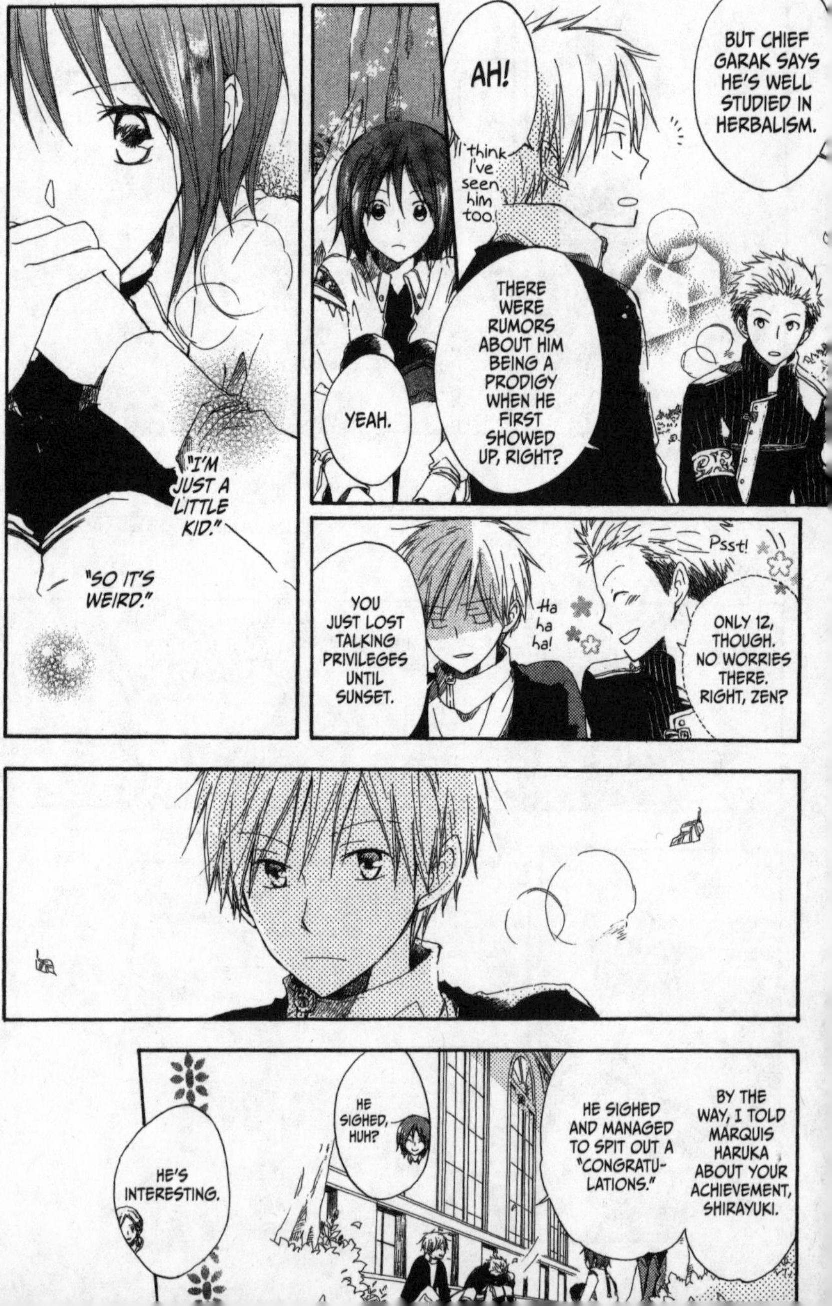
BUT CHIEF GARAK SAYS HE'S WELL STUDIED IN HERBALISM.
AH!
I think I've seen him too.
THERE WERE RUMORS ABOUT HIM BEING A PRODIGY WHEN HE FIRST SHOWED UP, RIGHT?
YEAH.
Psst!
ONLY 12, THOUGH. NO WORRIES THERE. RIGHT, ZEN?
Ha ha ha!
YOU JUST LOST TALKING PRIVILEGES UNTIL SUNSET.
"I'M JUST A LITTLE KID."
"SO IT'S WEIRD."
BY THE WAY, I TOLD MARQUIS HARUKA ABOUT YOUR ACHIEVEMENT, SHIRAYUKI.
HE SIGHED AND MANAGED TO SPIT OUT A "CONGRATU-LATIONS."
HE SIGHED, HUH?
HE'S INTERESTING.

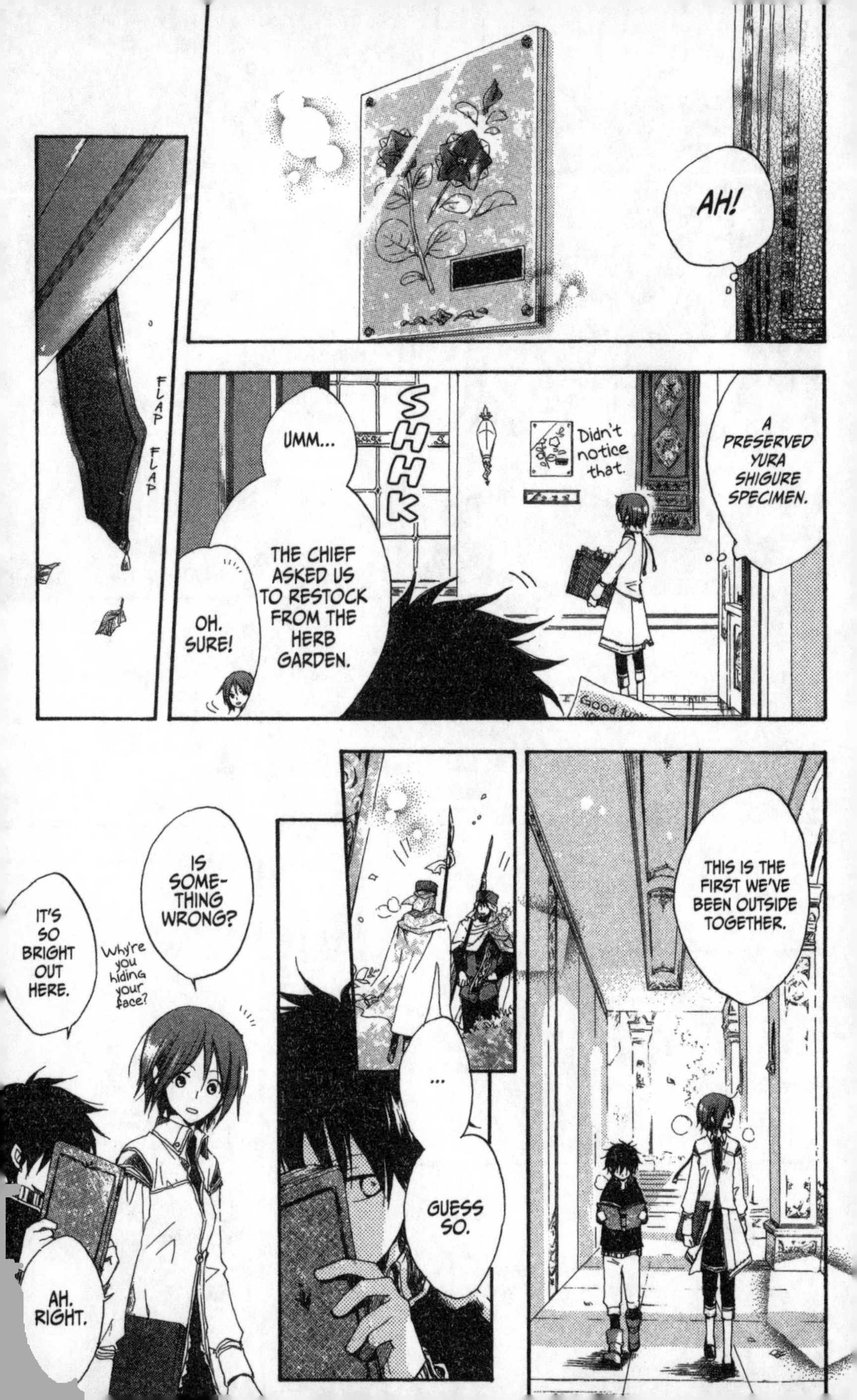
AH!
A PRESERVED YURA SHIGURE SPECIMEN.
Didn't notice that.
UMM...
SHHK
THE CHIEF ASKED US TO RESTOCK FROM THE HERB GARDEN.
OH. SURE!
FLAP FLAP
THIS IS THE FIRST WE'VE BEEN OUTSIDE TOGETHER.
...
GUESS SO.
IS SOME-THING WRONG?
Why're you hiding your face?
IT'S SO BRIGHT OUT HERE.
AH. RIGHT.

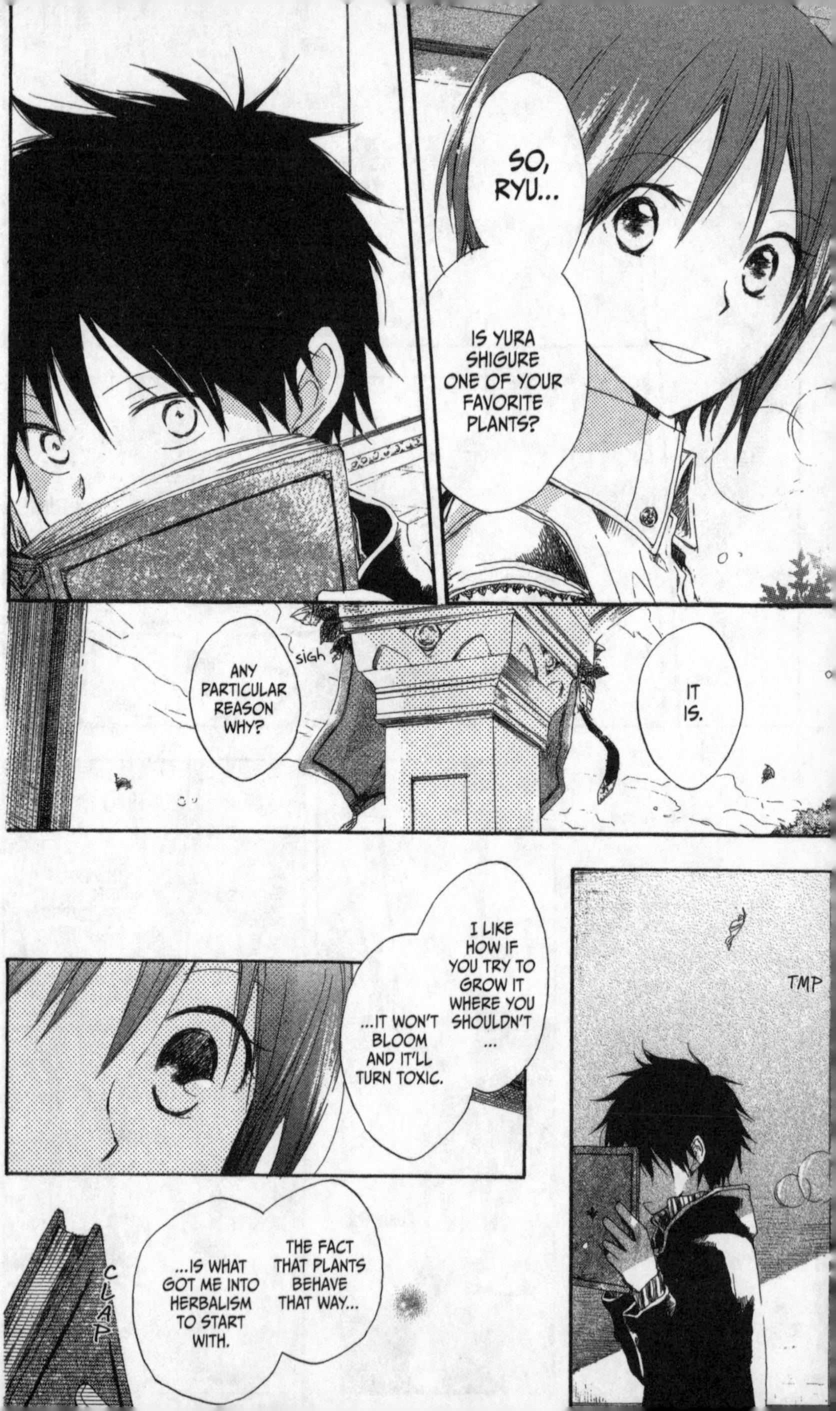
SO, RYU...
IS YURA SHIGURE ONE OF YOUR FAVORITE PLANTS?
IT IS.
sigh
ANY PARTICULAR REASON WHY?
TMP
I LIKE HOW IF YOU TRY TO GROW IT WHERE YOU SHOULDN'T ...
...IT WON'T BLOOM AND IT'LL TURN TOXIC.
THE FACT THAT PLANTS BEHAVE THAT WAY...
...IS WHAT GOT ME INTO HERBALISM TO START WITH.
CLAP

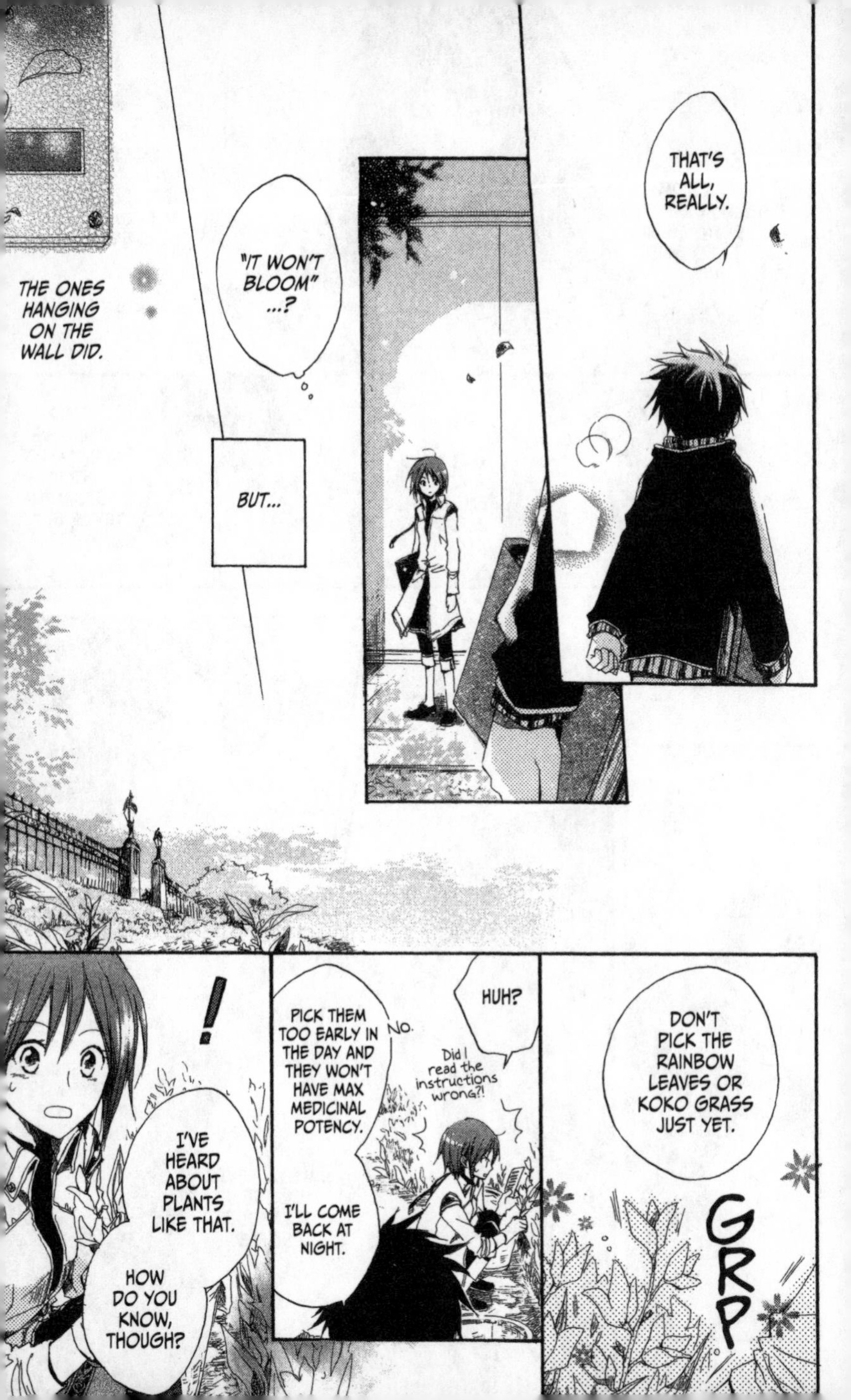
THAT'S ALL, REALLY.
"IT WON'T BLOOM" ...?
THE ONES HANGING ON THE WALL DID.
BUT...
DON'T PICK THE RAINBOW LEAVES OR KOKO GRASS JUST YET.
GRP
HUH?
Did I read the instructions wrong?!
No.
PICK THEM TOO EARLY IN THE DAY AND THEY WON'T HAVE MAX MEDICINAL POTENCY.
I'LL COME BACK AT NIGHT.
!
I'VE HEARD ABOUT PLANTS LIKE THAT.
HOW DO YOU KNOW, THOUGH?

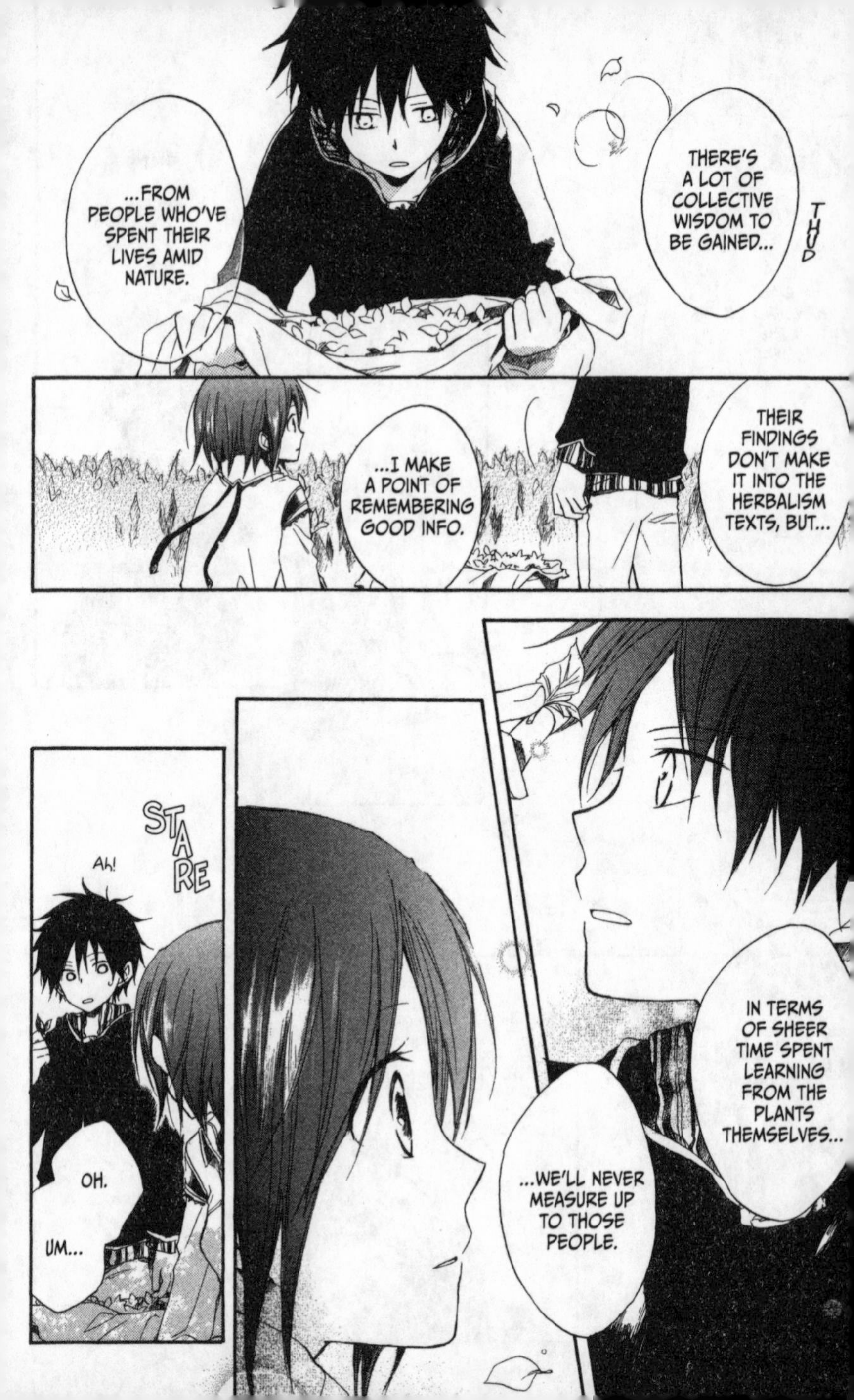
THERE'S A LOT OF COLLECTIVE WISDOM TO BE GAINED...
THUD
...FROM PEOPLE WHO'VE SPENT THEIR LIVES AMID NATURE.
THEIR FINDINGS DON'T MAKE IT INTO THE HERBALISM TEXTS, BUT...
...I MAKE A POINT OF REMEMBERING GOOD INFO.
IN TERMS OF SHEER TIME SPENT LEARNING FROM THE PLANTS THEMSELVES...
...WE'LL NEVER MEASURE UP TO THOSE PEOPLE.
STARE
Ah!
OH.
UM...

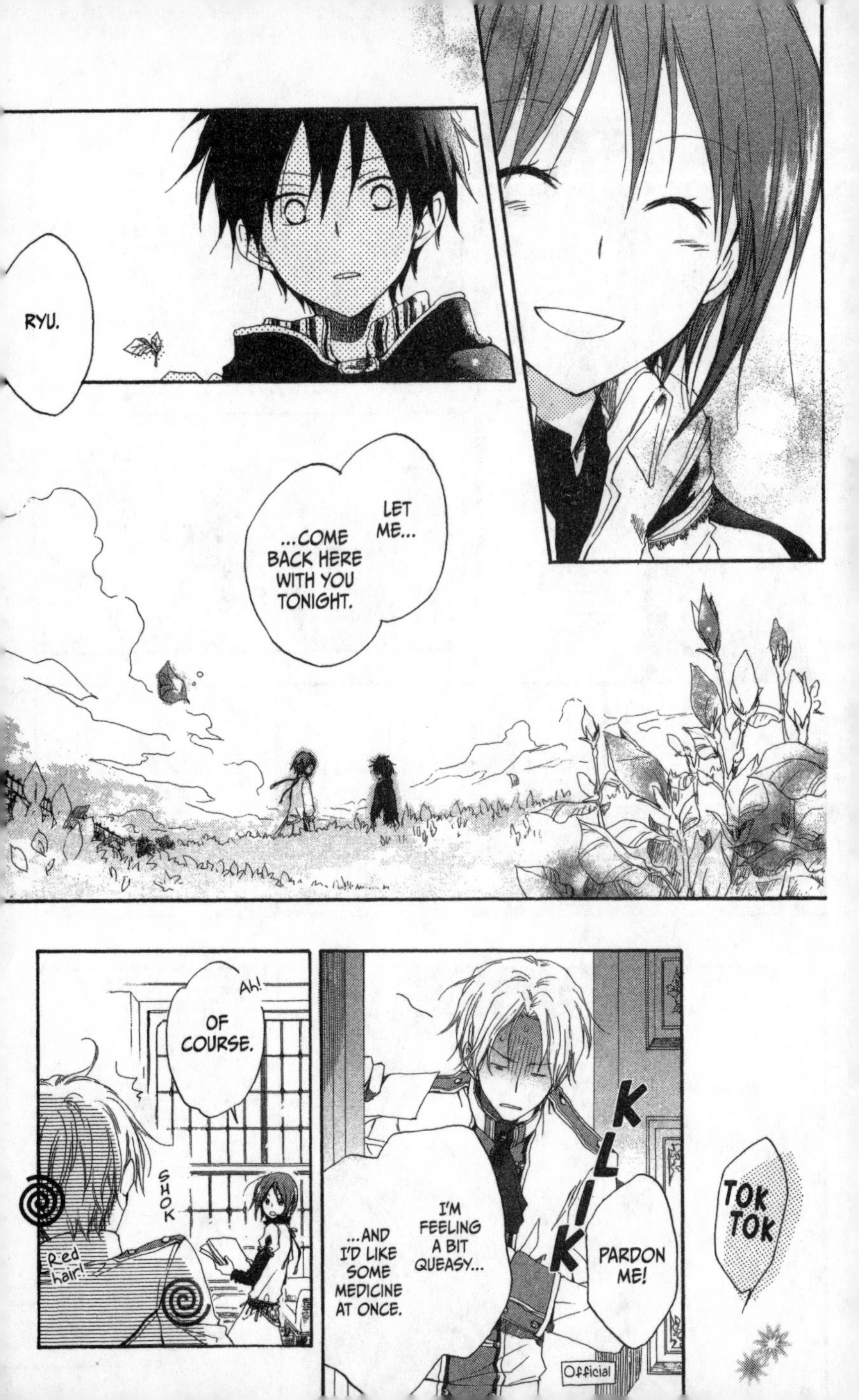
RYU.
LET ME... ...COME BACK HERE WITH YOU TONIGHT.
TOK TOK
PARDON ME!
KLIK
I'M FEELING A BIT QUEASY...
...AND I'D LIKE SOME MEDICINE AT ONCE.
Official
Ah! OF COURSE.
SHOK
Red hair!

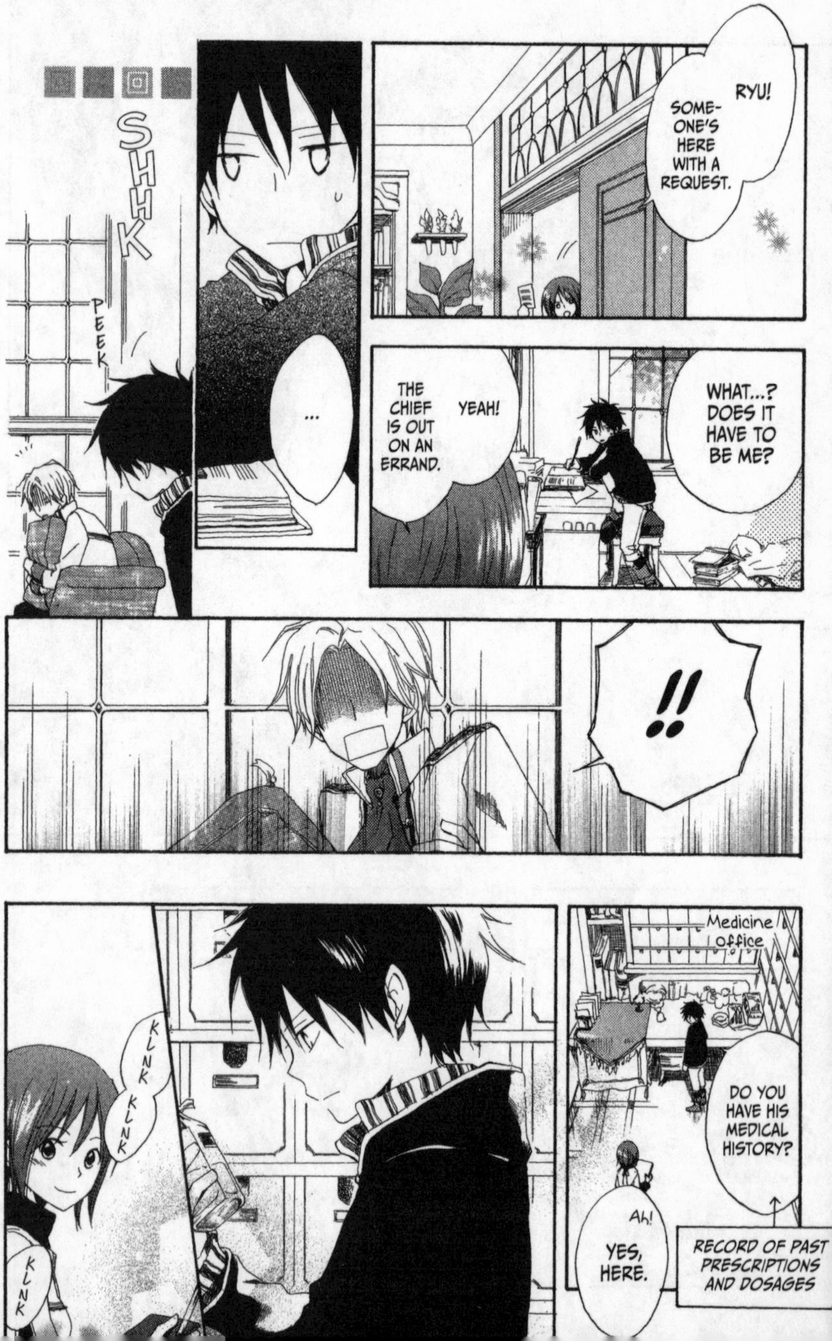
RYU!
SOME-ONE'S HERE WITH A REQUEST.
WHAT...? DOES IT HAVE TO BE ME?
YEAH!
THE CHIEF IS OUT ON AN ERRAND.
...
SHHK
PEEK
!!
Medicine office
DO YOU HAVE HIS MEDICAL HISTORY?
Ah!
YES, HERE.
RECORD OF PAST PRESCRIPTIONS AND DOSAGES
KLNK KLNK KLNK
KLNK

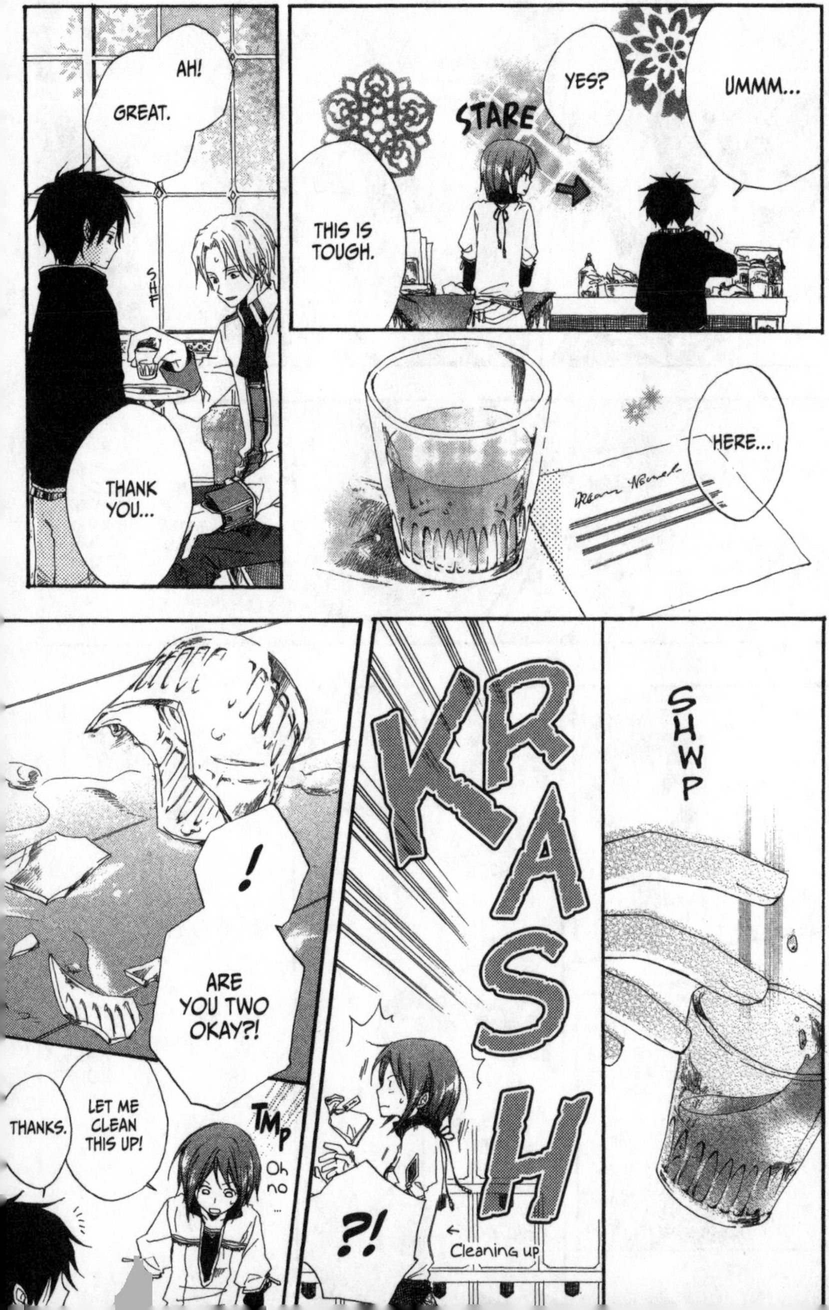
UMMM...
YES?
STARE
THIS IS TOUGH.
HERE...
AH! GREAT.
SHF
THANK YOU...
SHWP
KRASH
?!
Cleaning up
!
ARE YOU TWO OKAY?!
TMP
Oh no ...
LET ME CLEAN THIS UP!
THANKS.

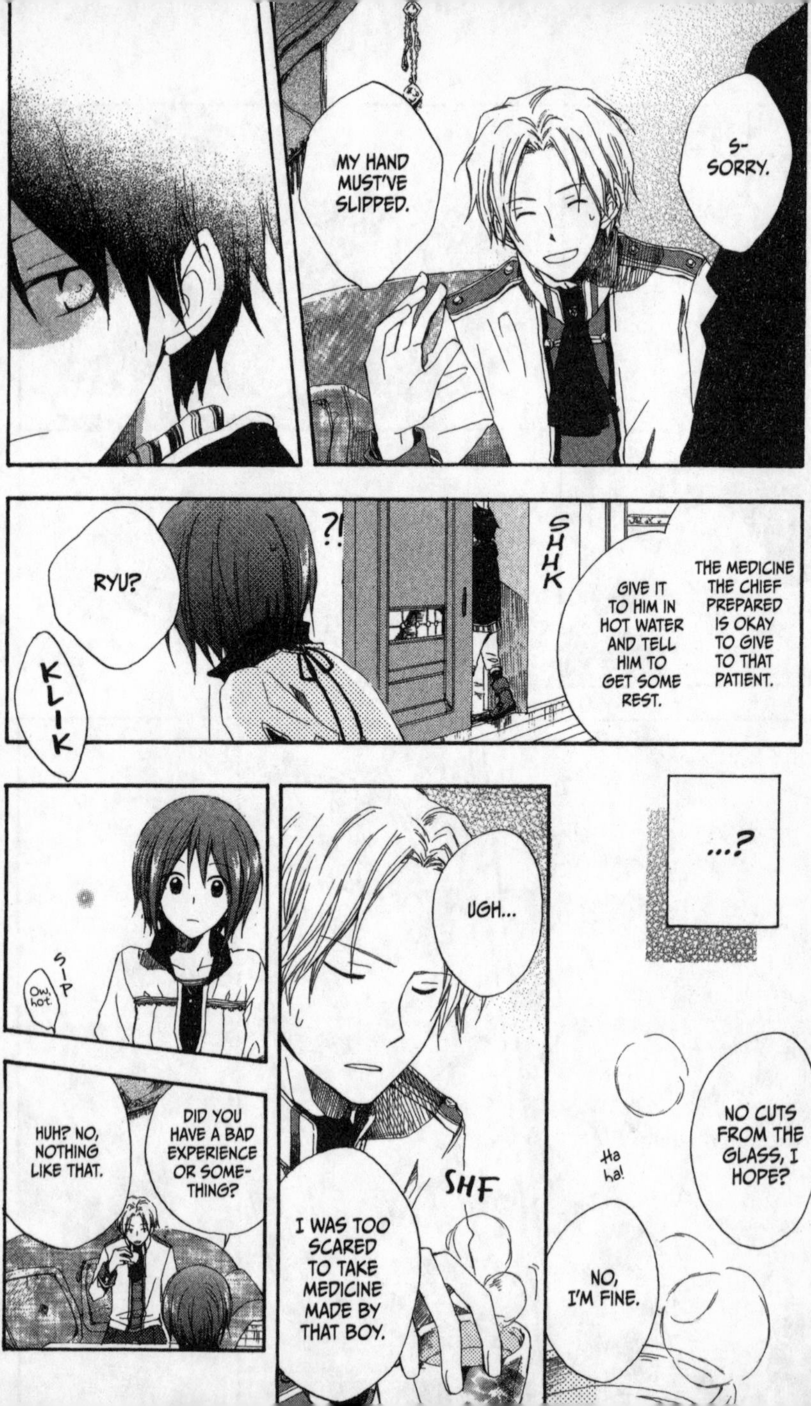
S- SORRY.
MY HAND MUST'VE SLIPPED.
THE MEDICINE THE CHIEF PREPARED IS OKAY TO GIVE TO THAT PATIENT.
GIVE IT TO HIM IN HOT WATER AND TELL HIM TO GET SOME REST.
SHHK
?!
RYU?
KLIK
...?
UGH...
NO CUTS FROM THE GLASS, I HOPE?
Ha ha!
NO, I'M FINE.
SHF
I WAS TOO SCARED TO TAKE MEDICINE MADE BY THAT BOY.
SIP
Ow, hot.
DID YOU HAVE A BAD EXPERIENCE OR SOME-THING?
HUH? NO, NOTHING LIKE THAT.

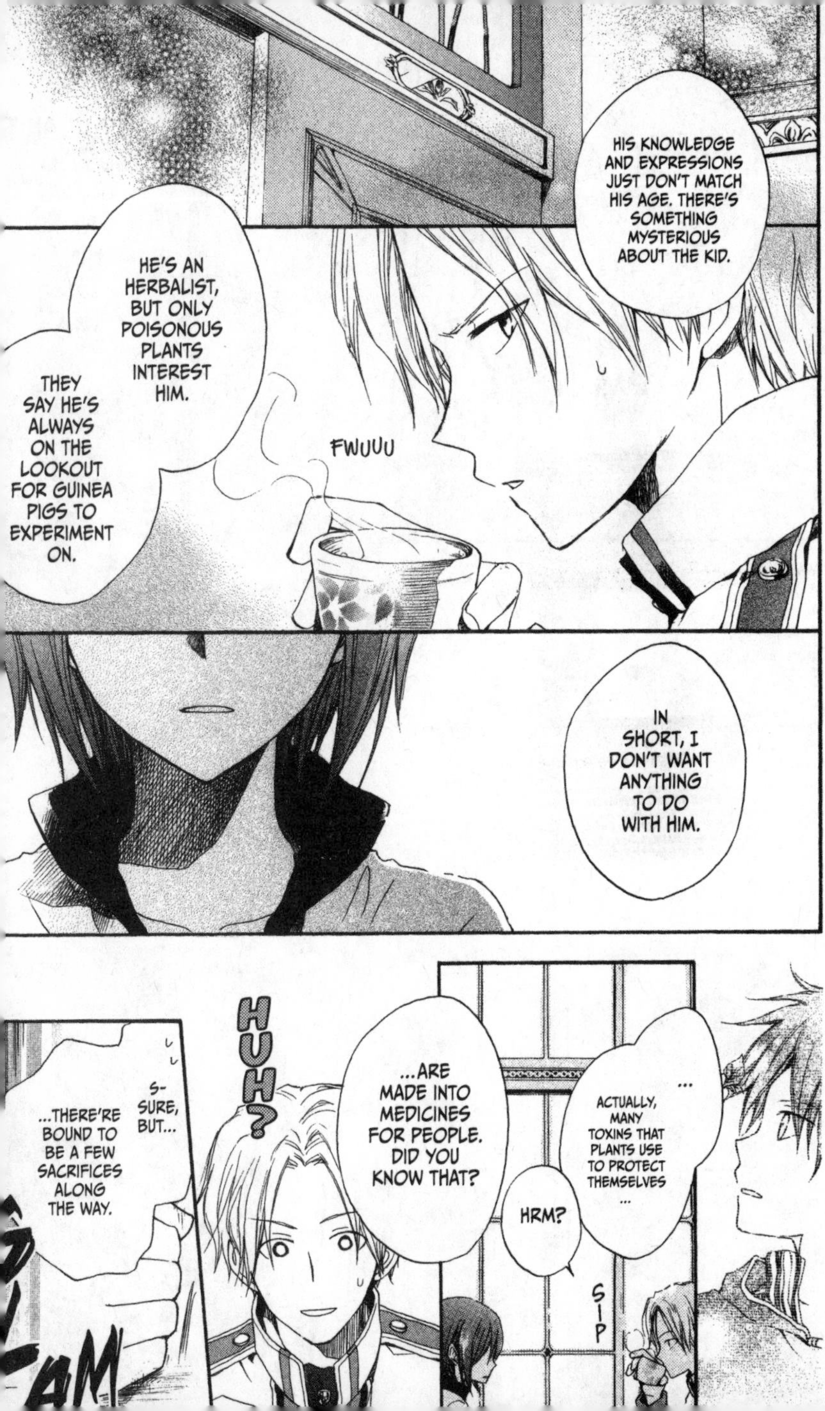
HIS KNOWLEDGE AND EXPRESSIONS JUST DON'T MATCH HIS AGE. THERE'S SOMETHING MYSTERIOUS ABOUT THE KID.
HE'S AN HERBALIST, BUT ONLY POISONOUS PLANTS INTEREST HIM.
THEY SAY HE'S ALWAYS ON THE LOOKOUT FOR GUINEA PIGS TO EXPERIMENT ON.
FWUUU
IN SHORT, I DON'T WANT ANYTHING TO DO WITH HIM.
...
ACTUALLY, MANY TOXINS THAT PLANTS USE TO PROTECT THEMSELVES ...
HRM?
SIP
...ARE MADE INTO MEDICINES FOR PEOPLE. DID YOU KNOW THAT?
HUH?
S-SURE, BUT...
...THERE'RE BOUND TO BE A FEW SACRIFICES ALONG THE WAY.

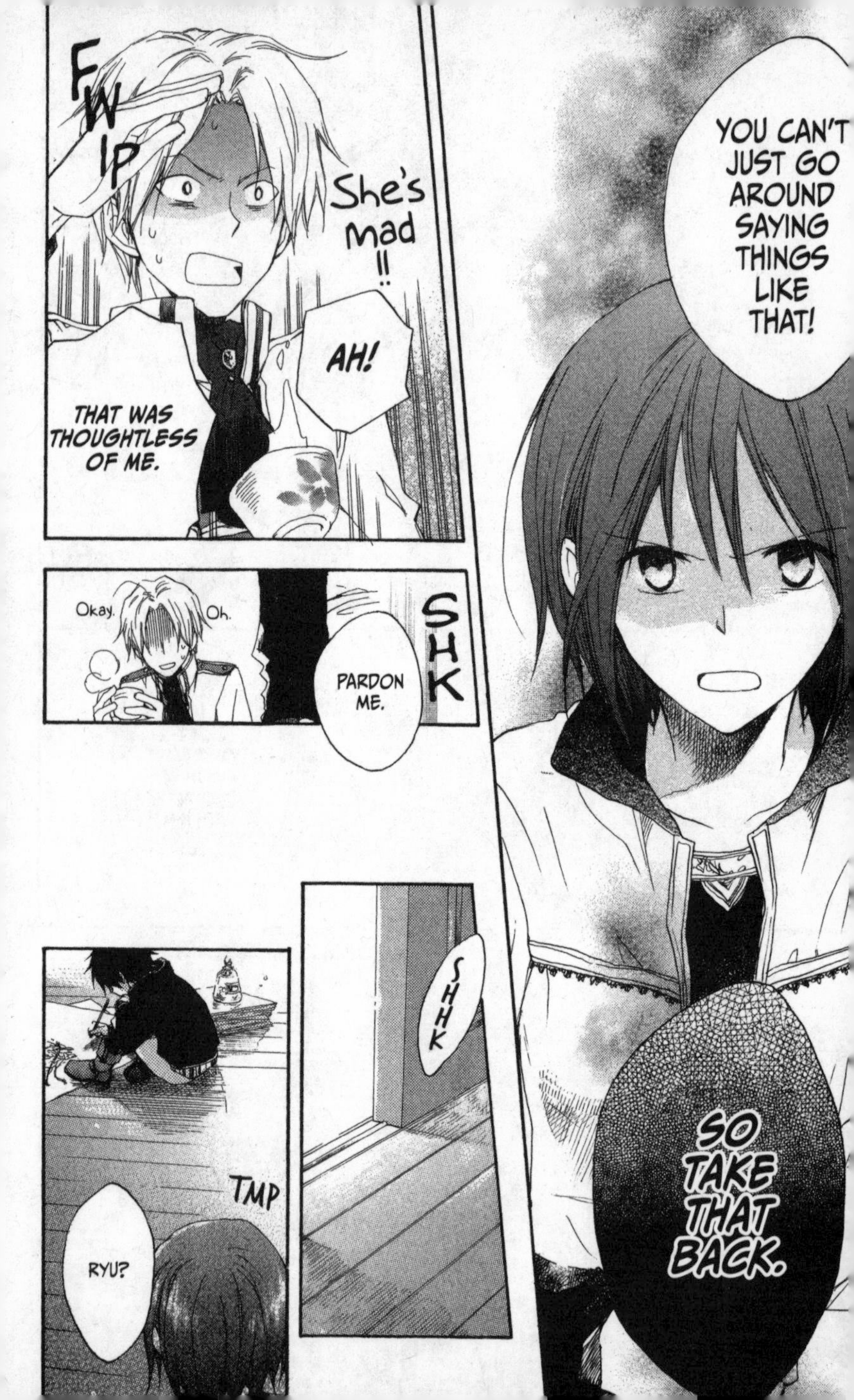
YOU CAN'T JUST GO AROUND SAYING THINGS LIKE THAT!
SO TAKE THAT BACK.
She's mad!!
FWIP
AH!
THAT WAS THOUGHTLESS OF ME.
SHK
PARDON ME.
Oh.
Okay.
SHHK
TMP
RYU?

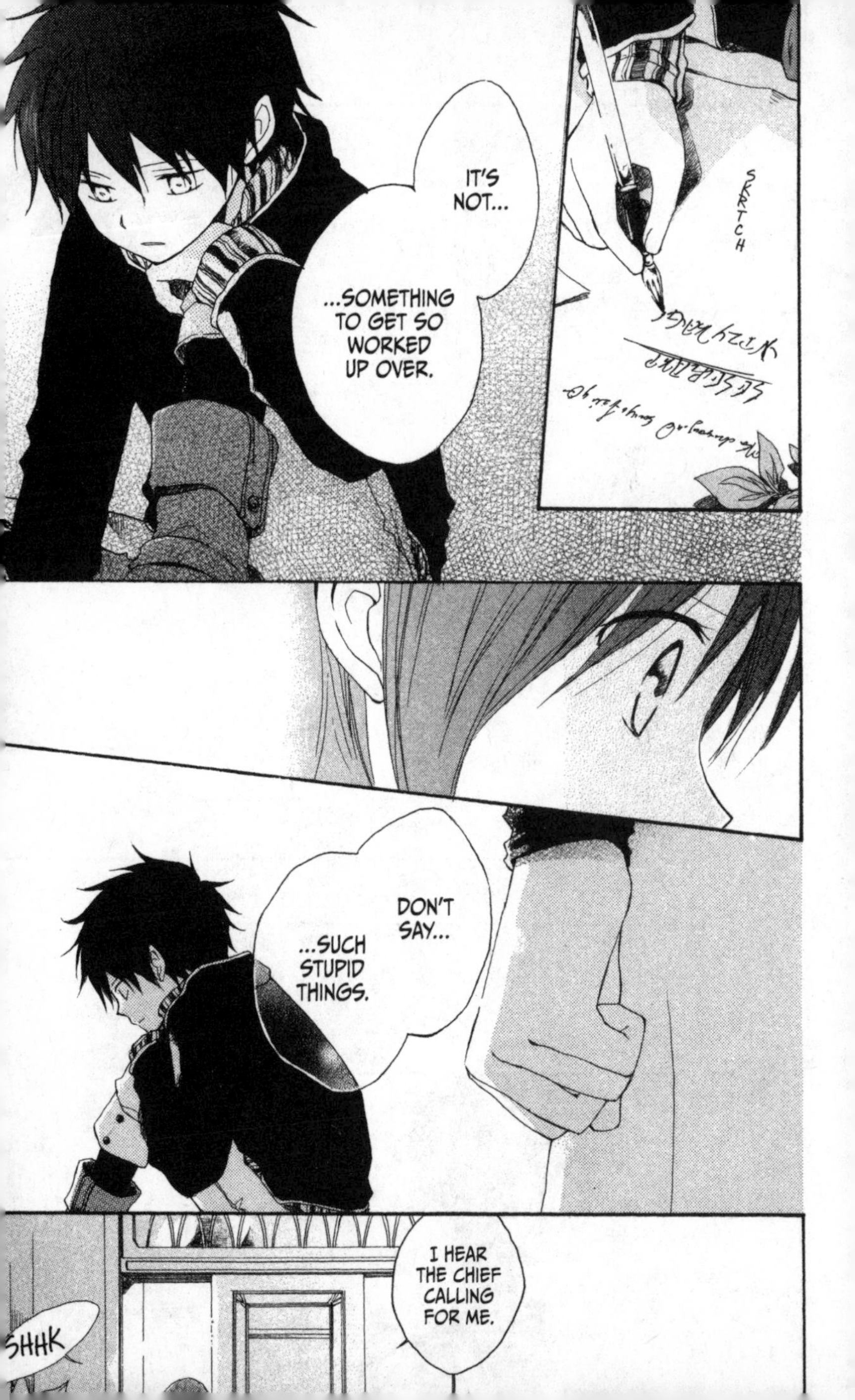
SKRTCH
IT'S NOT...
...SOMETHING TO GET SO WORKED UP OVER.
DON'T SAY...
...SUCH STUPID THINGS.
I HEAR THE CHIEF CALLING FOR ME.
SHHK

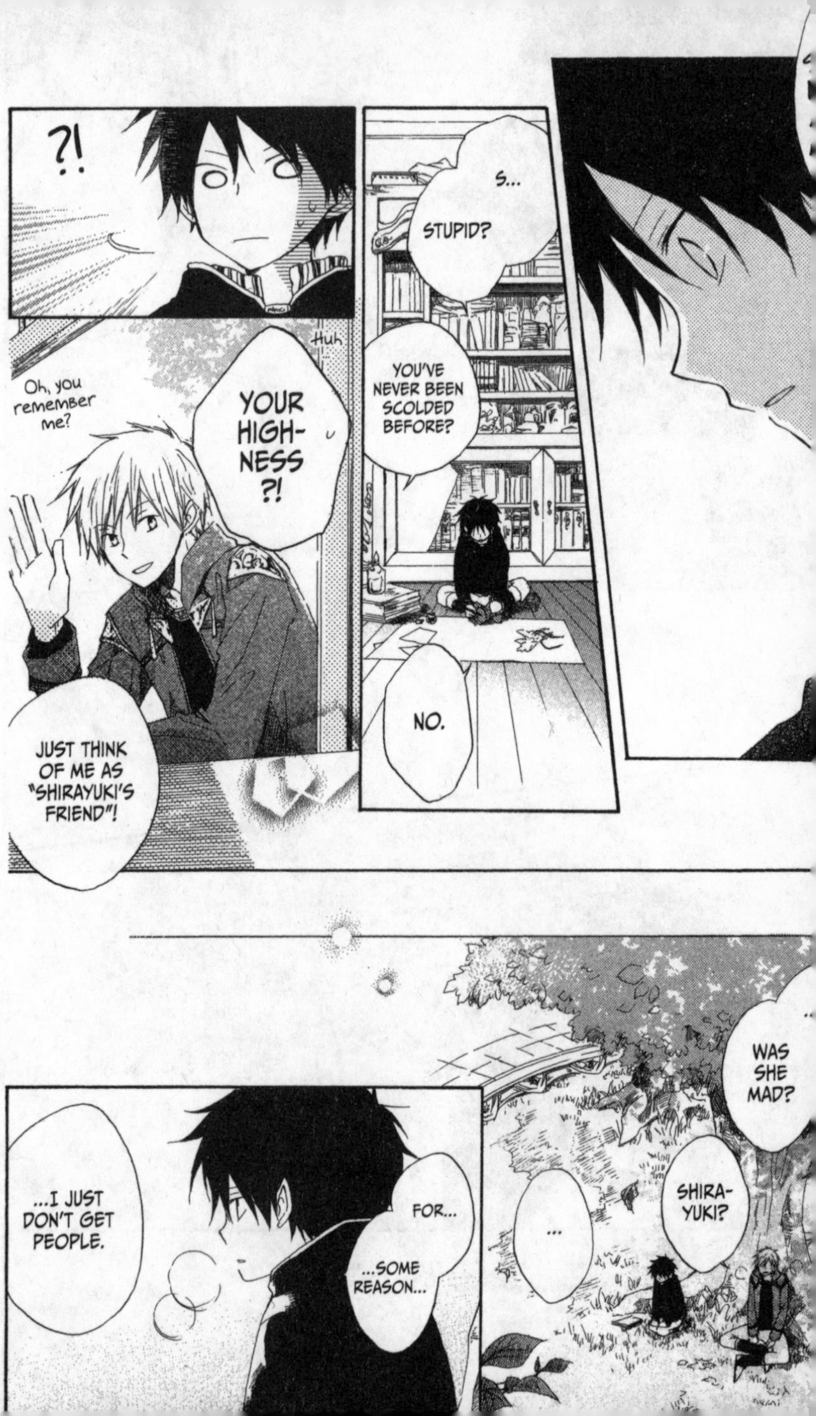
S...
STUPID?
YOU'VE NEVER BEEN SCOLDED BEFORE?
NO.
?!
Huh
YOUR HIGH-NESS ?!
Oh, you remember me?
JUST THINK OF ME AS "SHIRAYUKI'S FRIEND"!
WAS SHE MAD?
SHIRA-YUKI?
...
FOR...
...SOME REASON...
...I JUST DON'T GET PEOPLE.

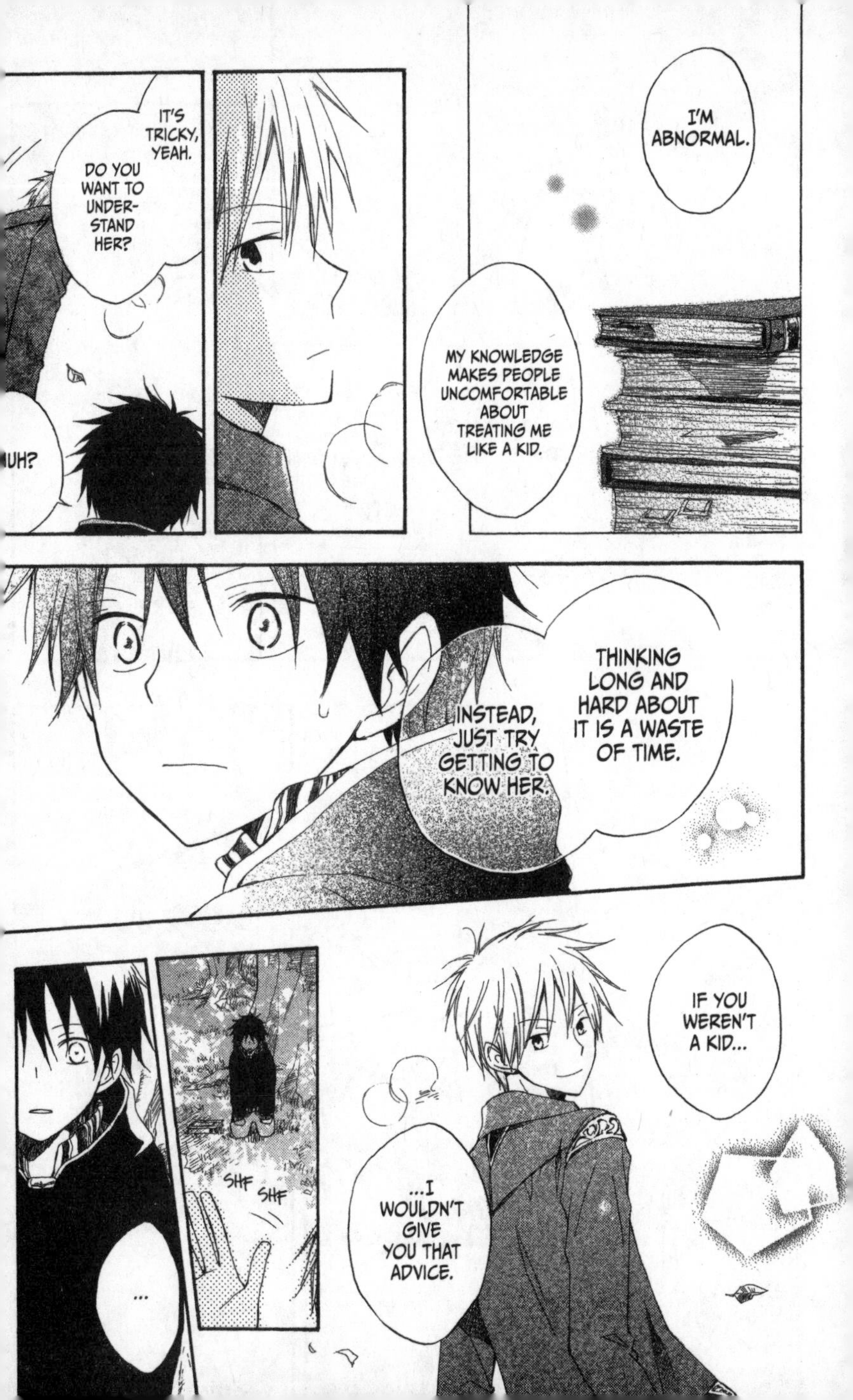
I'M ABNORMAL.
MY KNOWLEDGE MAKES PEOPLE UNCOMFORTABLE ABOUT TREATING ME LIKE A KID.
IT'S TRICKY, YEAH.
DO YOU WANT TO UNDERSTAND HER?
UH?
THINKING LONG AND HARD ABOUT IT IS A WASTE OF TIME.
INSTEAD, JUST TRY GETTING TO KNOW HER.
IF YOU WEREN'T A KID...
...I WOULDN'T GIVE YOU THAT ADVICE.
SHF SHF
...

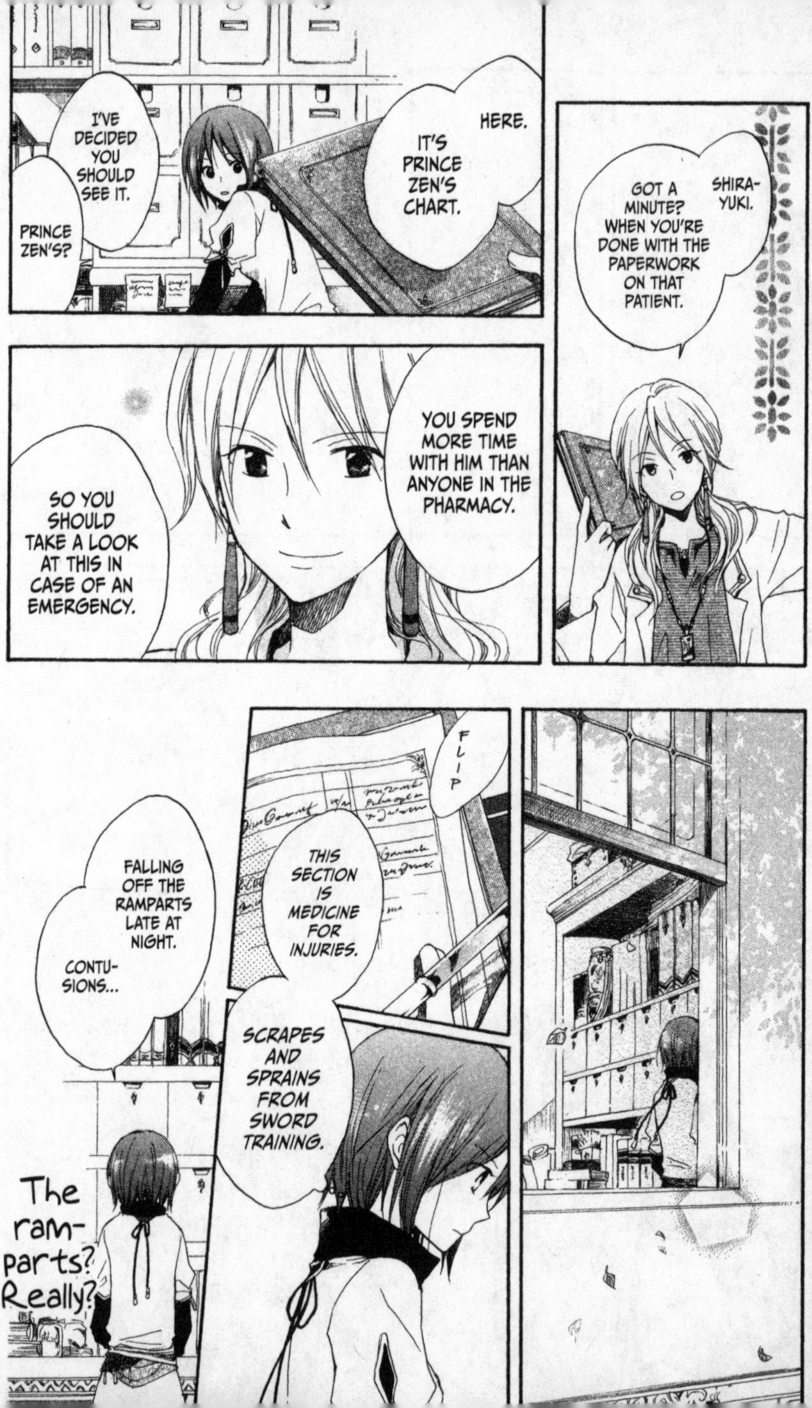
SHIRA-YUKI.
GOT A MINUTE? WHEN YOU'RE DONE WITH THE PAPERWORK ON THAT PATIENT.
HERE.
IT'S PRINCE ZEN'S CHART.
I'VE DECIDED YOU SHOULD SEE IT.
PRINCE ZEN'S?
YOU SPEND MORE TIME WITH HIM THAN ANYONE IN THE PHARMACY.
SO YOU SHOULD TAKE A LOOK AT THIS IN CASE OF AN EMERGENCY.
FLIP
THIS SECTION IS MEDICINE FOR INJURIES.
FALLING OFF THE RAMPARTS LATE AT NIGHT.
CONTU-SIONS...
SCRAPES AND SPRAINS FROM SWORD TRAINING.
The ram-parts? Really?

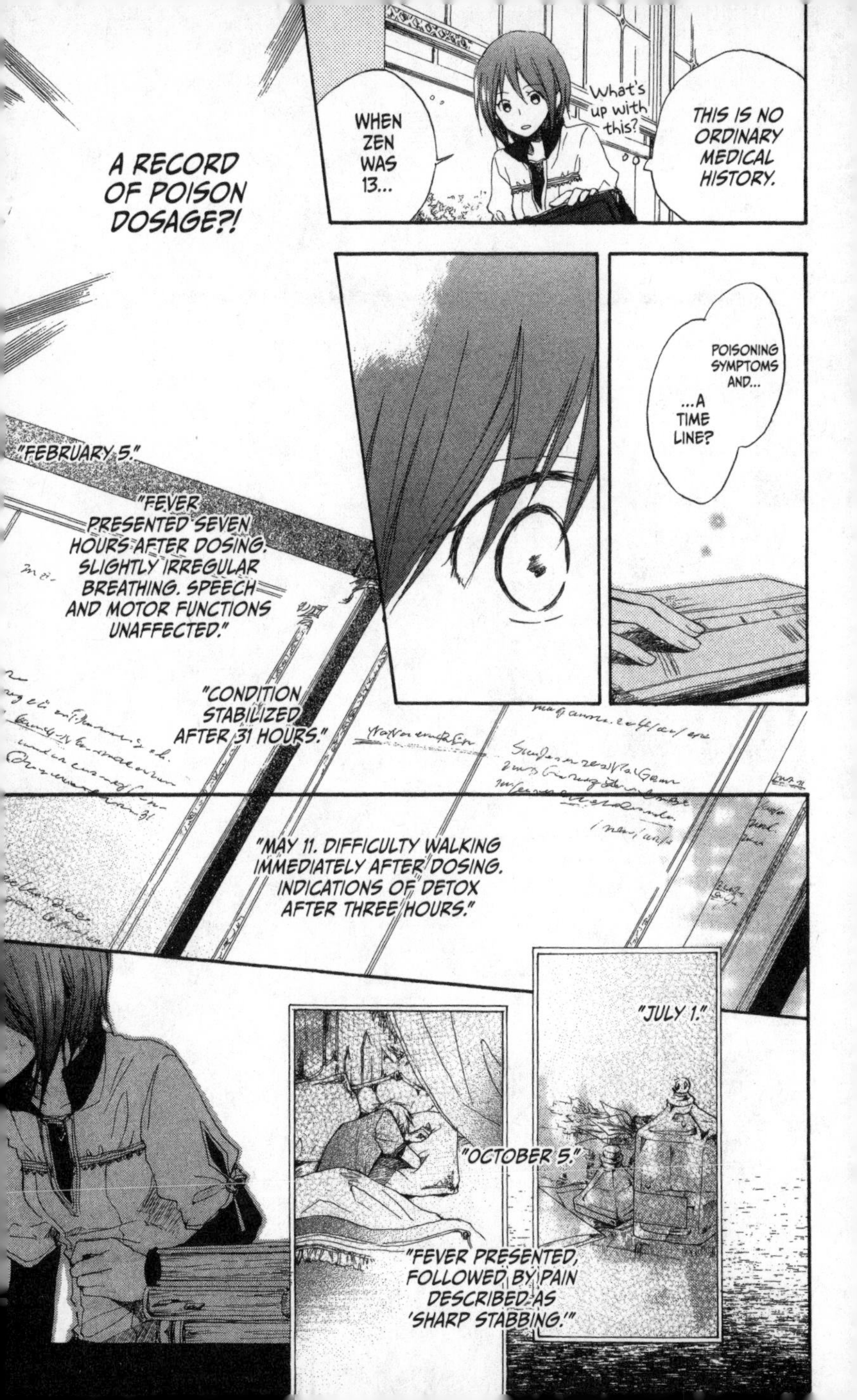
THIS IS NO ORDINARY MEDICAL HISTORY.
What's up with this?
WHEN ZEN WAS 13...
A RECORD OF POISON DOSAGE?!
POISONING SYMPTOMS AND...
...A TIME LINE?
"FEBRUARY 5."
"FEVER PRESENTED SEVEN HOURS AFTER DOSING. SLIGHTLY IRREGULAR BREATHING. SPEECH AND MOTOR FUNCTIONS UNAFFECTED."
"CONDITION STABILIZED AFTER 31 HOURS."
"MAY 11. DIFFICULTY WALKING IMMEDIATELY AFTER DOSING. INDICATIONS OF DETOX AFTER THREE HOURS."
"JULY 1."
"OCTOBER 5."
"FEVER PRESENTED, FOLLOWED BY PAIN DESCRIBED AS 'SHARP STABBING.'"

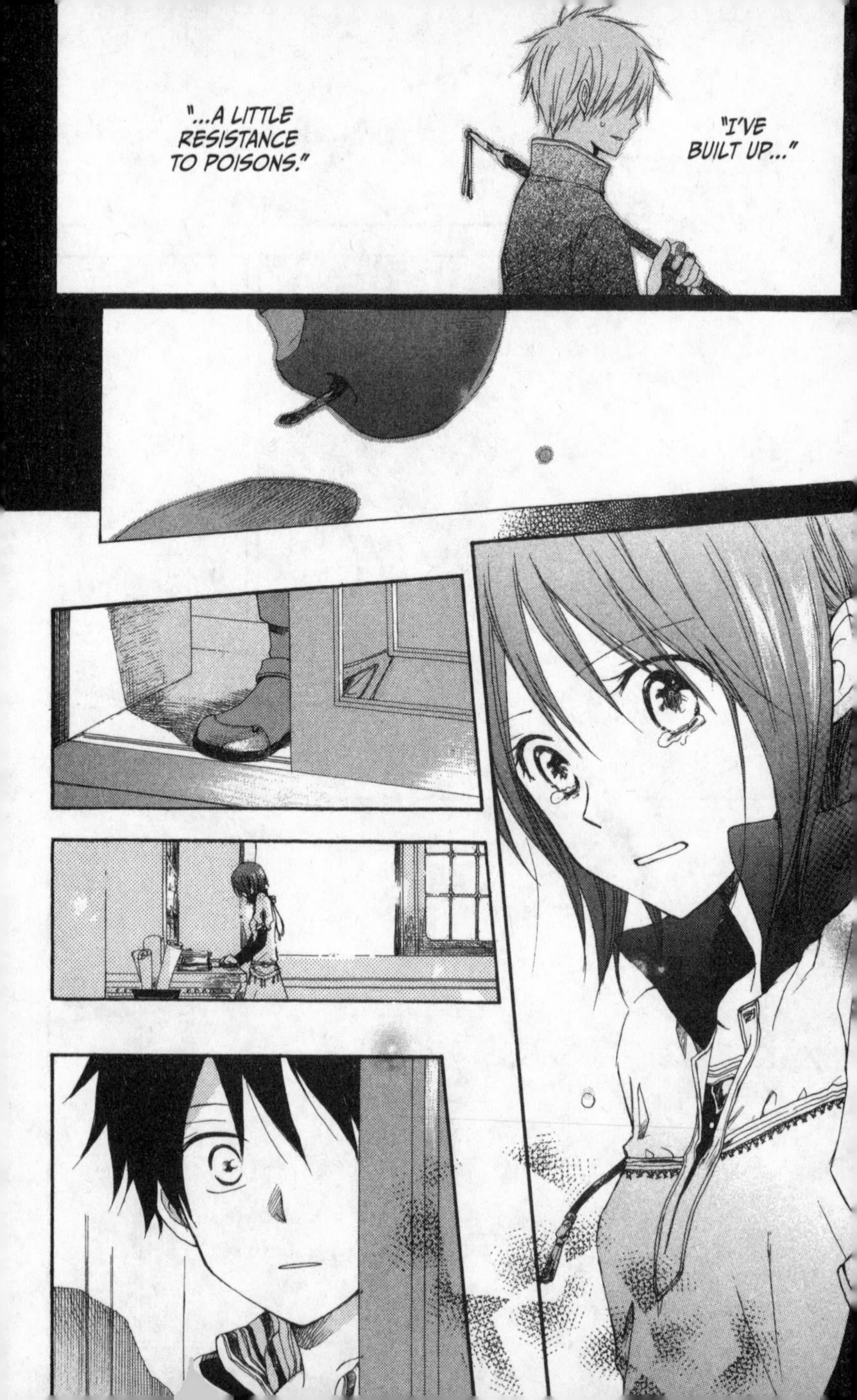
"I'VE BUILT UP..."
"...A LITTLE RESISTANCE TO POISONS."

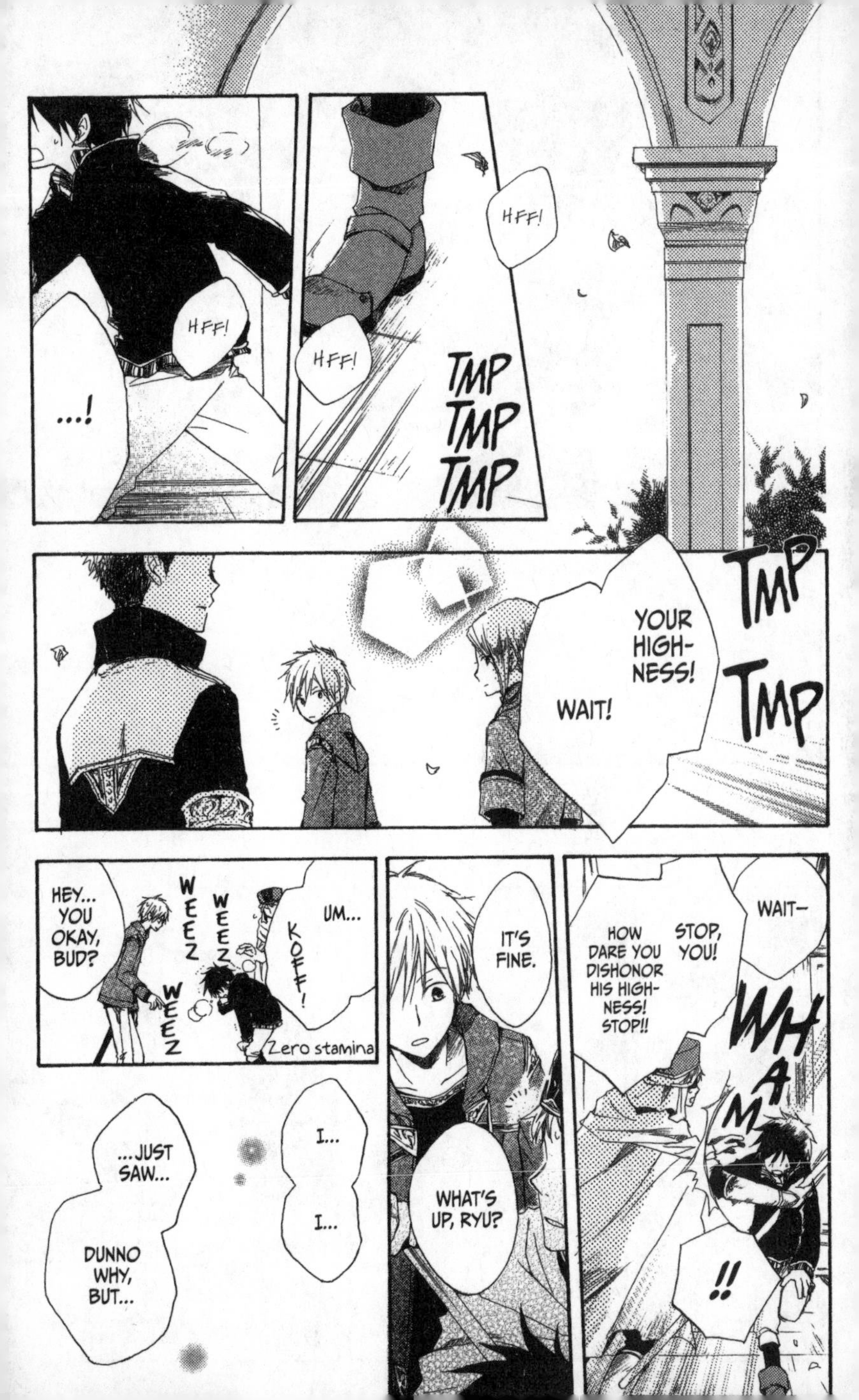
HFF!
HFF!
TMP TMP TMP
HFF!
...!
YOUR HIGHNESS!
WAIT!
TMP TMP
WAIT—
STOP, YOU!
HOW DARE YOU DISHONOR HIS HIGHNESS! STOP!!
WHAMM
!!
IT'S FINE.
WHAT'S UP, RYU?
UM...
KOFF!
WEEZ WEEZ
WEEZ WEEZ
HEY... YOU OKAY, BUD?
Zero stamina
I...
I...
...JUST SAW...
DUNNO WHY, BUT...

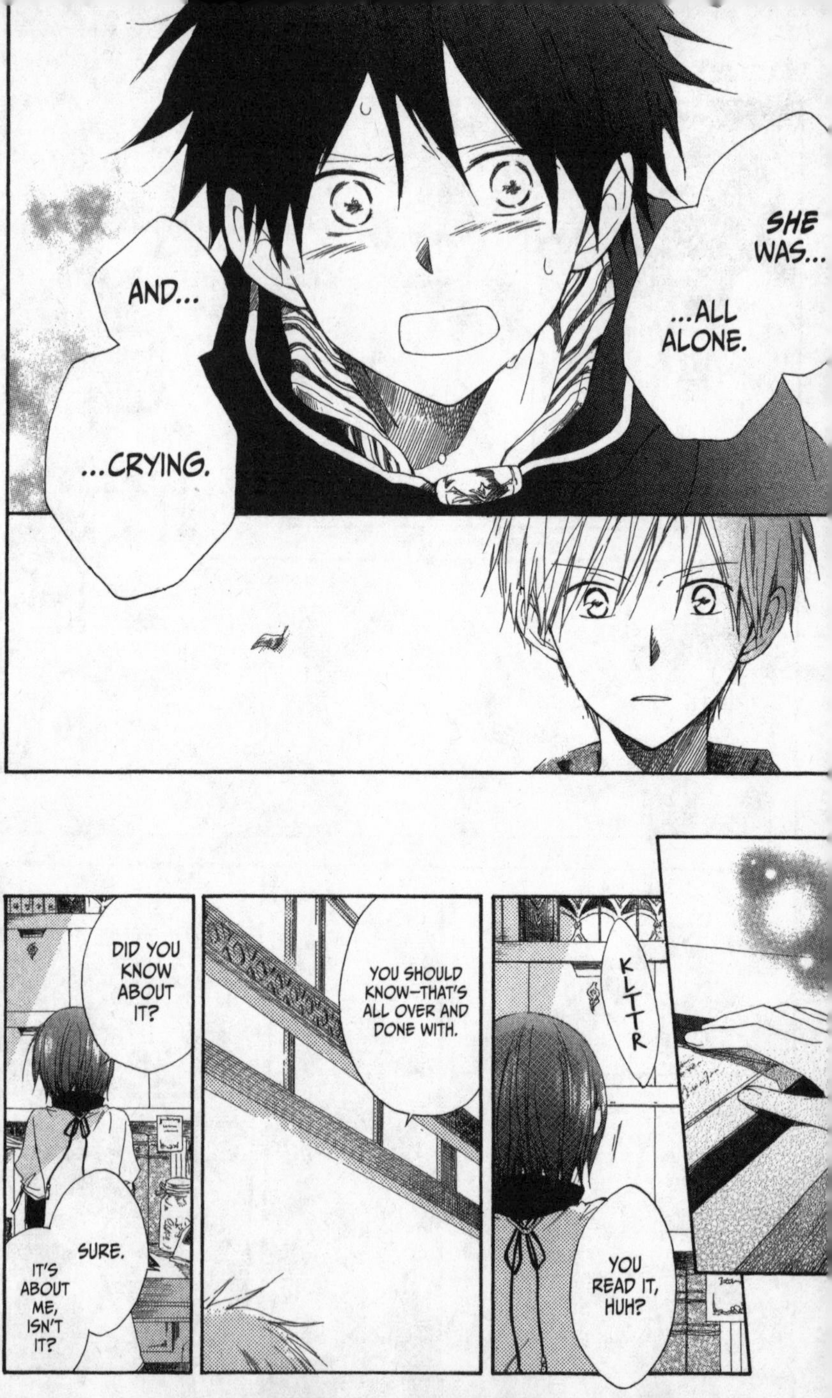
SHE WAS...
...ALL ALONE.
AND...
...CRYING.
KLTTR
YOU READ IT, HUH?
YOU SHOULD KNOW—THAT'S ALL OVER AND DONE WITH.
DID YOU KNOW ABOUT IT?
SURE.
IT'S ABOUT ME, ISN'T IT?

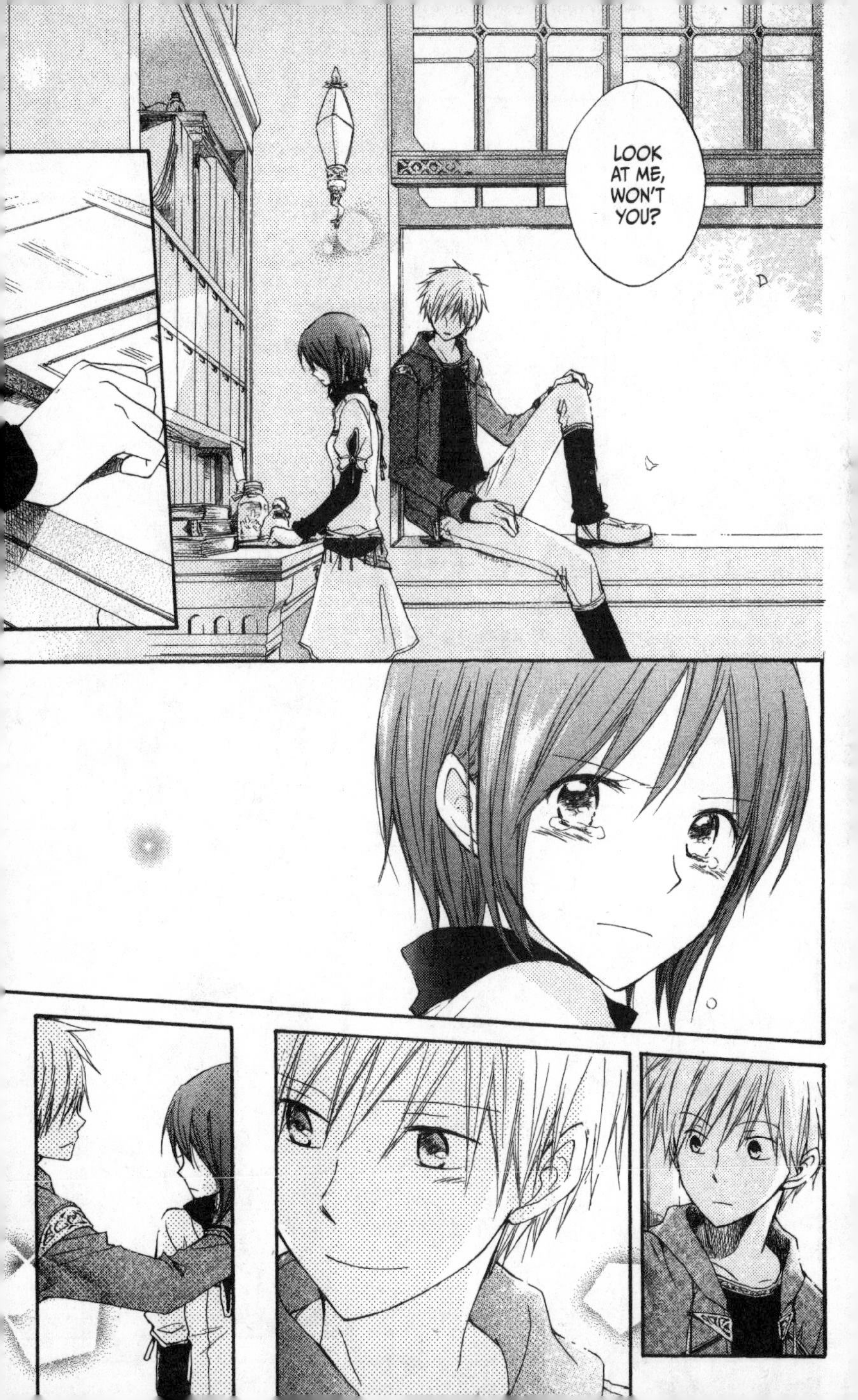
LOOK AT ME, WON'T YOU?

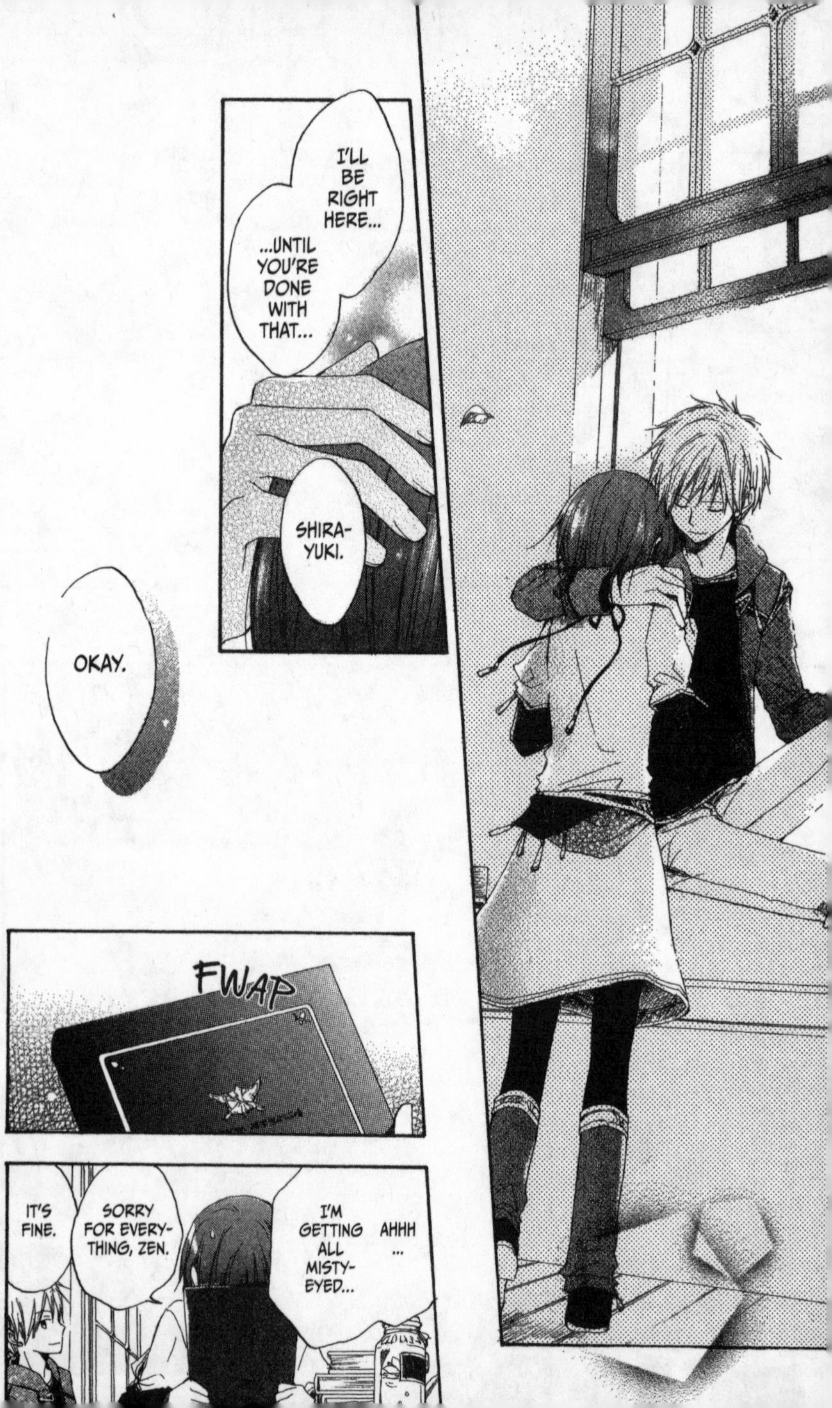
I'LL BE RIGHT HERE...
...UNTIL YOU'RE DONE WITH THAT...
SHIRA-YUKI.
OKAY.
FWAP
AHHH...
I'M GETTING ALL MISTY-EYED...
SORRY FOR EVERY-THING, ZEN.
IT'S FINE.

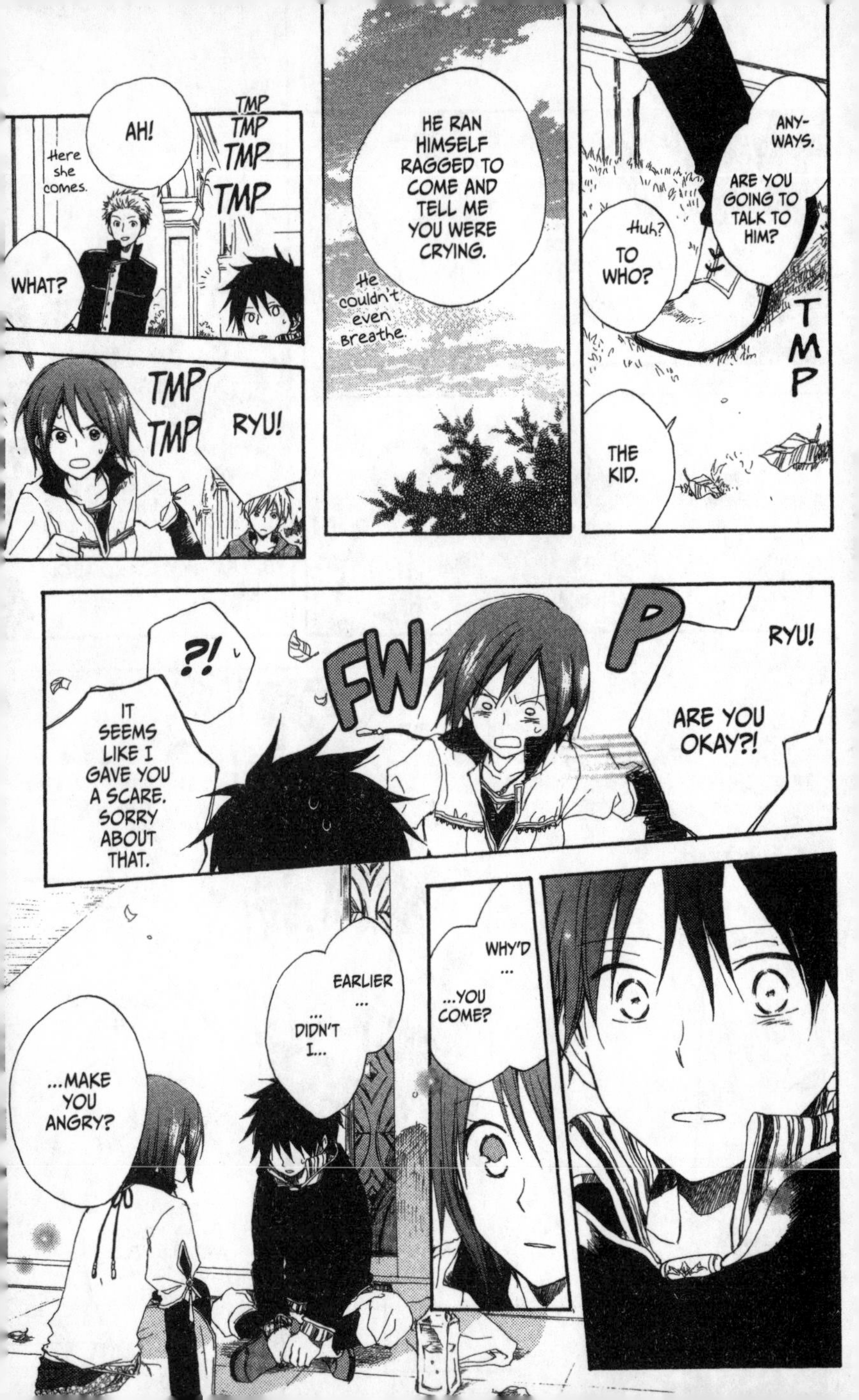
ANY-WAYS.
ARE YOU GOING TO TALK TO HIM?
Huh?
TO WHO?
TMP
THE KID.
HE RAN HIMSELF RAGGED TO COME AND TELL ME YOU WERE CRYING.
He couldn't even breathe.
TMP TMP TMP TMP
AH!
Here she comes.
WHAT?
TMP TMP
RYU!
RYU!
ARE YOU OKAY?!
FWP
?!
IT SEEMS LIKE I GAVE YOU A SCARE. SORRY ABOUT THAT.
WHY'D ...
...YOU COME?
EARLIER ...
... DIDN'T I...
...MAKE YOU ANGRY?

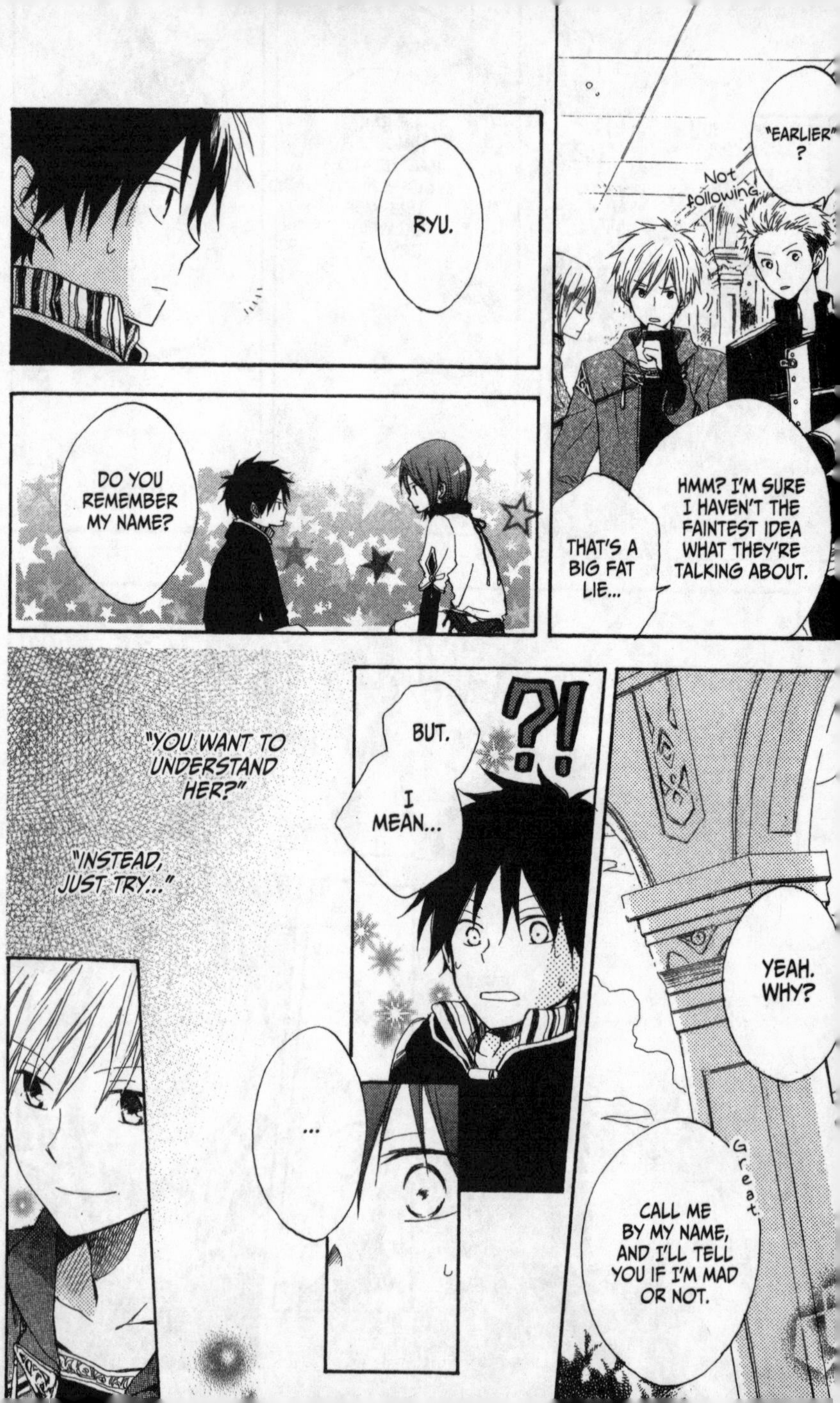
"EARLIER"?
Not following.
HMM? I'M SURE I HAVEN'T THE FAINTEST IDEA WHAT THEY'RE TALKING ABOUT.
THAT'S A BIG FAT LIE...
RYU.
DO YOU REMEMBER MY NAME?
YEAH. WHY?
Great.
CALL ME BY MY NAME, AND I'LL TELL YOU IF I'M MAD OR NOT.
?!
BUT.
I MEAN...
...
"YOU WANT TO UNDERSTAND HER?"
"INSTEAD, JUST TRY..."

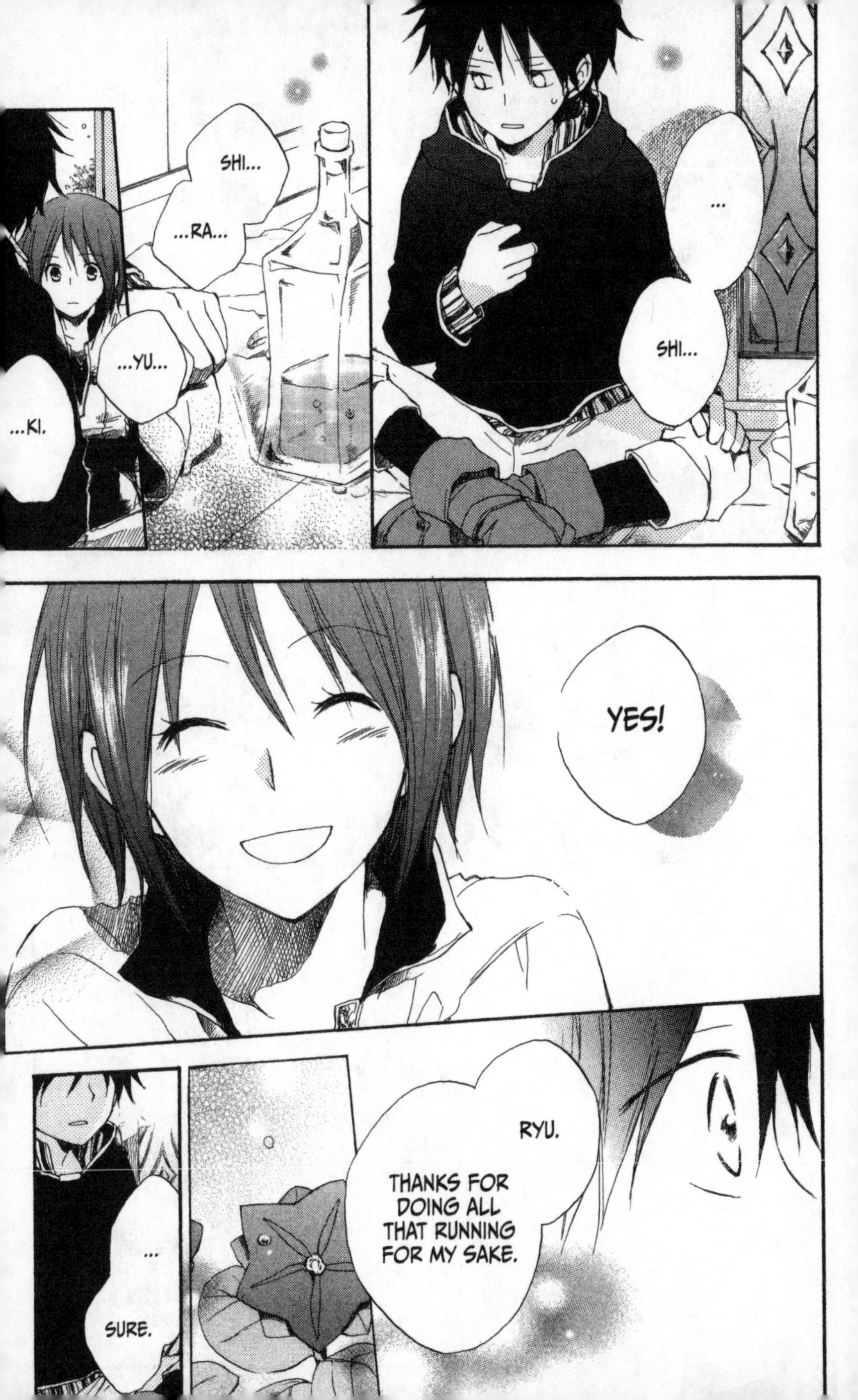
...
SHI...
SHI...
...RA...
...YU...
...KI.
YES!
RYU.
THANKS FOR DOING ALL THAT RUNNING FOR MY SAKE.
...
SURE.

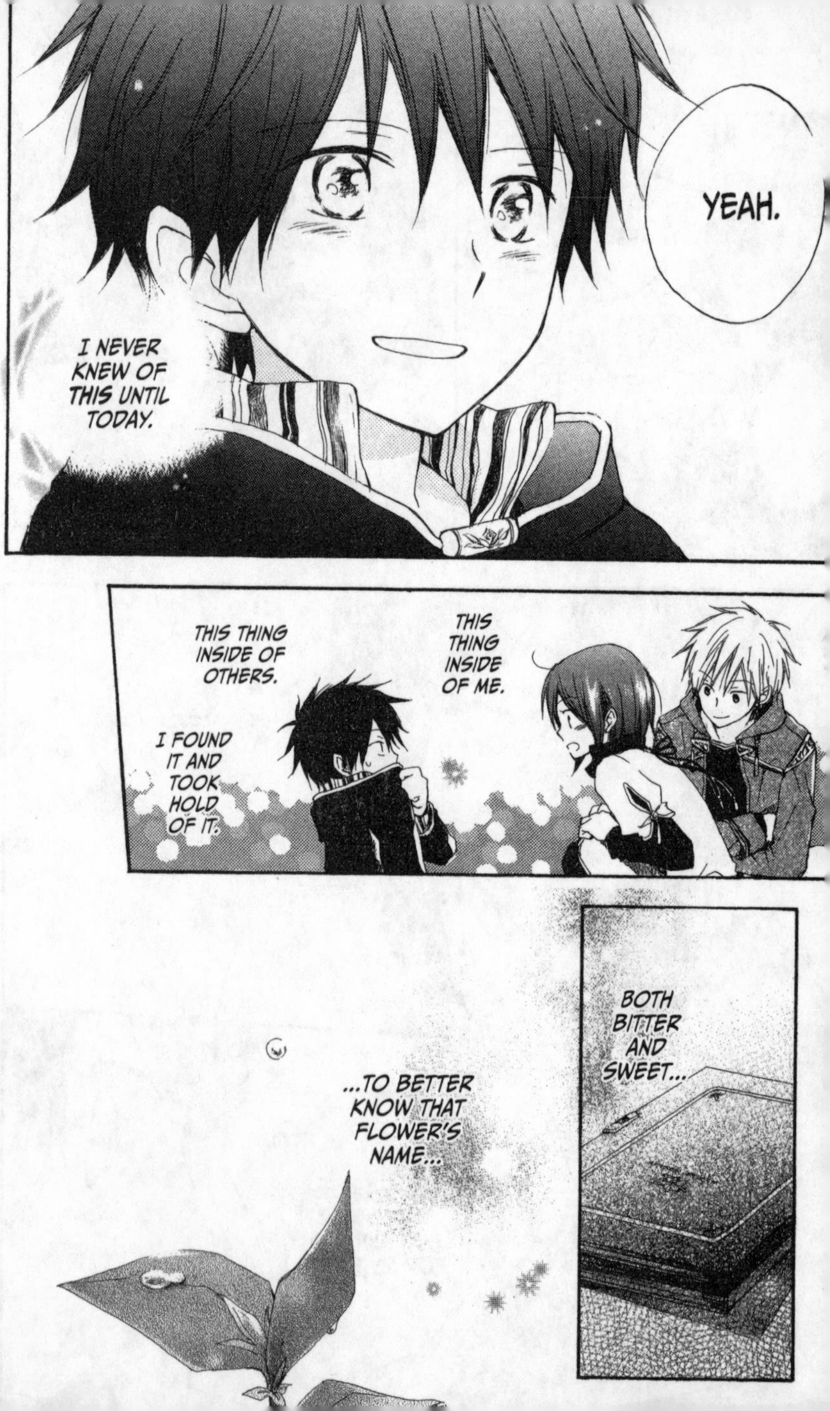
YEAH.
I NEVER KNEW OF THIS UNTIL TODAY.
THIS THING INSIDE OF ME.
THIS THING INSIDE OF OTHERS.
I FOUND IT AND TOOK HOLD OF IT.
BOTH BITTER AND SWEET...
...TO BETTER KNOW THAT FLOWER'S NAME...

Chapter 6

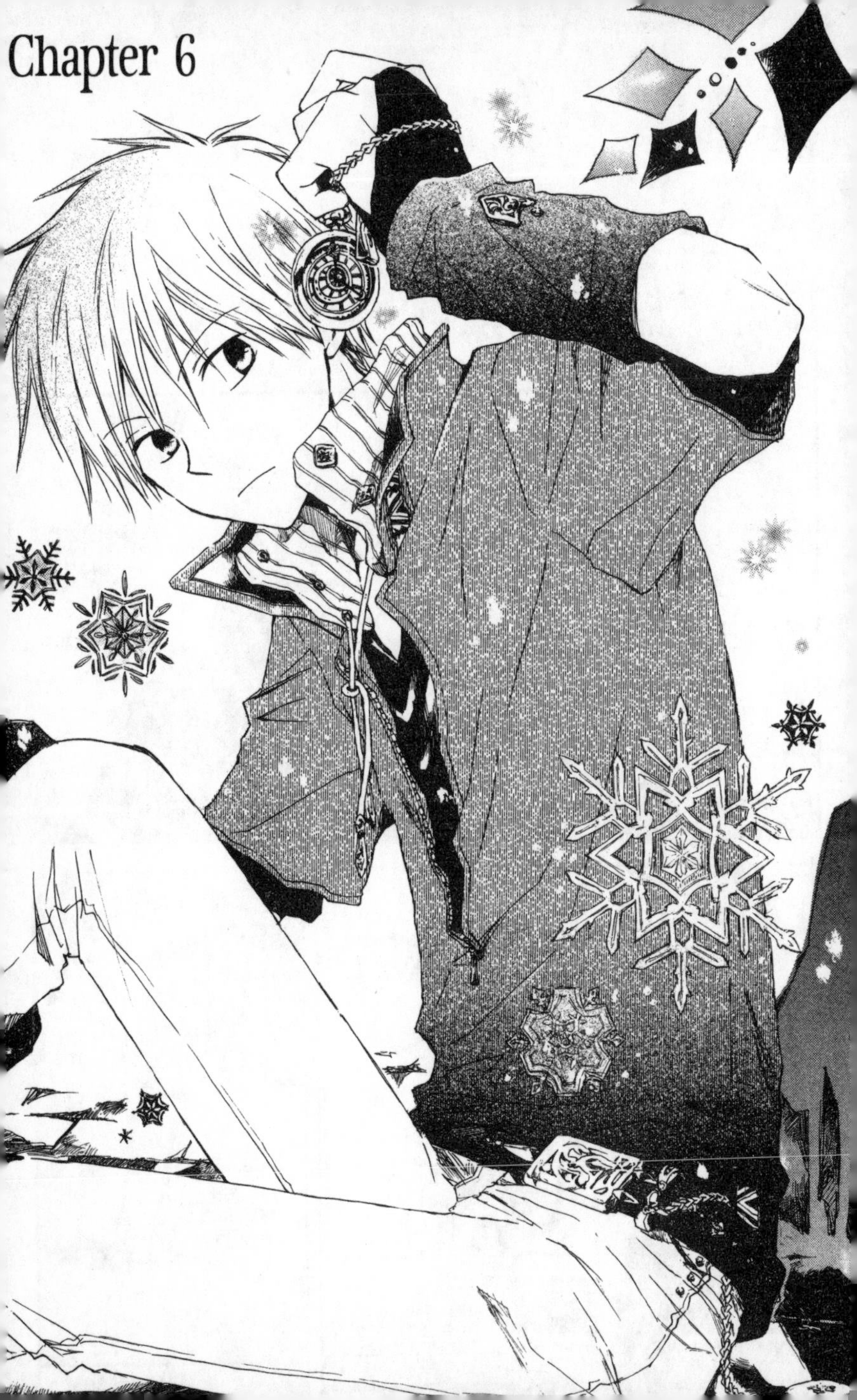

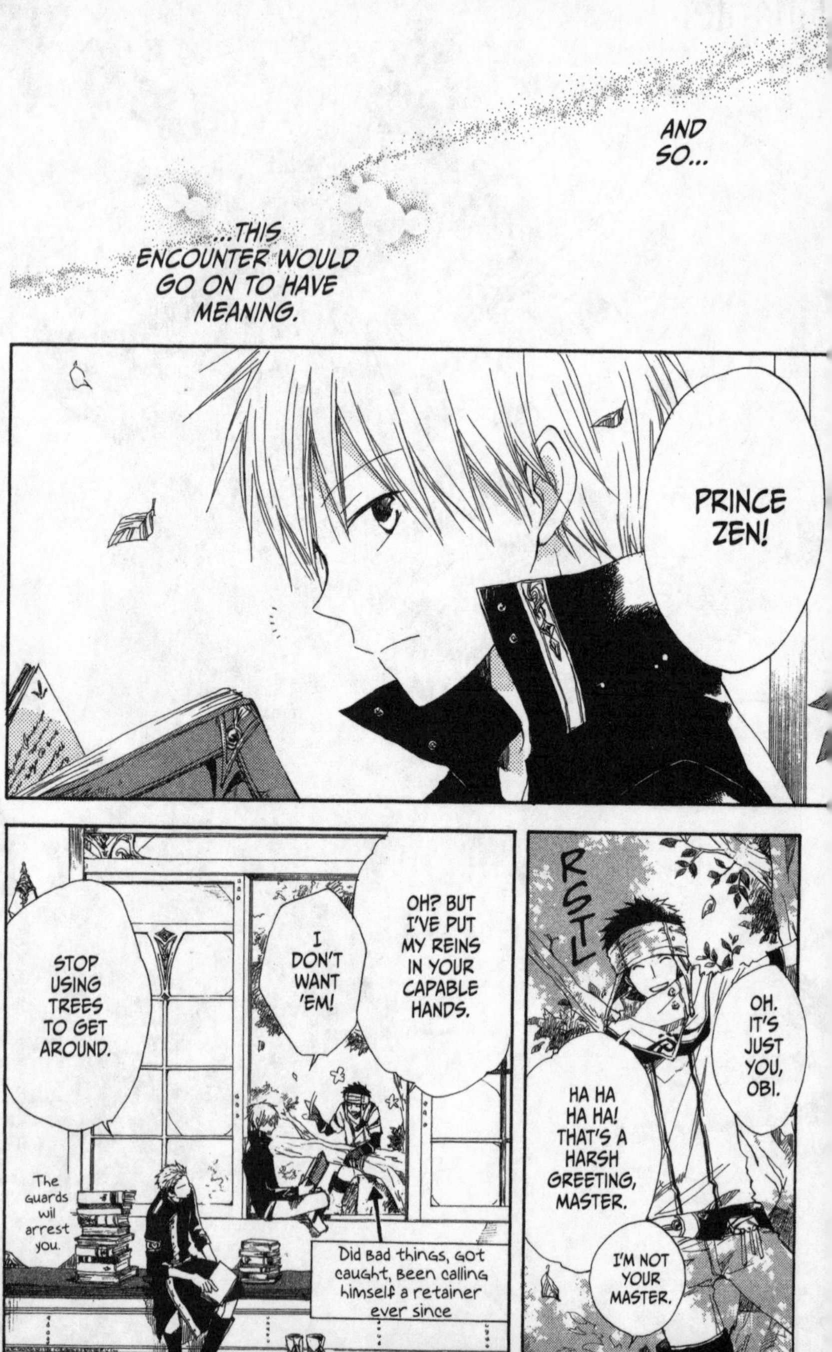
AND SO...
...THIS ENCOUNTER WOULD GO ON TO HAVE MEANING.
PRINCE ZEN!
RSTL
OH. IT'S JUST YOU, OBI.
HA HA HA HA! THAT'S A HARSH GREETING, MASTER.
I'M NOT YOUR MASTER.
OH? BUT I'VE PUT MY REINS IN YOUR CAPABLE HANDS.
I DON'T WANT 'EM!
STOP USING TREES TO GET AROUND.
The Guards wil arrest you.
Did bad things, got caught, been calling himself a retainer ever since

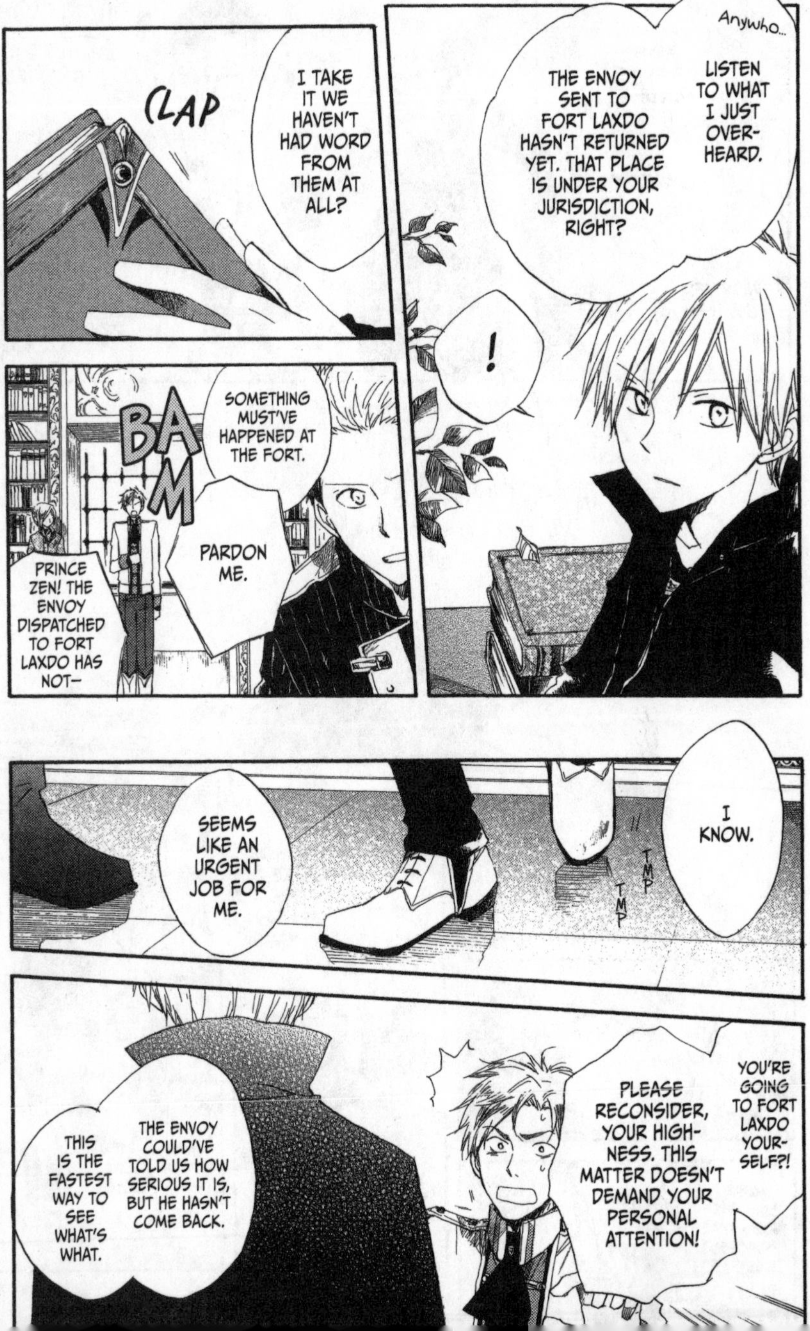
Anywho...
LISTEN TO WHAT I JUST OVER-HEARD.
THE ENVOY SENT TO FORT LAXDO HASN'T RETURNED YET. THAT PLACE IS UNDER YOUR JURISDICTION, RIGHT?
!
I TAKE IT WE HAVEN'T HAD WORD FROM THEM AT ALL?
CLAP
SOMETHING MUST'VE HAPPENED AT THE FORT.
BAM
PARDON ME.
PRINCE ZEN! THE ENVOY DISPATCHED TO FORT LAXDO HAS NOT—
I KNOW.
TMP
TMP
SEEMS LIKE AN URGENT JOB FOR ME.
YOU'RE GOING TO FORT LAXDO YOUR-SELF?!
PLEASE RECONSIDER, YOUR HIGH-NESS. THIS MATTER DOESN'T DEMAND YOUR PERSONAL ATTENTION!
THE ENVOY COULD'VE TOLD US HOW SERIOUS IT IS, BUT HE HASN'T COME BACK.
THIS IS THE FASTEST WAY TO SEE WHAT'S WHAT.

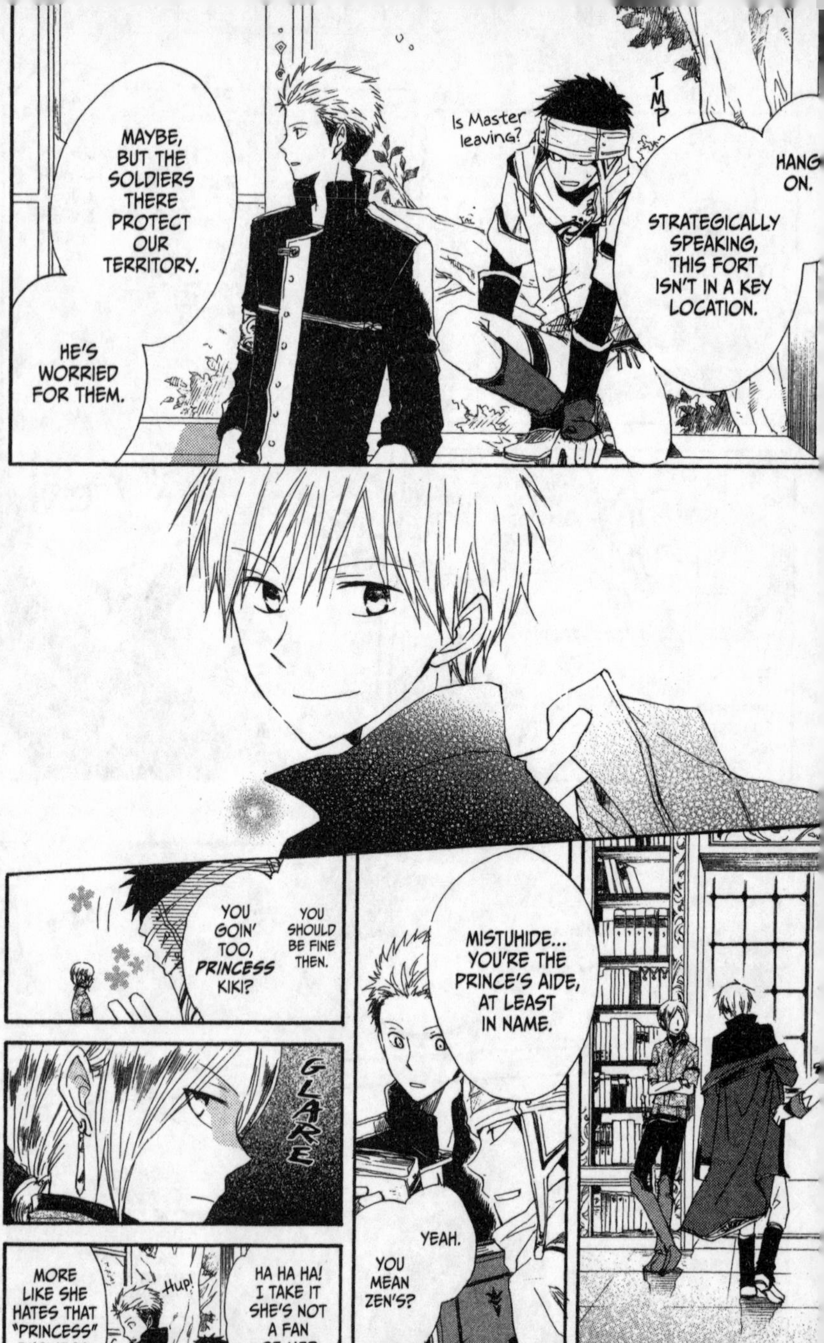
TMP
HANG ON.
STRATEGICALLY SPEAKING, THIS FORT ISN'T IN A KEY LOCATION.
Is Master leaving?
MAYBE, BUT THE SOLDIERS THERE PROTECT OUR TERRITORY.
HE'S WORRIED FOR THEM.
MISTUHIDE... YOU'RE THE PRINCE'S AIDE, AT LEAST IN NAME.
YEAH.
YOU MEAN ZEN'S?
YOU SHOULD BE FINE THEN.
YOU GOIN' TOO, PRINCESS KIKI?
GLARE
HA HA HA! I TAKE IT SHE'S NOT A FAN OF ME?
Hup!
MORE LIKE SHE HATES THAT "PRINCESS" BUSINESS.

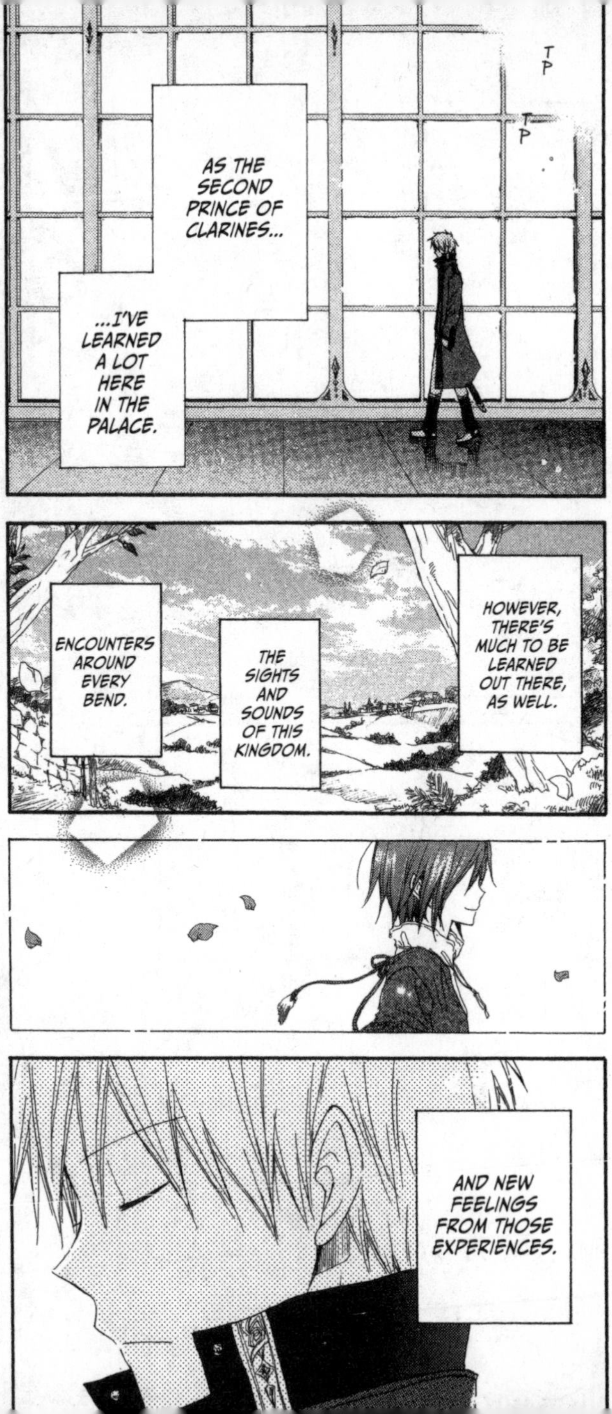
TP
TP
AS THE SECOND PRINCE OF CLARINES...
...I'VE LEARNED A LOT HERE IN THE PALACE.
HOWEVER, THERE'S MUCH TO BE LEARNED OUT THERE, AS WELL.
THE SIGHTS AND SOUNDS OF THIS KINGDOM.
ENCOUNTERS AROUND EVERY BEND.
AND NEW FEELINGS FROM THOSE EXPERIENCES.

Chapter 6

A tale from Zen's perspective.

It's fun taking on Zen like this.

At the time, my editor said, "You'd also better start defining how exactly Kiki and Mitsuhide fit into the story."

Really! How to go about that? (smiles)

That lit a fire under me, and I went on to craft this chapter.

The timing of this overlapped with another one-shot, so I found myself in deadline hell. I barely remember doing the second half of this chapter...

I'd better keep honing my skills.

I also hope to draw some really solid battle scenes someday.

3

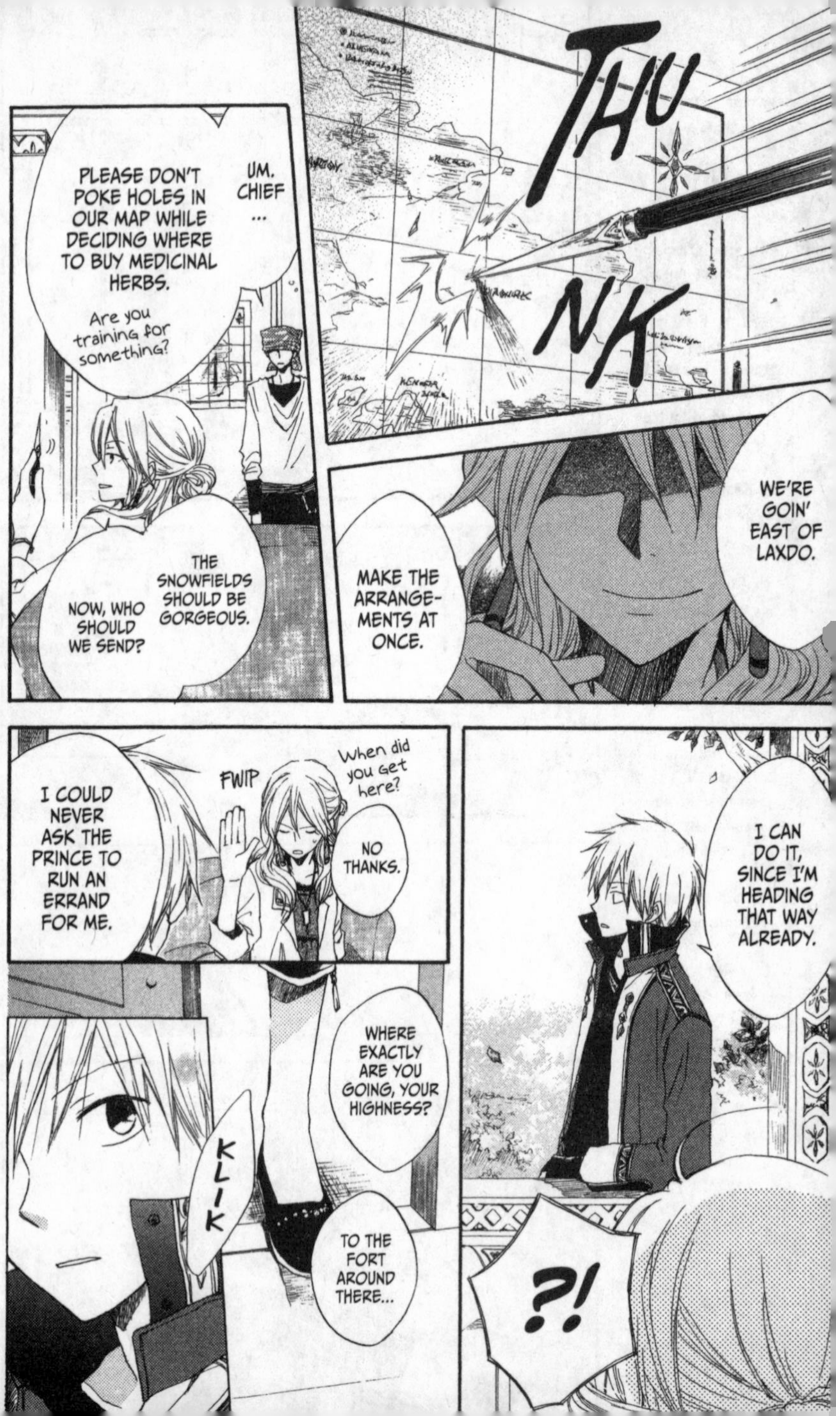
THUNK
WE'RE GOIN' EAST OF LAXDO.
MAKE THE ARRANGEMENTS AT ONCE.
UM. CHIEF ...
PLEASE DON'T POKE HOLES IN OUR MAP WHILE DECIDING WHERE TO BUY MEDICINAL HERBS.
Are you training for something?
THE SNOWFIELDS SHOULD BE GORGEOUS.
NOW, WHO SHOULD WE SEND?
I CAN DO IT, SINCE I'M HEADING THAT WAY ALREADY.
?!
When did you get here?
NO THANKS.
FWIP
I COULD NEVER ASK THE PRINCE TO RUN AN ERRAND FOR ME.
WHERE EXACTLY ARE YOU GOING, YOUR HIGHNESS?
TO THE FORT AROUND THERE...
KLIK

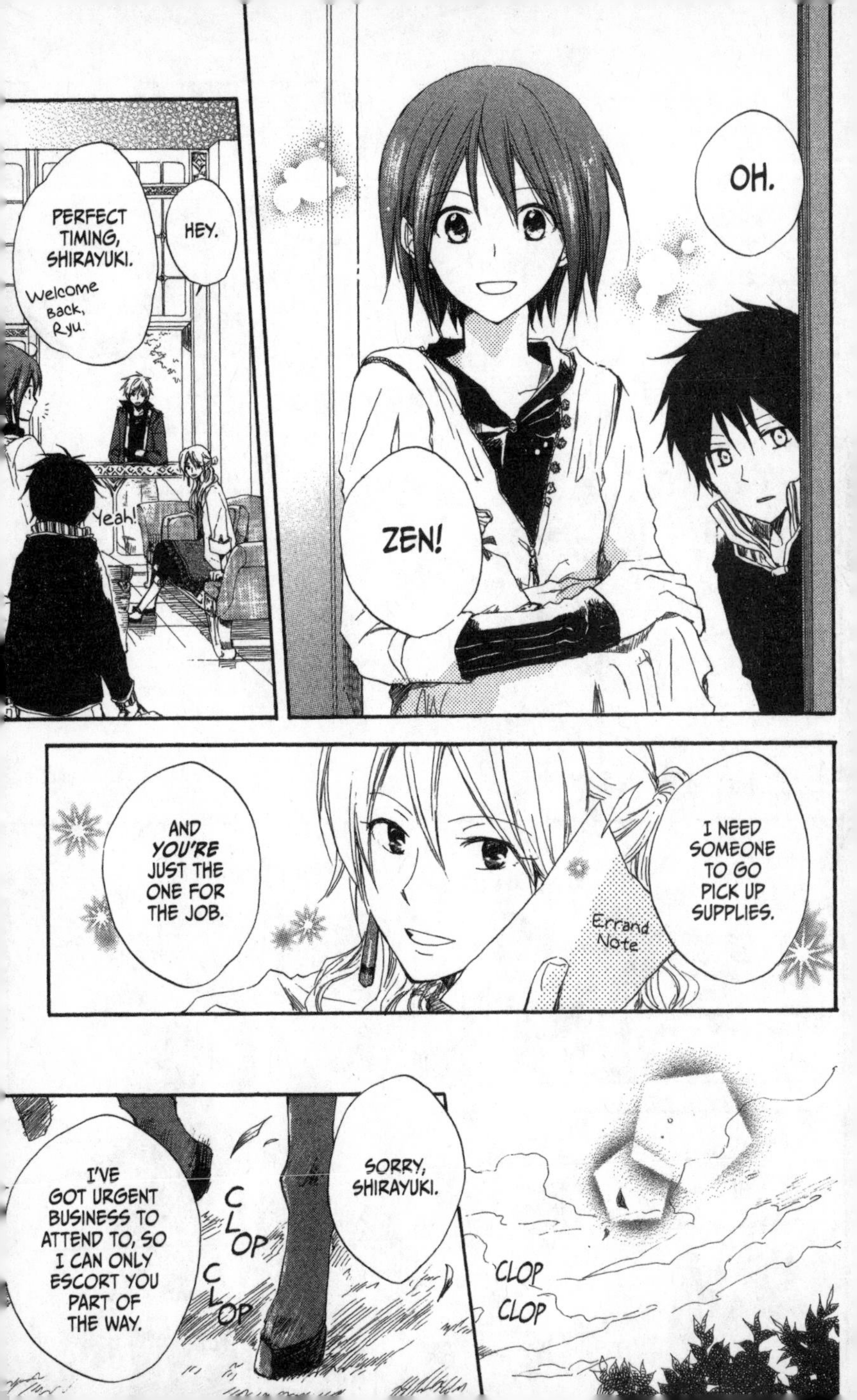
OH.
ZEN!
HEY.
PERFECT TIMING, SHIRAYUKI.
Welcome back, Ryu.
Yeah!
I NEED SOMEONE TO GO PICK UP SUPPLIES.
Errand Note
AND *YOU'RE* JUST THE ONE FOR THE JOB.
CLOP CLOP
SORRY, SHIRAYUKI.
CLOP CLOP
I'VE GOT URGENT BUSINESS TO ATTEND TO, SO I CAN ONLY ESCORT YOU PART OF THE WAY.

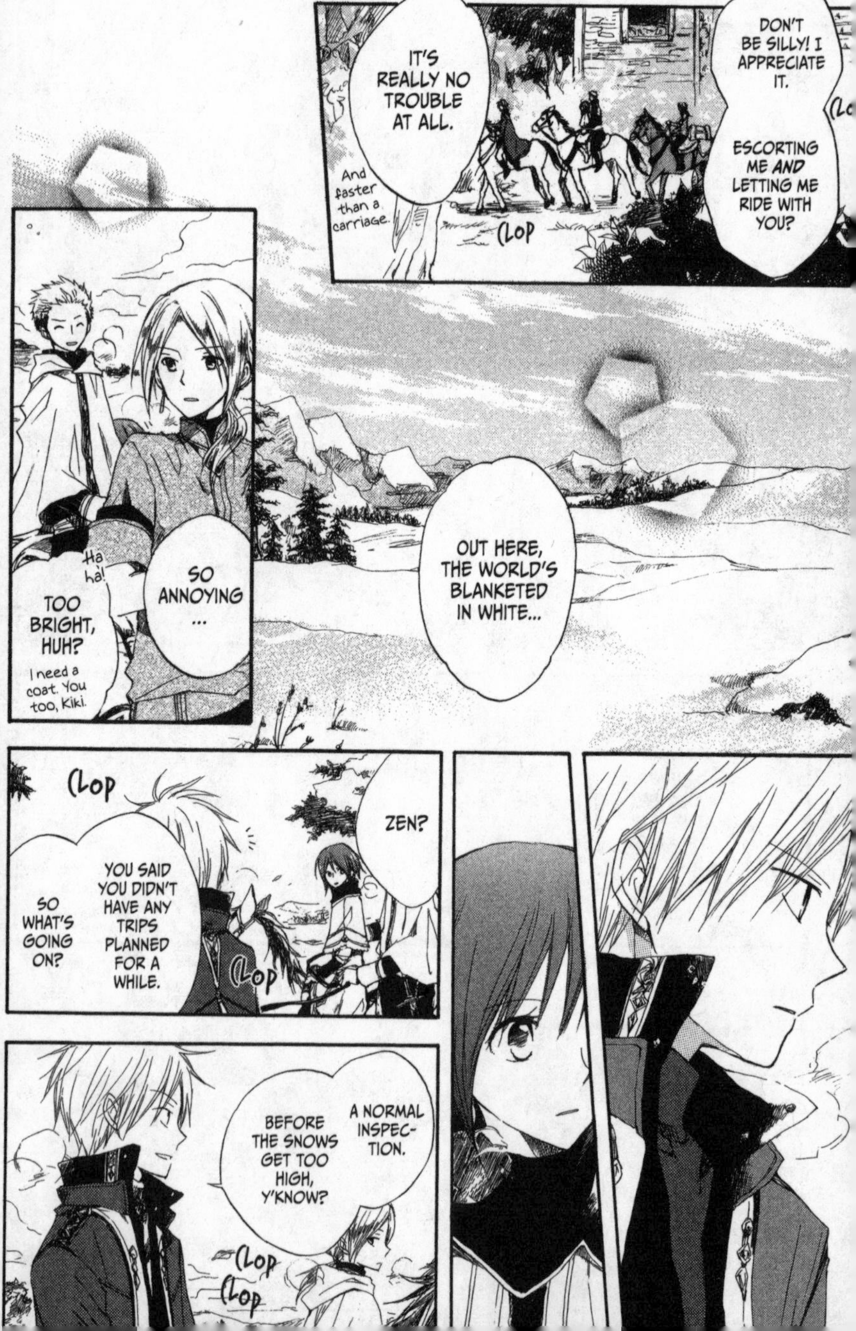
DON'T BE SILLY! I APPRECIATE IT.
ESCORTING ME AND LETTING ME RIDE WITH YOU?
IT'S REALLY NO TROUBLE AT ALL.
And faster than a carriage.
CLOP
OUT HERE, THE WORLD'S BLANKETED IN WHITE...
SO ANNOYING...
Ha ha!
TOO BRIGHT, HUH?
I need a coat. You too, Kiki.
CLOP
ZEN?
YOU SAID YOU DIDN'T HAVE ANY TRIPS PLANNED FOR A WHILE.
SO WHAT'S GOING ON?
CLOP
A NORMAL INSPECTION.
BEFORE THE SNOWS GET TOO HIGH, Y'KNOW?
CLOP
CLOP

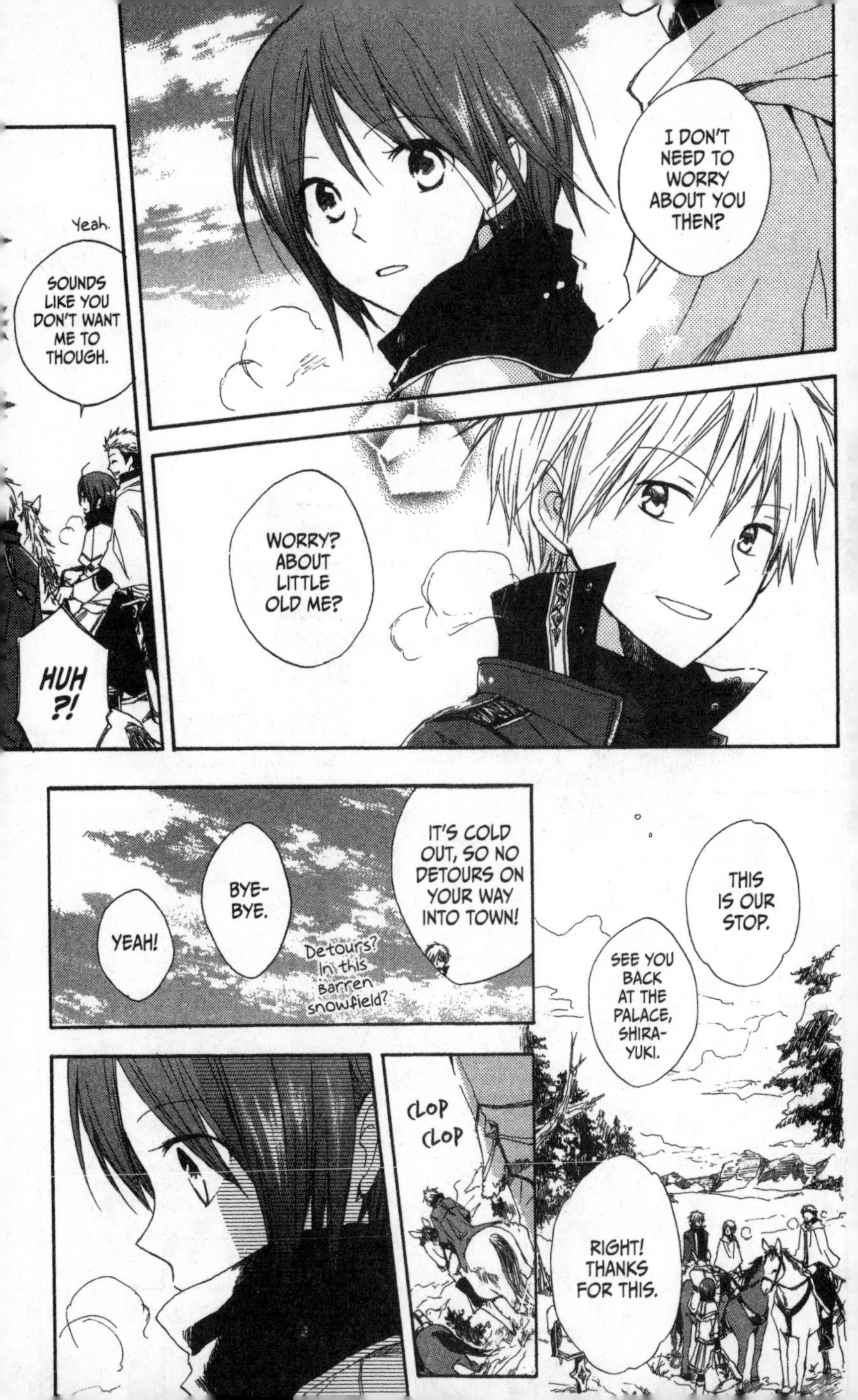
I DON'T NEED TO WORRY ABOUT YOU THEN?
WORRY? ABOUT LITTLE OLD ME?
Yeah.
SOUNDS LIKE YOU DON'T WANT ME TO THOUGH.
HUH ?!
THIS IS OUR STOP.
SEE YOU BACK AT THE PALACE, SHIRAYUKI.
RIGHT! THANKS FOR THIS.
IT'S COLD OUT, SO NO DETOURS ON YOUR WAY INTO TOWN!
BYE-BYE.
Detours? In this barren snowfield?
YEAH!
CLOP CLOP

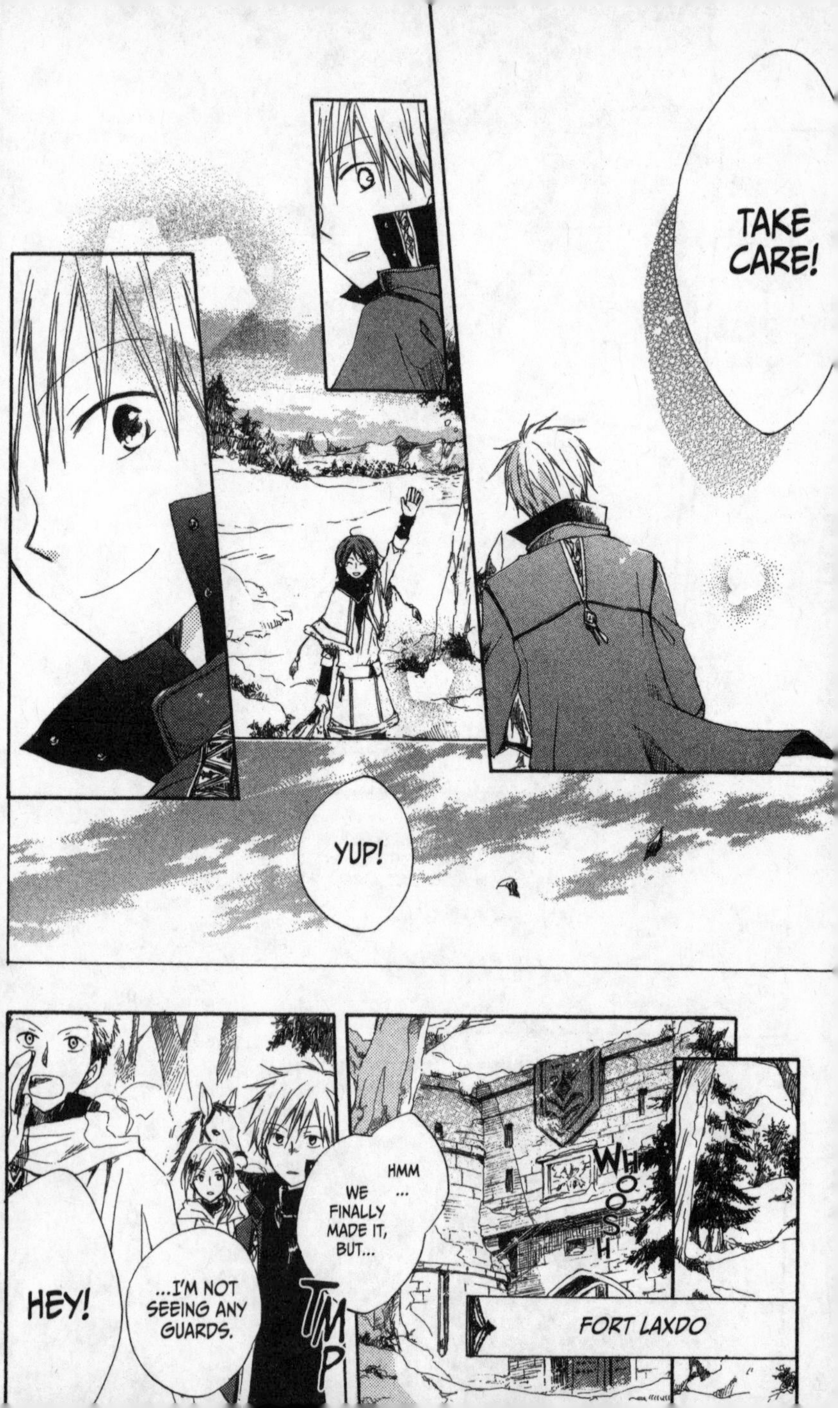
TAKE CARE!
YUP!
WHOOSH
FORT LAXDO
HMM ...
WE FINALLY MADE IT, BUT...
...I'M NOT SEEING ANY GUARDS.
TMP
HEY!

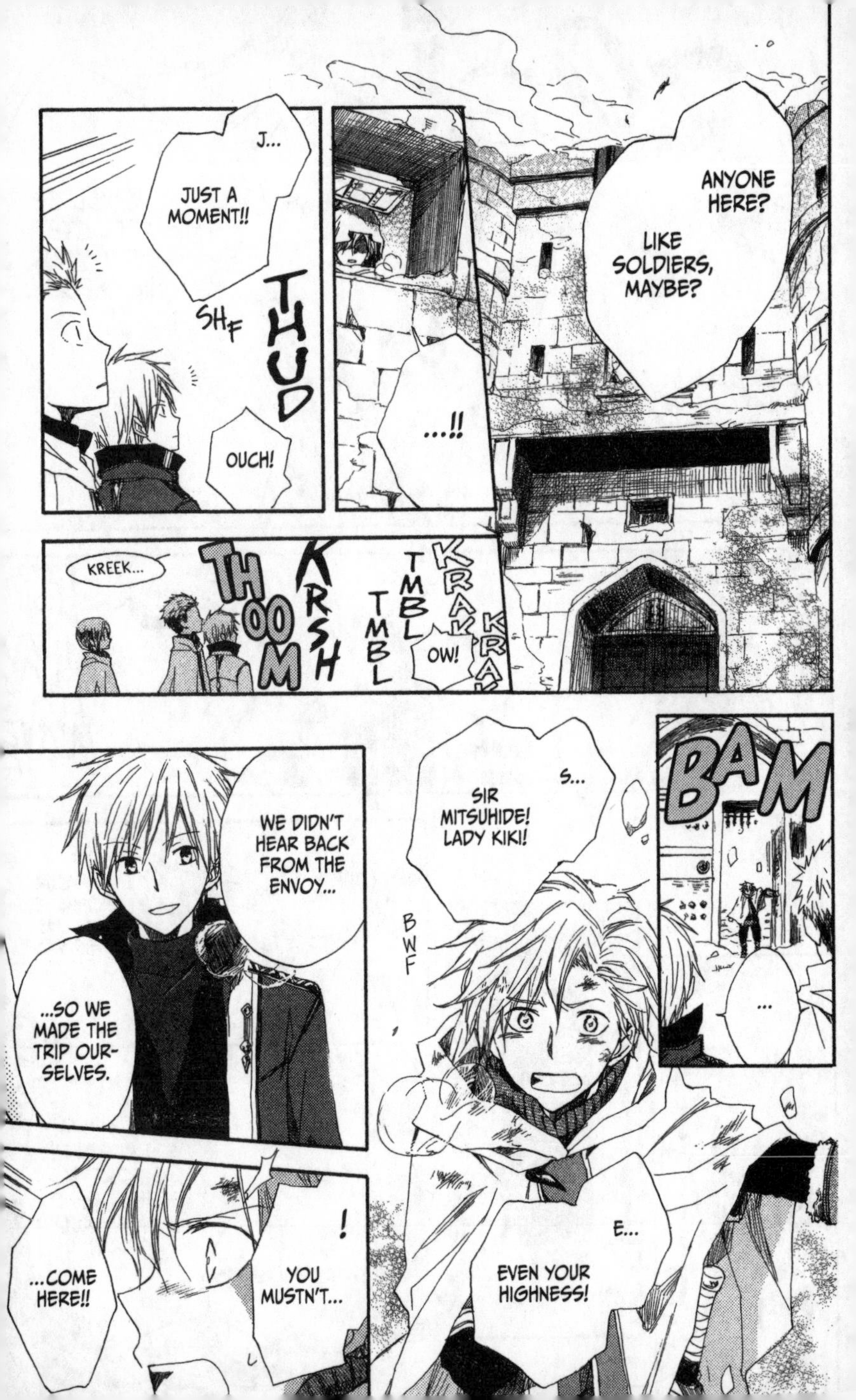
ANYONE HERE?
LIKE SOLDIERS, MAYBE?
...!!
J...
JUST A MOMENT!!
SHF
THUD
OUCH!
KRAK
KRAK
TMBL
TMBL
OW!
KRSH
THOOM
KREEK...
BAM
...
S...
SIR MITSUHIDE! LADY KIKI!
BWF
E...
EVEN YOUR HIGHNESS!
WE DIDN'T HEAR BACK FROM THE ENVOY...
...SO WE MADE THE TRIP OURSELVES.
!
YOU MUSTN'T...
...COME HERE!!

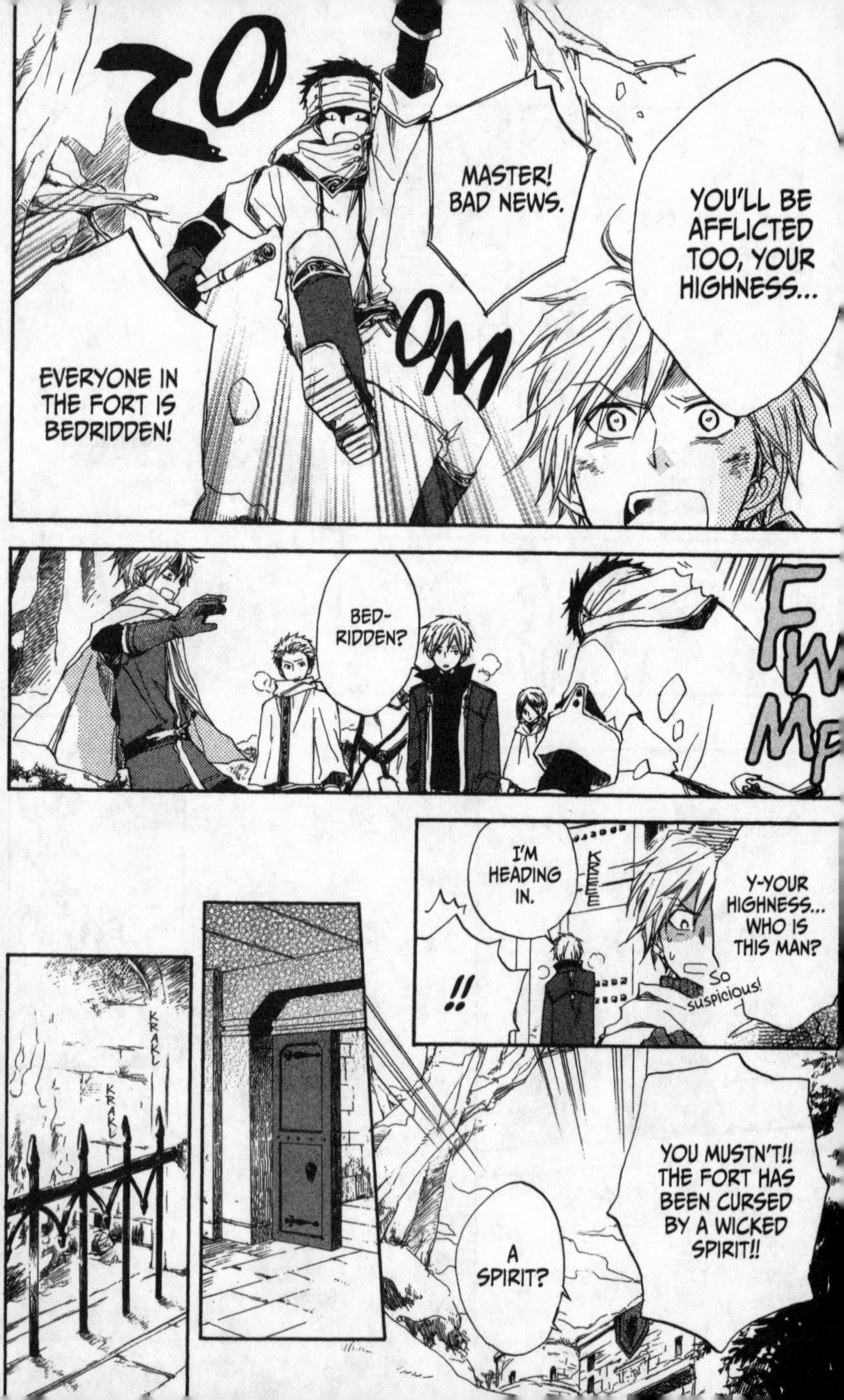
YOU'LL BE AFFLICTED TOO, YOUR HIGHNESS...
ZOOM
MASTER! BAD NEWS.
EVERYONE IN THE FORT IS BEDRIDDEN!
FWMP
BED-RIDDEN?
Y-YOUR HIGHNESS... WHO IS THIS MAN?
So suspicious!
KREEE
I'M HEADING IN.
!!
YOU MUSTN'T!! THE FORT HAS BEEN CURSED BY A WICKED SPIRIT!!
A SPIRIT?
KRAKL
KRAKL

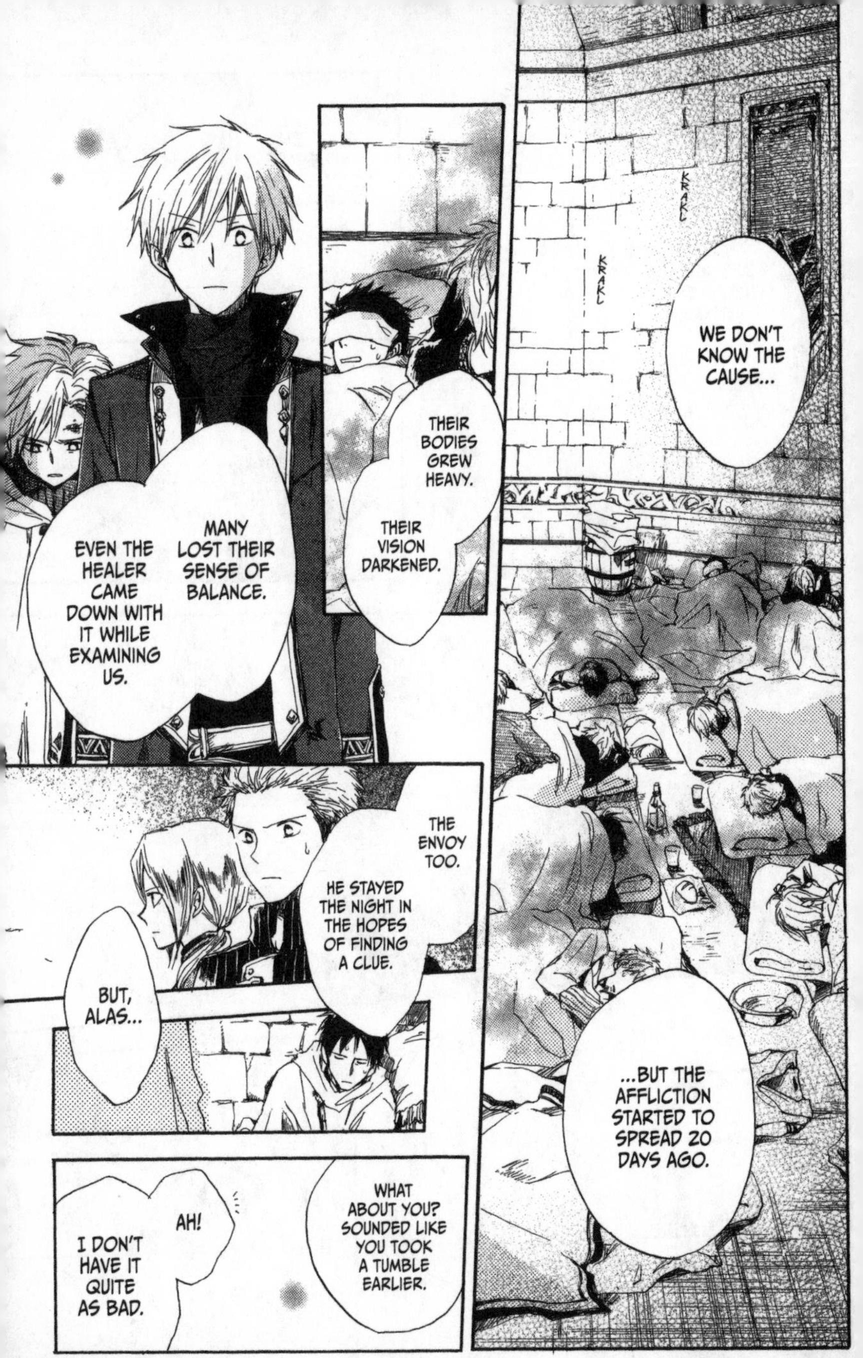
KRAKL
KRAKL
WE DON'T KNOW THE CAUSE...
...BUT THE AFFLICTION STARTED TO SPREAD 20 DAYS AGO.
THEIR BODIES GREW HEAVY.
THEIR VISION DARKENED.
MANY LOST THEIR SENSE OF BALANCE.
EVEN THE HEALER CAME DOWN WITH IT WHILE EXAMINING US.
THE ENVOY TOO.
HE STAYED THE NIGHT IN THE HOPES OF FINDING A CLUE.
BUT, ALAS...
WHAT ABOUT YOU? SOUNDED LIKE YOU TOOK A TUMBLE EARLIER.
AH!
I DON'T HAVE IT QUITE AS BAD.

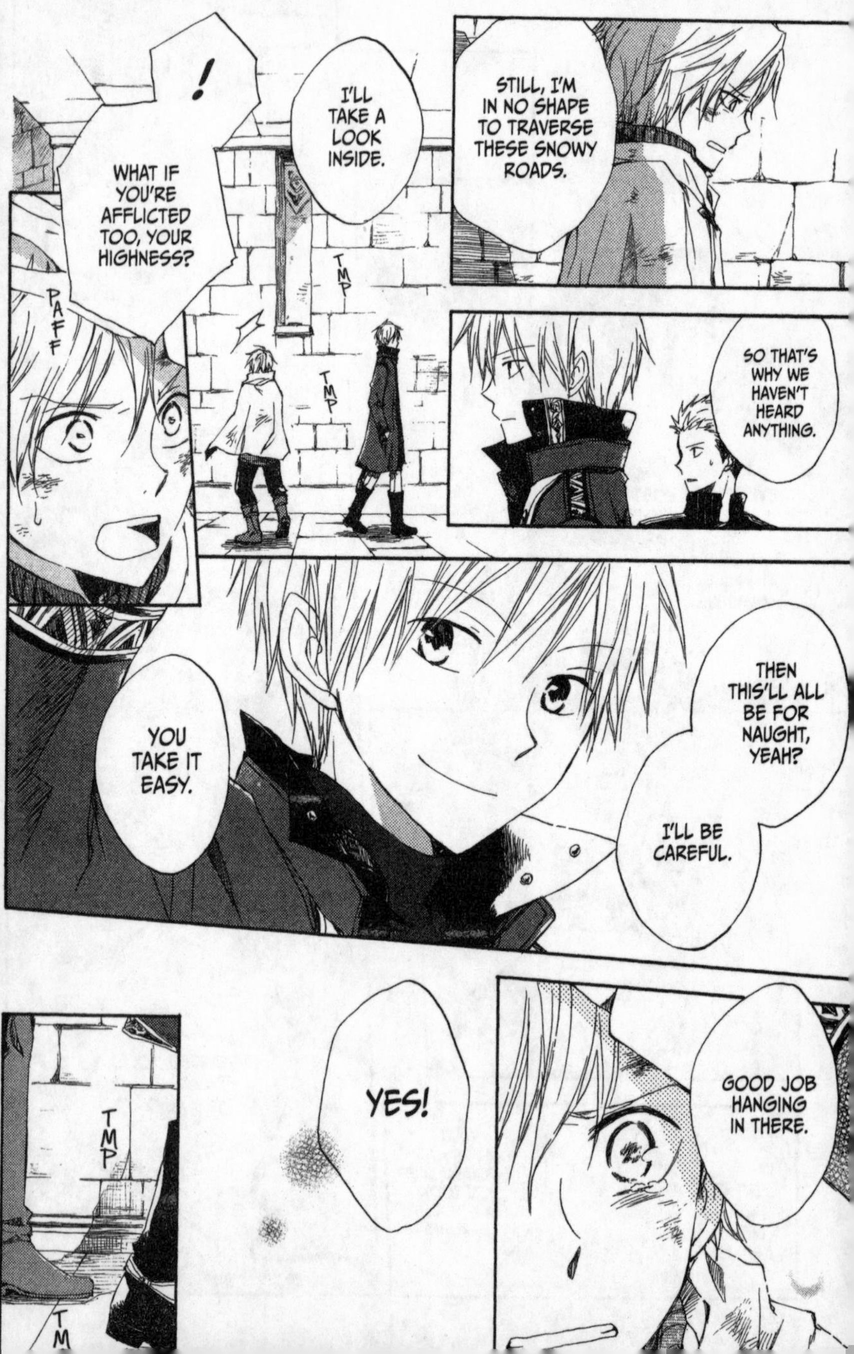
STILL, I'M IN NO SHAPE TO TRAVERSE THESE SNOWY ROADS.
SO THAT'S WHY WE HAVEN'T HEARD ANYTHING.
I'LL TAKE A LOOK INSIDE.
TMP
TMP
!
WHAT IF YOU'RE AFFLICTED TOO, YOUR HIGHNESS?
PAFF
THEN THIS'LL ALL BE FOR NAUGHT, YEAH?
I'LL BE CAREFUL.
YOU TAKE IT EASY.
GOOD JOB HANGING IN THERE.
YES!
TMP
TM

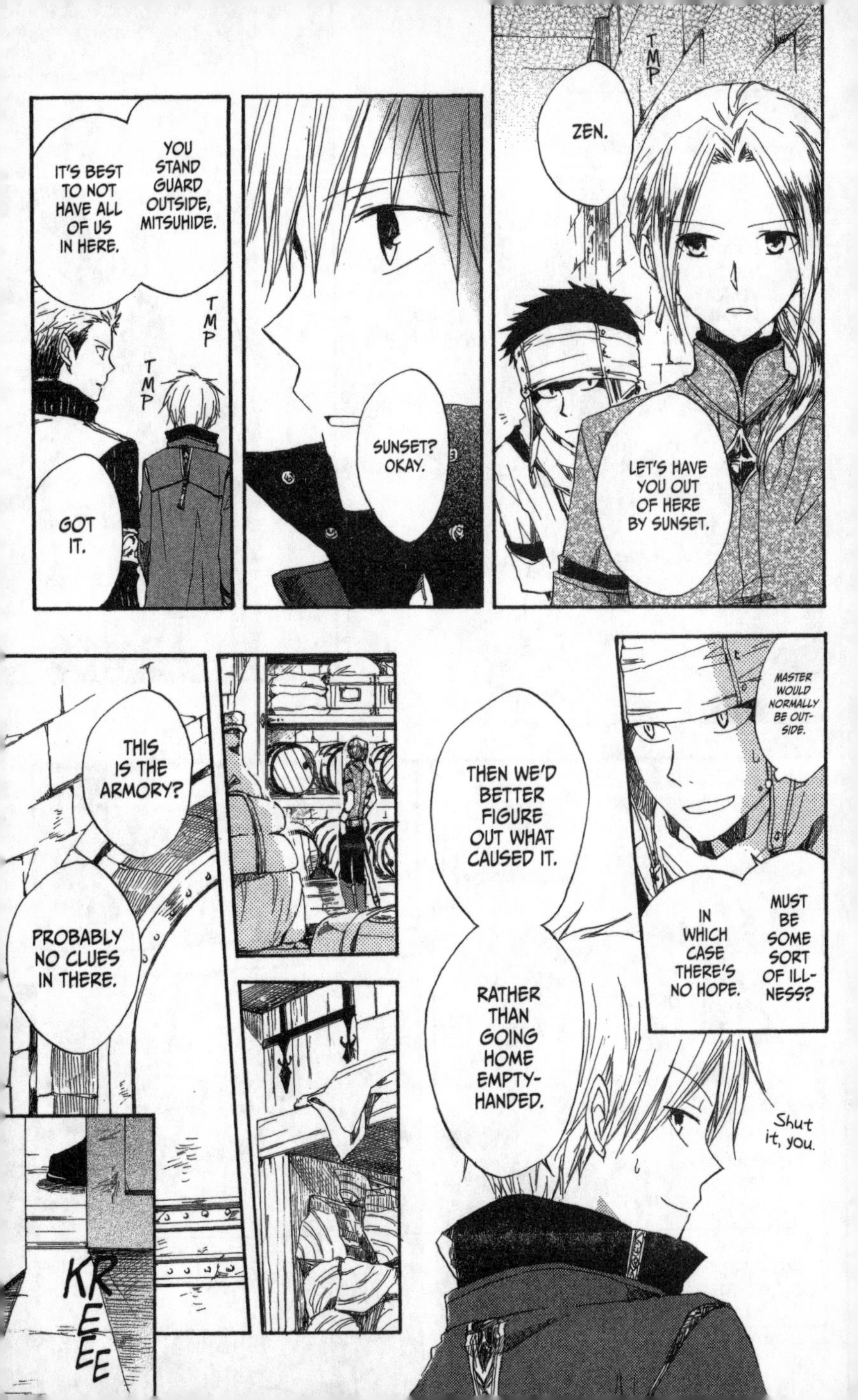
TMP
ZEN.
LET'S HAVE YOU OUT OF HERE BY SUNSET.
SUNSET? OKAY.
YOU STAND GUARD OUTSIDE, MITSUHIDE.
IT'S BEST TO NOT HAVE ALL OF US IN HERE.
TMP
TMP
GOT IT.
MASTER WOULD NORMALLY BE OUT-SIDE.
MUST BE SOME SORT OF ILL-NESS?
IN WHICH CASE THERE'S NO HOPE.
THEN WE'D BETTER FIGURE OUT WHAT CAUSED IT.
RATHER THAN GOING HOME EMPTY-HANDED.
Shut it, you.
THIS IS THE ARMORY?
PROBABLY NO CLUES IN THERE.
KREEE

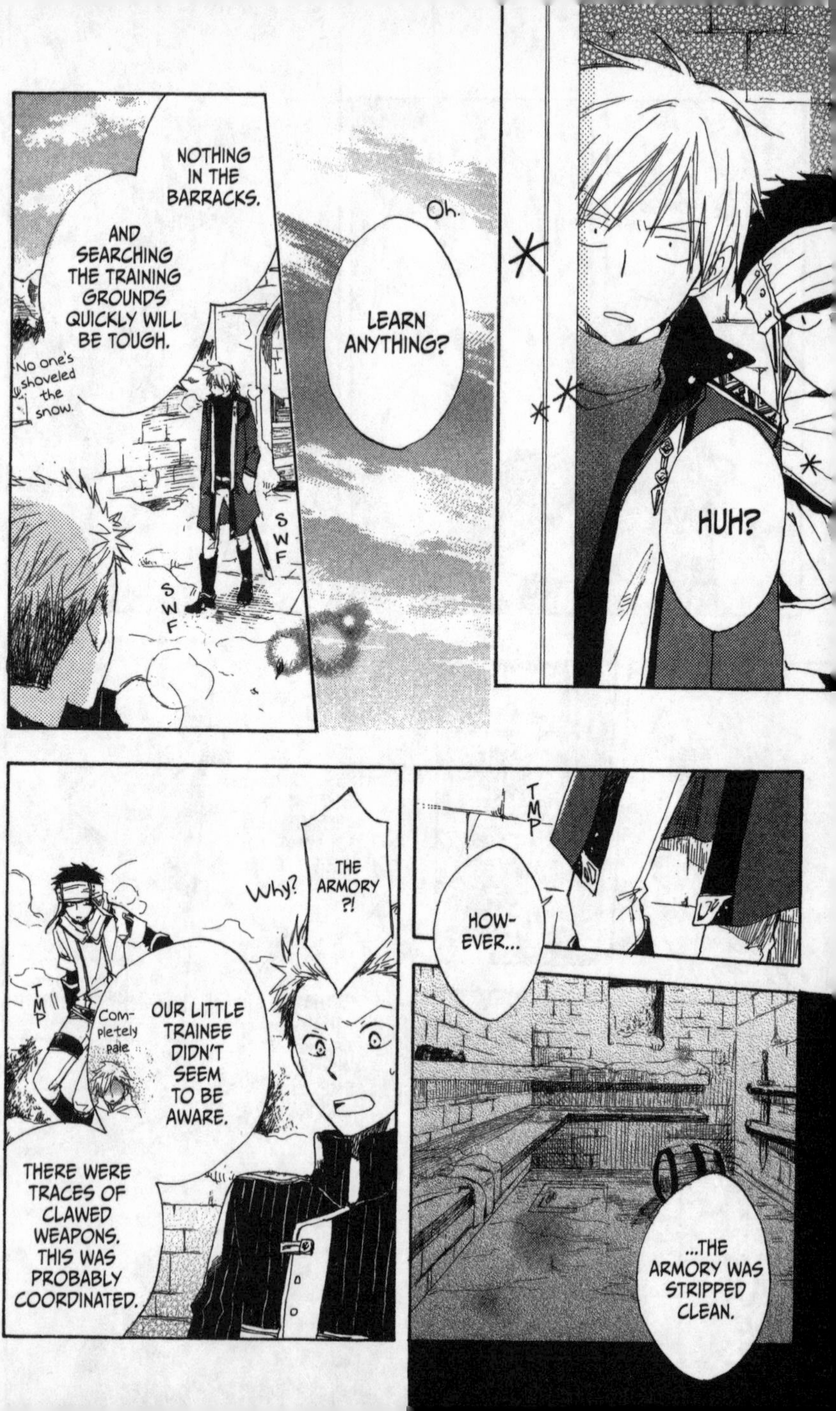
Oh.
LEARN ANYTHING?
HUH?
NOTHING IN THE BARRACKS.
AND SEARCHING THE TRAINING GROUNDS QUICKLY WILL BE TOUGH.
No one's shoveled the snow.
SWF
SWF
TMP
HOW-EVER...
...THE ARMORY WAS STRIPPED CLEAN.
THE ARMORY ?!
Why?
OUR LITTLE TRAINEE DIDN'T SEEM TO BE AWARE.
Com-pletely pale
TMP
THERE WERE TRACES OF CLAWED WEAPONS. THIS WAS PROBABLY COORDINATED.

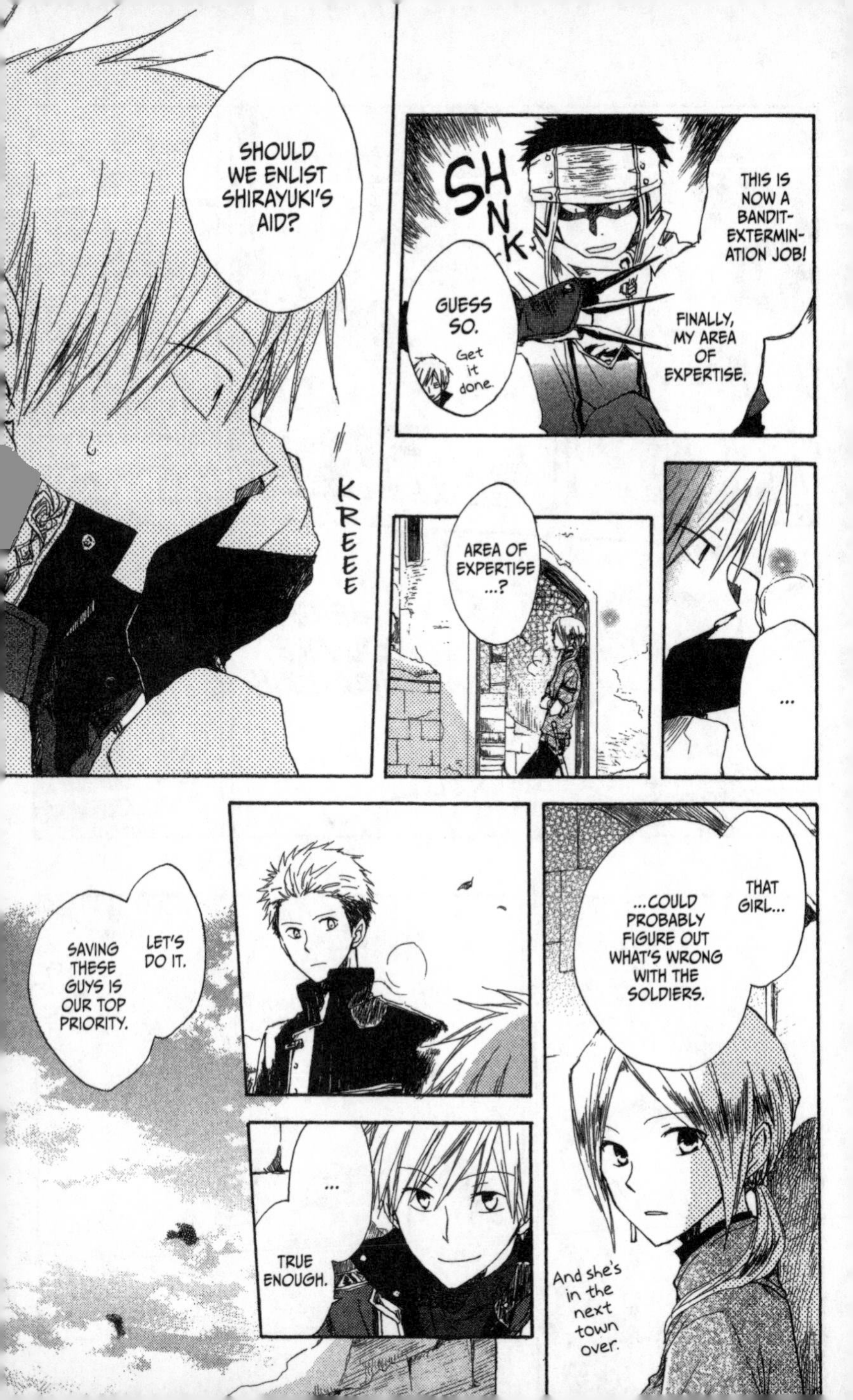
SHNK
THIS IS NOW A BANDIT-EXTERMINATION JOB!
FINALLY, MY AREA OF EXPERTISE.
GUESS SO.
Get it done.
...
AREA OF EXPERTISE ...?
SHOULD WE ENLIST SHIRAYUKI'S AID?
KREEE
THAT GIRL...
...COULD PROBABLY FIGURE OUT WHAT'S WRONG WITH THE SOLDIERS.
And she's in the next town over.
LET'S DO IT.
SAVING THESE GUYS IS OUR TOP PRIORITY.
...
TRUE ENOUGH.

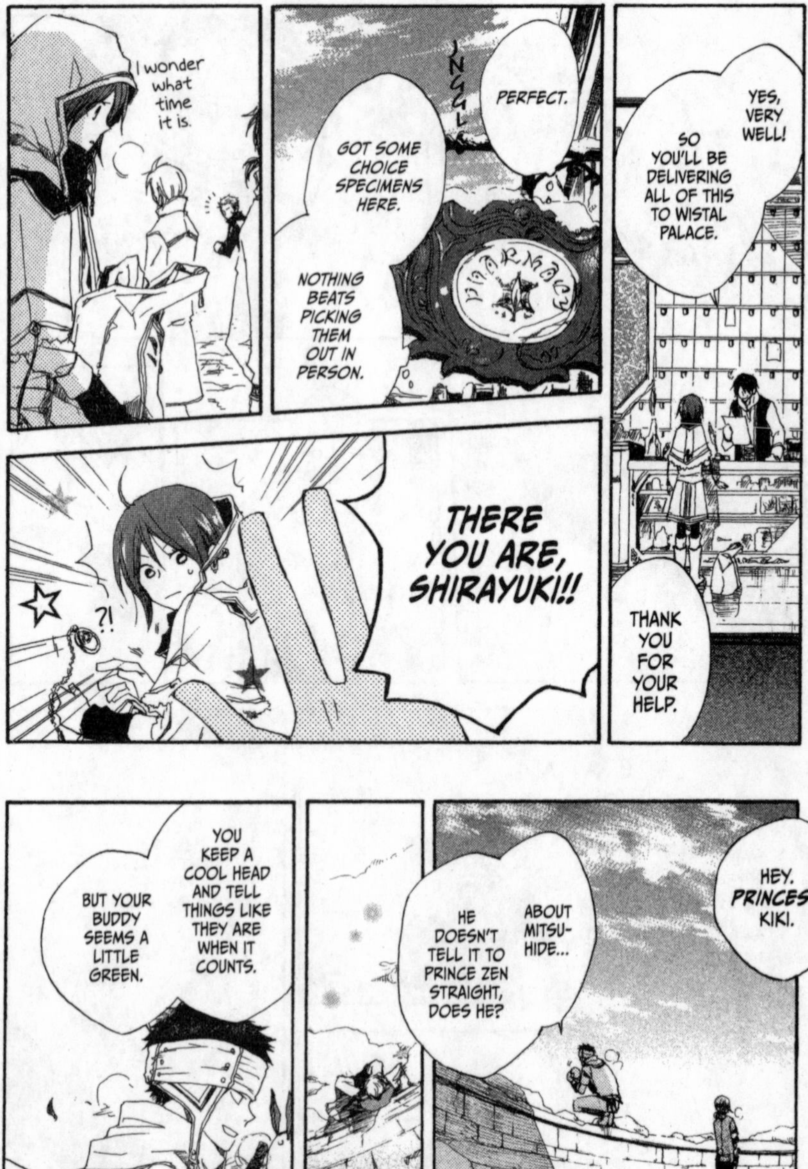

YES, VERY WELL!
SO YOU'LL BE DELIVERING ALL OF THIS TO WISTAL PALACE.
THANK YOU FOR YOUR HELP.
PERFECT.
GOT SOME CHOICE SPECIMENS HERE.
NOTHING BEATS PICKING THEM OUT IN PERSON.
I wonder what time it is.
THERE YOU ARE, SHIRAYUKI!!
?!
HEY. PRINCESS KIKI.
ABOUT MITSU-HIDE...
HE DOESN'T TELL IT TO PRINCE ZEN STRAIGHT, DOES HE?
YOU KEEP A COOL HEAD AND TELL THINGS LIKE THEY ARE WHEN IT COUNTS.
BUT YOUR BUDDY SEEMS A LITTLE GREEN.

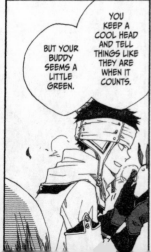

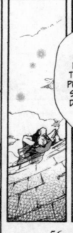

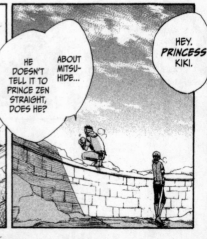

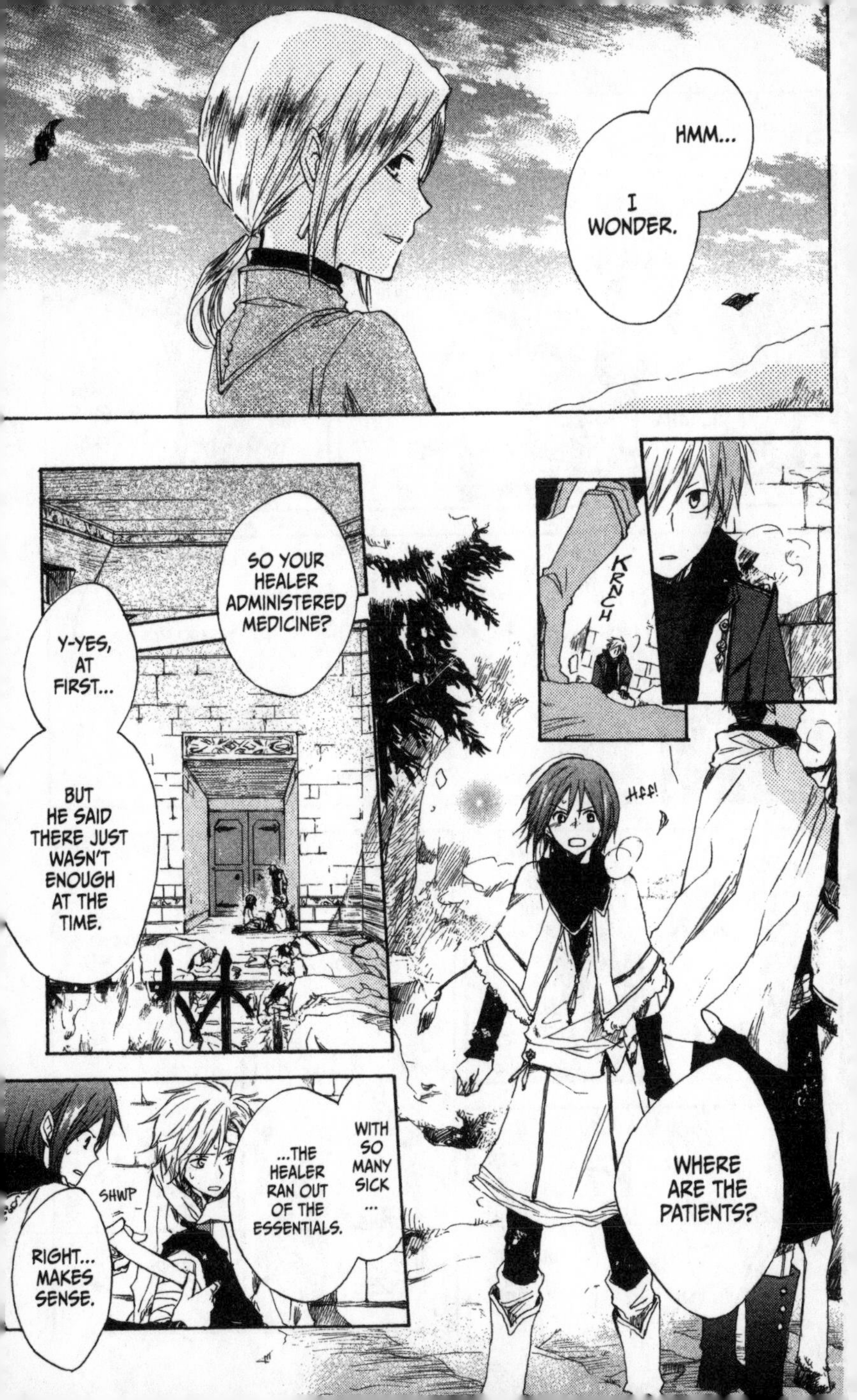
HMM...
I WONDER.
KRNCH
Hff!
WHERE ARE THE PATIENTS?
SO YOUR HEALER ADMINISTERED MEDICINE?
Y-YES, AT FIRST...
BUT HE SAID THERE JUST WASN'T ENOUGH AT THE TIME.
WITH SO MANY SICK...
...THE HEALER RAN OUT OF THE ESSENTIALS.
SHWP
RIGHT... MAKES SENSE.

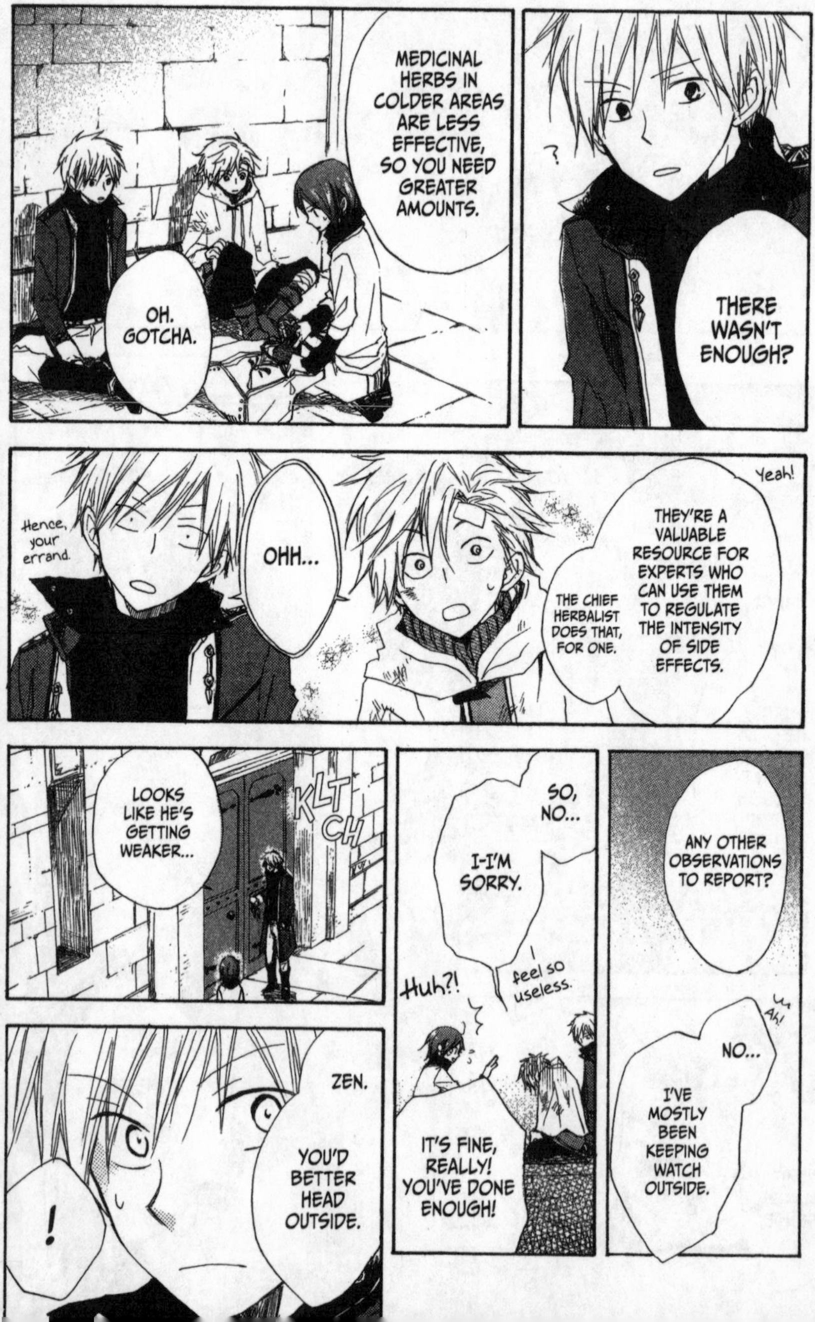
?
THERE WASN'T ENOUGH?
MEDICINAL HERBS IN COLDER AREAS ARE LESS EFFECTIVE, SO YOU NEED GREATER AMOUNTS.
OH. GOTCHA.
Yeah!
THEY'RE A VALUABLE RESOURCE FOR EXPERTS WHO CAN USE THEM TO REGULATE THE INTENSITY OF SIDE EFFECTS.
THE CHIEF HERBALIST DOES THAT, FOR ONE.
OHH...
Hence, your errand.
ANY OTHER OBSERVATIONS TO REPORT?
Ah!
NO...
I'VE MOSTLY BEEN KEEPING WATCH OUTSIDE.
SO, NO...
I-I'M SORRY.
I feel so useless.
Huh?!
IT'S FINE, REALLY! YOU'VE DONE ENOUGH!
LOOKS LIKE HE'S GETTING WEAKER...
KLTCH
ZEN.
YOU'D BETTER HEAD OUTSIDE.
!

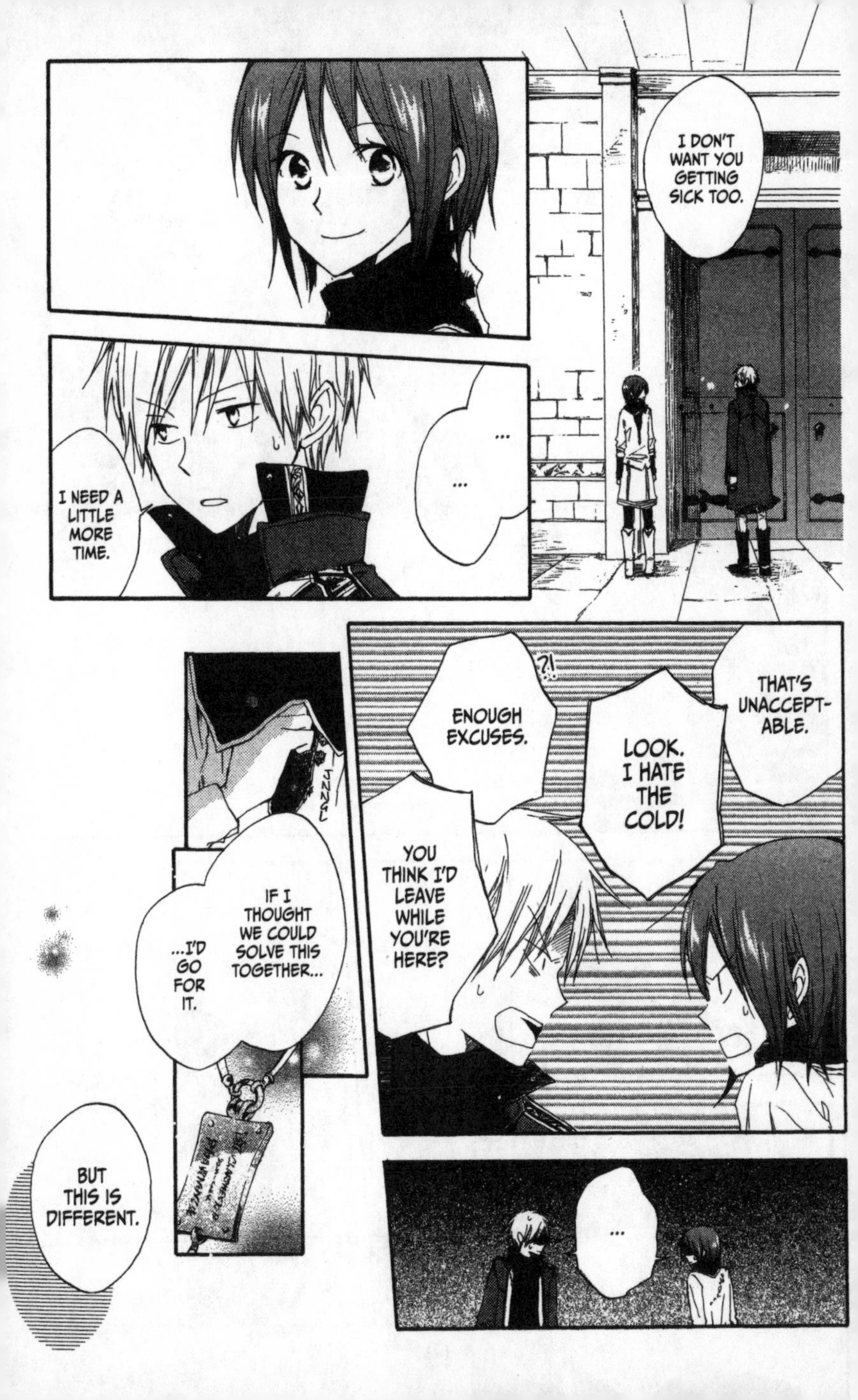
I DON'T WANT YOU GETTING SICK TOO.
... ...
I NEED A LITTLE MORE TIME.
THAT'S UNACCEPTABLE.
LOOK. I HATE THE COLD!
?!
ENOUGH EXCUSES.
YOU THINK I'D LEAVE WHILE YOU'RE HERE?
IF I THOUGHT WE COULD SOLVE THIS TOGETHER...
...I'D GO FOR IT.
...
BUT THIS IS DIFFERENT.

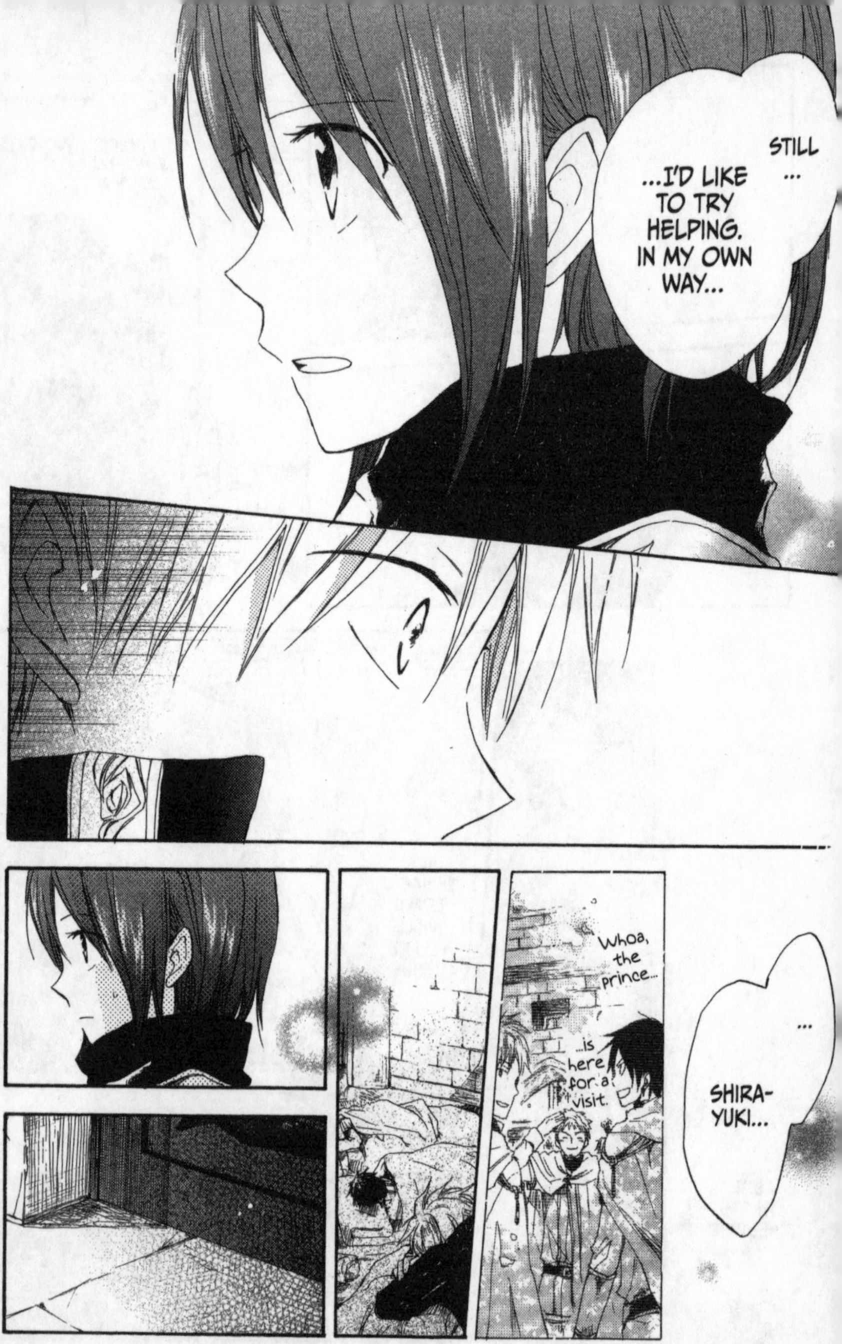
STILL ...
...I'D LIKE TO TRY HELPING. IN MY OWN WAY...
... SHIRA-YUKI...
Whoa, the prince...
...is here for a visit.

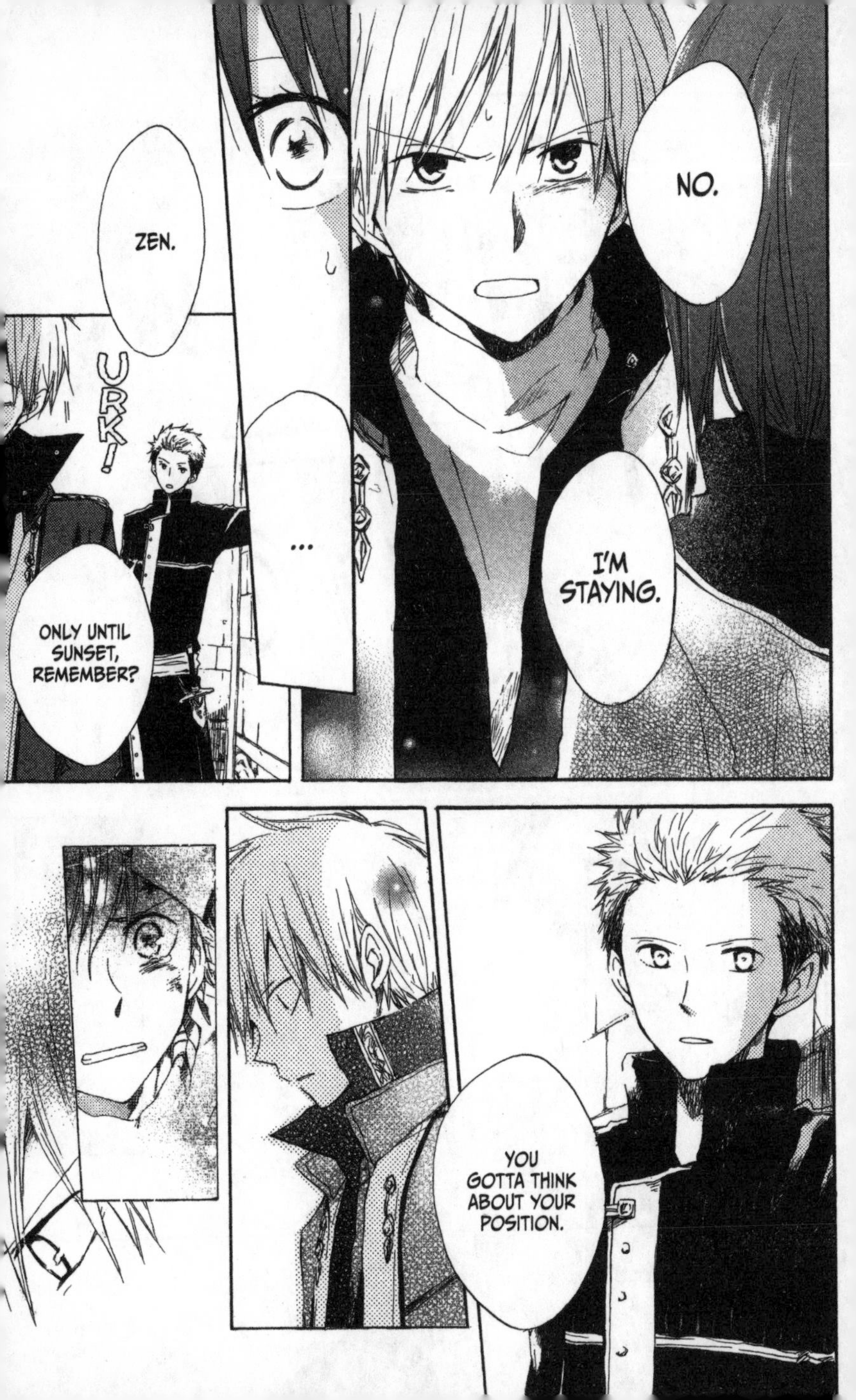
NO.
I'M STAYING.
...
ZEN.
URK!
ONLY UNTIL SUNSET, REMEMBER?
YOU GOTTA THINK ABOUT YOUR POSITION.

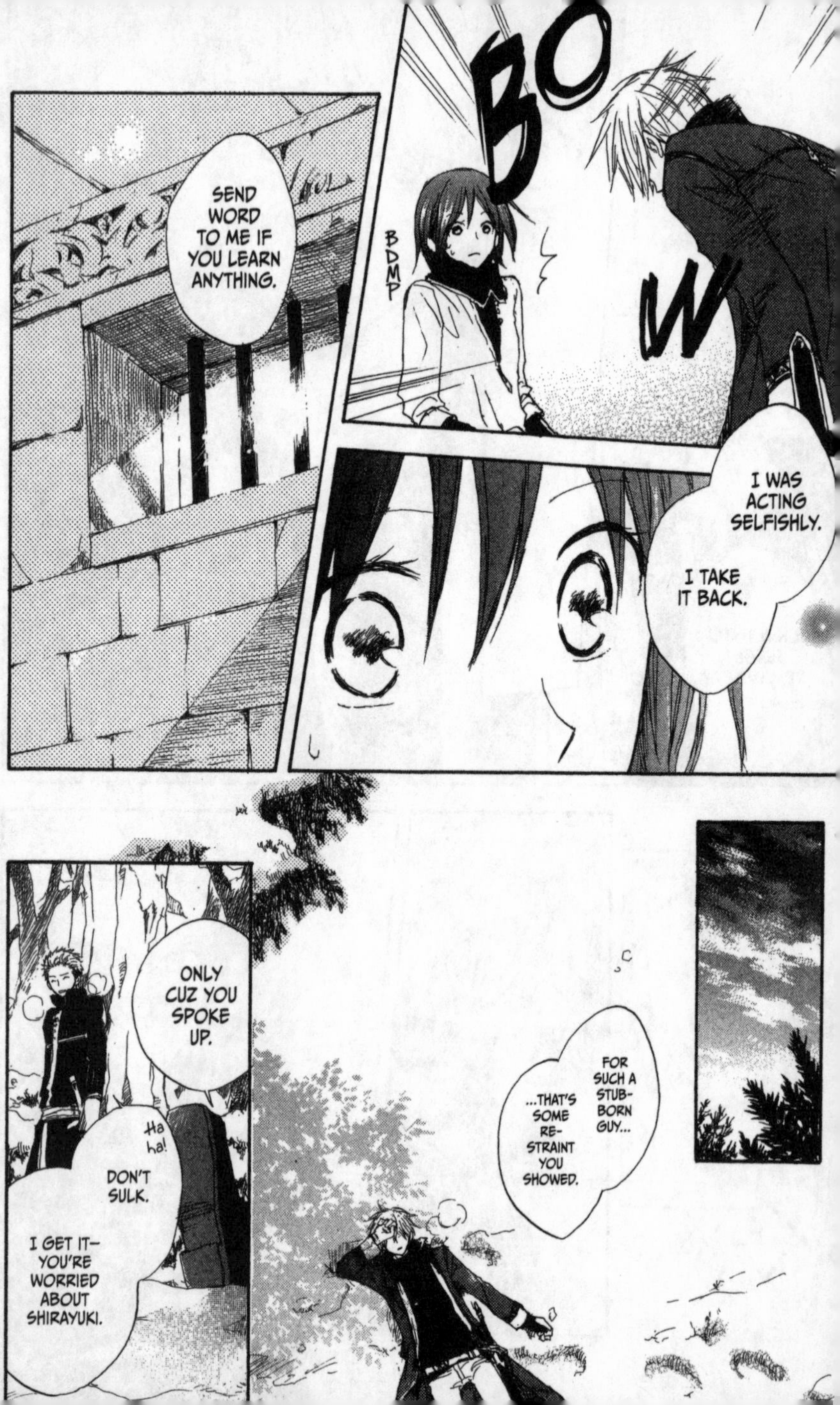
BOW
BDMP
I WAS ACTING SELFISHLY.
I TAKE IT BACK.
SEND WORD TO ME IF YOU LEARN ANYTHING.
FOR SUCH A STUB-BORN GUY...
...THAT'S SOME RE-STRAINT YOU SHOWED.
ONLY CUZ YOU SPOKE UP.
Ha ha!
DON'T SULK.
I GET IT— YOU'RE WORRIED ABOUT SHIRAYUKI.

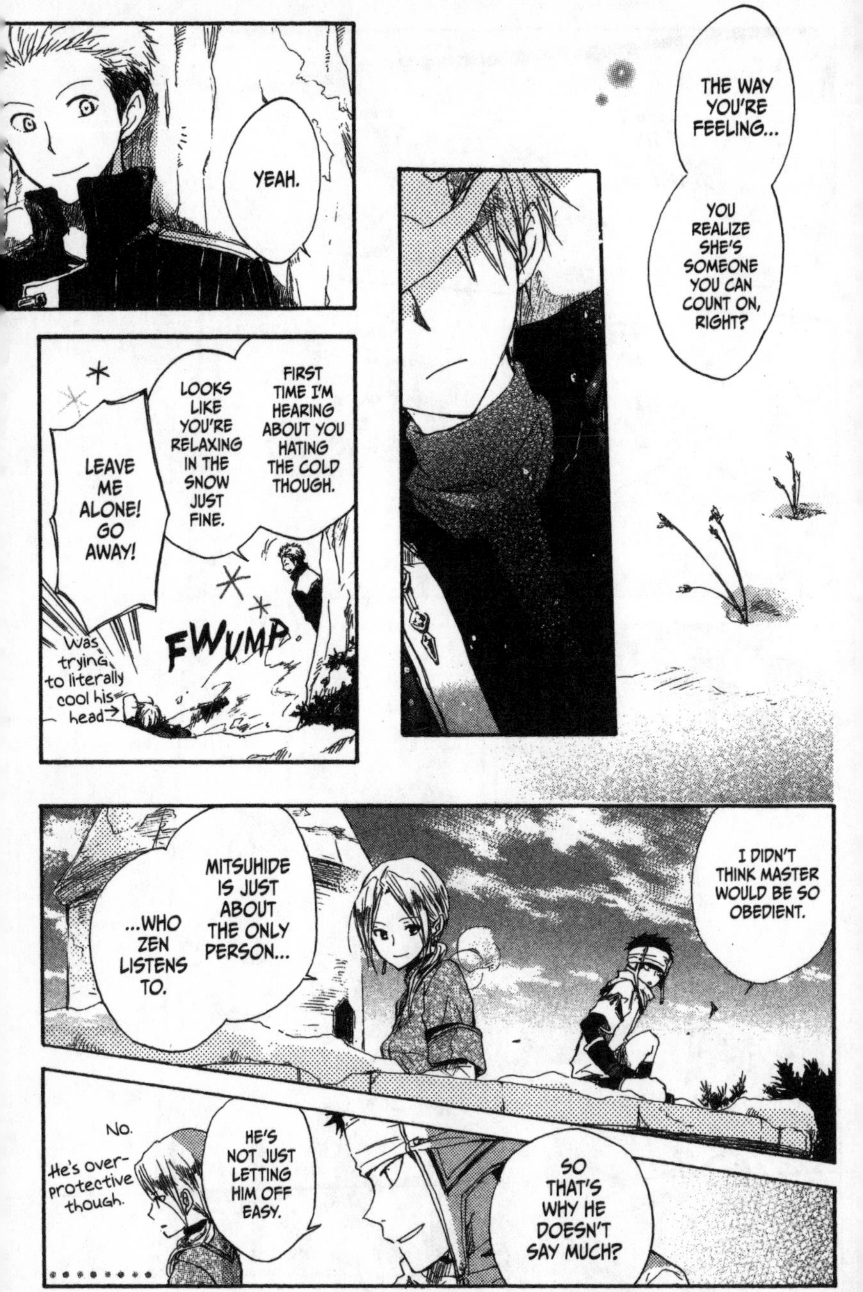

THE WAY YOU'RE FEELING...
YOU REALIZE SHE'S SOMEONE YOU CAN COUNT ON, RIGHT?
YEAH.
FIRST TIME I'M HEARING ABOUT YOU HATING THE COLD THOUGH.
LOOKS LIKE YOU'RE RELAXING IN THE SNOW JUST FINE.
LEAVE ME ALONE! GO AWAY!
FWUMP
Was trying to literally cool his head
I DIDN'T THINK MASTER WOULD BE SO OBEDIENT.
MITSUHIDE IS JUST ABOUT THE ONLY PERSON...
...WHO ZEN LISTENS TO.
SO THAT'S WHY HE DOESN'T SAY MUCH?
HE'S NOT JUST LETTING HIM OFF EASY.
No.
He's over-protective though.

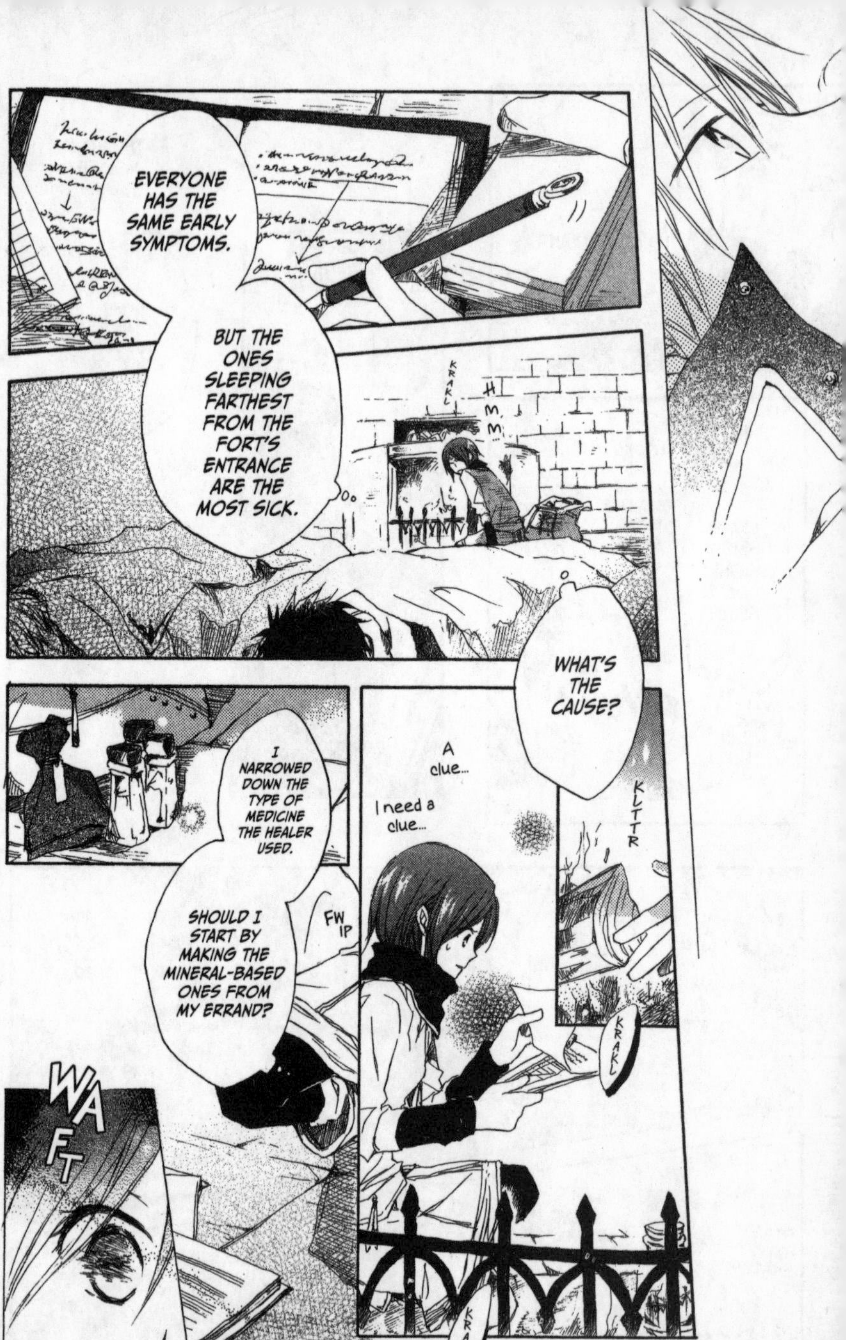
EVERYONE HAS THE SAME EARLY SYMPTOMS.
BUT THE ONES SLEEPING FARTHEST FROM THE FORT'S ENTRANCE ARE THE MOST SICK.
KRAKL
HMMM
WHAT'S THE CAUSE?
KLTTR
KRAKL
A clue...
I need a clue...
FWIP
I NARROWED DOWN THE TYPE OF MEDICINE THE HEALER USED.
SHOULD I START BY MAKING THE MINERAL-BASED ONES FROM MY ERRAND?
KRAKL
WAFT

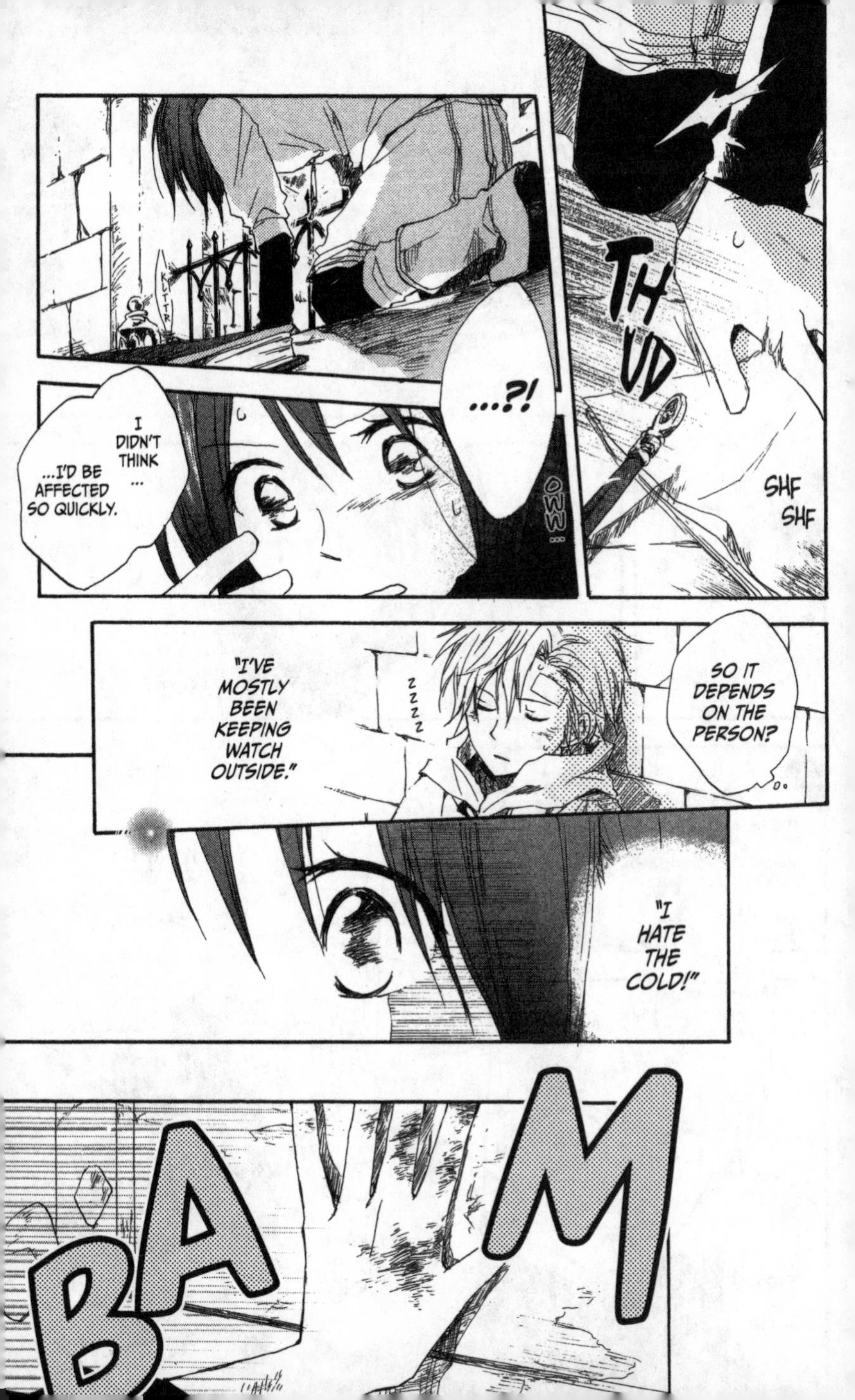
THUD
SHF SHF
KLTTR
...?!
OWW...
I DIDN'T THINK ...
...I'D BE AFFECTED SO QUICKLY.
SO IT DEPENDS ON THE PERSON?
ZZZZ
"I'VE MOSTLY BEEN KEEPING WATCH OUTSIDE."
"I HATE THE COLD!"
BAM

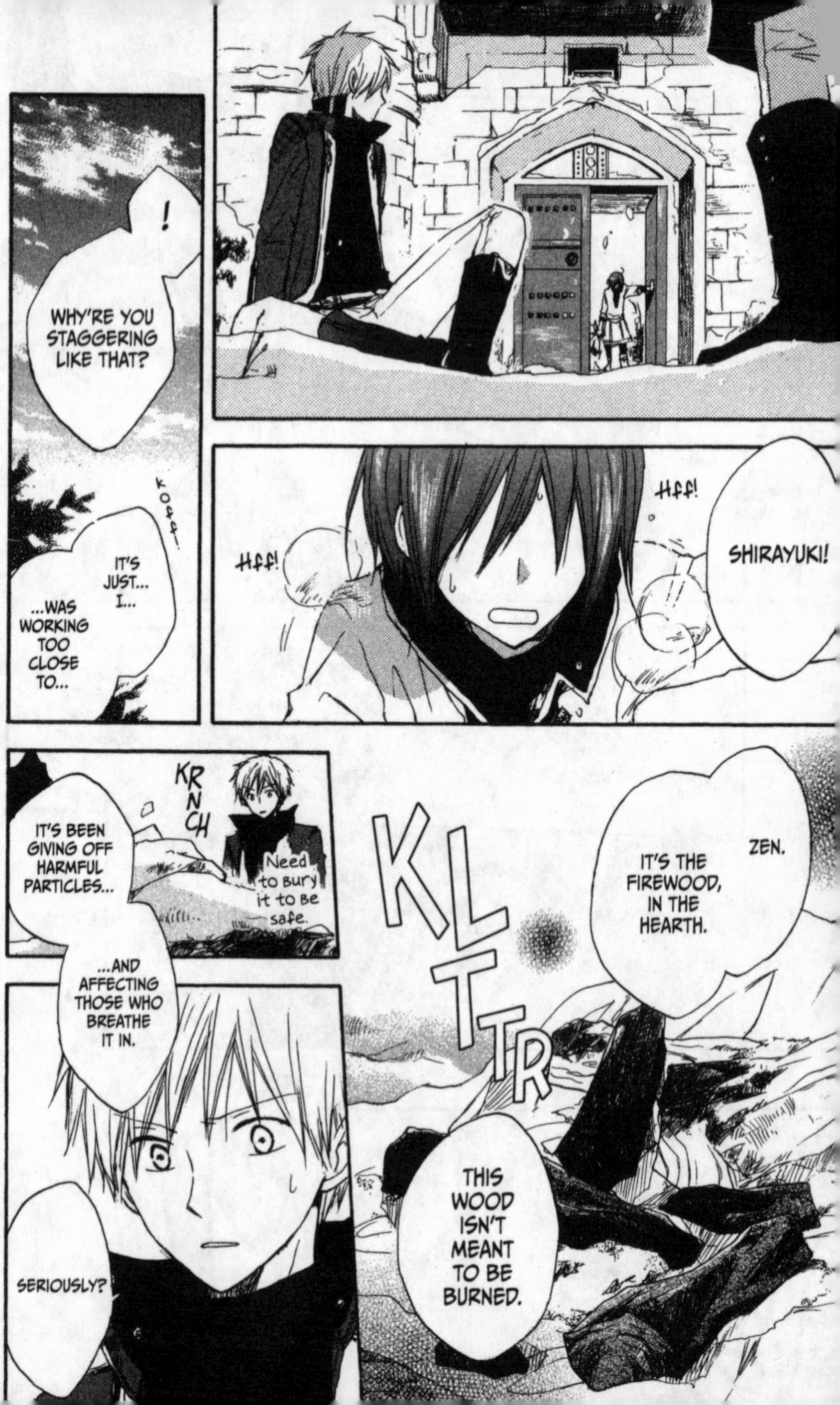
Hff!
SHIRAYUKI!
Hff!
!
WHY'RE YOU STAGGERING LIKE THAT?
koff!
IT'S JUST... I...
...WAS WORKING TOO CLOSE TO...
ZEN.
IT'S THE FIREWOOD, IN THE HEARTH.
KLTTR
THIS WOOD ISN'T MEANT TO BE BURNED.
IT'S BEEN GIVING OFF HARMFUL PARTICLES...
KRNCH
Need to bury it to be safe.
...AND AFFECTING THOSE WHO BREATHE IT IN.
SERIOUSLY?

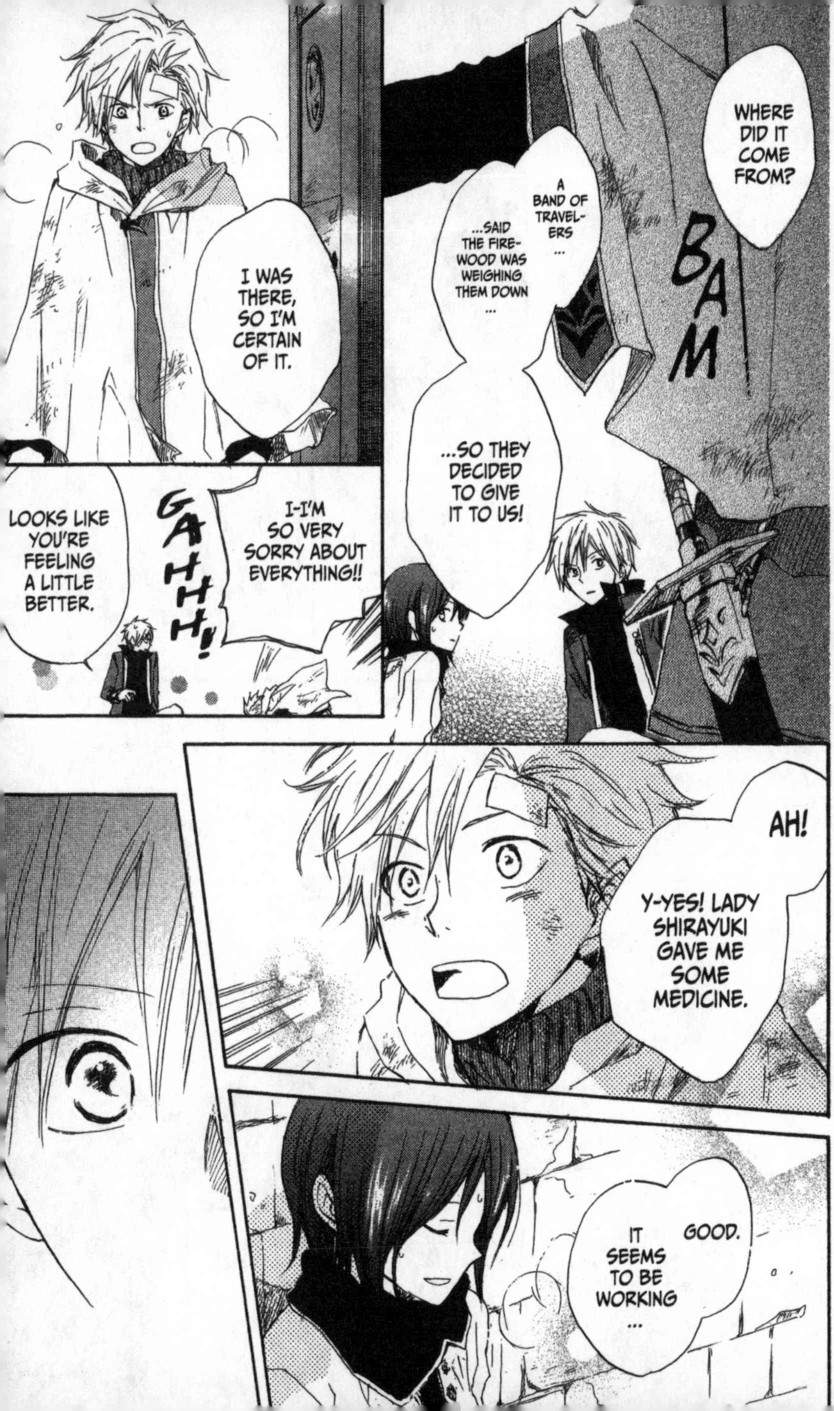
WHERE DID IT COME FROM?
BAM
A BAND OF TRAVELERS...
...SAID THE FIREWOOD WAS WEIGHING THEM DOWN...
...SO THEY DECIDED TO GIVE IT TO US!
I WAS THERE, SO I'M CERTAIN OF IT.
I-I'M SO VERY SORRY ABOUT EVERYTHING!!
GAHHHH!
LOOKS LIKE YOU'RE FEELING A LITTLE BETTER.
AH!
Y-YES! LADY SHIRAYUKI GAVE ME SOME MEDICINE.
GOOD.
IT SEEMS TO BE WORKING...

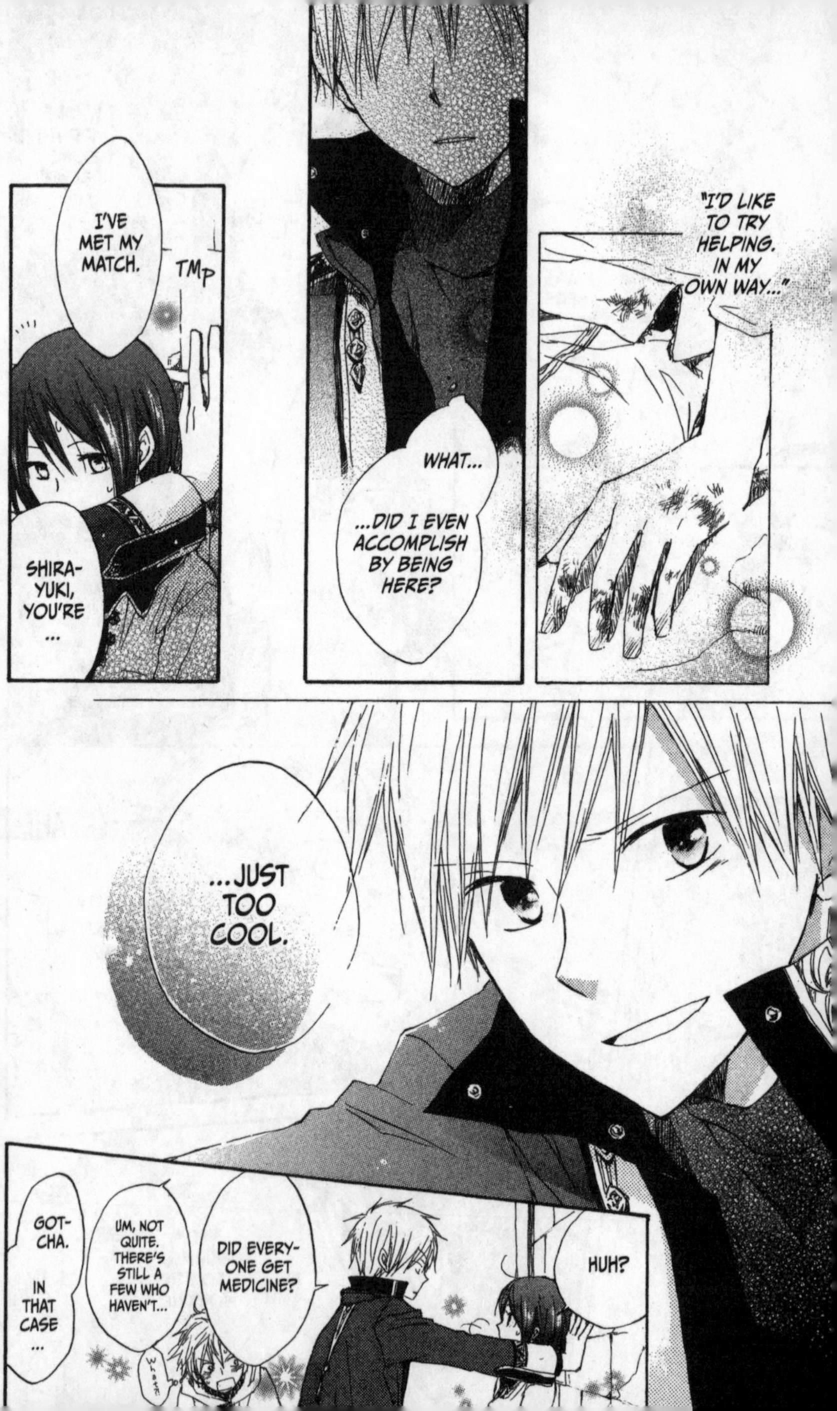
"I'D LIKE TO TRY HELPING. IN MY OWN WAY..."
WHAT...
...DID I EVEN ACCOMPLISH BY BEING HERE?
I'VE MET MY MATCH.
TMP
SHIRA-YUKI, YOU'RE ...
...JUST TOO COOL.
HUH?
DID EVERY-ONE GET MEDICINE?
UM, NOT QUITE. THERE'S STILL A FEW WHO HAVEN'T...
GOT-CHA.
IN THAT CASE ...

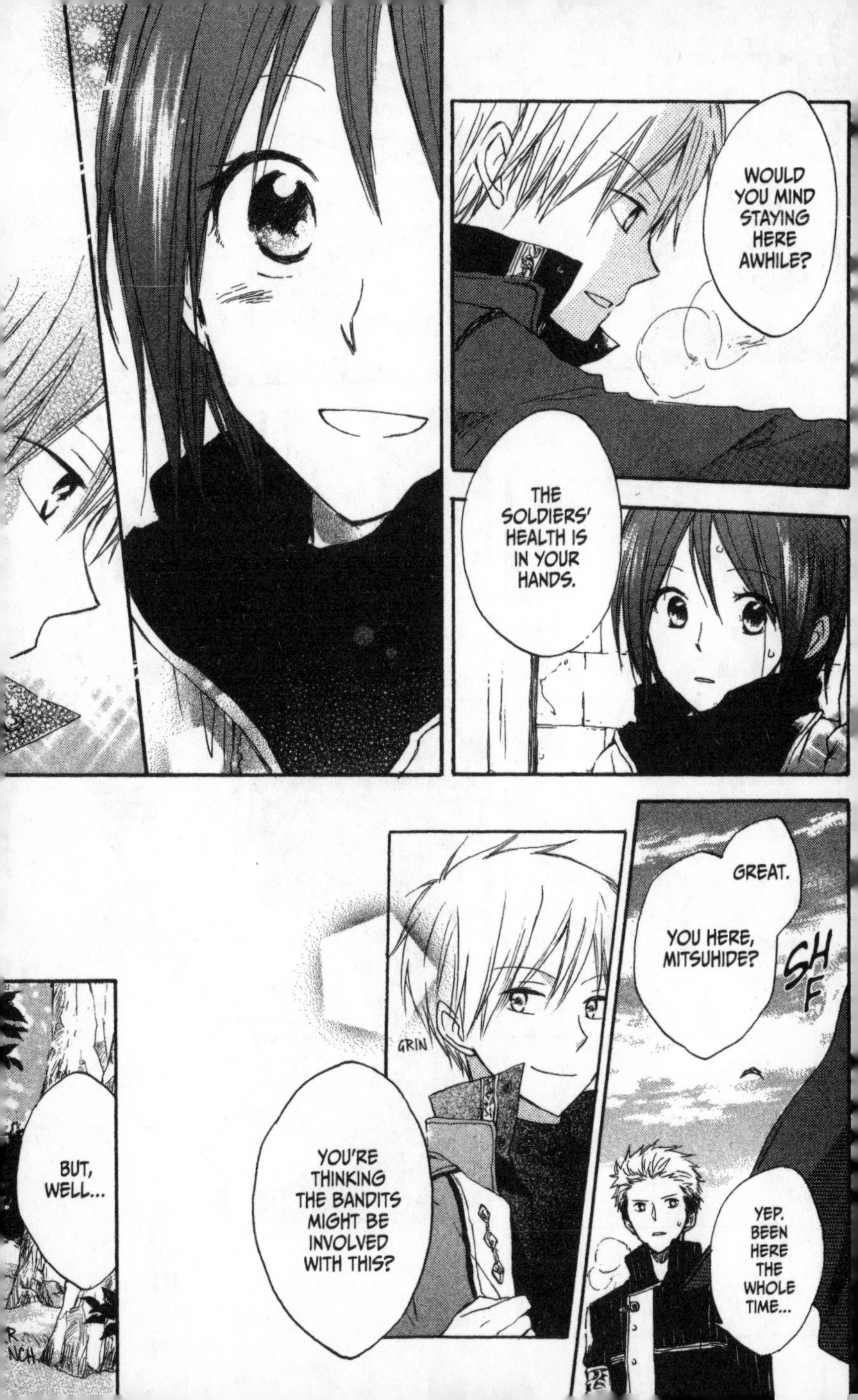
WOULD YOU MIND STAYING HERE AWHILE?
THE SOLDIERS' HEALTH IS IN YOUR HANDS.
GREAT.
YOU HERE, MITSUHIDE?
SHF
YEP. BEEN HERE THE WHOLE TIME...
GRIN
YOU'RE THINKING THE BANDITS MIGHT BE INVOLVED WITH THIS?
BUT, WELL...

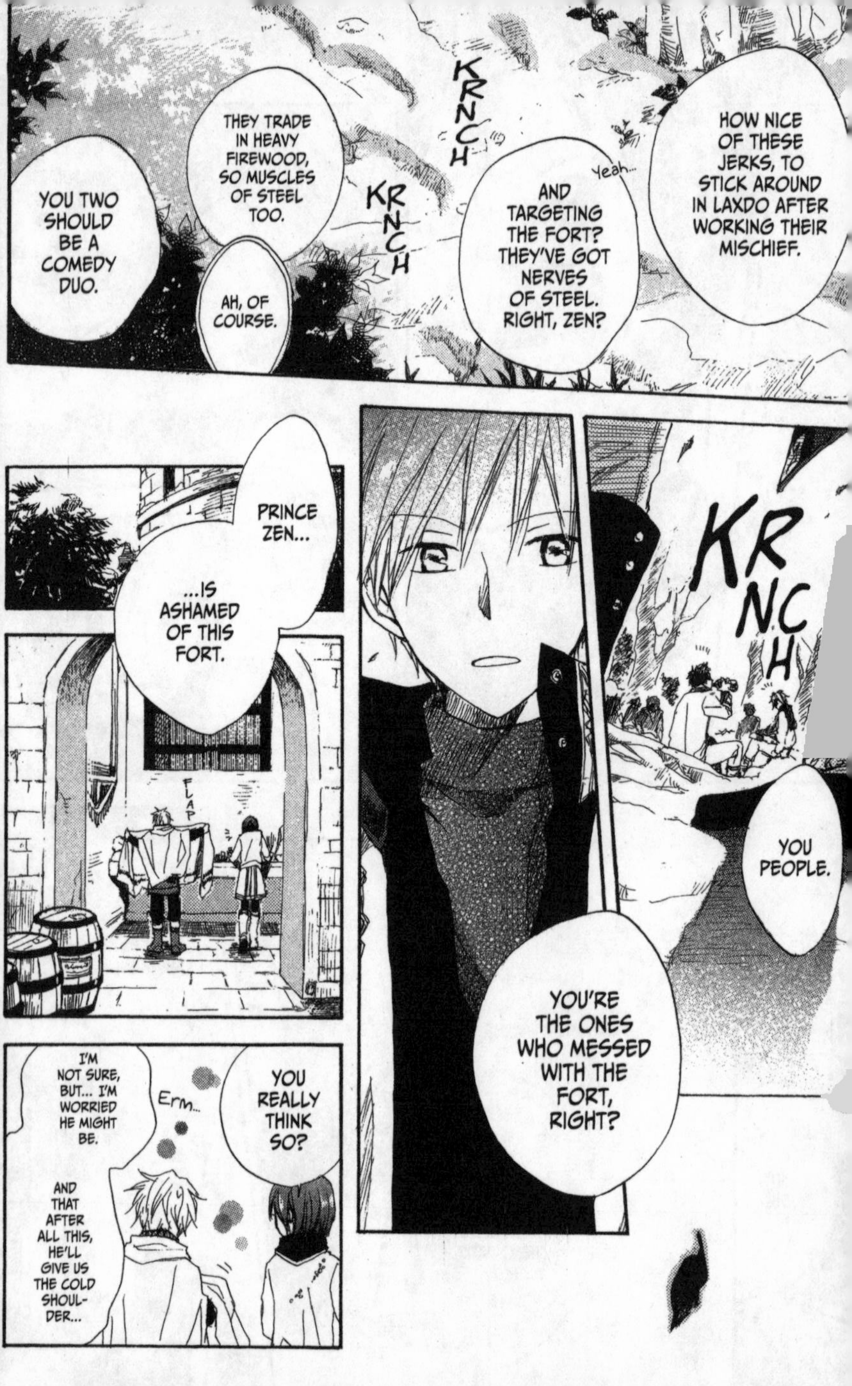
HOW NICE OF THESE JERKS, TO STICK AROUND IN LAXDO AFTER WORKING THEIR MISCHIEF.
Yeah...
AND TARGETING THE FORT? THEY'VE GOT NERVES OF STEEL. RIGHT, ZEN?
KRNCH
KRNCH
THEY TRADE IN HEAVY FIREWOOD, SO MUSCLES OF STEEL TOO.
AH, OF COURSE.
YOU TWO SHOULD BE A COMEDY DUO.
KRNCH
YOU PEOPLE.
YOU'RE THE ONES WHO MESSED WITH THE FORT, RIGHT?
PRINCE ZEN...
...IS ASHAMED OF THIS FORT.
FLAP
YOU REALLY THINK SO?
Erm...
I'M NOT SURE, BUT... I'M WORRIED HE MIGHT BE.
AND THAT AFTER ALL THIS, HE'LL GIVE US THE COLD SHOULDER...

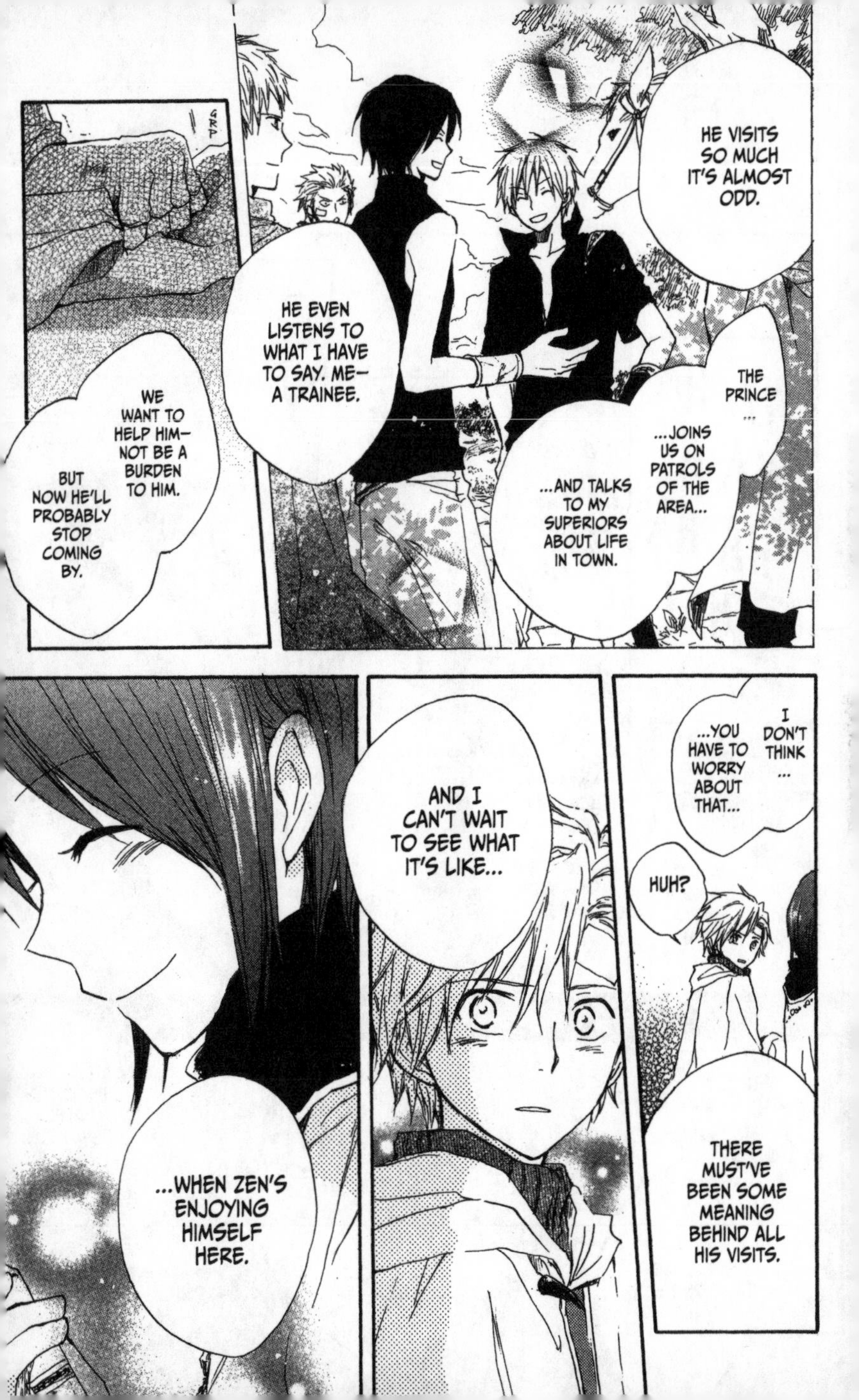
HE VISITS SO MUCH IT'S ALMOST ODD.
THE PRINCE...
...JOINS US ON PATROLS OF THE AREA...
...AND TALKS TO MY SUPERIORS ABOUT LIFE IN TOWN.
HE EVEN LISTENS TO WHAT I HAVE TO SAY. ME—A TRAINEE.
GRP
WE WANT TO HELP HIM—NOT BE A BURDEN TO HIM.
BUT NOW HE'LL PROBABLY STOP COMING BY.
I DON'T THINK...
...YOU HAVE TO WORRY ABOUT THAT...
HUH?
THERE MUST'VE BEEN SOME MEANING BEHIND ALL HIS VISITS.
AND I CAN'T WAIT TO SEE WHAT IT'S LIKE...
...WHEN ZEN'S ENJOYING HIMSELF HERE.

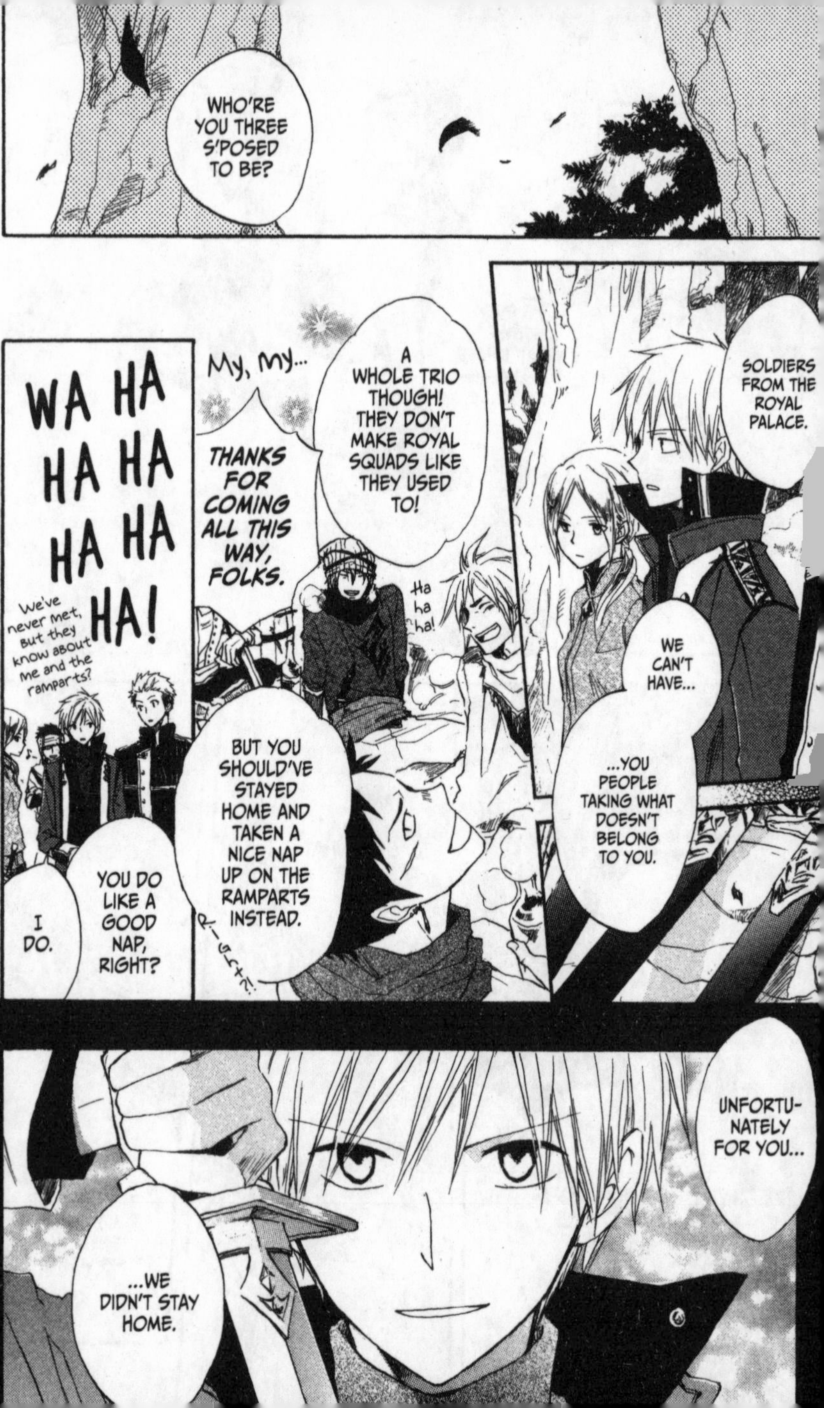
WHO'RE YOU THREE S'POSED TO BE?
SOLDIERS FROM THE ROYAL PALACE.
WE CAN'T HAVE...
...YOU PEOPLE TAKING WHAT DOESN'T BELONG TO YOU.
A WHOLE TRIO THOUGH! THEY DON'T MAKE ROYAL SQUADS LIKE THEY USED TO!
Ha ha ha!
My, my...
THANKS FOR COMING ALL THIS WAY, FOLKS.
BUT YOU SHOULD'VE STAYED HOME AND TAKEN A NICE NAP UP ON THE RAMPARTS INSTEAD.
R-Right?!
WA HA HA HA HA HA HA!
We've never met, but they know about me and the ramparts?
YOU DO LIKE A GOOD NAP, RIGHT?
I DO.
UNFORTUNATELY FOR YOU...
...WE DIDN'T STAY HOME.

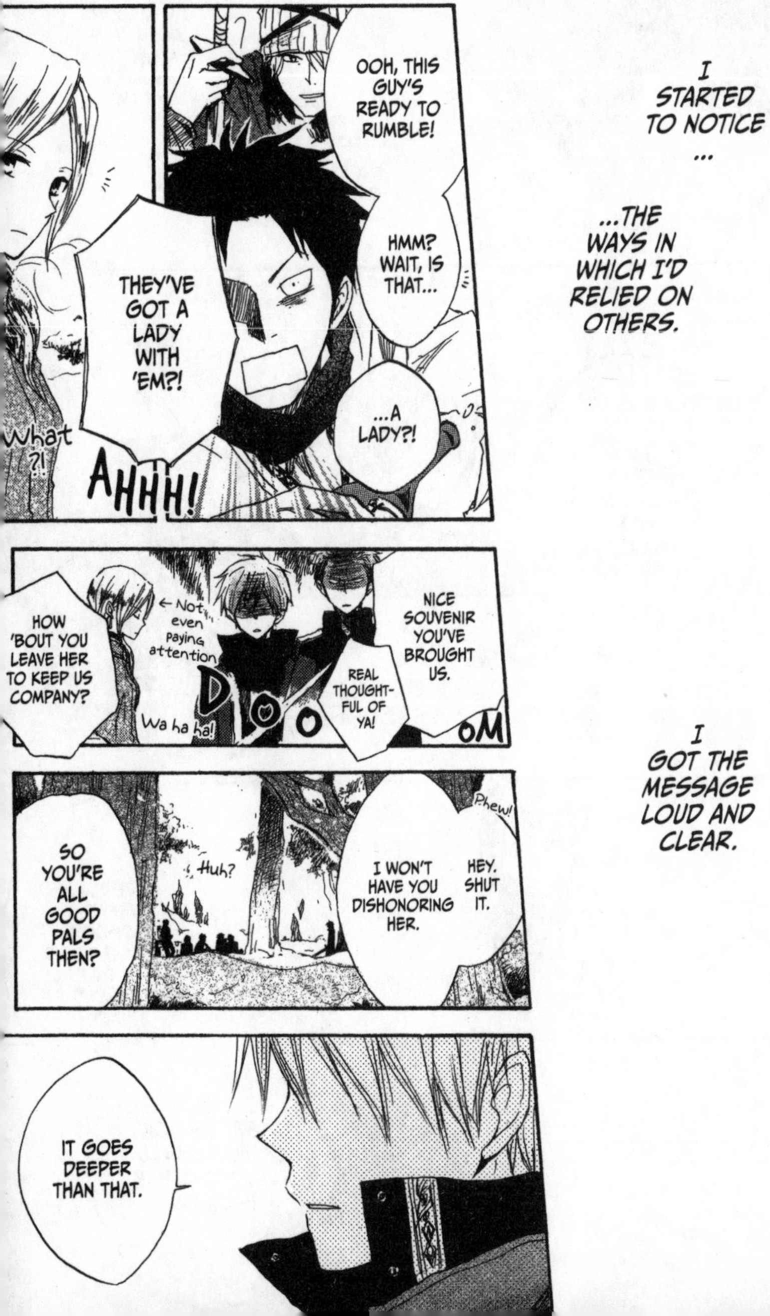
I STARTED TO NOTICE ...
...THE WAYS IN WHICH I'D RELIED ON OTHERS.
OOH, THIS GUY'S READY TO RUMBLE!
HMM? WAIT, IS THAT...
...A LADY?!
THEY'VE GOT A LADY WITH 'EM?!
AHHH!
What?!
NICE SOUVENIR YOU'VE BROUGHT US.
REAL THOUGHT-FUL OF YA!
DOOOM
← Not even paying attention
HOW 'BOUT YOU LEAVE HER TO KEEP US COMPANY?
Wa ha ha!
I GOT THE MESSAGE LOUD AND CLEAR.
Phew!
HEY. SHUT IT.
I WON'T HAVE YOU DISHONORING HER.
Huh?
SO YOU'RE ALL GOOD PALS THEN?
IT GOES DEEPER THAN THAT.

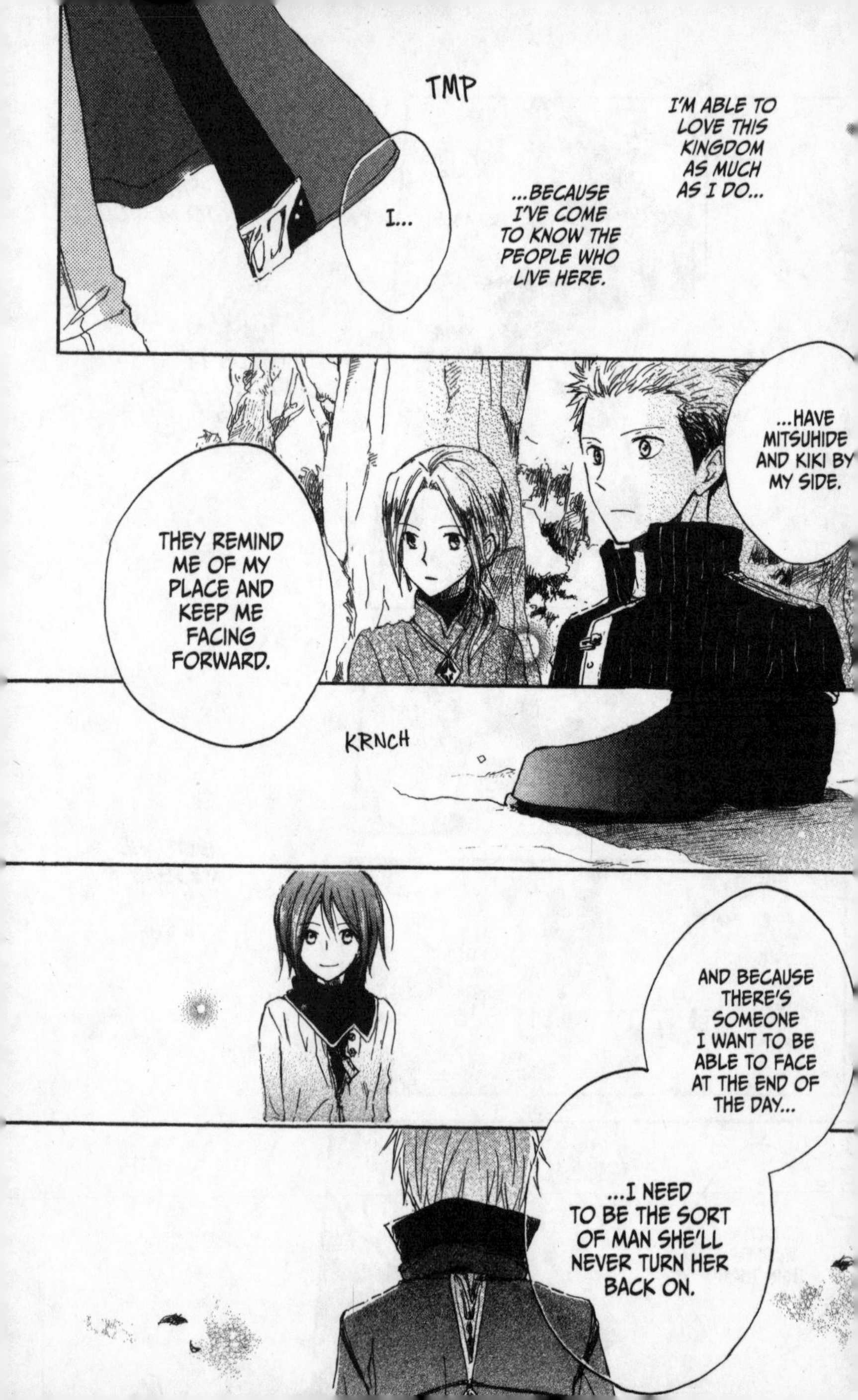
I'M ABLE TO LOVE THIS KINGDOM AS MUCH AS I DO...
...BECAUSE I'VE COME TO KNOW THE PEOPLE WHO LIVE HERE.
TMP
I...
...HAVE MITSUHIDE AND KIKI BY MY SIDE.
THEY REMIND ME OF MY PLACE AND KEEP ME FACING FORWARD.
KRNCH
AND BECAUSE THERE'S SOMEONE I WANT TO BE ABLE TO FACE AT THE END OF THE DAY...
...I NEED TO BE THE SORT OF MAN SHE'LL NEVER TURN HER BACK ON.

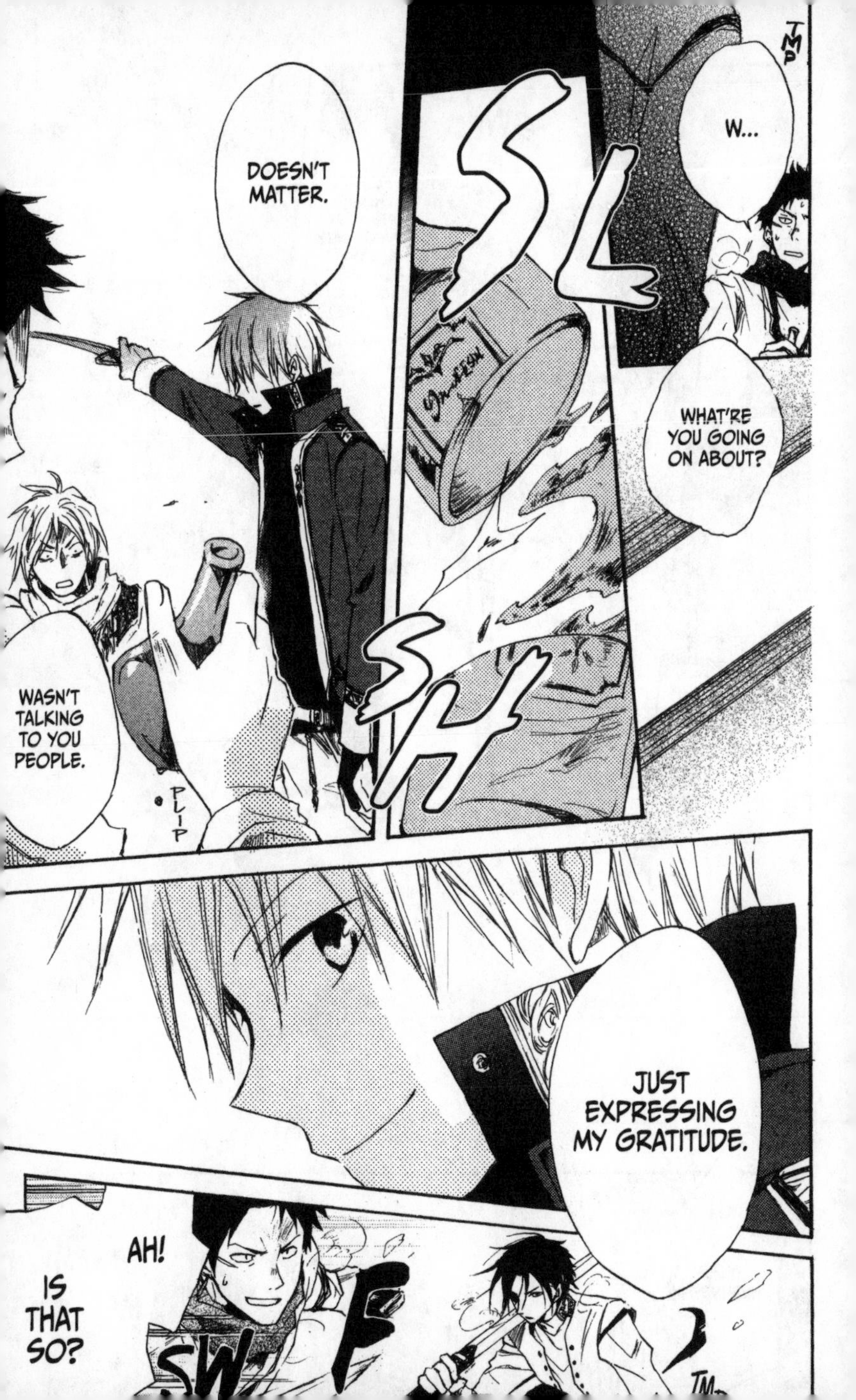
TMP
W...
WHAT'RE YOU GOING ON ABOUT?
SLSH
DOESN'T MATTER.
WASN'T TALKING TO YOU PEOPLE.
PLIP
JUST EXPRESSING MY GRATITUDE.
AH!
IS THAT SO?
SWF

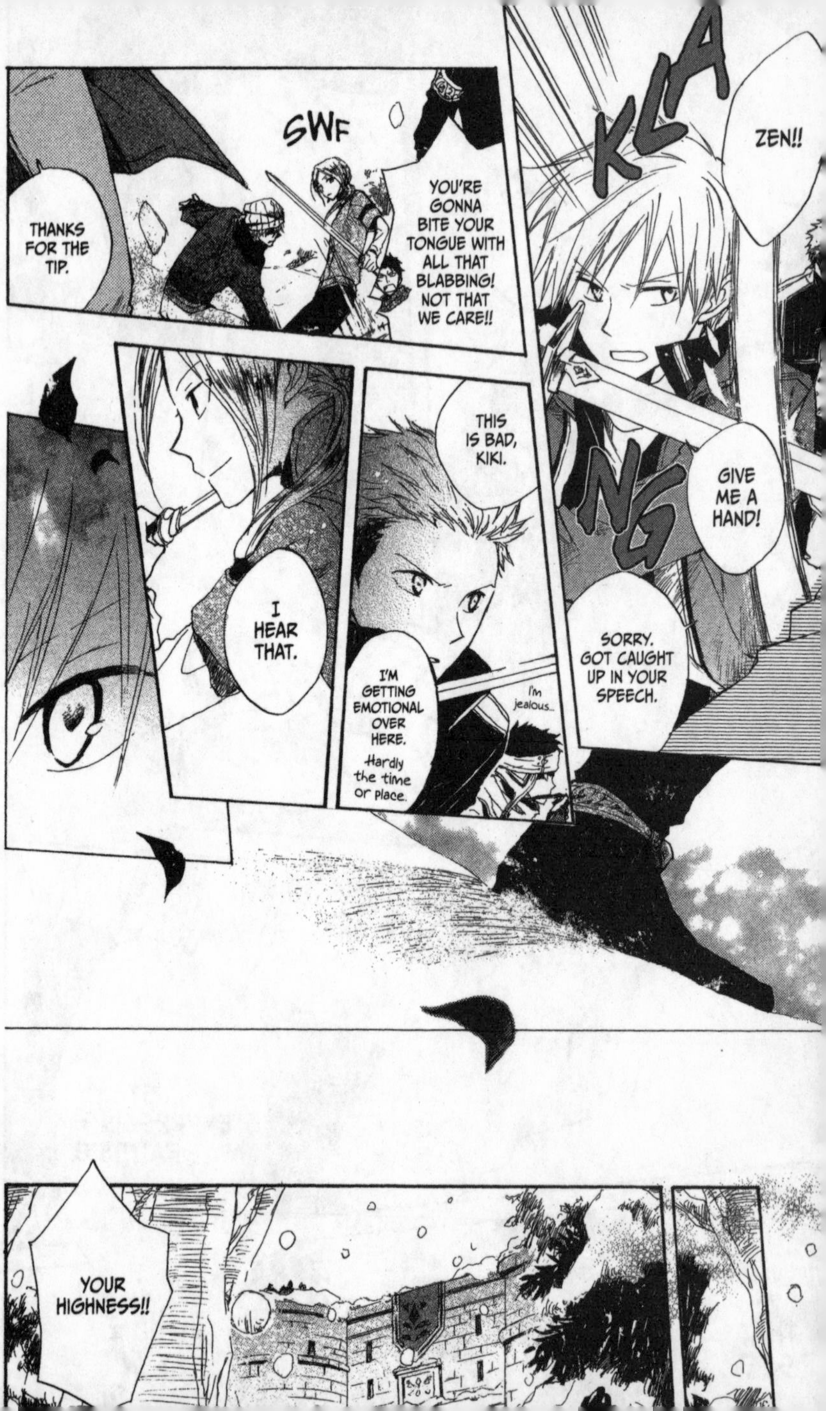
ZEN!!
KLANG
GIVE ME A HAND!
SORRY. GOT CAUGHT UP IN YOUR SPEECH.
SWF
YOU'RE GONNA BITE YOUR TONGUE WITH ALL THAT BLABBING! NOT THAT WE CARE!!
THANKS FOR THE TIP.
THIS IS BAD, KIKI.
I'm jealous...
I'M GETTING EMOTIONAL OVER HERE.
Hardly the time or place.
I HEAR THAT.
YOUR HIGHNESS!!

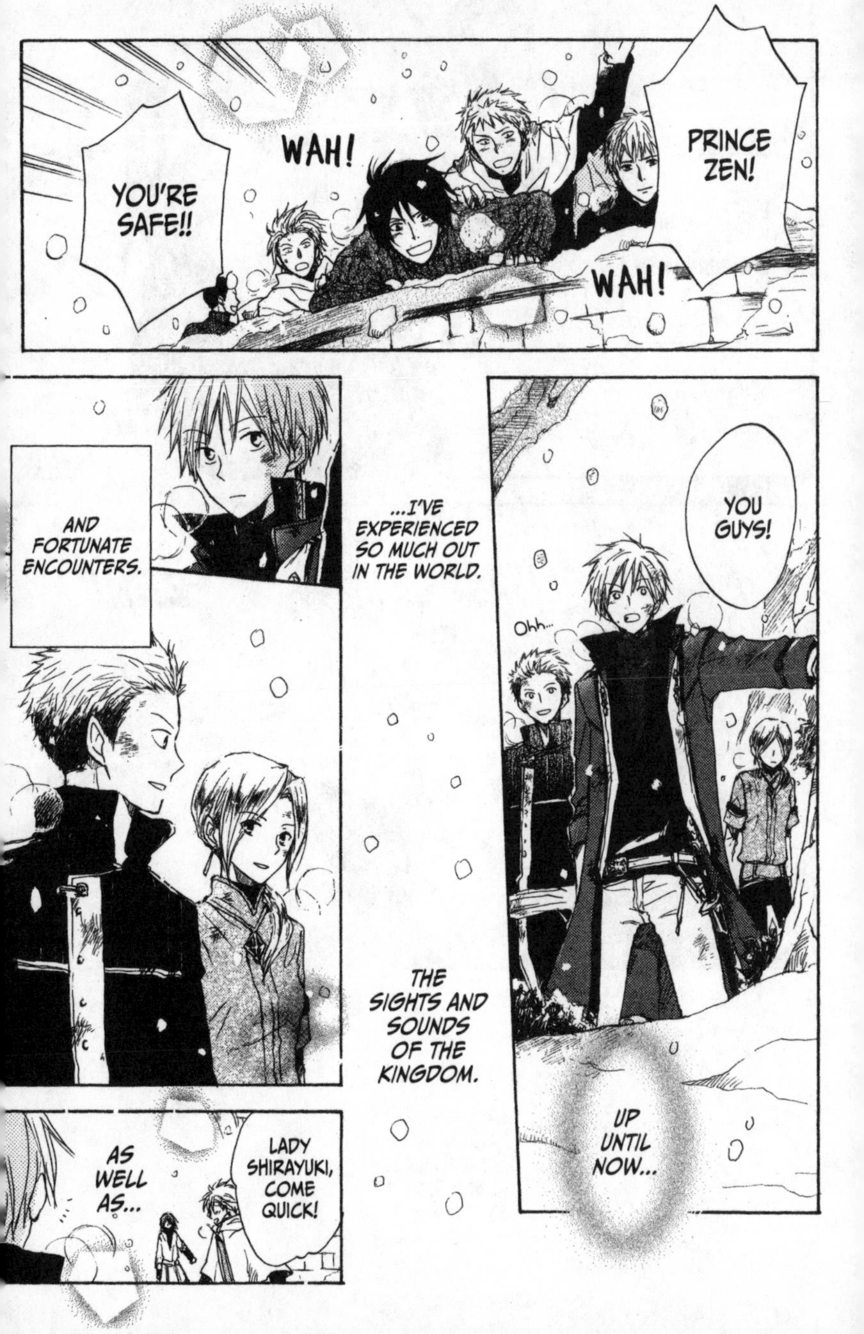
PRINCE ZEN!
WAH!
WAH!
YOU'RE SAFE!!
YOU GUYS!
Ohh...
UP UNTIL NOW...
...I'VE EXPERIENCED SO MUCH OUT IN THE WORLD.
THE SIGHTS AND SOUNDS OF THE KINGDOM.
AND FORTUNATE ENCOUNTERS.
LADY SHIRAYUKI, COME QUICK!
AS WELL AS...

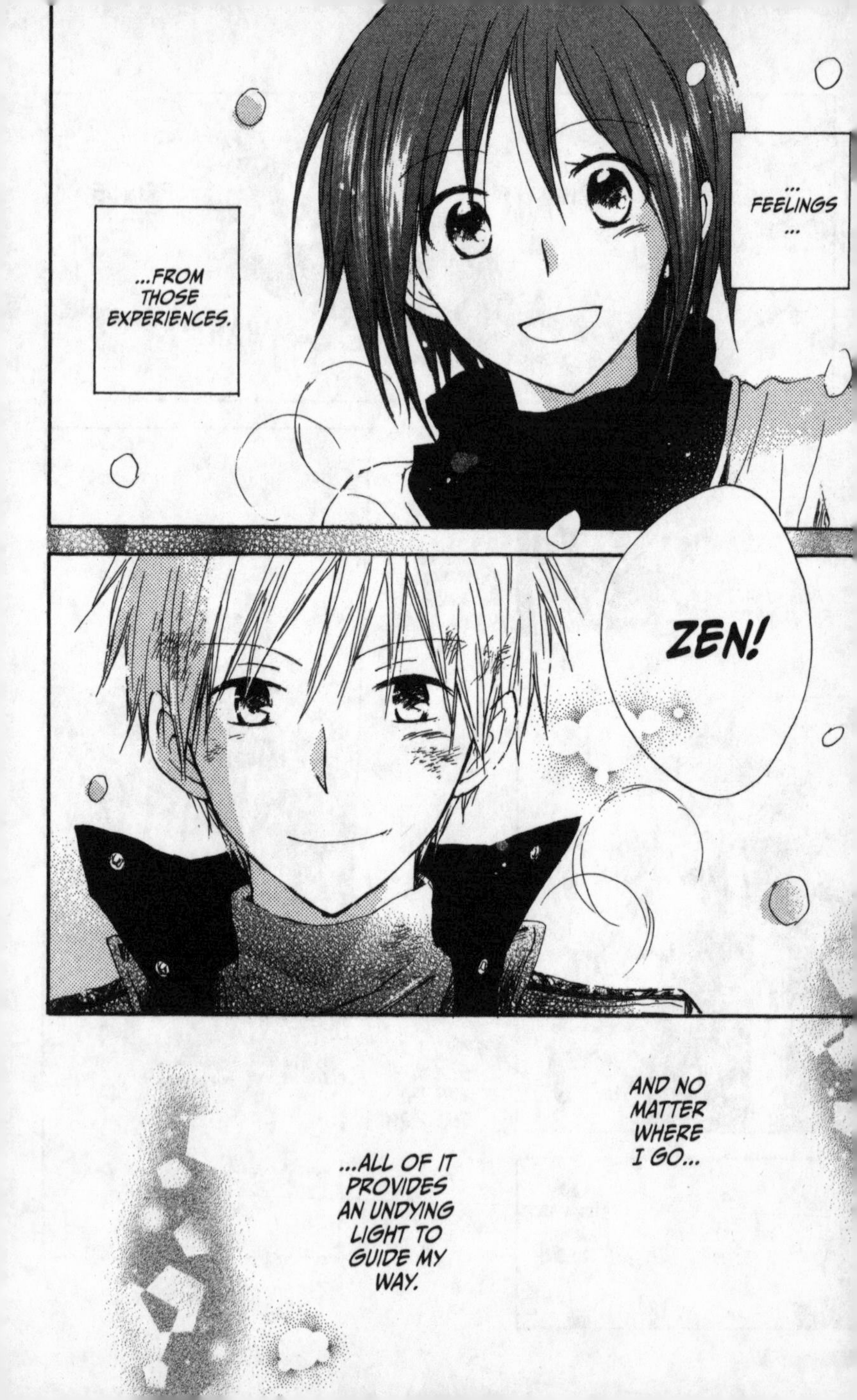
...FEELINGS...
...FROM THOSE EXPERIENCES.
ZEN!
AND NO MATTER WHERE I GO...
...ALL OF IT PROVIDES AN UNDYING LIGHT TO GUIDE MY WAY.

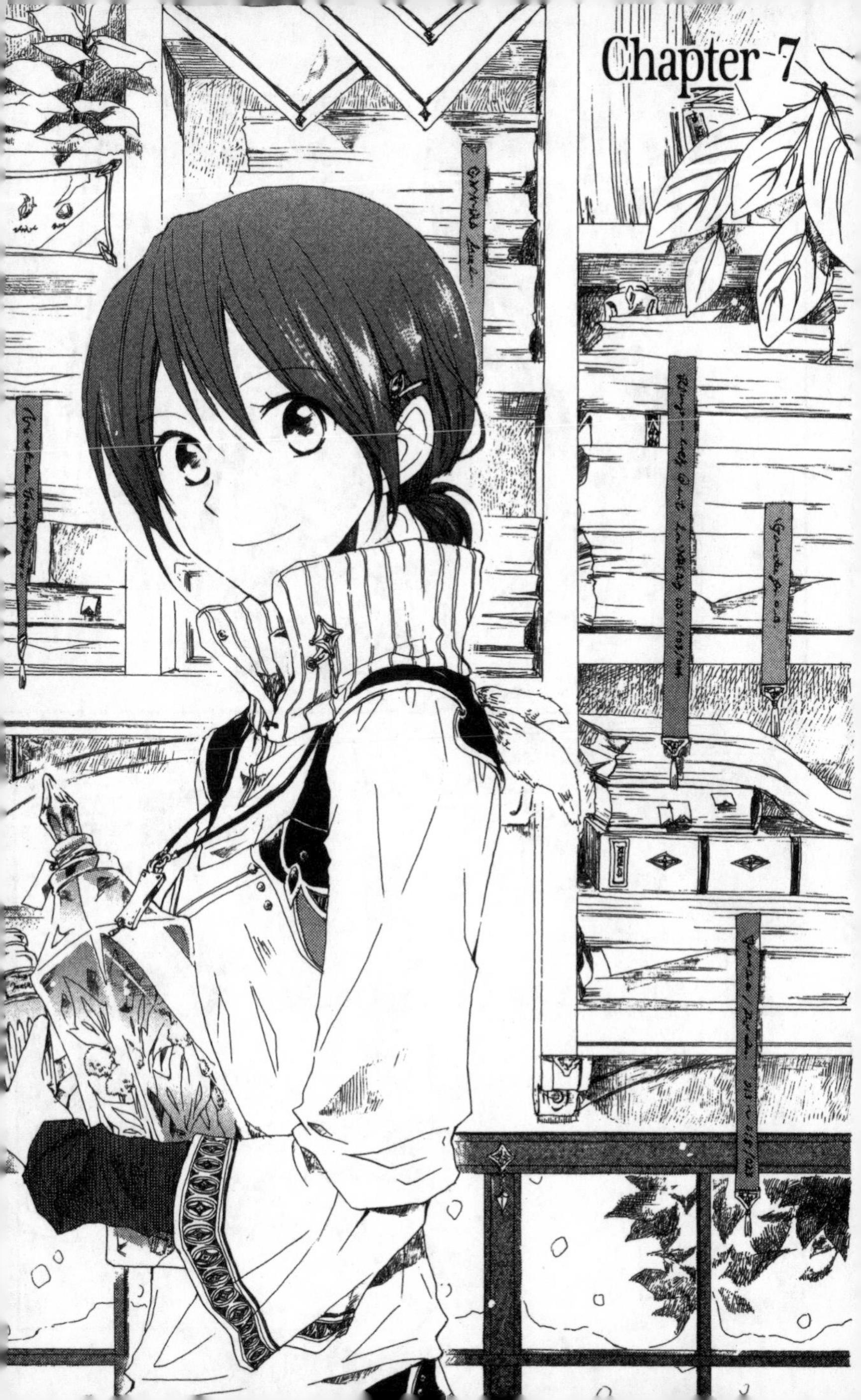
Chapter 7

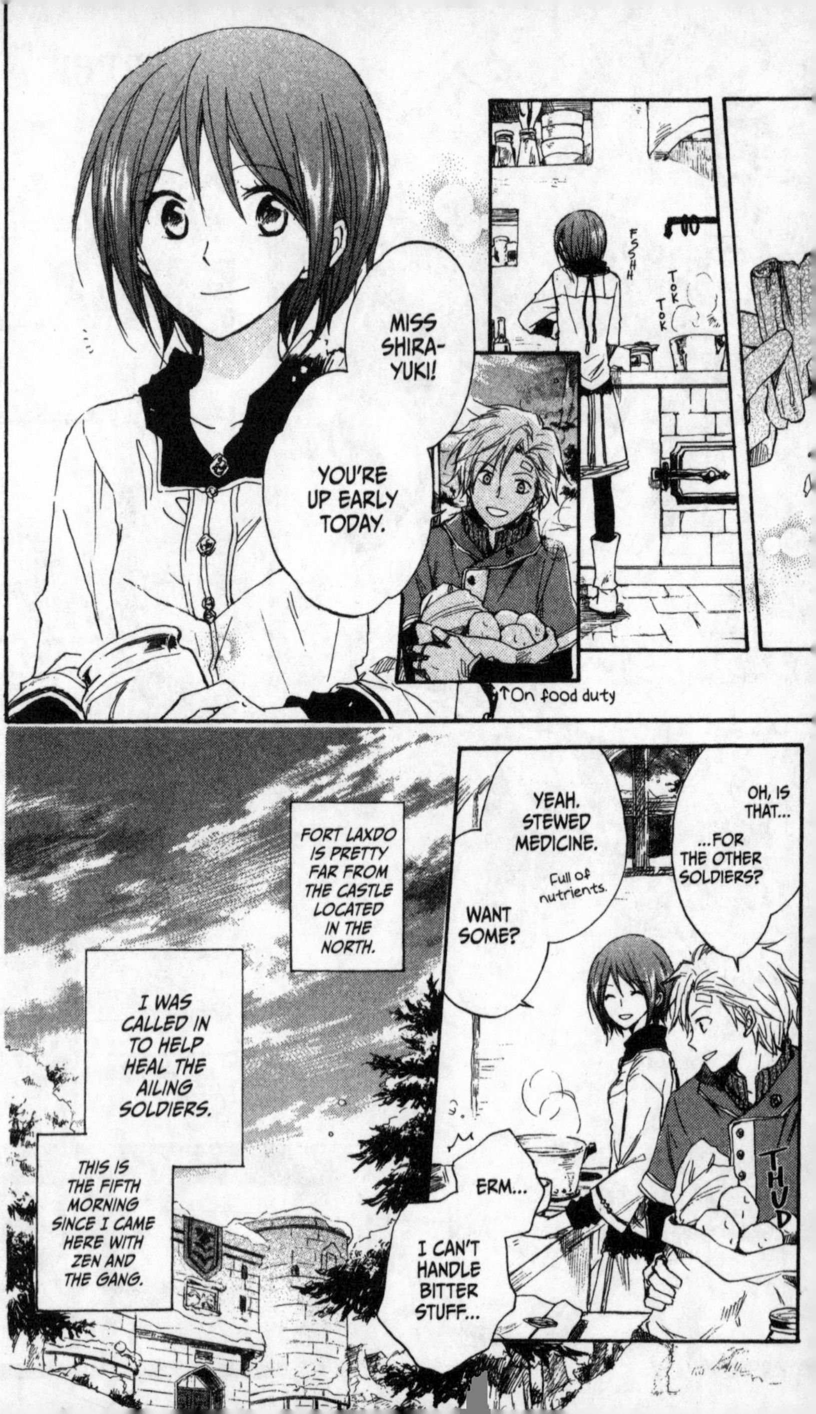
FSSH
TOK TOK
MISS SHIRA-YUKI!
YOU'RE UP EARLY TODAY.
↑On food duty
OH, IS THAT...
...FOR THE OTHER SOLDIERS?
YEAH. STEWED MEDICINE.
Full of nutrients.
WANT SOME?
THUD
ERM...
I CAN'T HANDLE BITTER STUFF...
FORT LAXDO IS PRETTY FAR FROM THE CASTLE LOCATED IN THE NORTH.
I WAS CALLED IN TO HELP HEAL THE AILING SOLDIERS.
THIS IS THE FIFTH MORNING SINCE I CAME HERE WITH ZEN AND THE GANG.

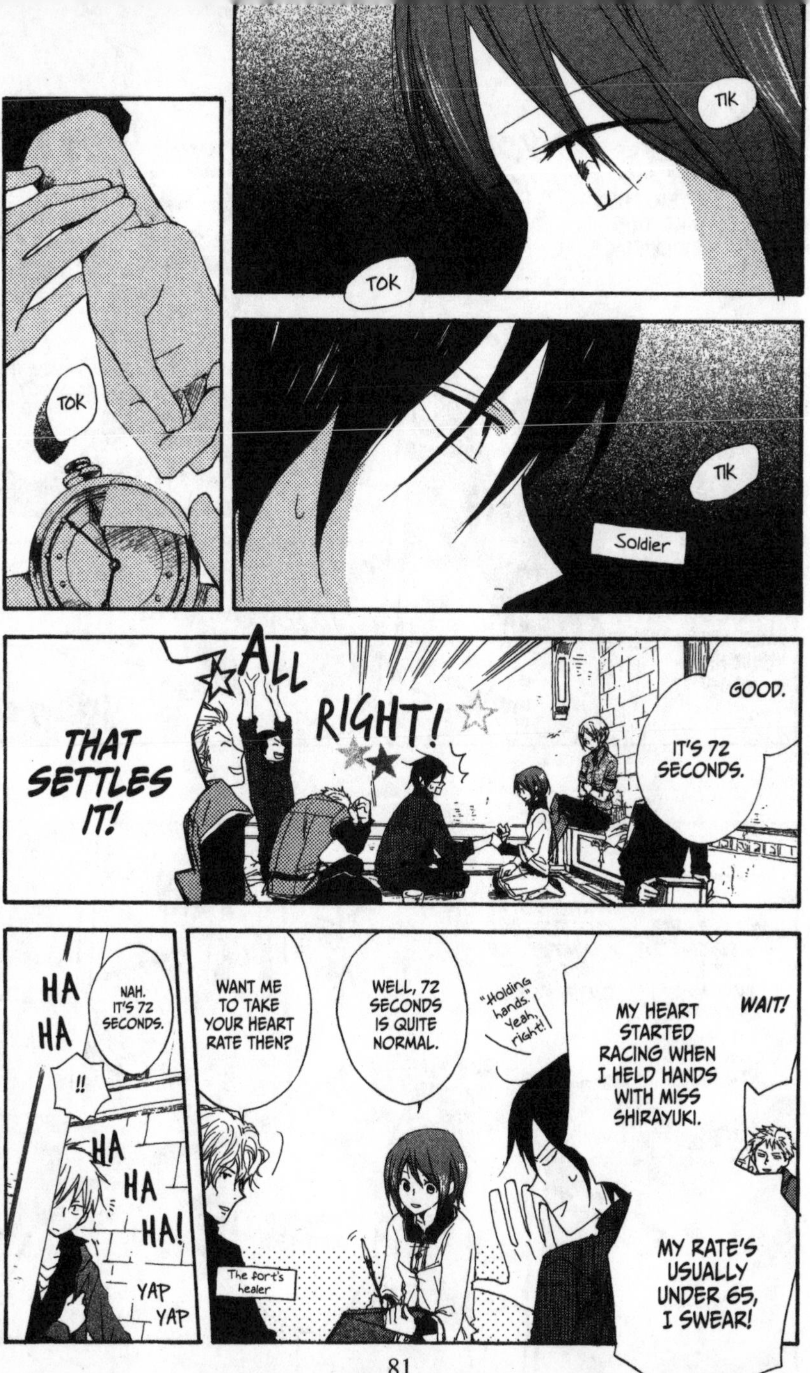
TIK
TOK
TIK
Soldier
TOK
GOOD.
IT'S 72 SECONDS.
ALL RIGHT!
THAT SETTLES IT!
WAIT!
MY HEART STARTED RACING WHEN I HELD HANDS WITH MISS SHIRAYUKI.
MY RATE'S USUALLY UNDER 65, I SWEAR!
"Holding hands." Yeah, right!
WELL, 72 SECONDS IS QUITE NORMAL.
WANT ME TO TAKE YOUR HEART RATE THEN?
The fort's healer
HA HA
NAH. IT'S 72 SECONDS.
!!
HA HA HA!
YAP YAP

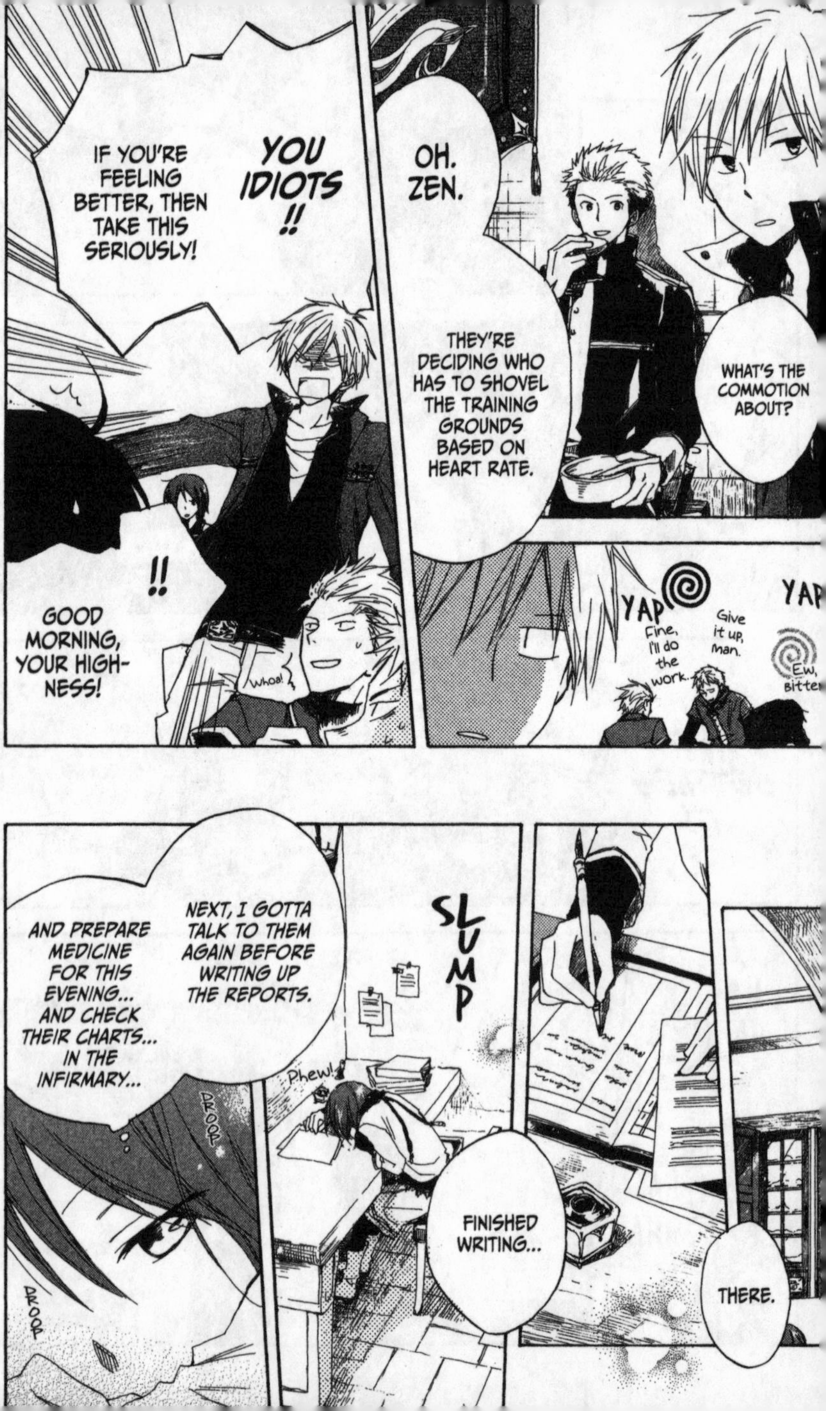
WHAT'S THE COMMOTION ABOUT?
OH. ZEN.
THEY'RE DECIDING WHO HAS TO SHOVEL THE TRAINING GROUNDS BASED ON HEART RATE.
YAP
YAP
Ew, bitter
Give it up, man.
Fine, I'll do the work.
YOU IDIOTS!!
IF YOU'RE FEELING BETTER, THEN TAKE THIS SERIOUSLY!
!!
GOOD MORNING, YOUR HIGHNESS!
Whoa!
THERE.
FINISHED WRITING...
SLUMP
Phew!
NEXT, I GOTTA TALK TO THEM AGAIN BEFORE WRITING UP THE REPORTS.
AND PREPARE MEDICINE FOR THIS EVENING... AND CHECK THEIR CHARTS... IN THE INFIRMARY...
DROOP
DROOP

FW IP

YEESH!

YAP YAP

NO...

YOU SURE?

OH?

SORRY, WERE YOU SLEEPING?

KLTR KLTR

KLTR

NOT THAT YOU COULD SLEEP WITH ALL THIS NOISE.

Woo, let's go!

YEAH!

I said hang on!

NOW THAT THEY'VE RECOVERED, THEY DON'T SHUT UP.

BAM

BANG

YOU LOOK SO RELIEVED.

Whoa chilly!

KLANG

Tch!

PRINCE ZEN.

4

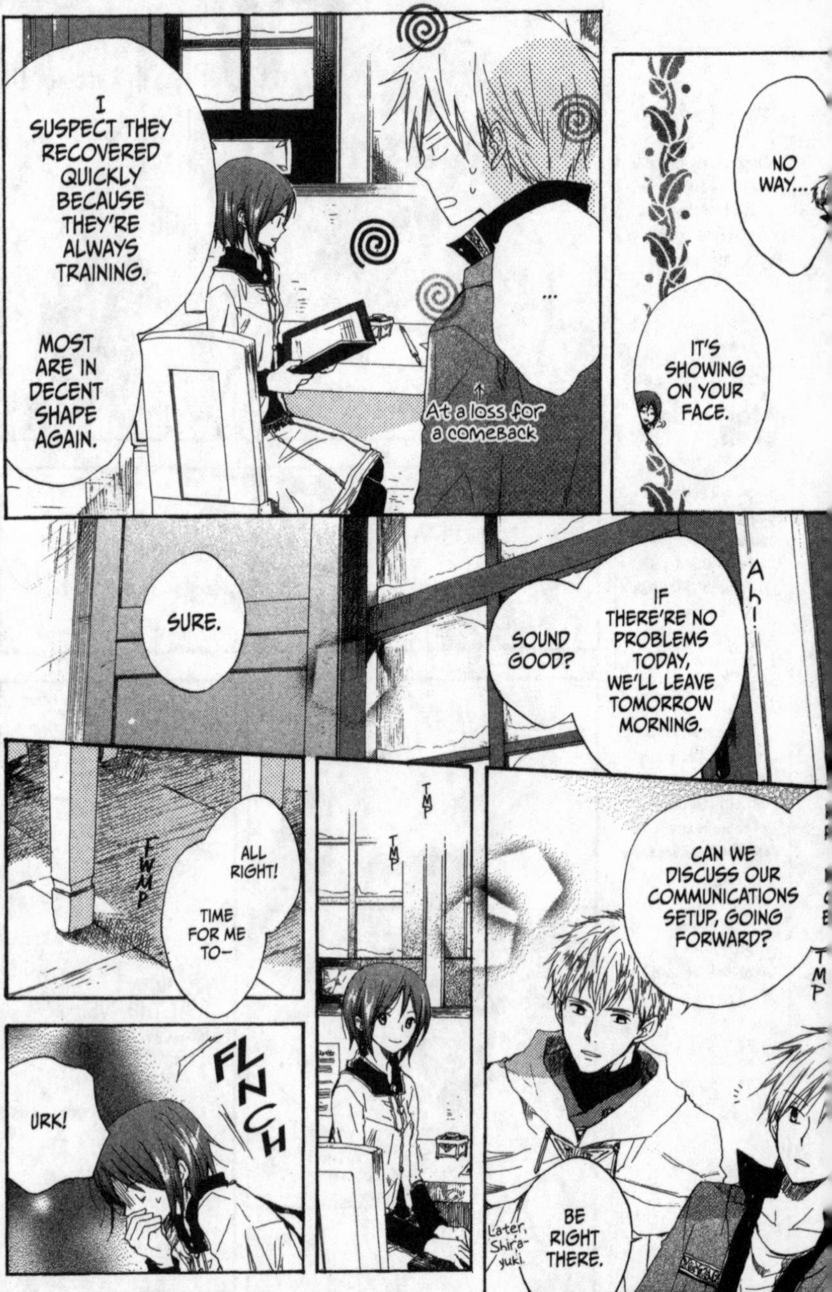
NO WAY...
IT'S SHOWING ON YOUR FACE.
I SUSPECT THEY RECOVERED QUICKLY BECAUSE THEY'RE ALWAYS TRAINING.
MOST ARE IN DECENT SHAPE AGAIN.
...
At a loss for a comeback
Ah!
IF THERE'RE NO PROBLEMS TODAY, WE'LL LEAVE TOMORROW MORNING.
SOUND GOOD?
SURE.
TMP
CAN WE DISCUSS OUR COMMUNICATIONS SETUP, GOING FORWARD?
BE RIGHT THERE.
Later, Shirayuki.
TMP
TMP
ALL RIGHT!
TIME FOR ME TO-
FWMP
FLINCH
URK!

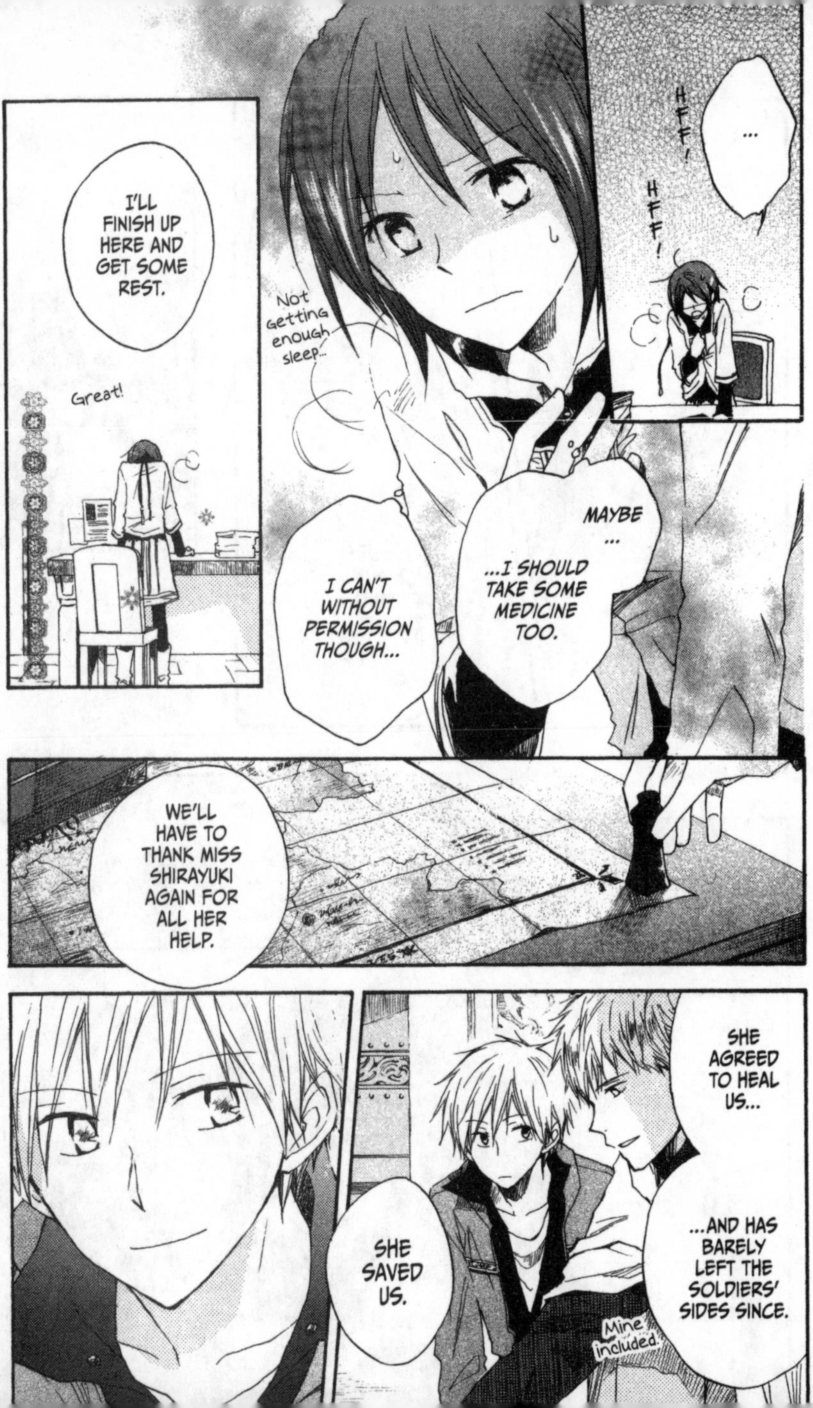
HFF! HFF!
...
Not getting enough sleep...
MAYBE... ...I SHOULD TAKE SOME MEDICINE TOO.
I CAN'T WITHOUT PERMISSION THOUGH...
I'LL FINISH UP HERE AND GET SOME REST.
Great!
WE'LL HAVE TO THANK MISS SHIRAYUKI AGAIN FOR ALL HER HELP.
SHE AGREED TO HEAL US...
...AND HAS BARELY LEFT THE SOLDIERS' SIDES SINCE.
Mine included.
SHE SAVED US.

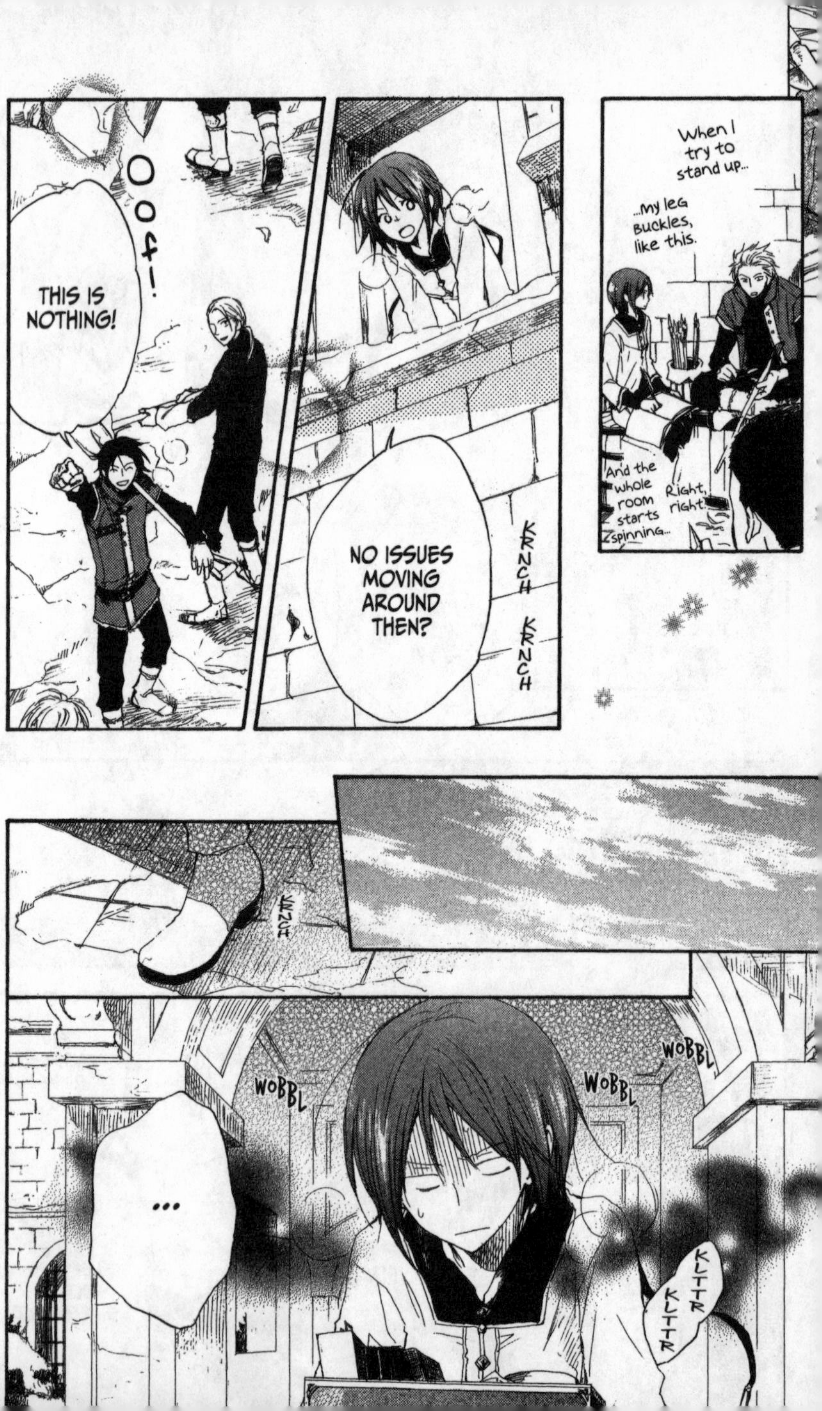
When I try to stand up...
...My leg buckles, like this.
And the whole room starts spinning...
Right, right!
NO ISSUES MOVING AROUND THEN?
KRNCH KRNCH
Oof!
THIS IS NOTHING!
KRNCH
WOBBL
WOBBL
WOBBL
KLTTR KLTTR
...

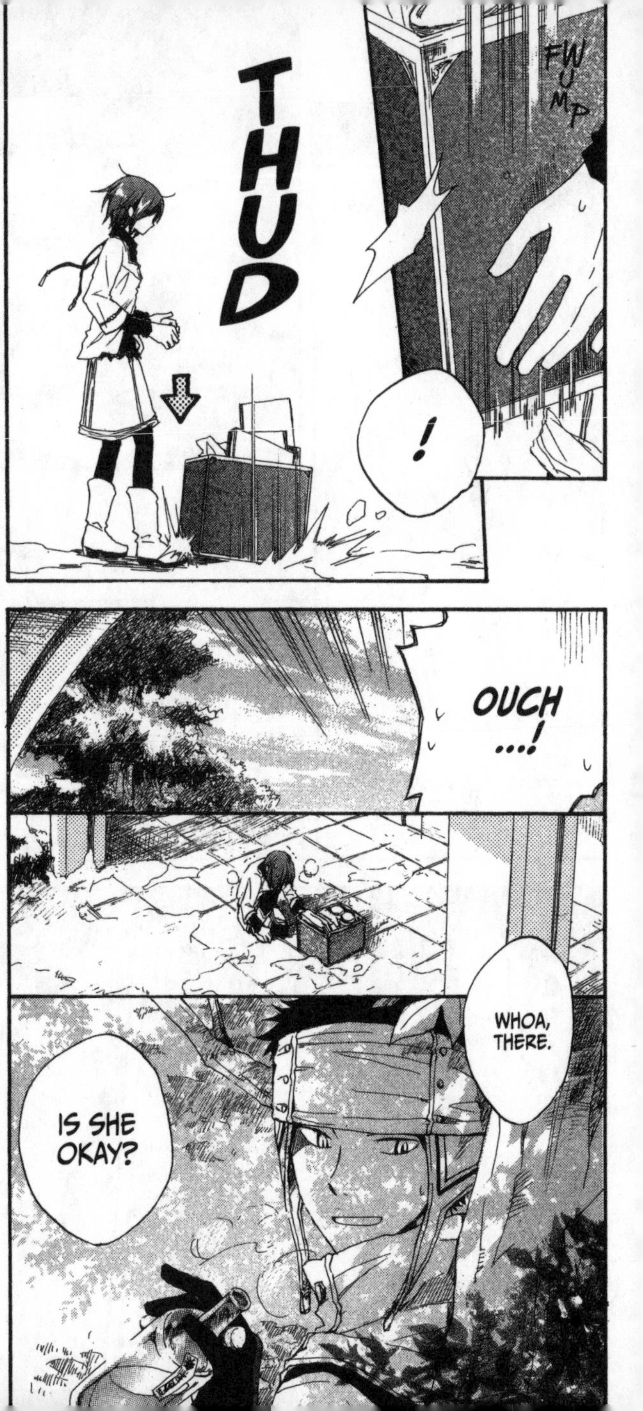
FWUMP
!
THUD
OUCH...!
WHOA, THERE.
IS SHE OKAY?

Chapter 7

This chapter comes right before the plot really gets moving. I remember asking my older sister (we were out eating ramen), "How does this sound?"

With chopsticks in my hand, I was going on and on about Shirayuki and Zen, but my sister only wanted to talk about Obi.

I prefer ramen with either a soy sauce base or a salt base.

Here, Shirayuki (who's been relying on Zen) takes on a little too much.

It was weirdly nerve-racking portraying their relationship in this chapter.

5

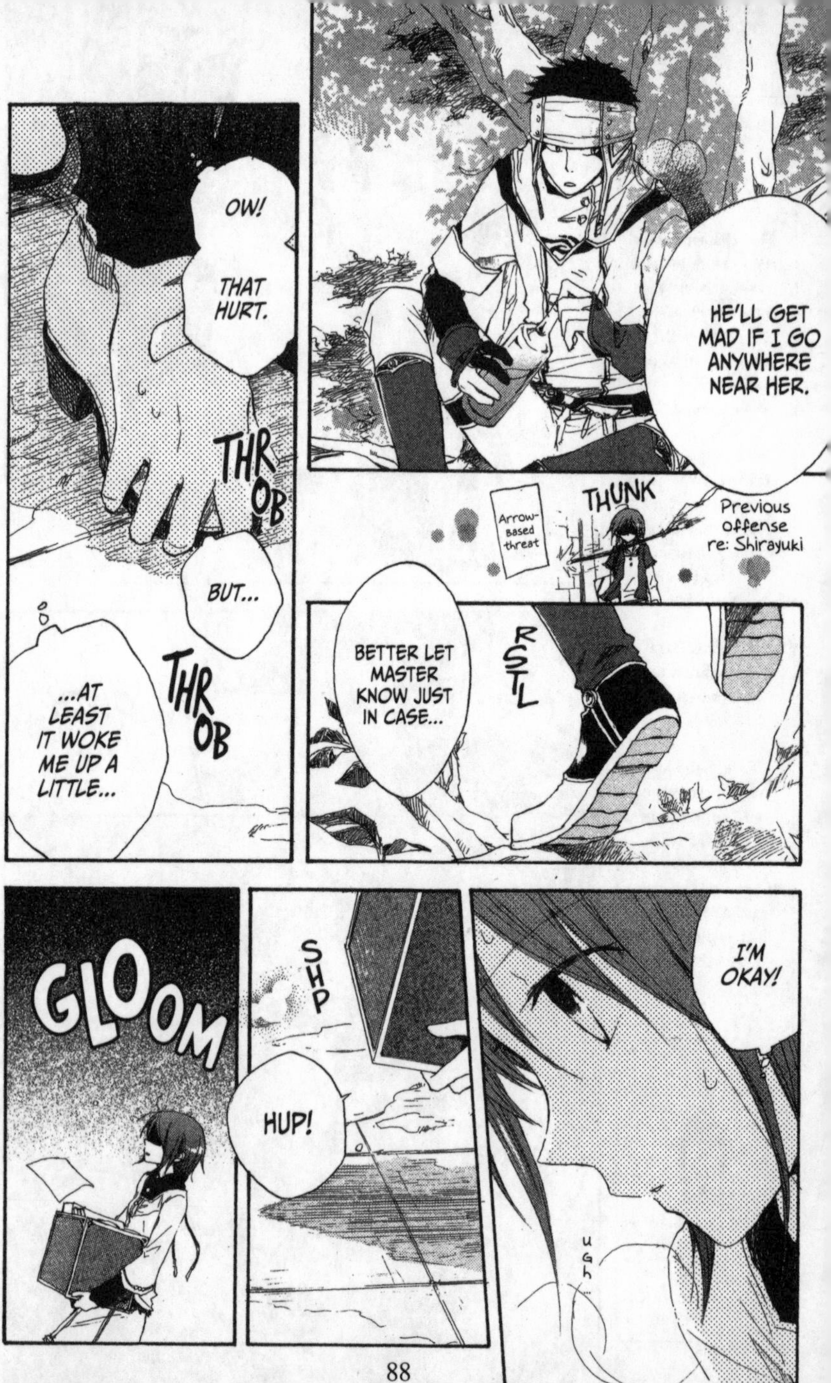
HE'LL GET MAD IF I GO ANYWHERE NEAR HER.
THUNK
Arrow-based threat
Previous offense re: Shirayuki
BETTER LET MASTER KNOW JUST IN CASE...
RSTL
OW!
THAT HURT.
THROB
BUT...
THROB
...AT LEAST IT WOKE ME UP A LITTLE...
I'M OKAY!
ugh...
SHP
HUP!
GLOOM

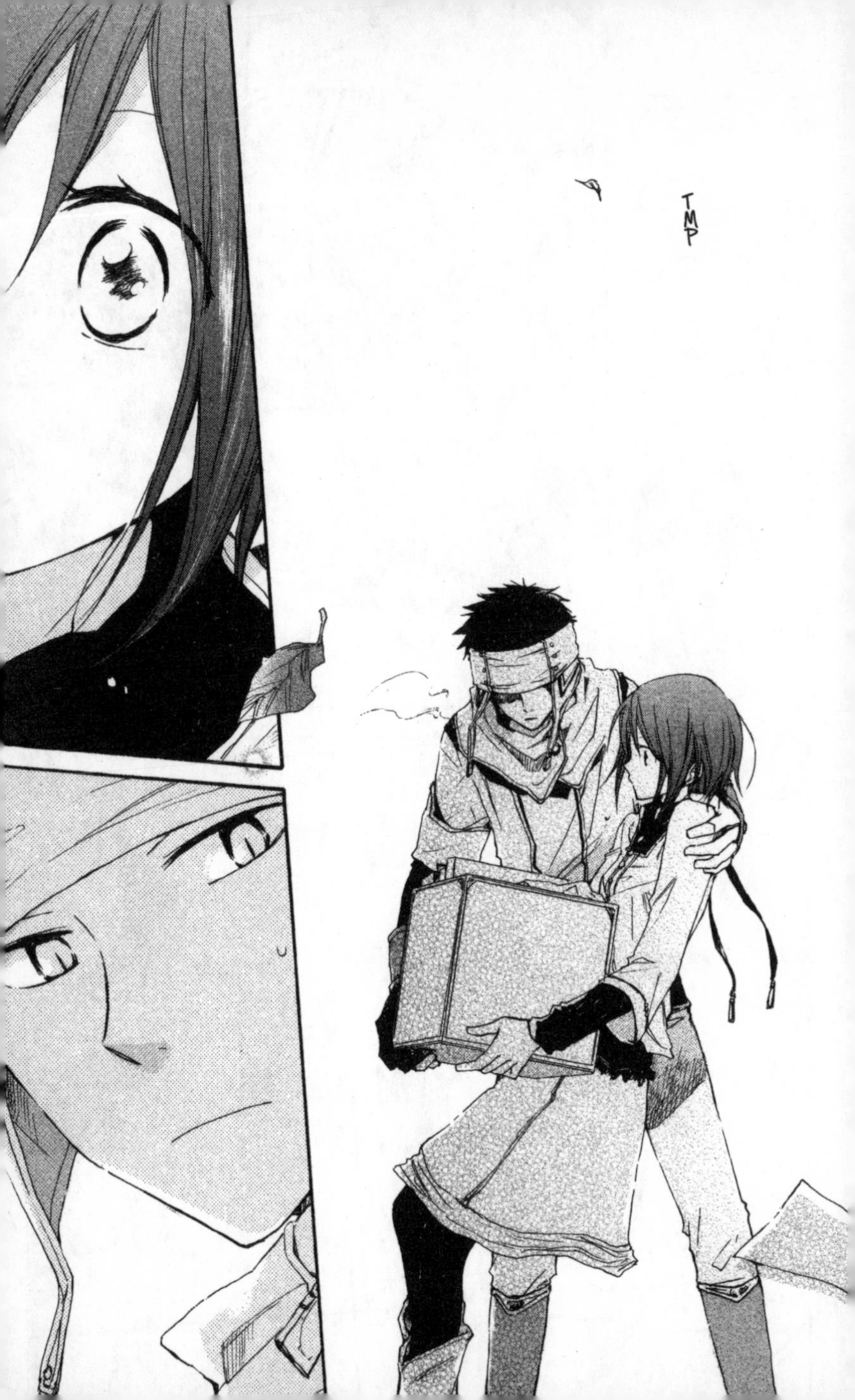
TMP

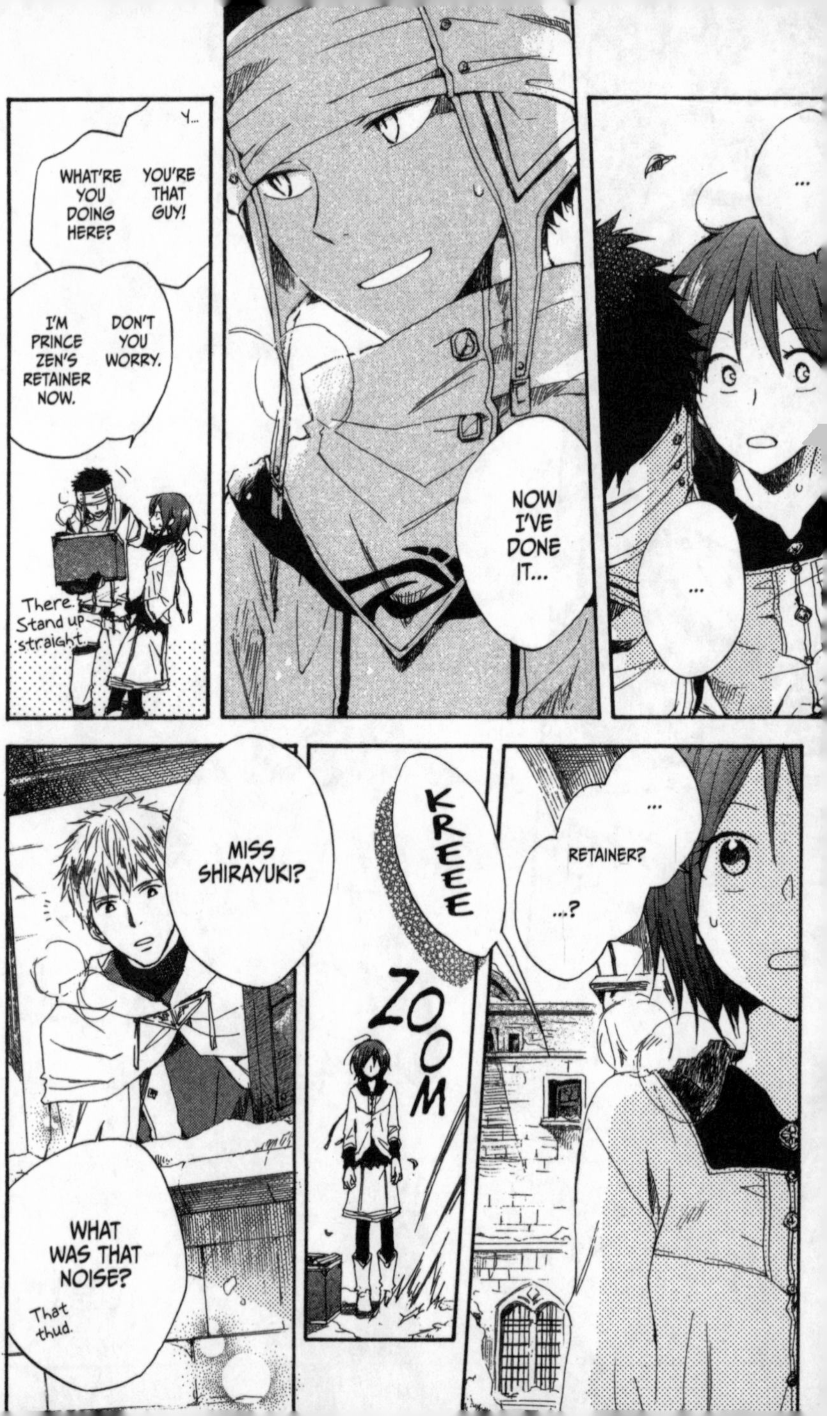
...
...
NOW I'VE DONE IT...
Y...
YOU'RE THAT GUY!
WHAT'RE YOU DOING HERE?
DON'T YOU WORRY.
I'M PRINCE ZEN'S RETAINER NOW.
There. Stand up straight.
...
RETAINER?
...?
KREEE
ZOOM
MISS SHIRAYUKI?
WHAT WAS THAT NOISE?
That thud.

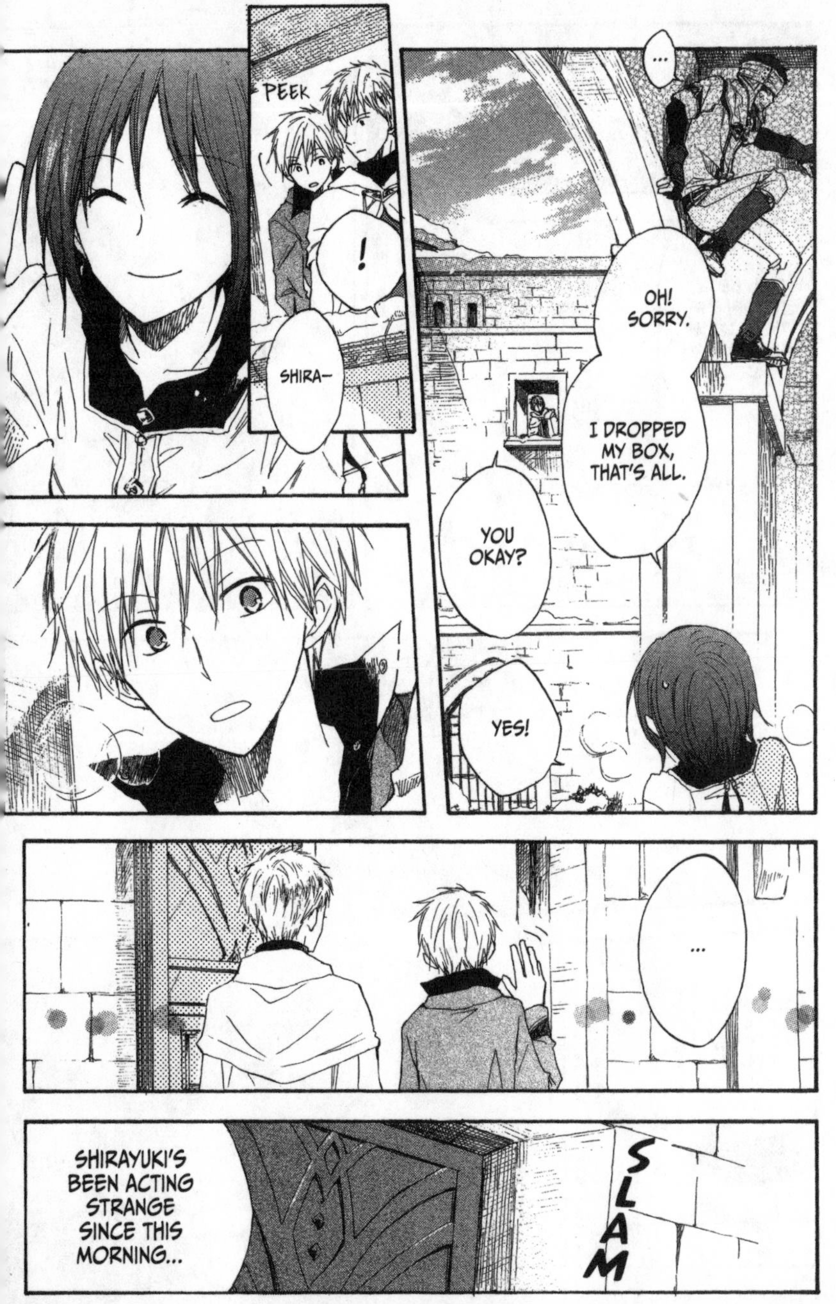
...
OH! SORRY.
I DROPPED MY BOX, THAT'S ALL.
YOU OKAY?
YES!
PEEK
!
SHIRA—
...
SLAM
SHIRAYUKI'S BEEN ACTING STRANGE SINCE THIS MORNING...

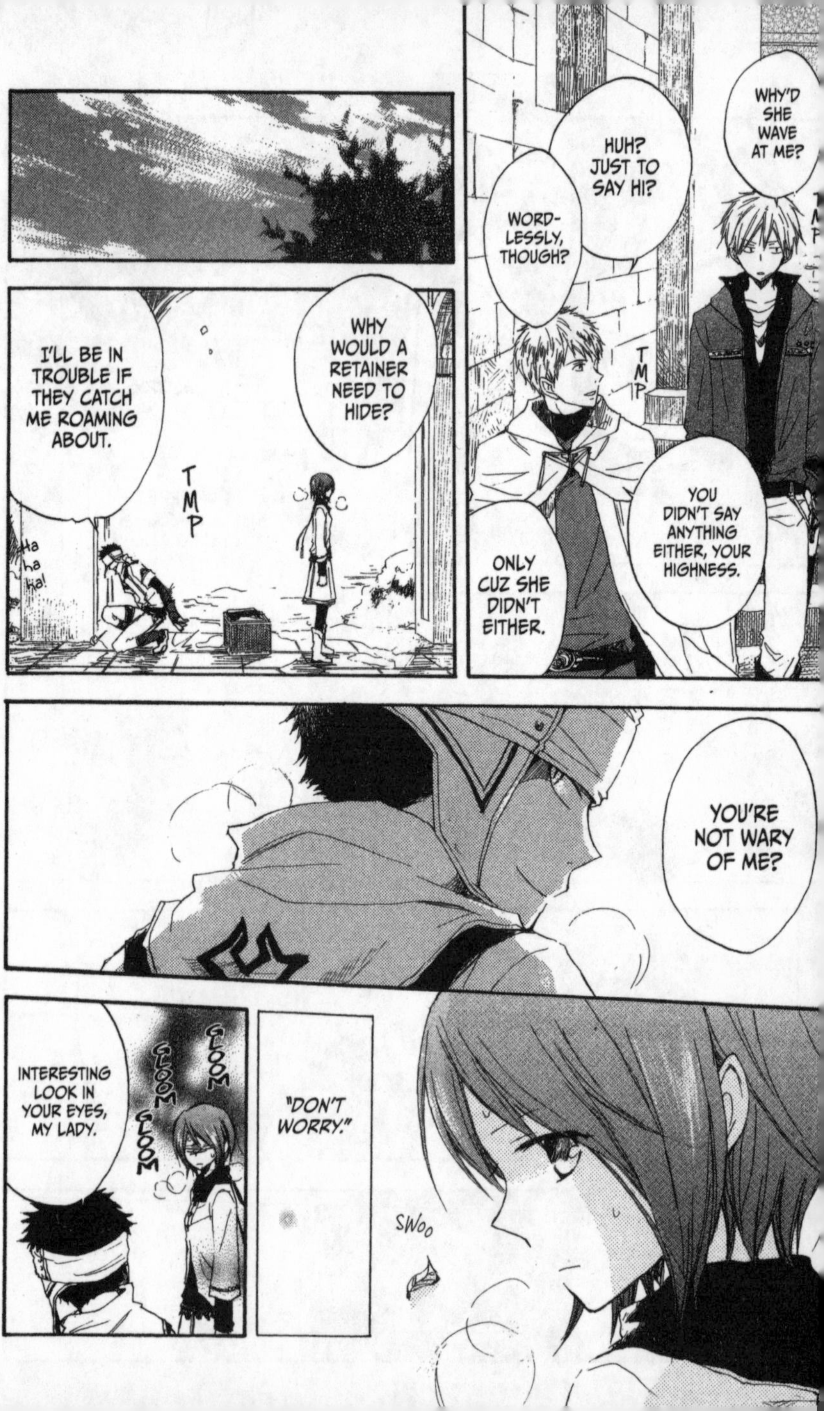
WHY'D SHE WAVE AT ME?
HUH? JUST TO SAY HI?
WORD-LESSLY, THOUGH?
TMP
TMP
YOU DIDN'T SAY ANYTHING EITHER, YOUR HIGHNESS.
ONLY CUZ SHE DIDN'T EITHER.
WHY WOULD A RETAINER NEED TO HIDE?
I'LL BE IN TROUBLE IF THEY CATCH ME ROAMING ABOUT.
TMP
Ha ha ha!
YOU'RE NOT WARY OF ME?
SWoo
"DON'T WORRY."
GLOOM
GLOOM
GLOOM
INTERESTING LOOK IN YOUR EYES, MY LADY.

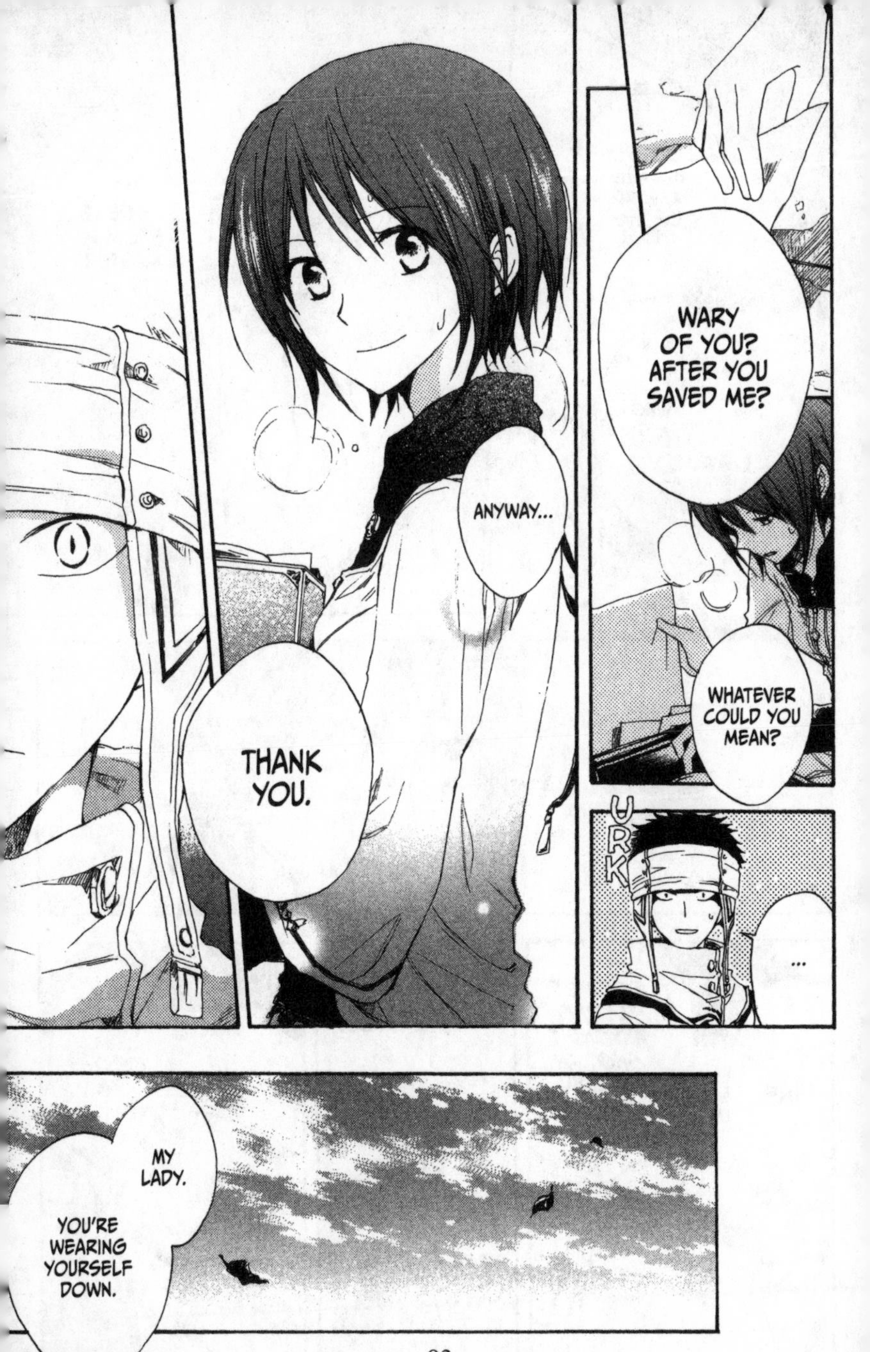
WARY OF YOU? AFTER YOU SAVED ME?
WHATEVER COULD YOU MEAN?
URK
...
ANYWAY...
THANK YOU.
MY LADY.
YOU'RE WEARING YOURSELF DOWN.

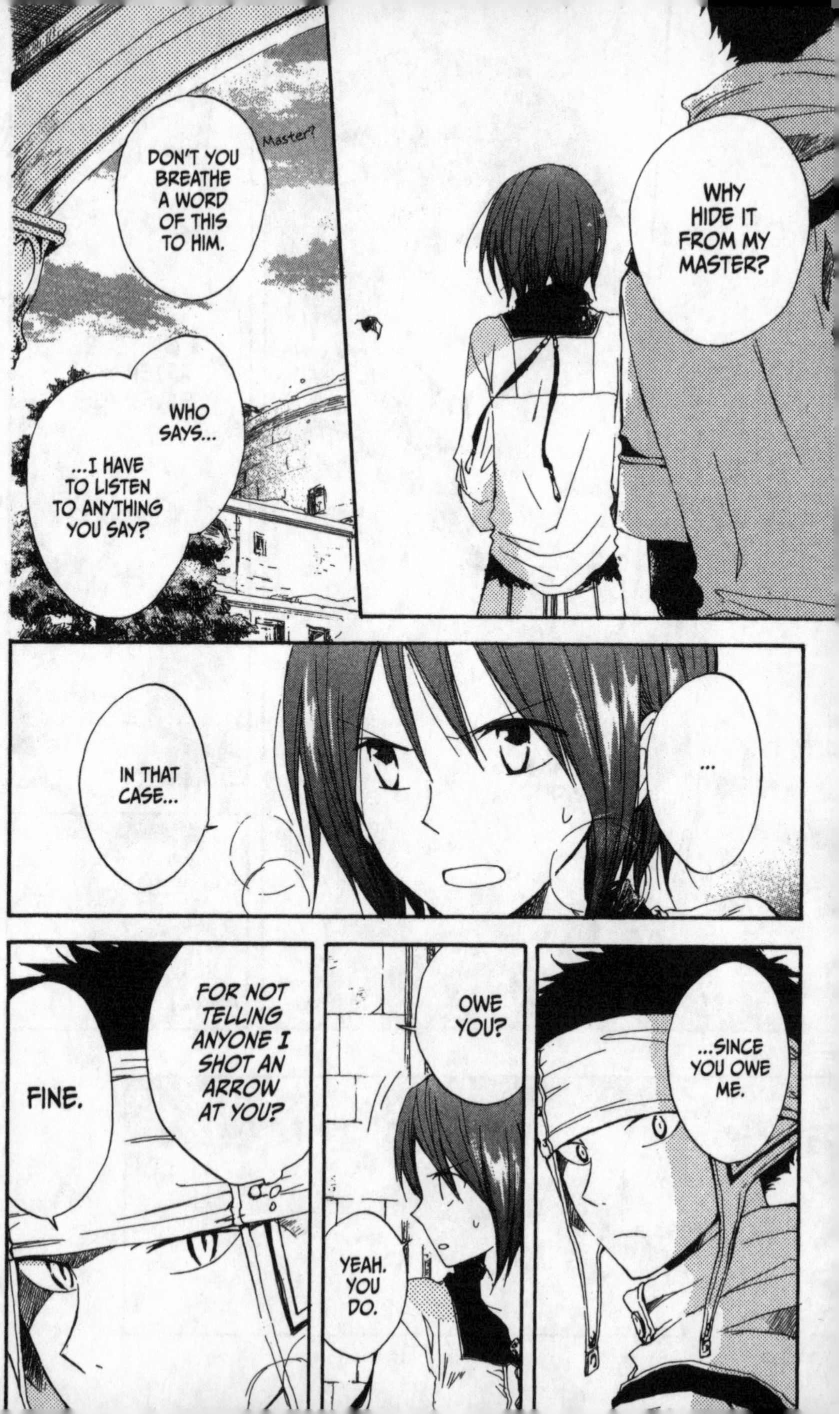
WHY HIDE IT FROM MY MASTER?
DON'T YOU BREATHE A WORD OF THIS TO HIM.
Master?
WHO SAYS...
...I HAVE TO LISTEN TO ANYTHING YOU SAY?
...
IN THAT CASE...
...SINCE YOU OWE ME.
OWE YOU?
YEAH. YOU DO.
FOR NOT TELLING ANYONE I SHOT AN ARROW AT YOU?
FINE.

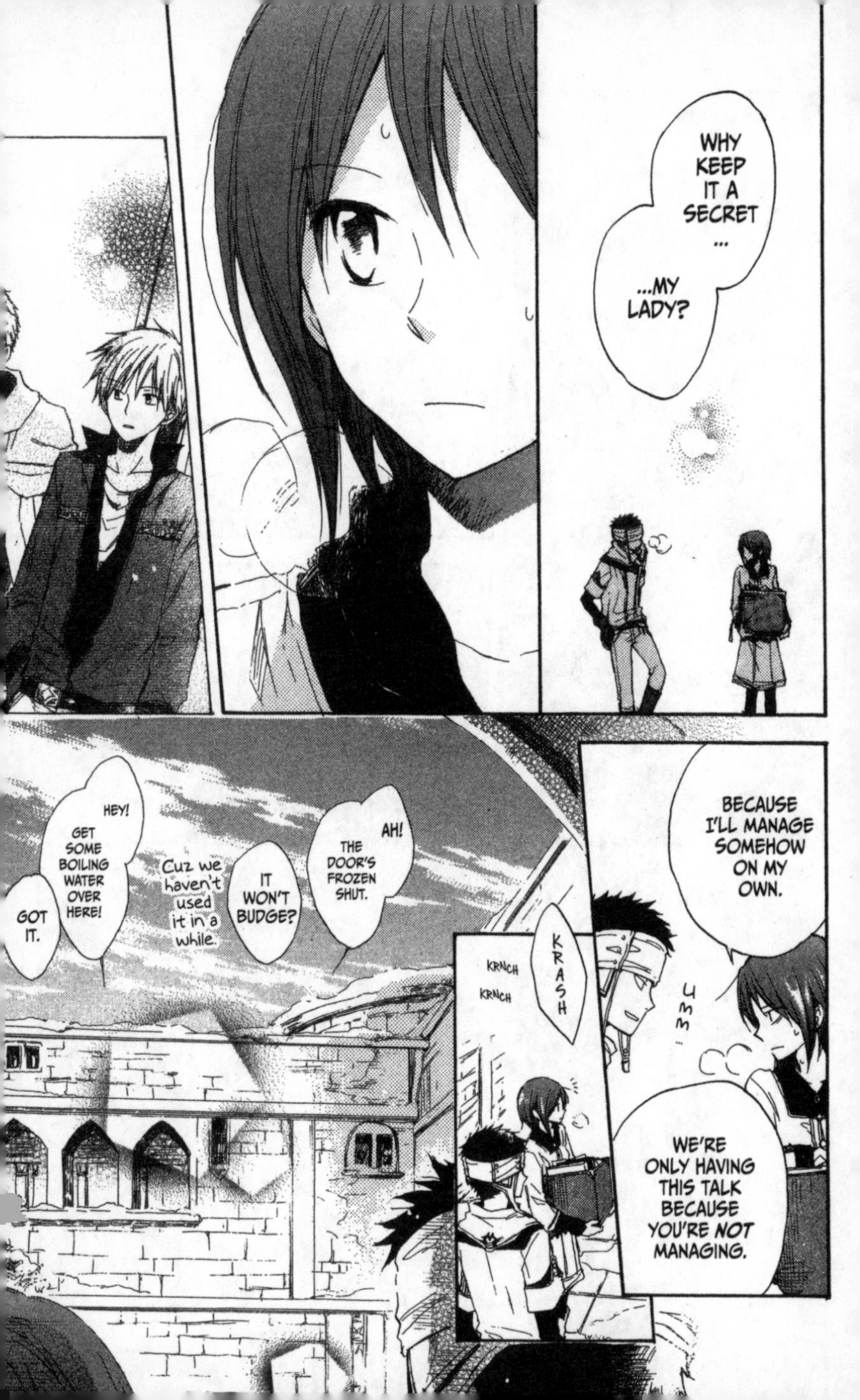
WHY KEEP IT A SECRET ...
...MY LADY?
BECAUSE I'LL MANAGE SOMEHOW ON MY OWN.
UMM...
WE'RE ONLY HAVING THIS TALK BECAUSE YOU'RE *NOT* MANAGING.
KRASH
KRNCH
KRNCH
AH! THE DOOR'S FROZEN SHUT.
IT WON'T BUDGE?
Cuz we haven't used it in a while.
HEY! GET SOME BOILING WATER OVER HERE!
GOT IT.

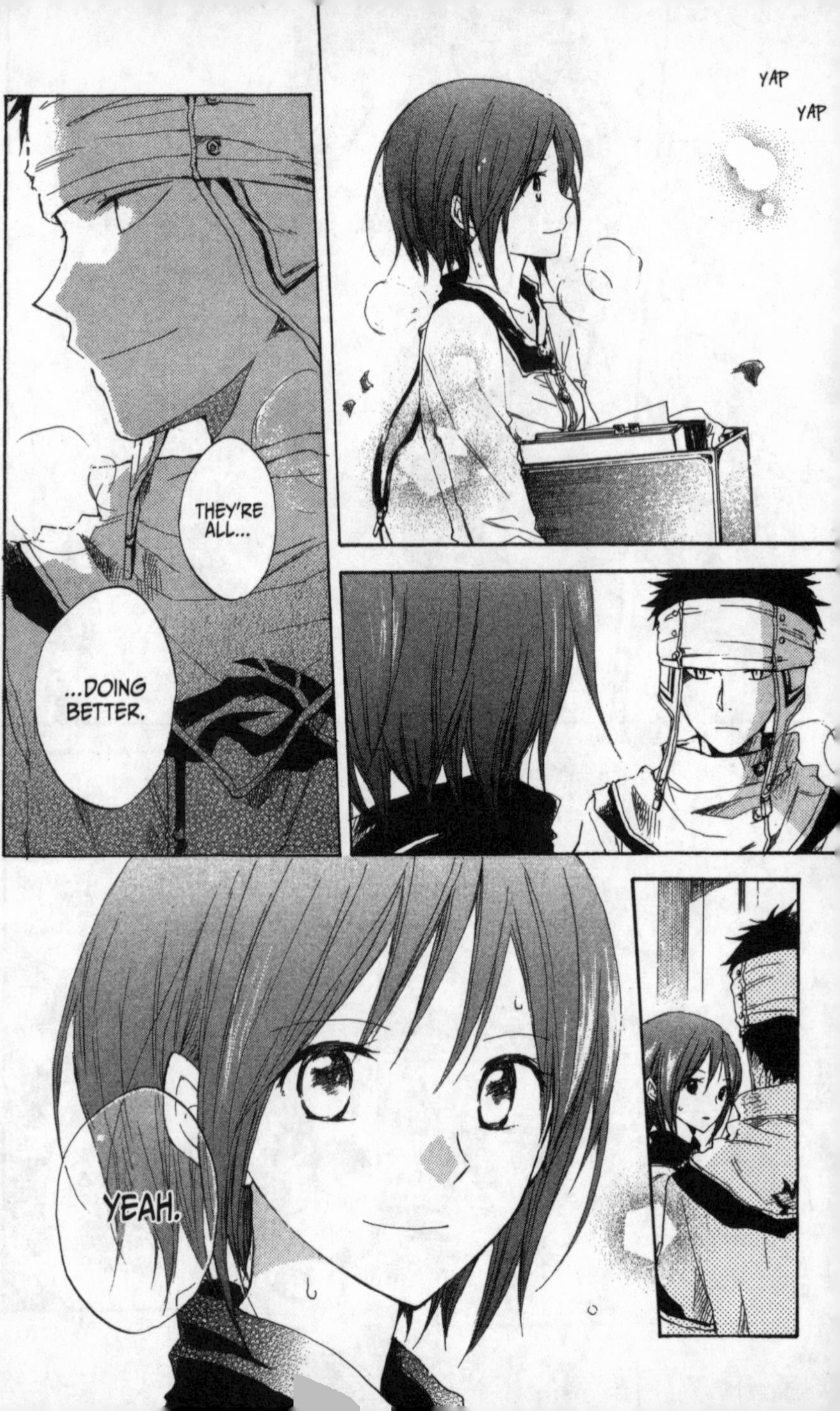
YAP
YAP
THEY'RE ALL...
...DOING BETTER.
YEAH.

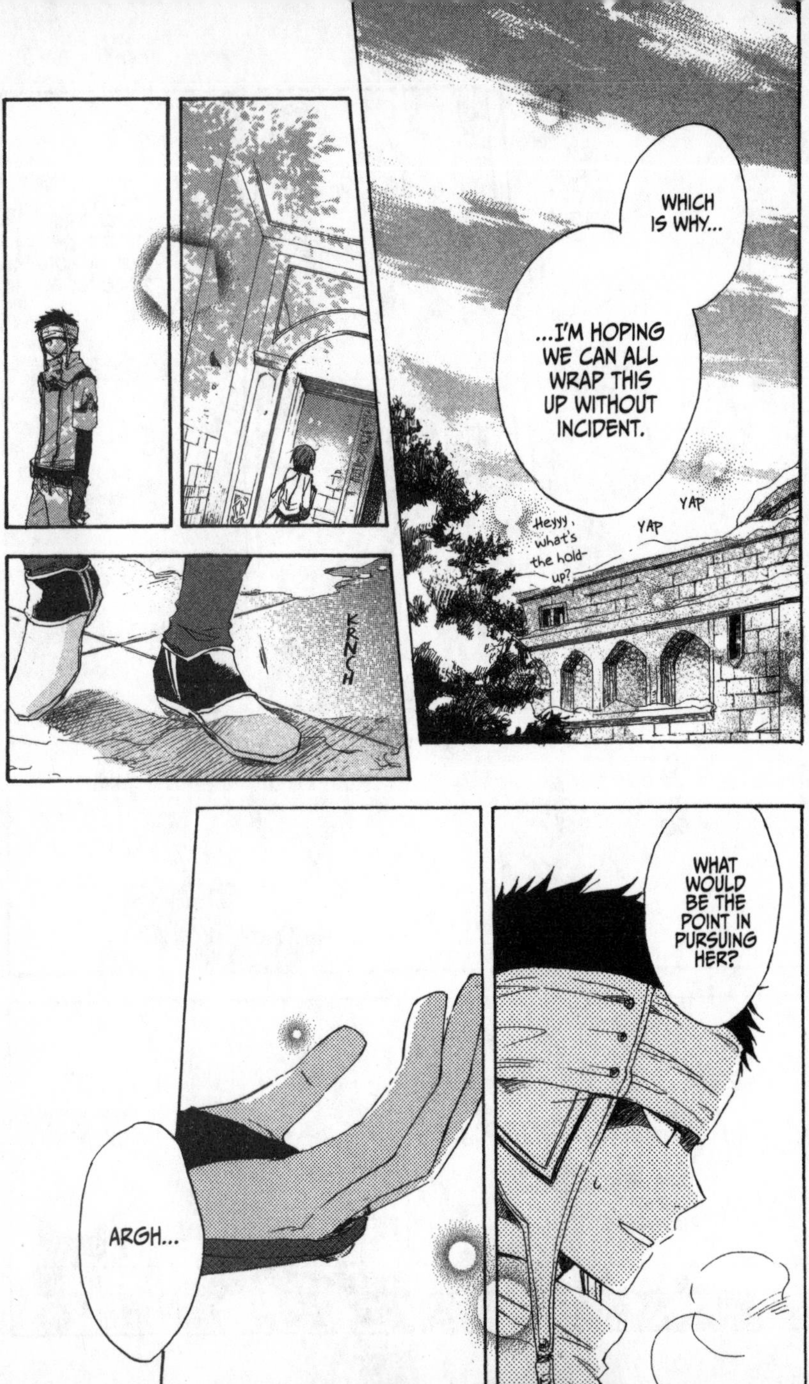
WHICH IS WHY...
...I'M HOPING WE CAN ALL WRAP THIS UP WITHOUT INCIDENT.
YAP
YAP
Heyyy, what's the hold-up?
KRNCH
WHAT WOULD BE THE POINT IN PURSUING HER?
ARGH...

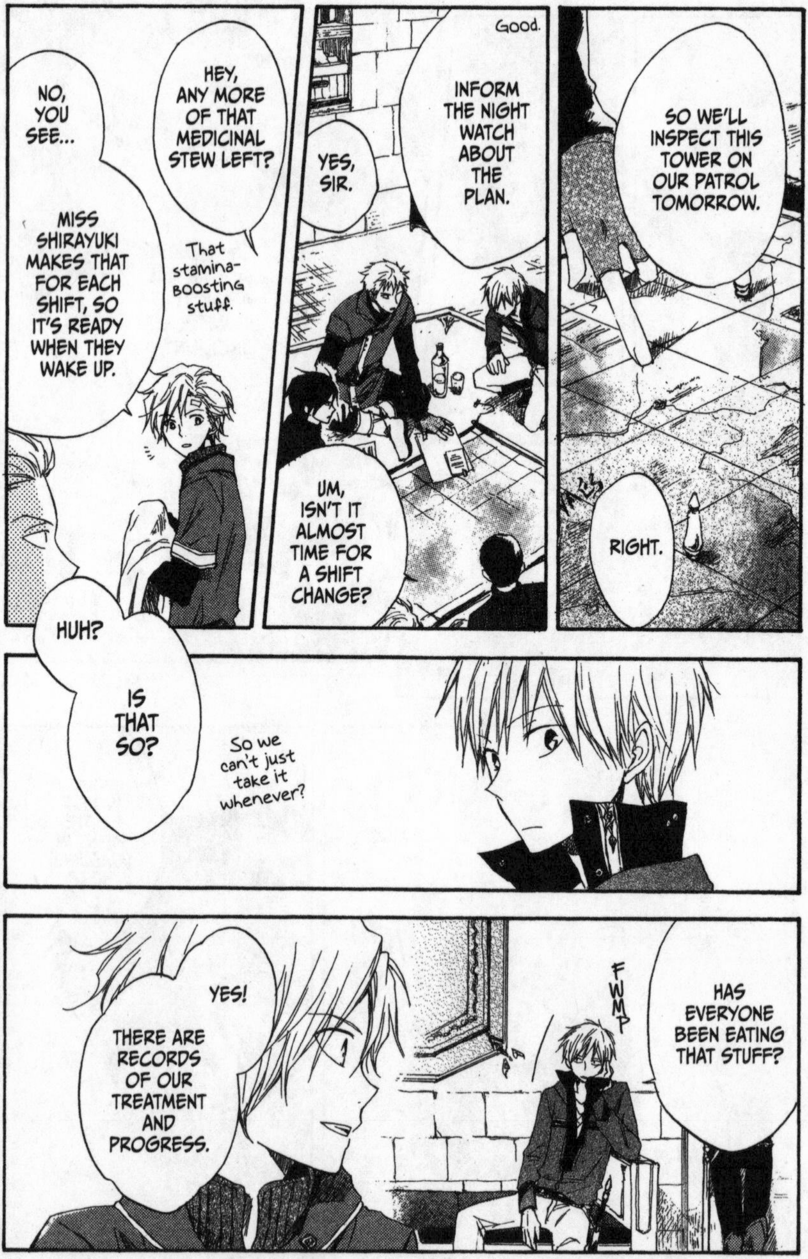
SO WE'LL INSPECT THIS TOWER ON OUR PATROL TOMORROW.
RIGHT.
Good.
INFORM THE NIGHT WATCH ABOUT THE PLAN.
YES, SIR.
UM, ISN'T IT ALMOST TIME FOR A SHIFT CHANGE?
HEY, ANY MORE OF THAT MEDICINAL STEW LEFT?
That stamina-boosting stuff.
NO, YOU SEE...
MISS SHIRAYUKI MAKES THAT FOR EACH SHIFT, SO IT'S READY WHEN THEY WAKE UP.
HUH?
IS THAT SO?
So we can't just take it whenever?
HAS EVERYONE BEEN EATING THAT STUFF?
FWMP
YES!
THERE ARE RECORDS OF OUR TREATMENT AND PROGRESS.

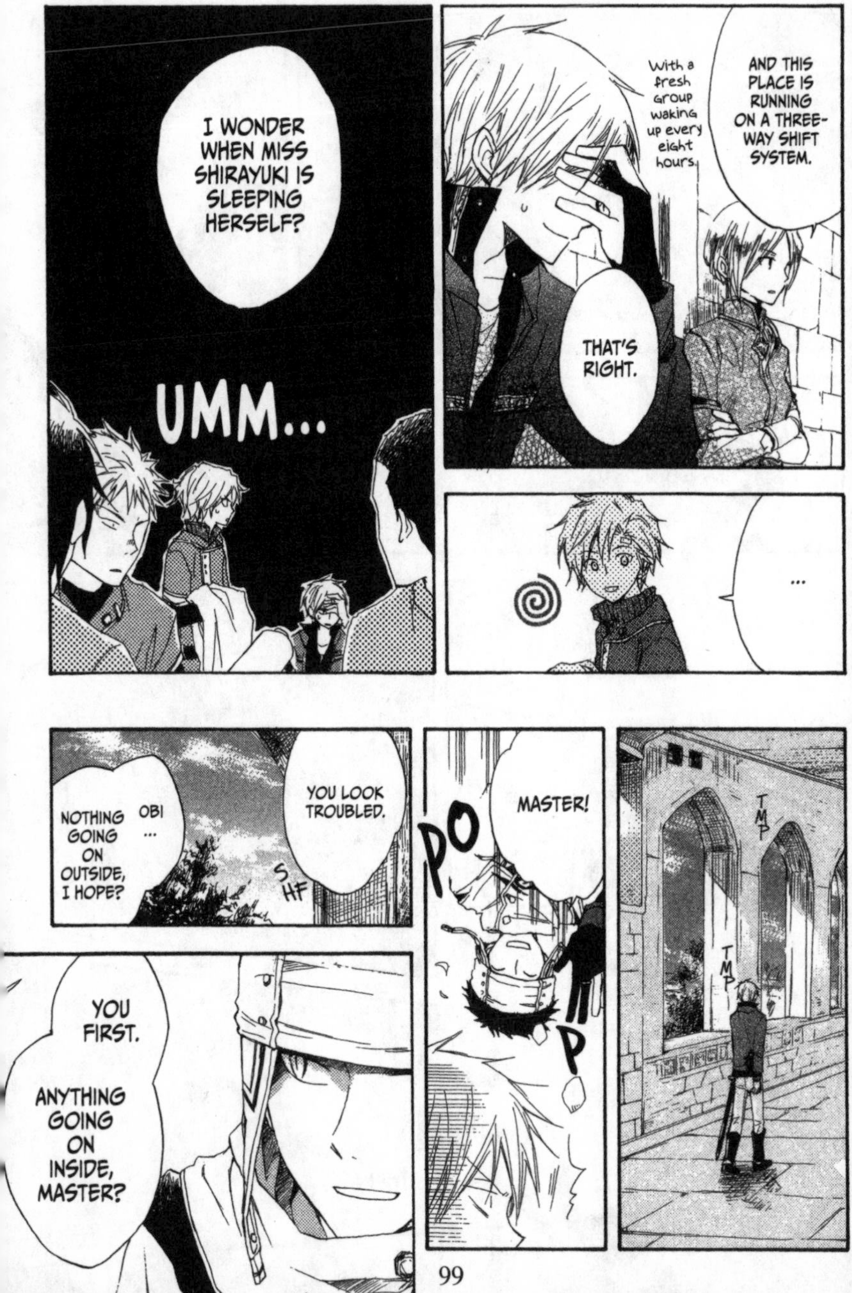
AND THIS PLACE IS RUNNING ON A THREE-WAY SHIFT SYSTEM.
With a fresh group waking up every eight hours.
THAT'S RIGHT.
...
I WONDER WHEN MISS SHIRAYUKI IS SLEEPING HERSELF?
UMM...
TMP
TMP
MASTER!
POP
YOU LOOK TROUBLED.
OBI ...
SHF
NOTHING GOING ON OUTSIDE, I HOPE?
YOU FIRST.
ANYTHING GOING ON INSIDE, MASTER?

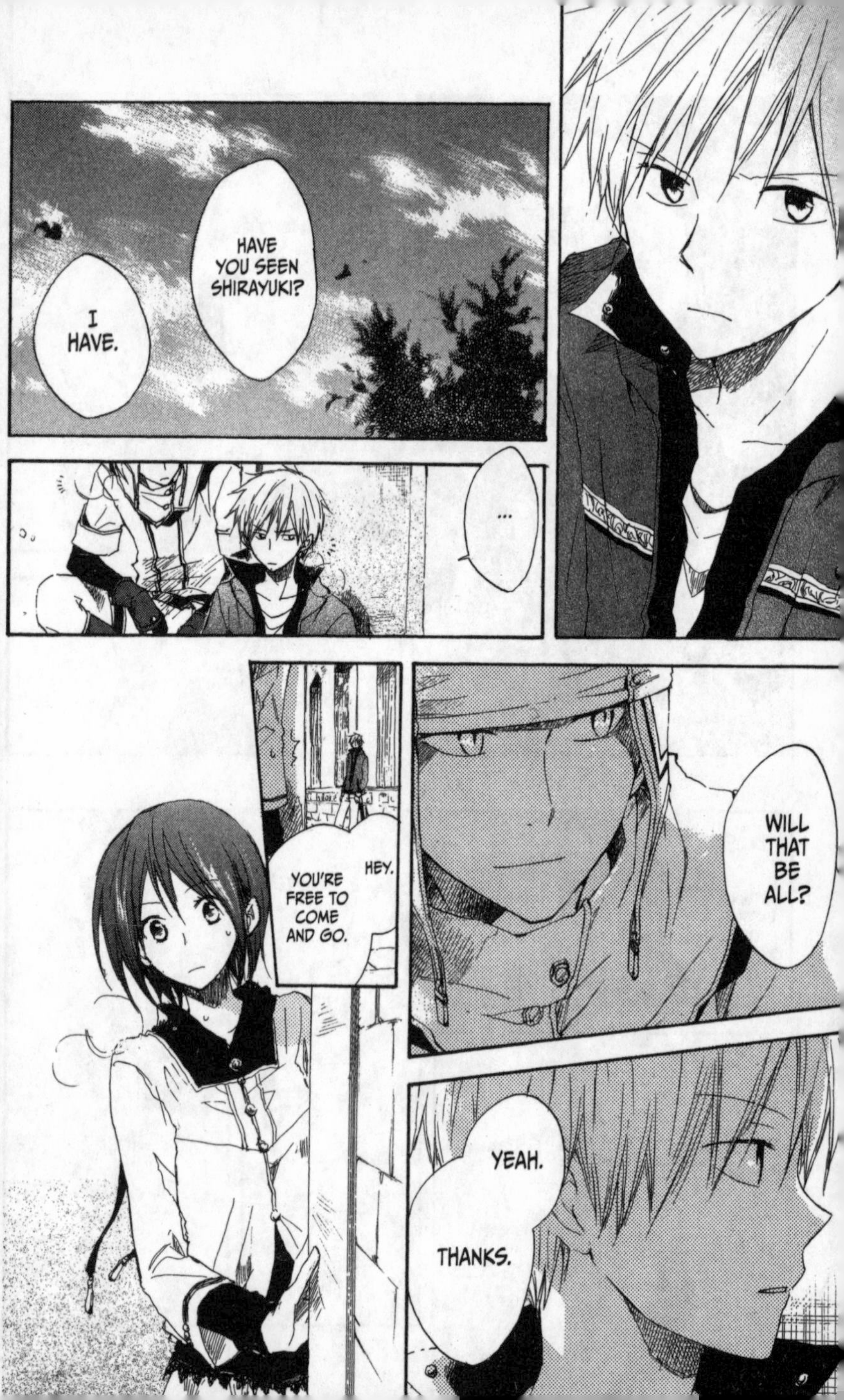
HAVE YOU SEEN SHIRAYUKI?
I HAVE.
...
WILL THAT BE ALL?
YEAH.
THANKS.
HEY.
YOU'RE FREE TO COME AND GO.

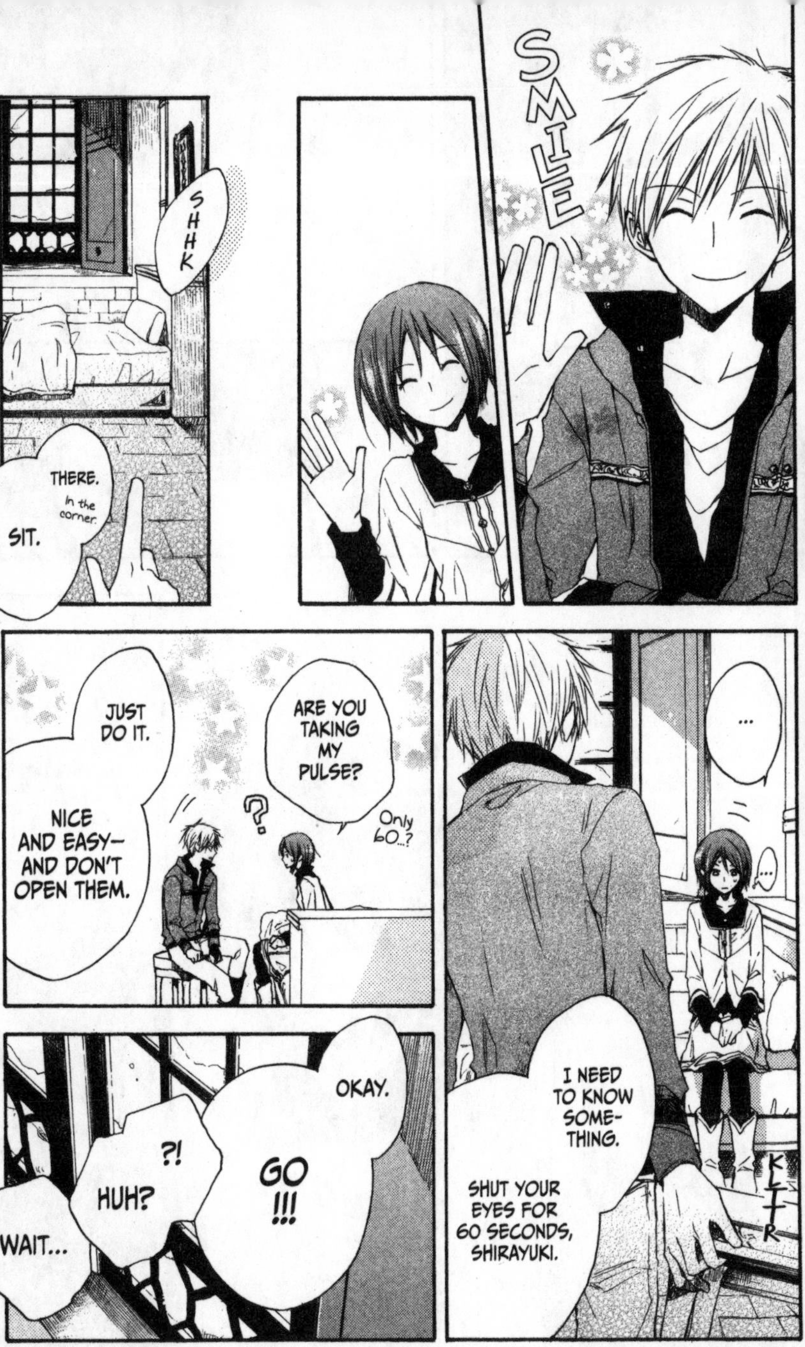
SMILE
SHHK
THERE.
In the corner.
SIT.
...
...
I NEED TO KNOW SOME-THING.
SHUT YOUR EYES FOR 60 SECONDS, SHIRAYUKI.
KLTTR
ARE YOU TAKING MY PULSE?
Only 60..?
?
JUST DO IT.
NICE AND EASY— AND DON'T OPEN THEM.
OKAY.
GO!!!
?!
HUH?
WAIT...

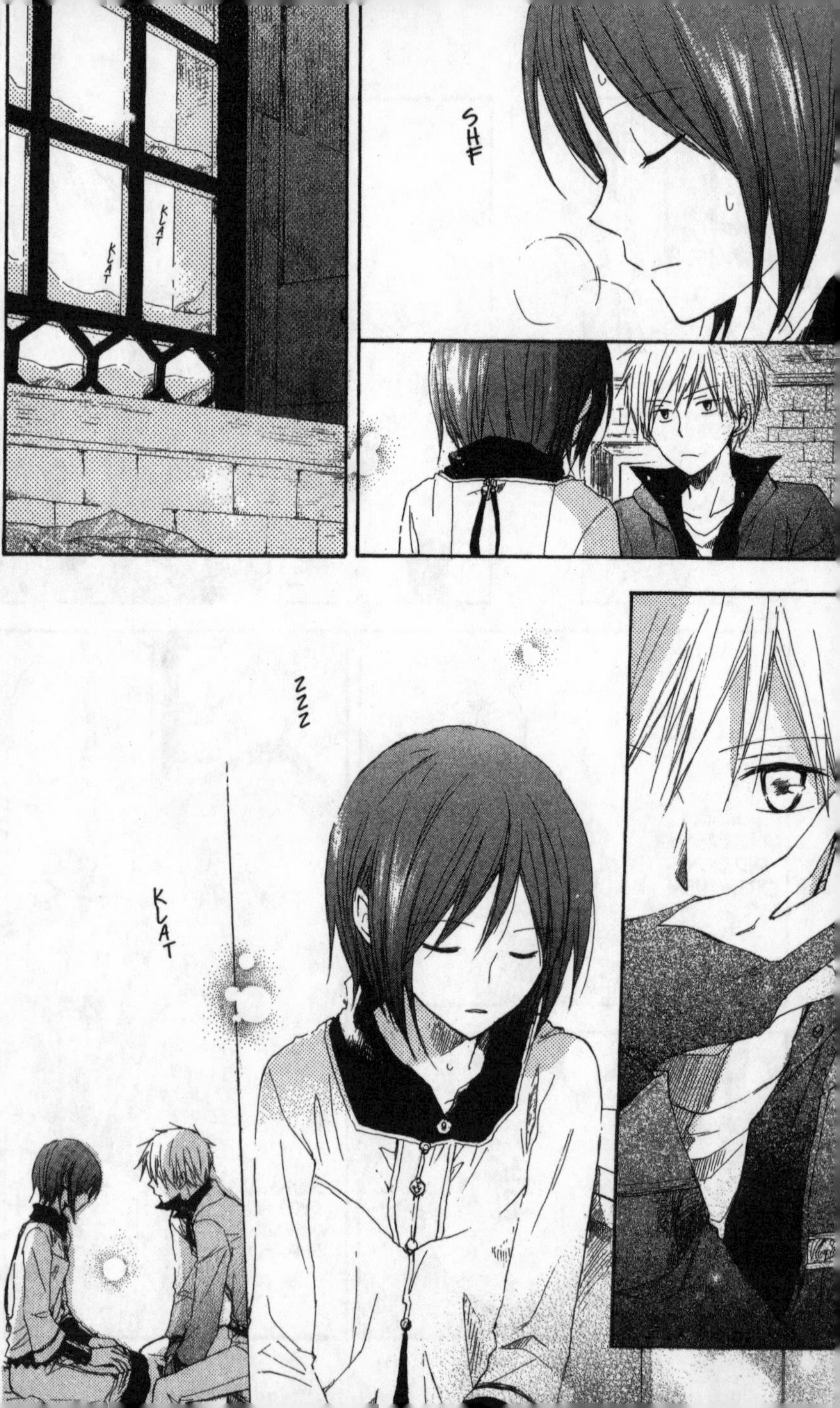
SHF
KLAT
KLAT
ZZZ
KLAT

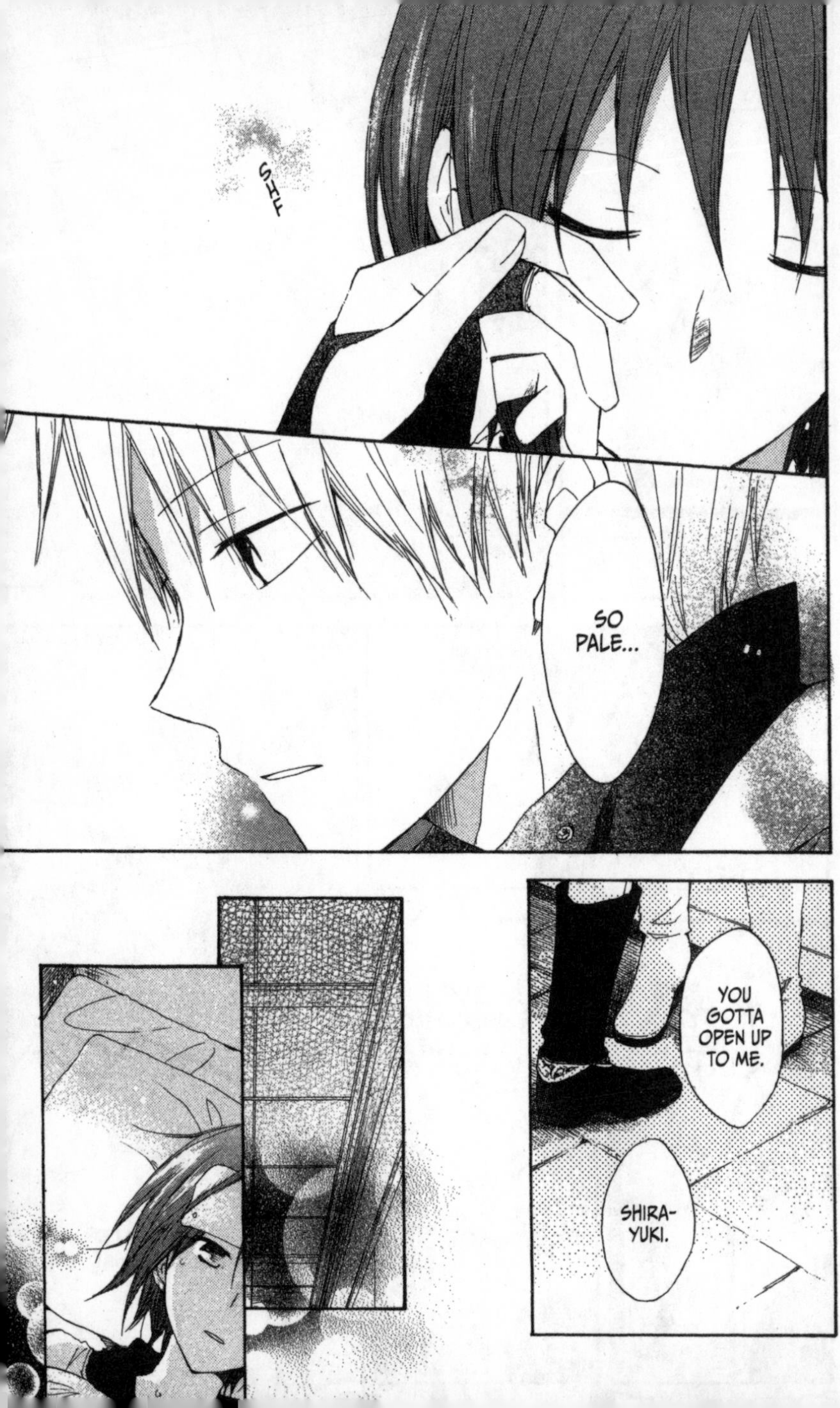
SHF
SO PALE...
YOU GOTTA OPEN UP TO ME.
SHIRA-YUKI.

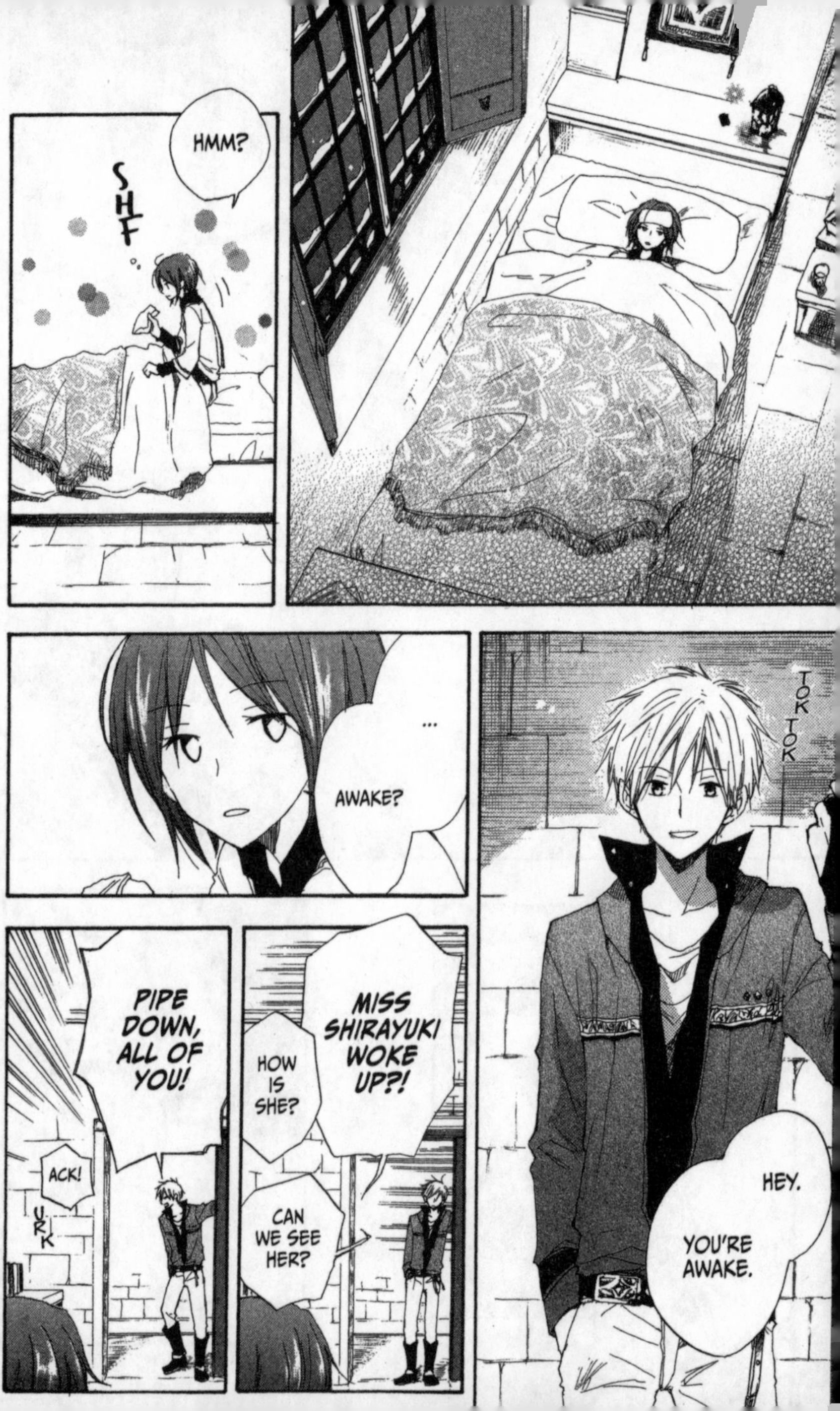
HMM?
SHF
TOK TOK
HEY.
YOU'RE AWAKE.
...
AWAKE?
MISS SHIRAYUKI WOKE UP?!
HOW IS SHE?
CAN WE SEE HER?
PIPE DOWN, ALL OF YOU!
ACK!
URK

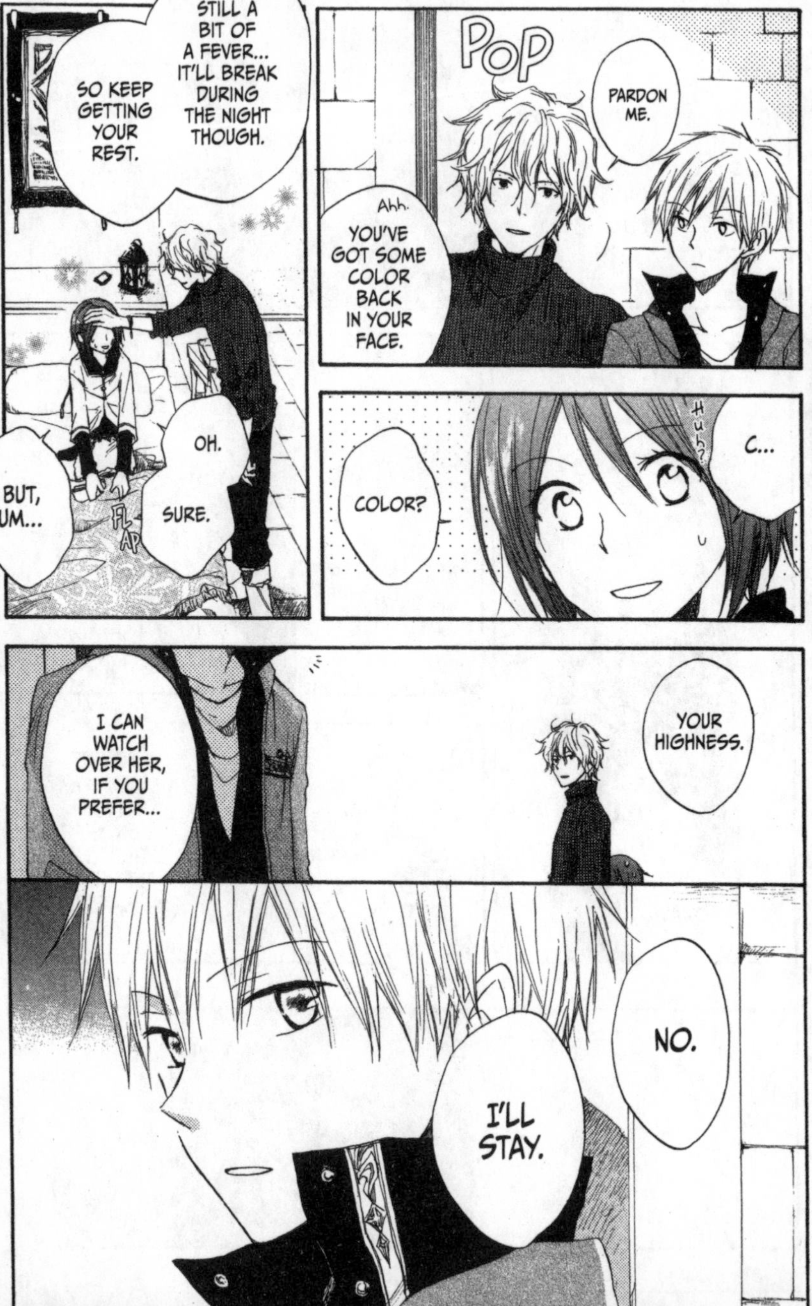
POP
PARDON ME.
Ahh. YOU'VE GOT SOME COLOR BACK IN YOUR FACE.
C...
Huh?
COLOR?
STILL A BIT OF A FEVER... IT'LL BREAK DURING THE NIGHT THOUGH.
SO KEEP GETTING YOUR REST.
OH.
SURE.
FLAP
BUT, UM...
YOUR HIGHNESS.
I CAN WATCH OVER HER, IF YOU PREFER...
NO.
I'LL STAY.

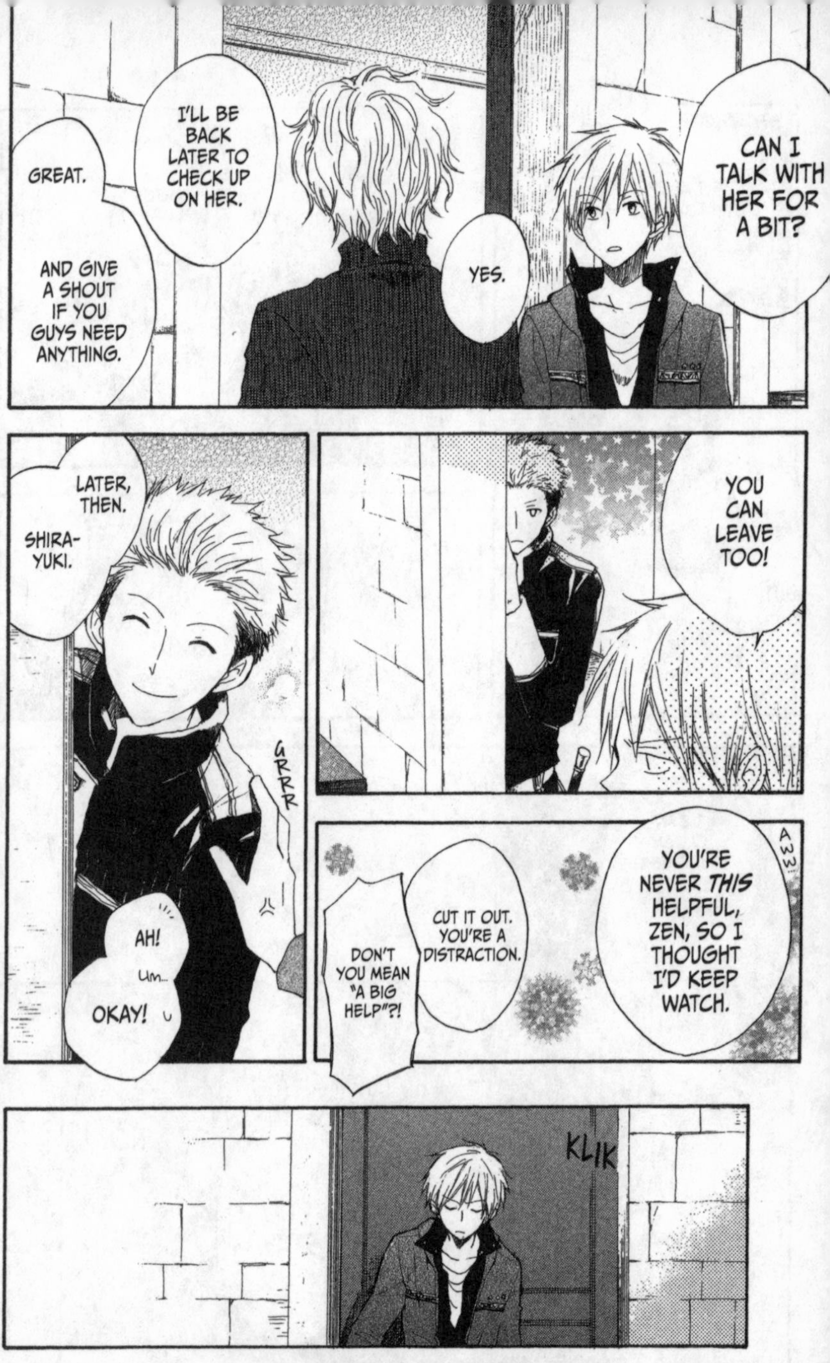
CAN I TALK WITH HER FOR A BIT?
YES.
I'LL BE BACK LATER TO CHECK UP ON HER.
GREAT.
AND GIVE A SHOUT IF YOU GUYS NEED ANYTHING.
YOU CAN LEAVE TOO!
AWW...
YOU'RE NEVER *THIS* HELPFUL, ZEN, SO I THOUGHT I'D KEEP WATCH.
CUT IT OUT. YOU'RE A DISTRACTION.
DON'T YOU MEAN "A BIG HELP"?!
LATER, THEN.
SHIRA-YUKI.
GRRR
AH!
Um...
OKAY!
KLIK

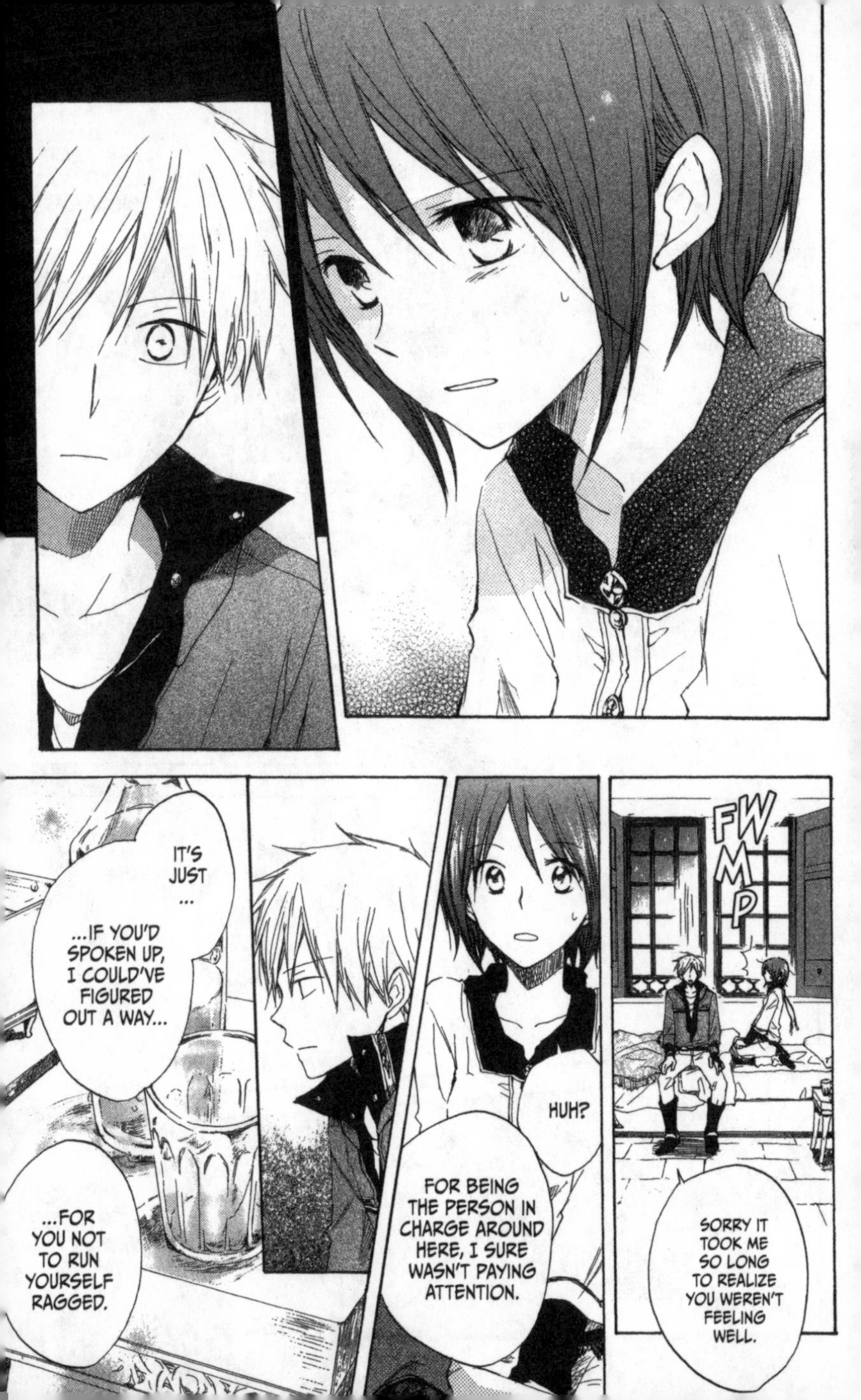
FWMP
SORRY IT TOOK ME SO LONG TO REALIZE YOU WEREN'T FEELING WELL.
HUH?
FOR BEING THE PERSON IN CHARGE AROUND HERE, I SURE WASN'T PAYING ATTENTION.
IT'S JUST ...
...IF YOU'D SPOKEN UP, I COULD'VE FIGURED OUT A WAY...
...FOR YOU NOT TO RUN YOURSELF RAGGED.

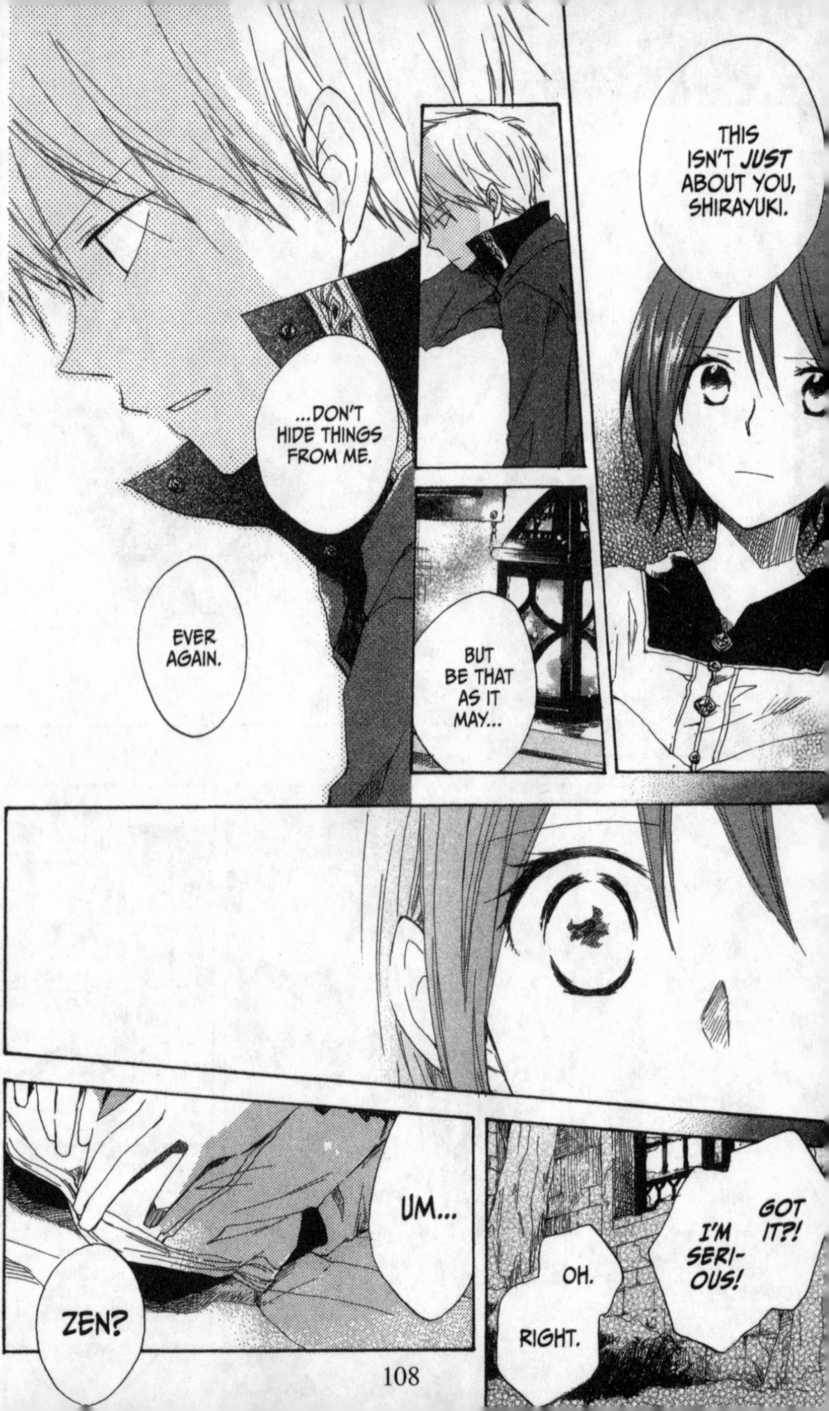
THIS ISN'T JUST ABOUT YOU, SHIRAYUKI.
BUT BE THAT AS IT MAY...
...DON'T HIDE THINGS FROM ME.
EVER AGAIN.
GOT IT?!
I'M SERI-OUS!
OH.
RIGHT.
UM...
ZEN?

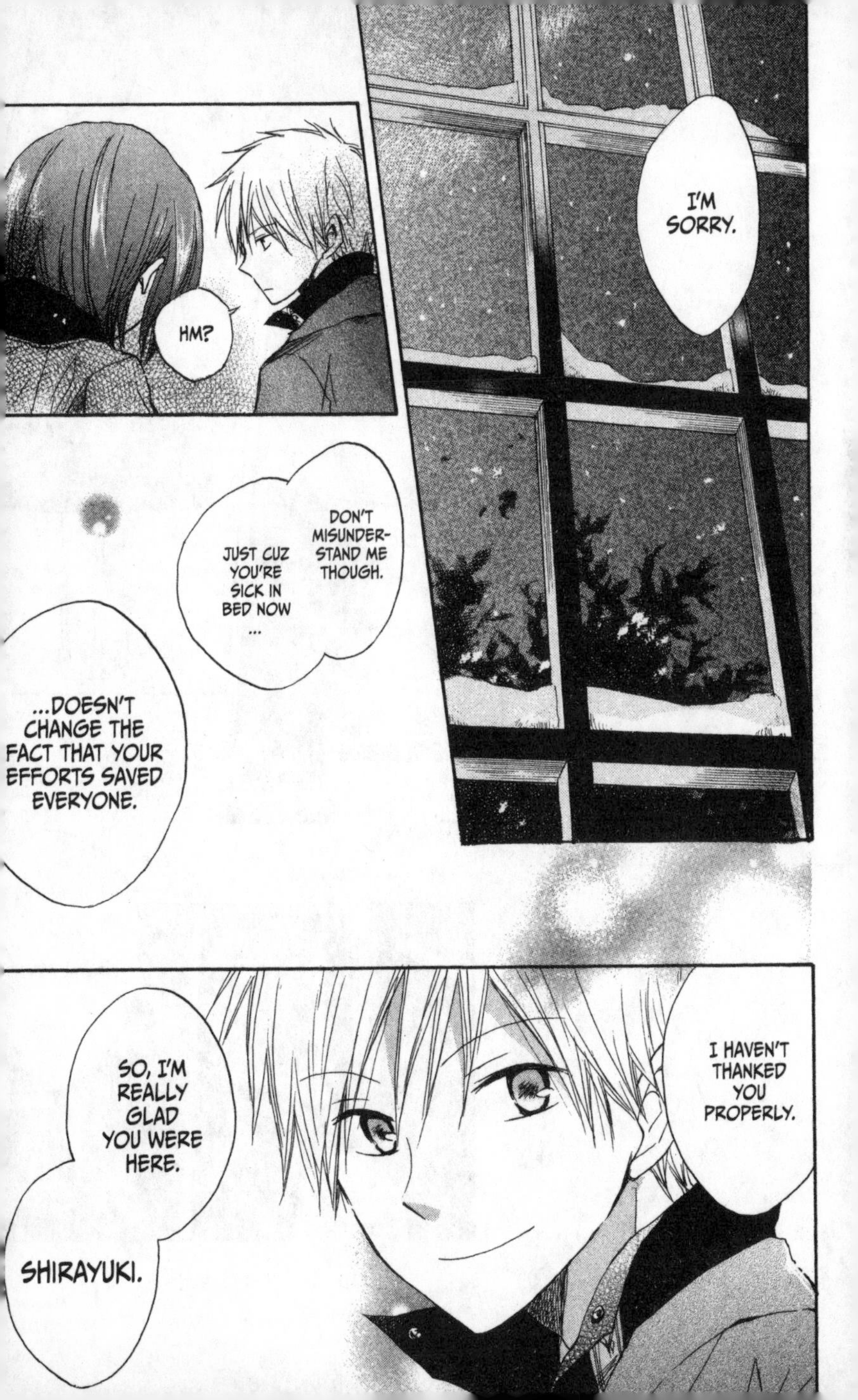
I'M SORRY.
HM?
DON'T MISUNDER-STAND ME THOUGH.
JUST CUZ YOU'RE SICK IN BED NOW ...
...DOESN'T CHANGE THE FACT THAT YOUR EFFORTS SAVED EVERYONE.
I HAVEN'T THANKED YOU PROPERLY.
SO, I'M REALLY GLAD YOU WERE HERE.
SHIRAYUKI.

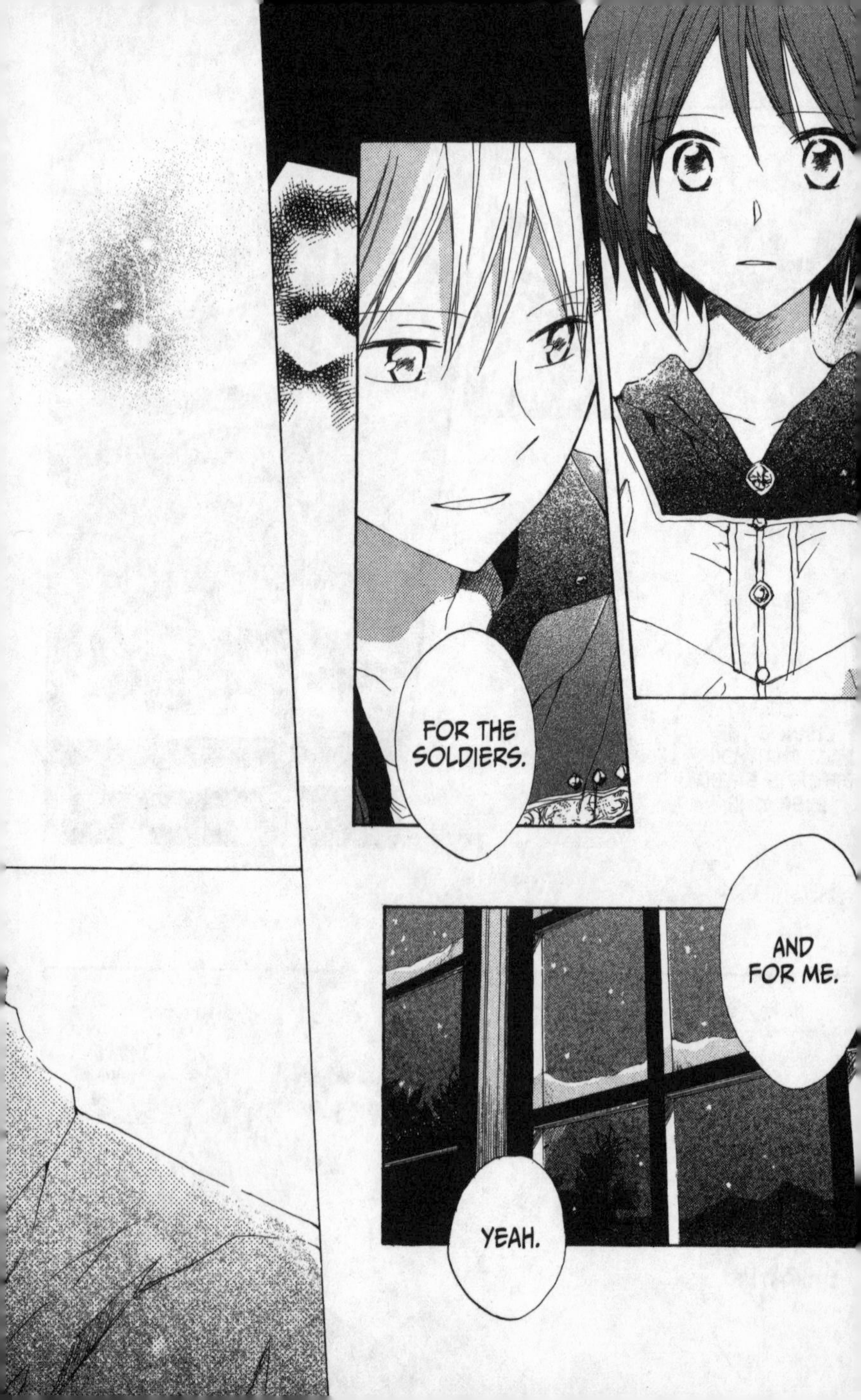
FOR THE SOLDIERS.
AND FOR ME.
YEAH.

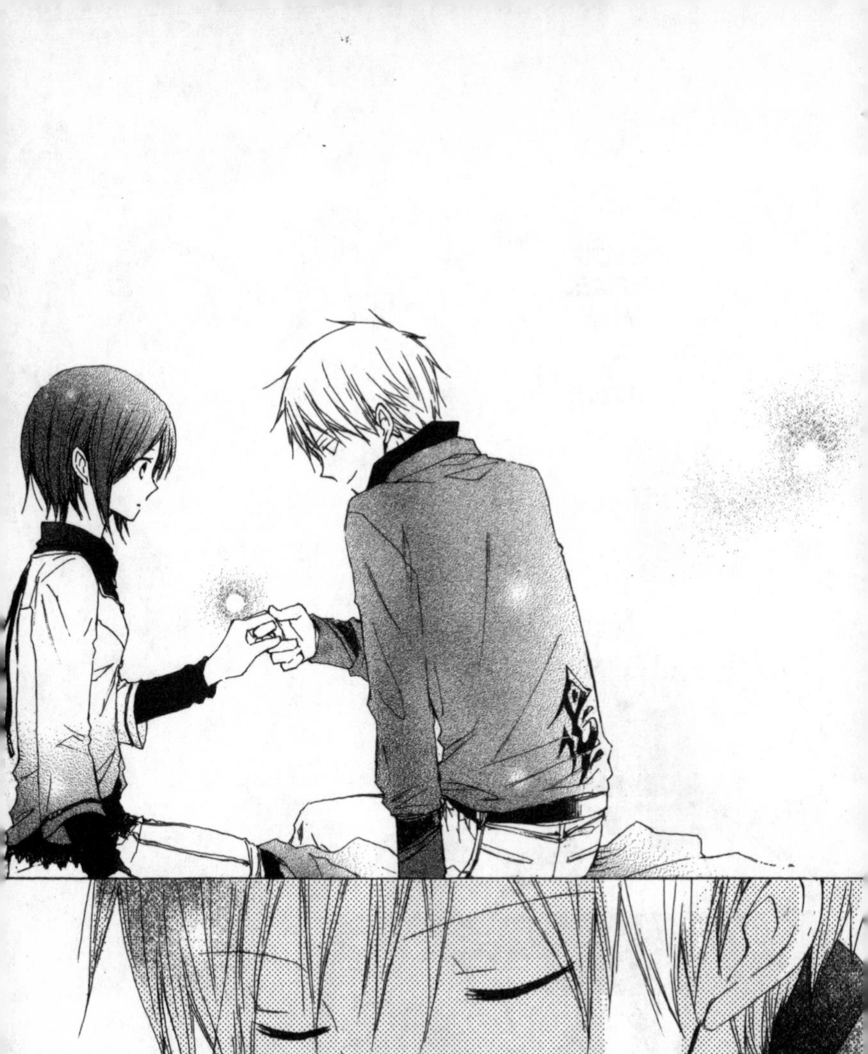
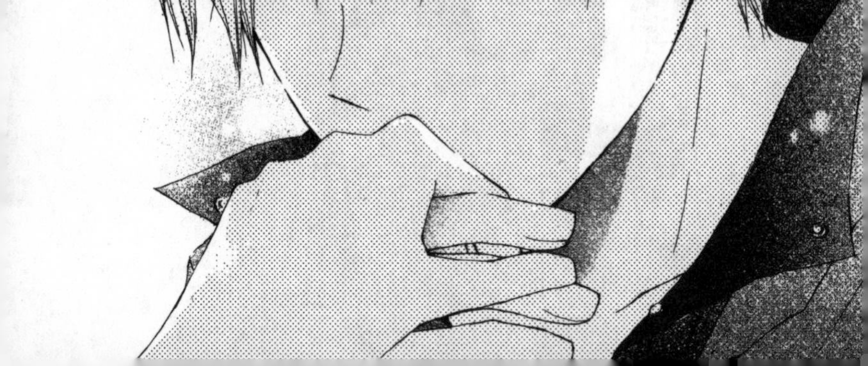

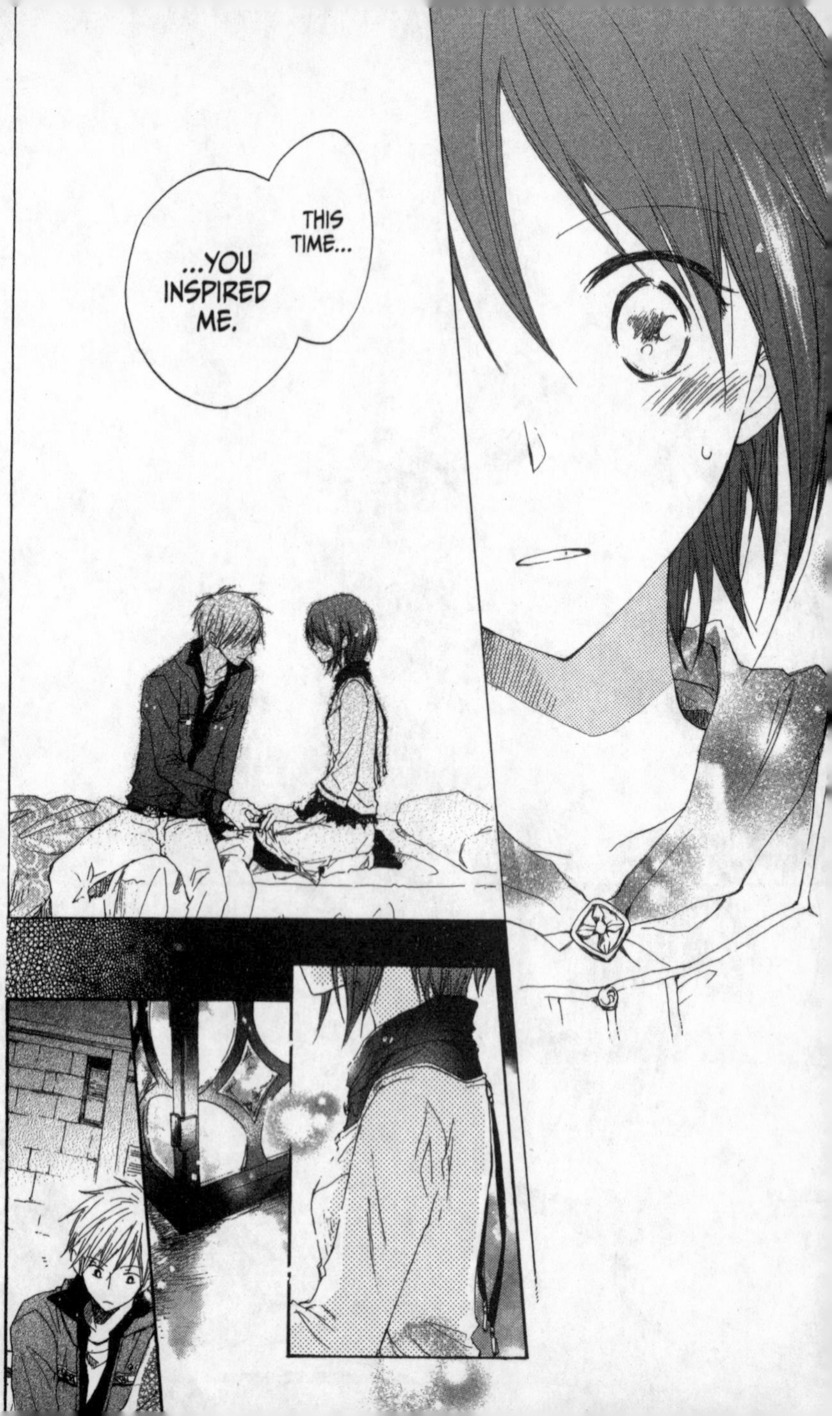
THIS TIME...
...YOU INSPIRED ME.

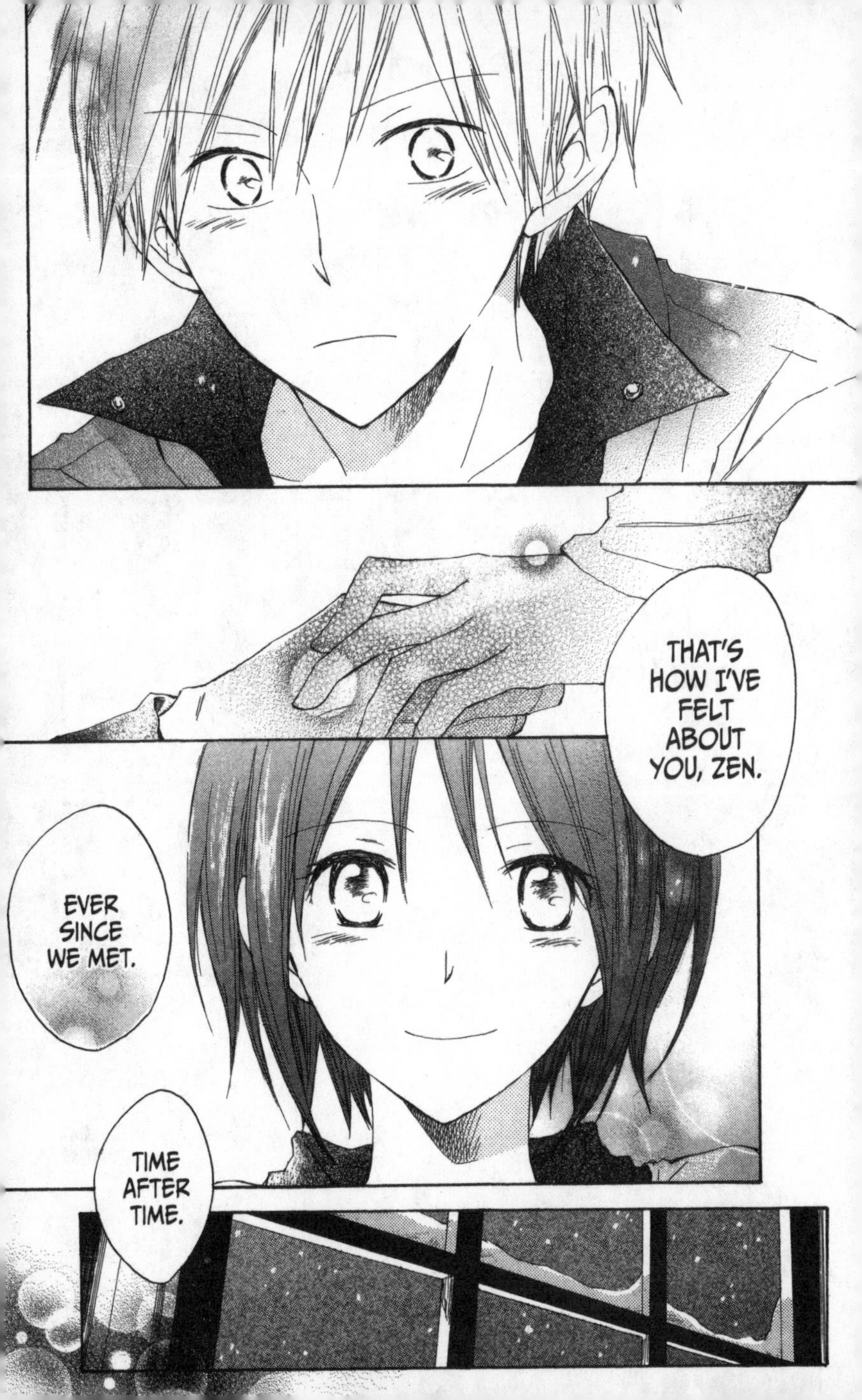
THAT'S HOW I'VE FELT ABOUT YOU, ZEN.
EVER SINCE WE MET.
TIME AFTER TIME.

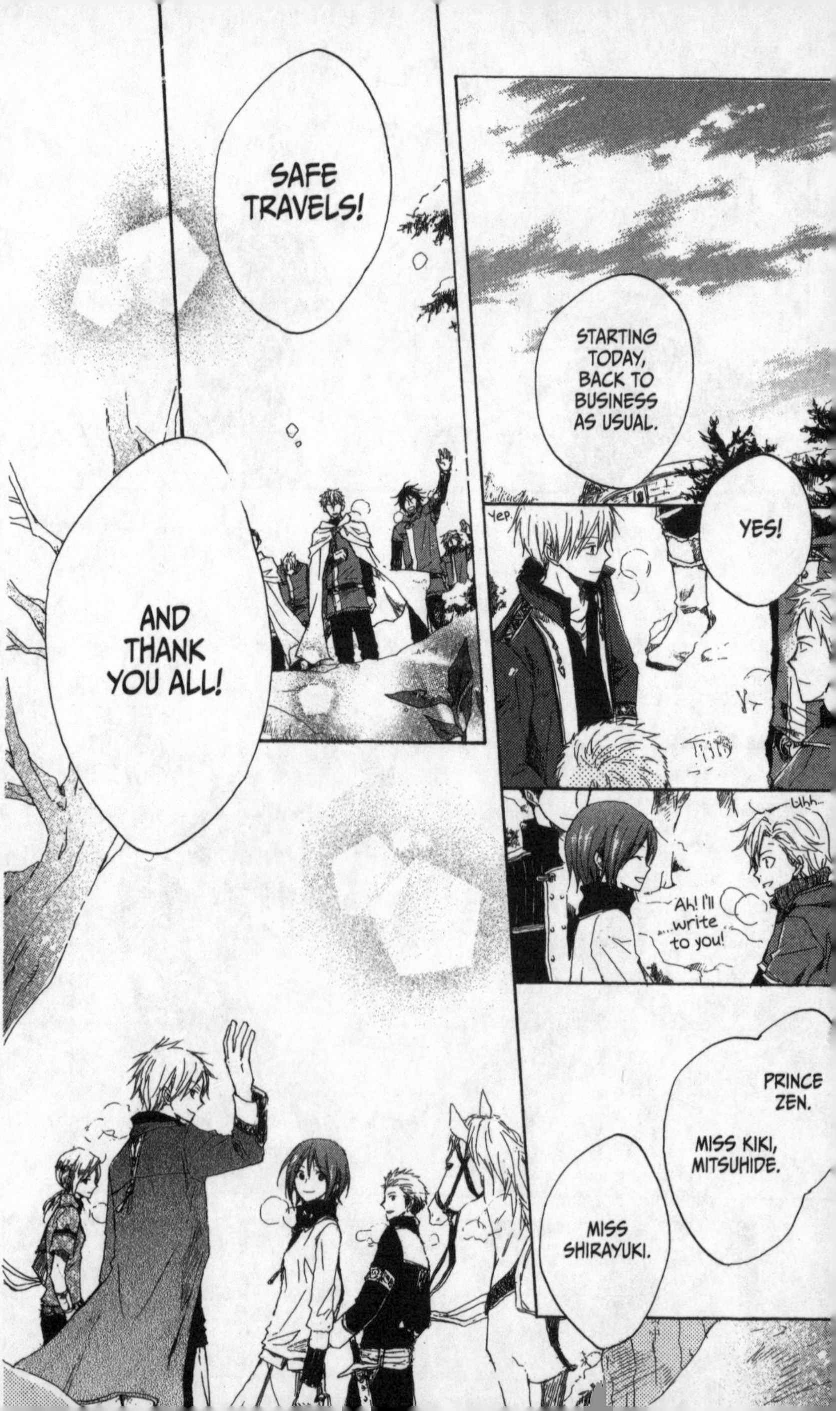
STARTING TODAY, BACK TO BUSINESS AS USUAL.
YES!
Yep.
Uhh...
Ah! I'll ...write to you!
PRINCE ZEN.
MISS KIKI, MITSUHIDE.
MISS SHIRAYUKI.
SAFE TRAVELS!
AND THANK YOU ALL!

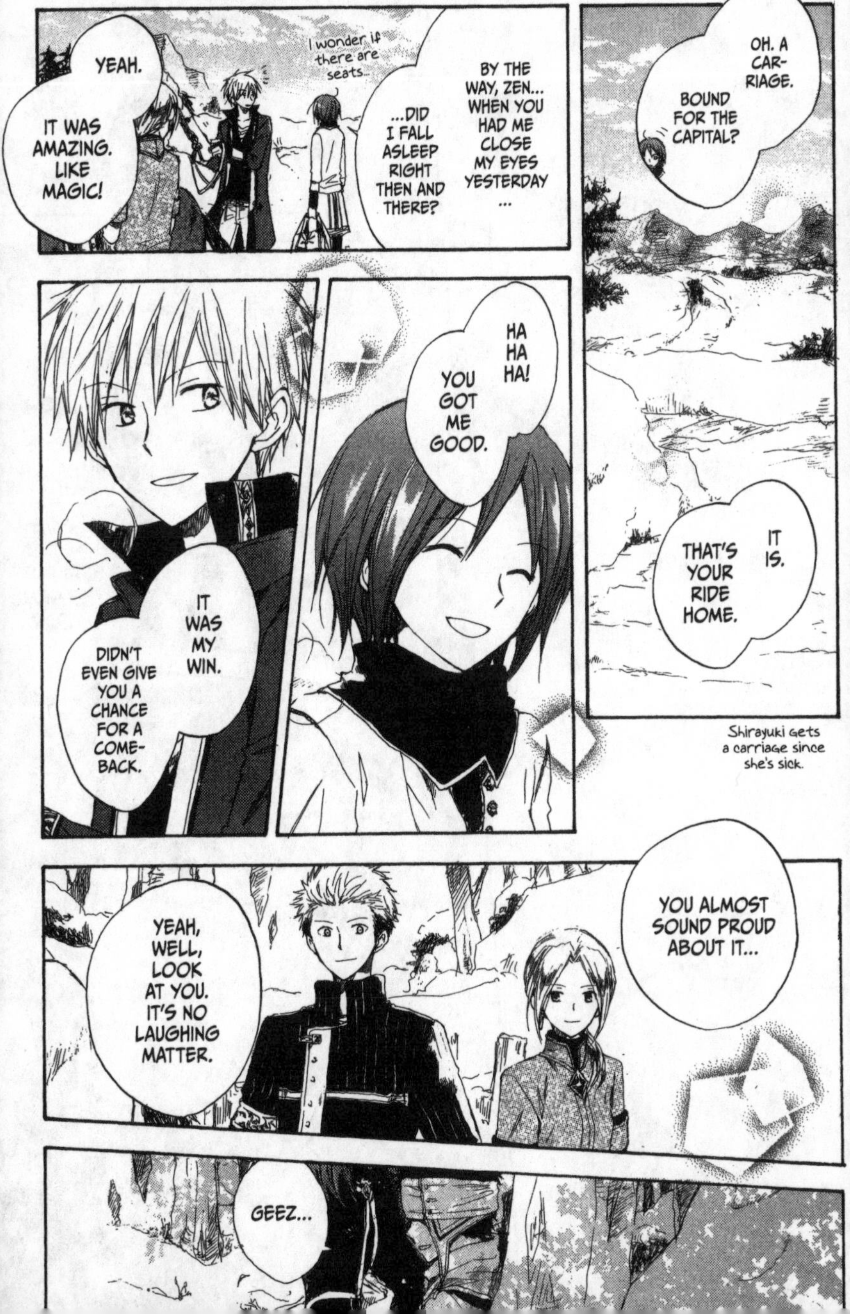
OH. A CARRIAGE.
BOUND FOR THE CAPITAL?
IT IS.
THAT'S YOUR RIDE HOME.
Shirayuki gets a carriage since she's sick.
BY THE WAY, ZEN... WHEN YOU HAD ME CLOSE MY EYES YESTERDAY ...
...DID I FALL ASLEEP RIGHT THEN AND THERE?
I wonder if there are seats...
YEAH.
IT WAS AMAZING. LIKE MAGIC!
HA HA HA!
YOU GOT ME GOOD.
IT WAS MY WIN.
DIDN'T EVEN GIVE YOU A CHANCE FOR A COME-BACK.
YOU ALMOST SOUND PROUD ABOUT IT...
YEAH, WELL, LOOK AT YOU. IT'S NO LAUGHING MATTER.
GEEZ...

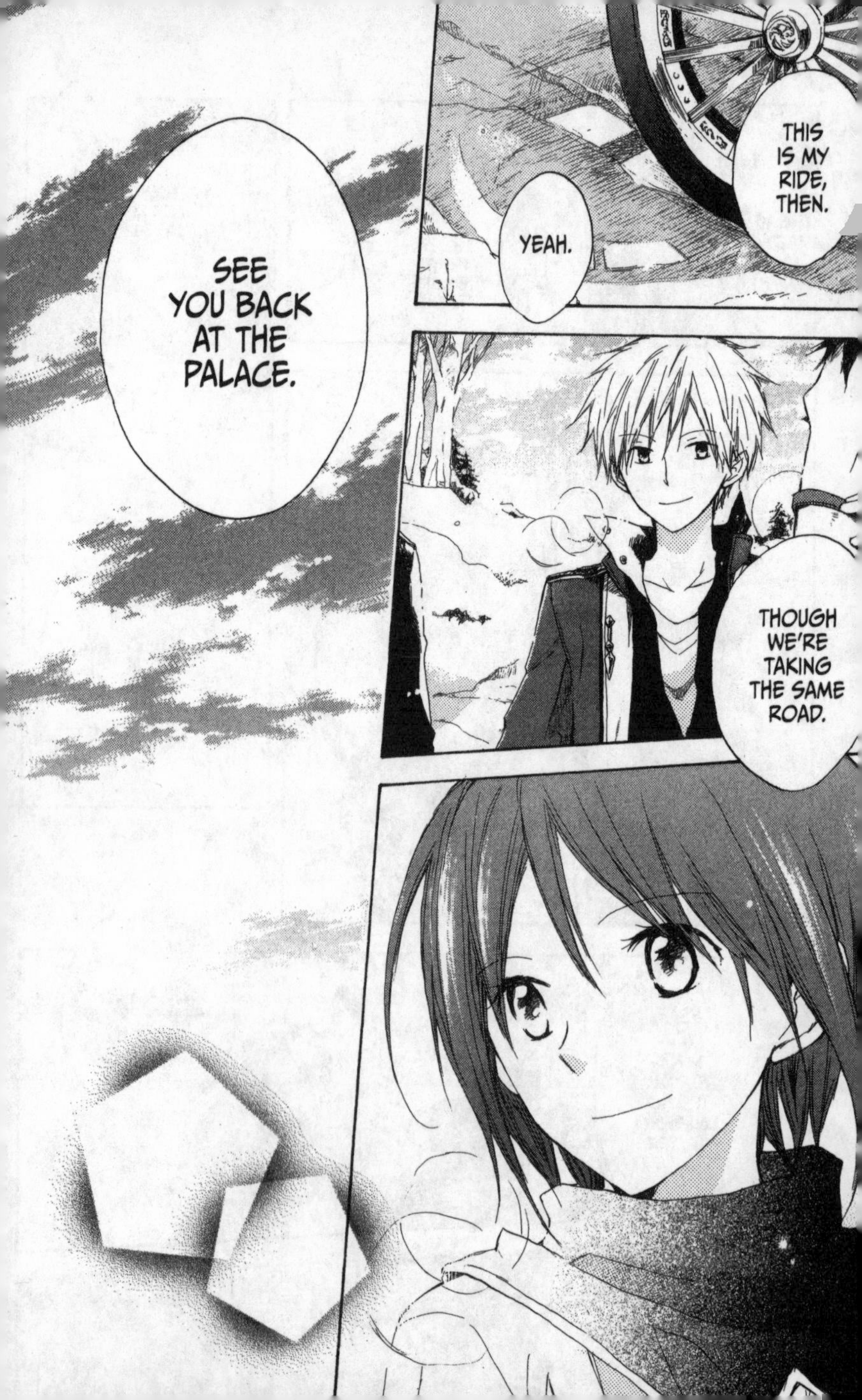
THIS IS MY RIDE, THEN.
YEAH.
THOUGH WE'RE TAKING THE SAME ROAD.
SEE YOU BACK AT THE PALACE.

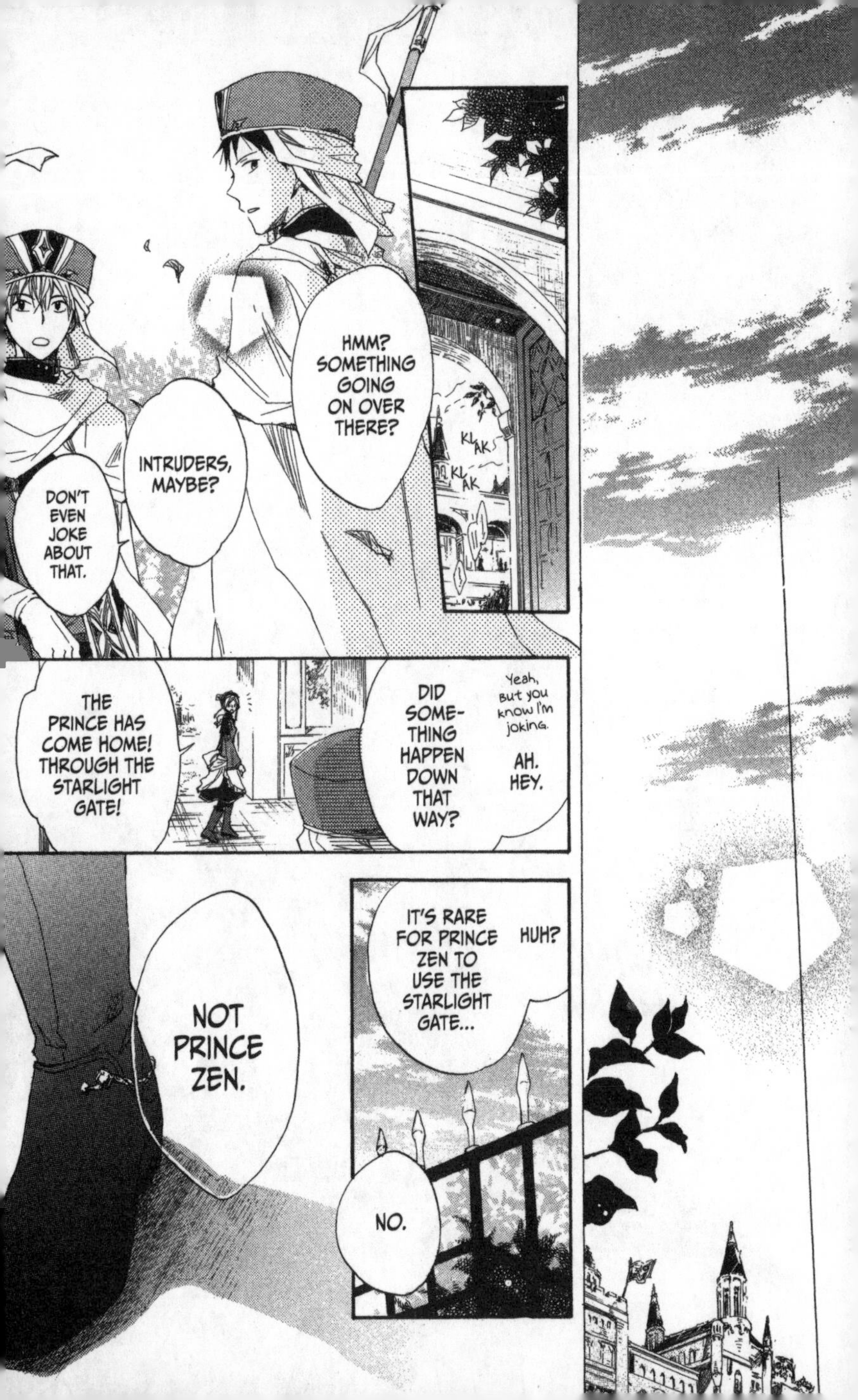
KLAK
KLAK
HMM? SOMETHING GOING ON OVER THERE?
INTRUDERS, MAYBE?
DON'T EVEN JOKE ABOUT THAT.
Yeah, but you know I'm joking.
AH. HEY.
DID SOME-THING HAPPEN DOWN THAT WAY?
THE PRINCE HAS COME HOME! THROUGH THE STARLIGHT GATE!
HUH?
IT'S RARE FOR PRINCE ZEN TO USE THE STARLIGHT GATE...
NO.
NOT PRINCE ZEN.

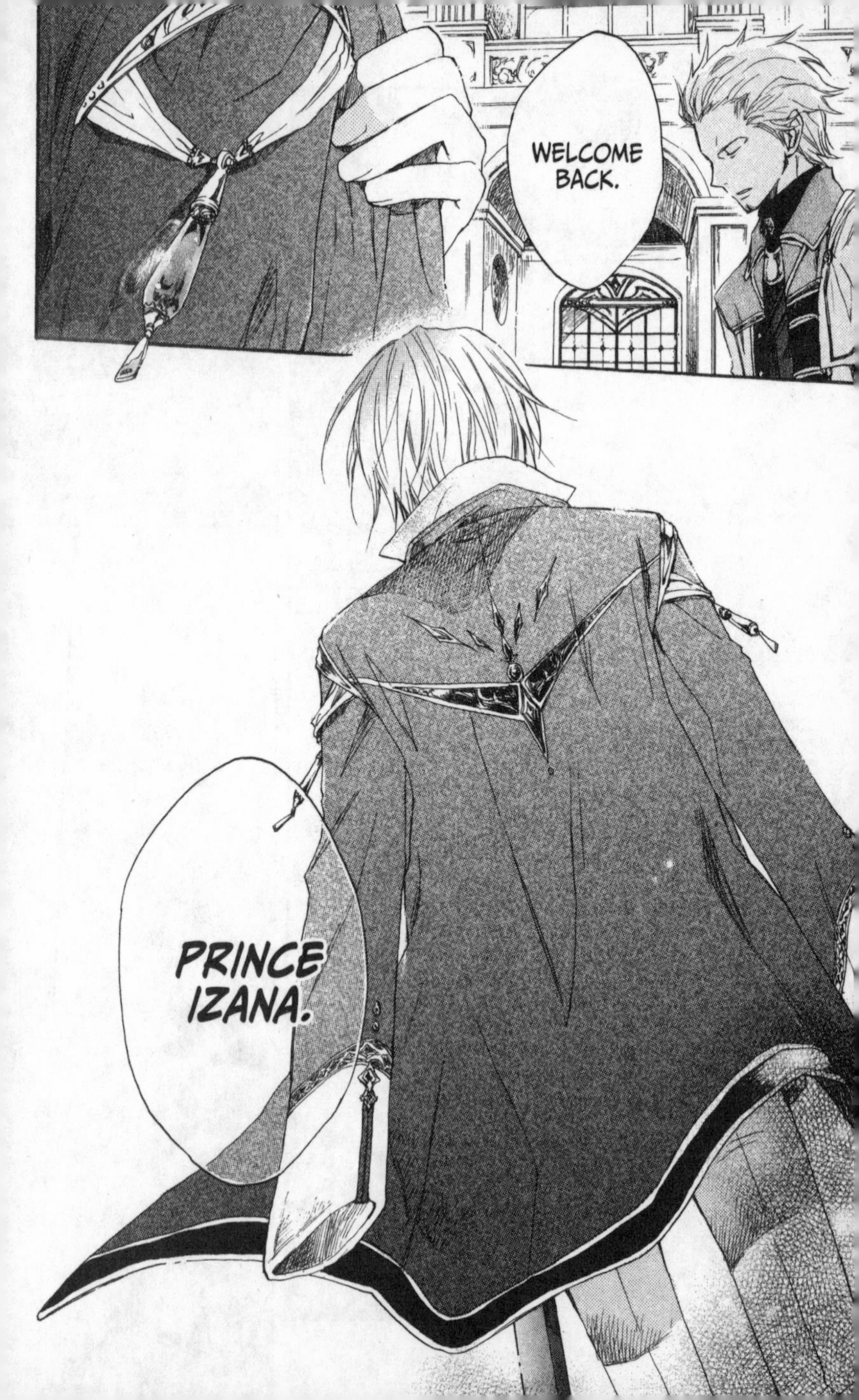
WELCOME BACK.
PRINCE IZANA.

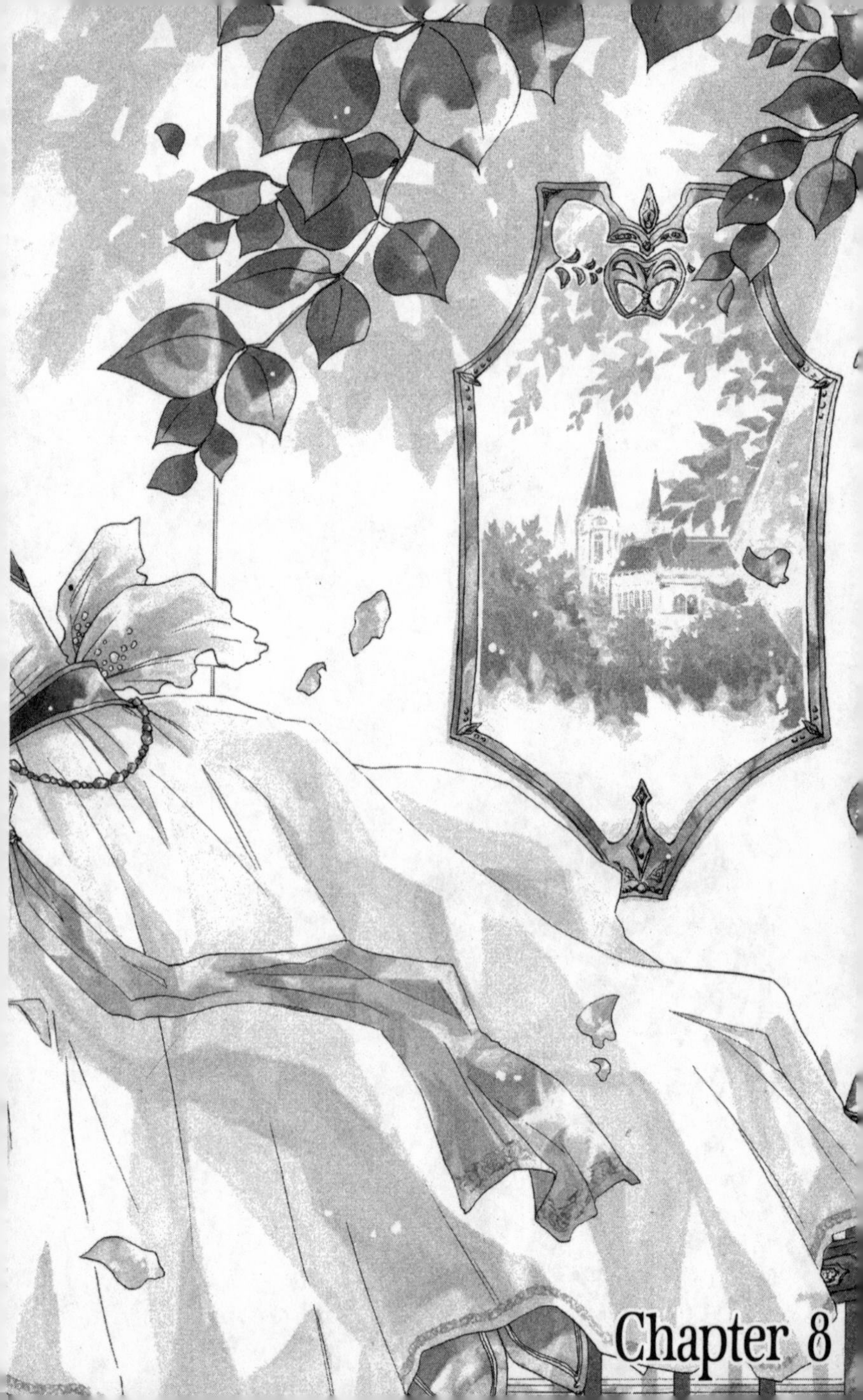
Chapter 8

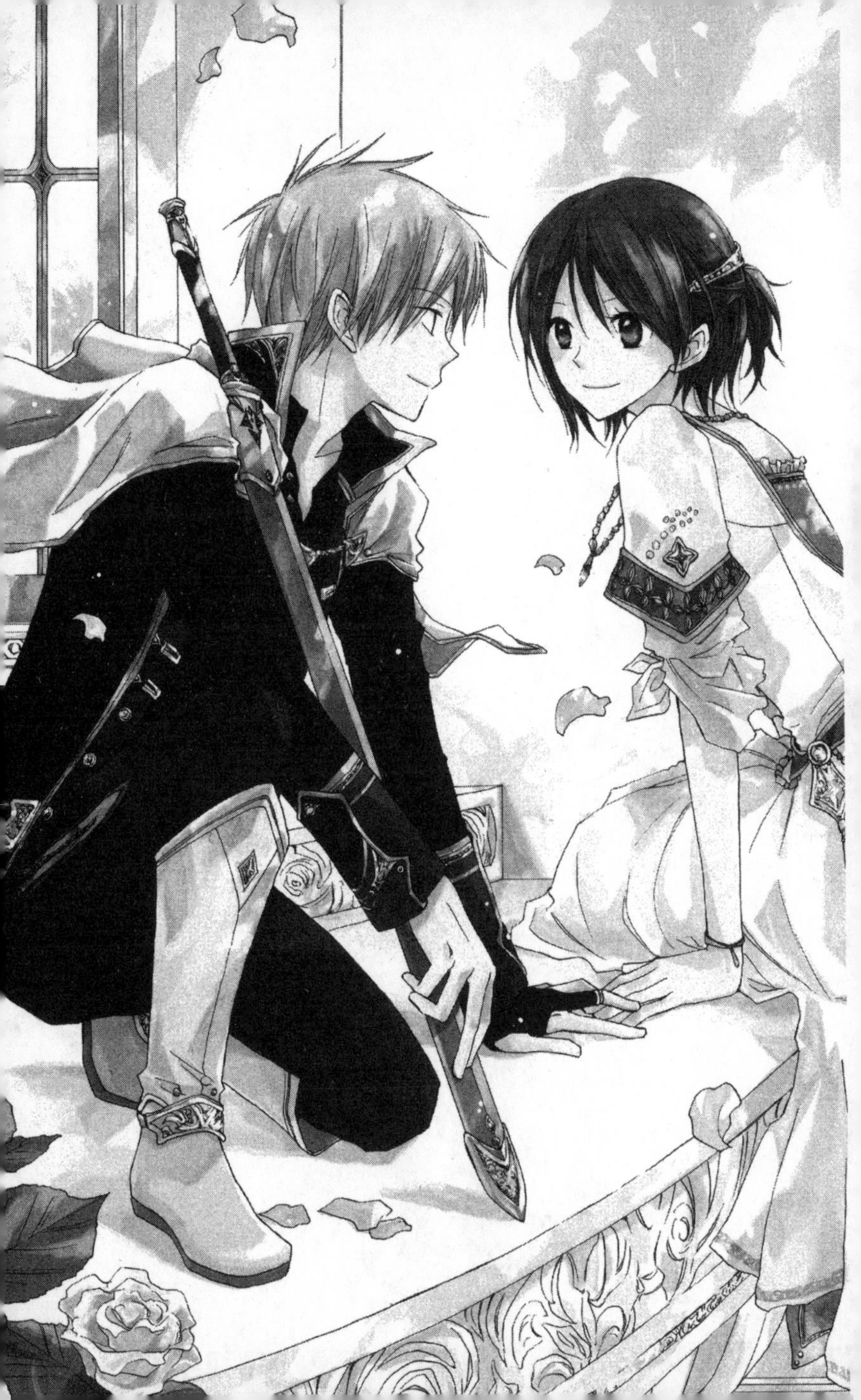

About one year
Before they met...

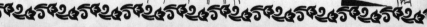

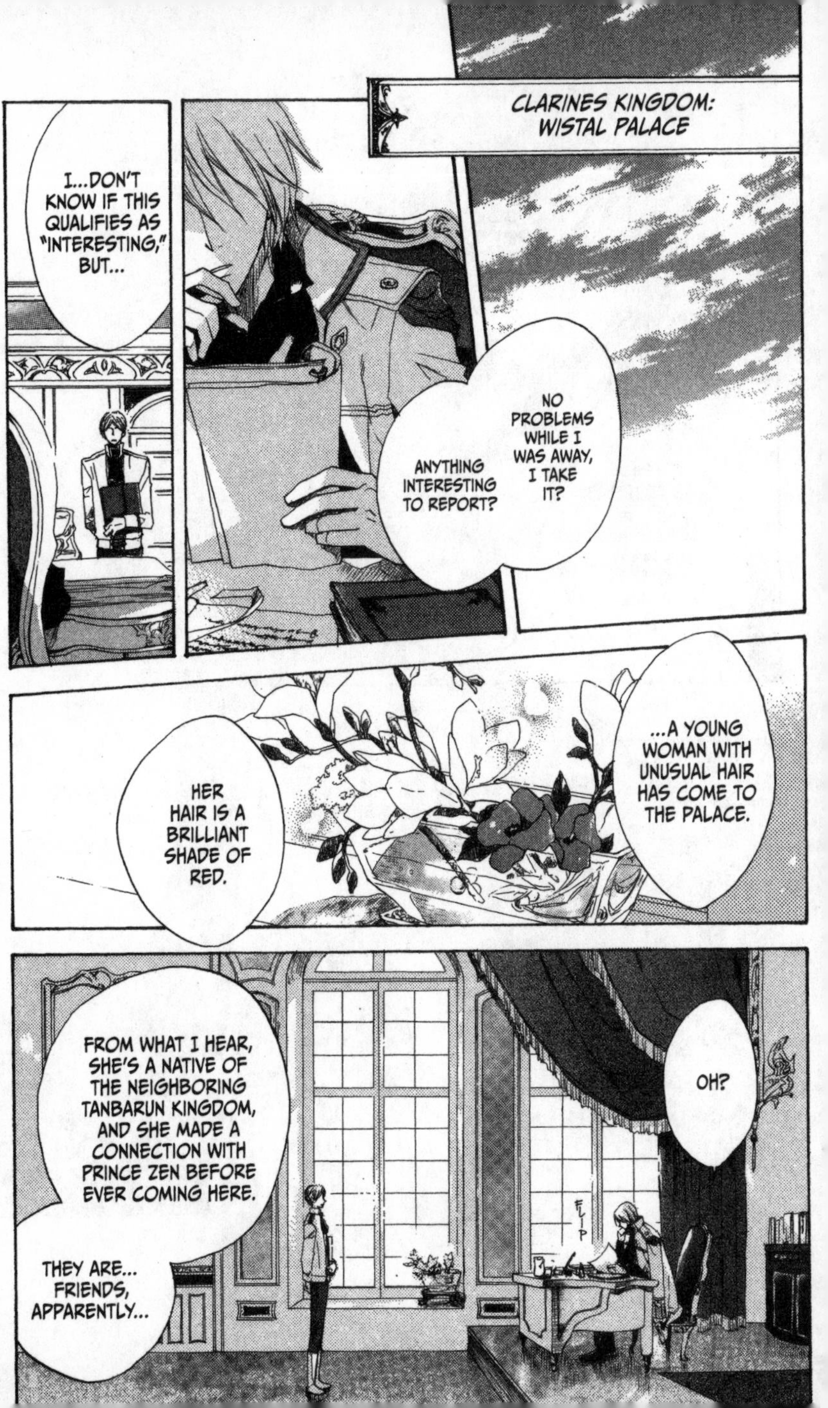
CLARINES KINGDOM: WISTAL PALACE
NO PROBLEMS WHILE I WAS AWAY, I TAKE IT?
ANYTHING INTERESTING TO REPORT?
I...DON'T KNOW IF THIS QUALIFIES AS "INTERESTING," BUT...
...A YOUNG WOMAN WITH UNUSUAL HAIR HAS COME TO THE PALACE.
HER HAIR IS A BRILLIANT SHADE OF RED.
OH?
FLIP
FROM WHAT I HEAR, SHE'S A NATIVE OF THE NEIGHBORING TANBARUN KINGDOM, AND SHE MADE A CONNECTION WITH PRINCE ZEN BEFORE EVER COMING HERE.
THEY ARE... FRIENDS, APPARENTLY...

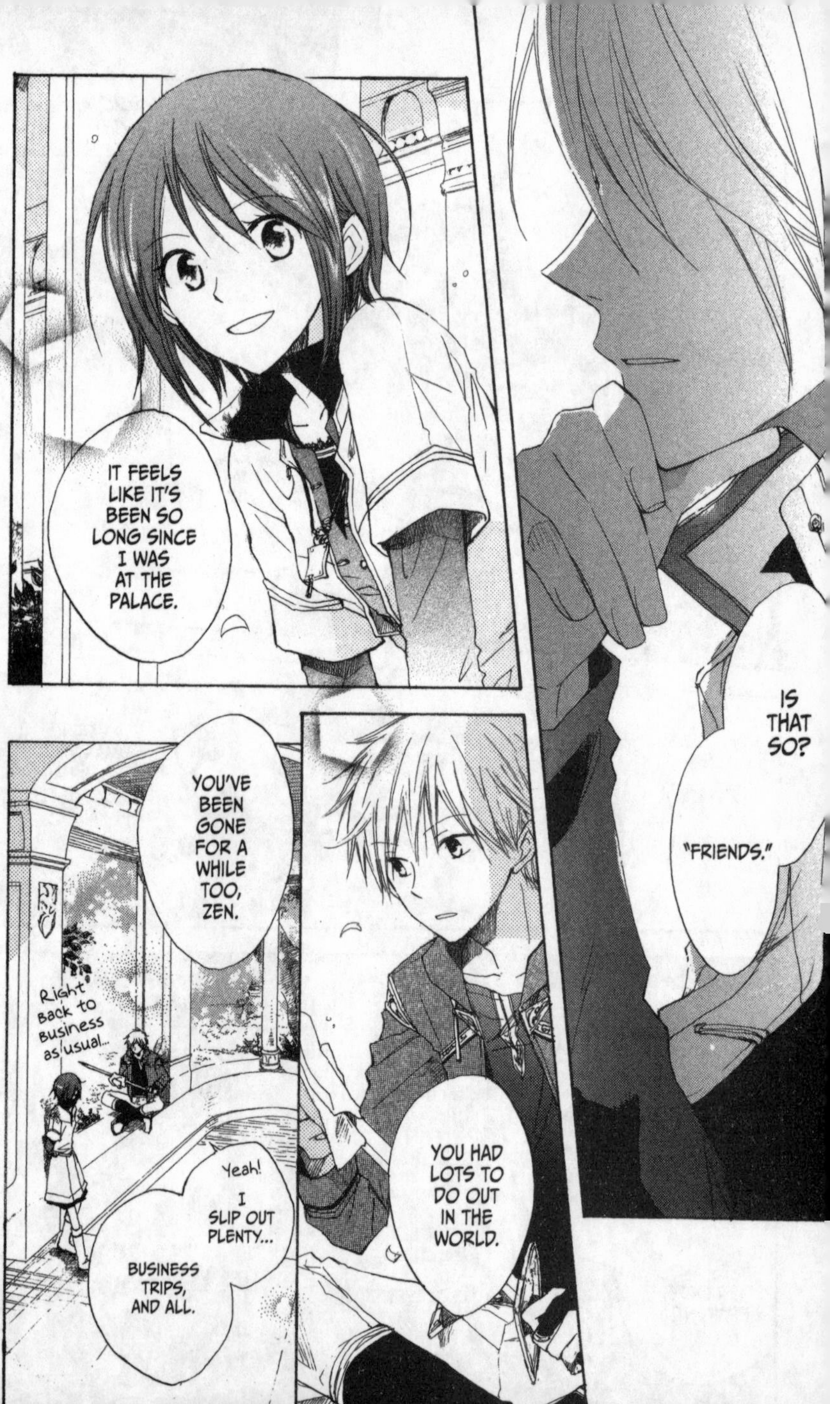
IS THAT SO?
"FRIENDS."
IT FEELS LIKE IT'S BEEN SO LONG SINCE I WAS AT THE PALACE.
YOU HAD LOTS TO DO OUT IN THE WORLD.
YOU'VE BEEN GONE FOR A WHILE TOO, ZEN.
Right back to business as usual...
Yeah!
I SLIP OUT PLENTY...
BUSINESS TRIPS, AND ALL.

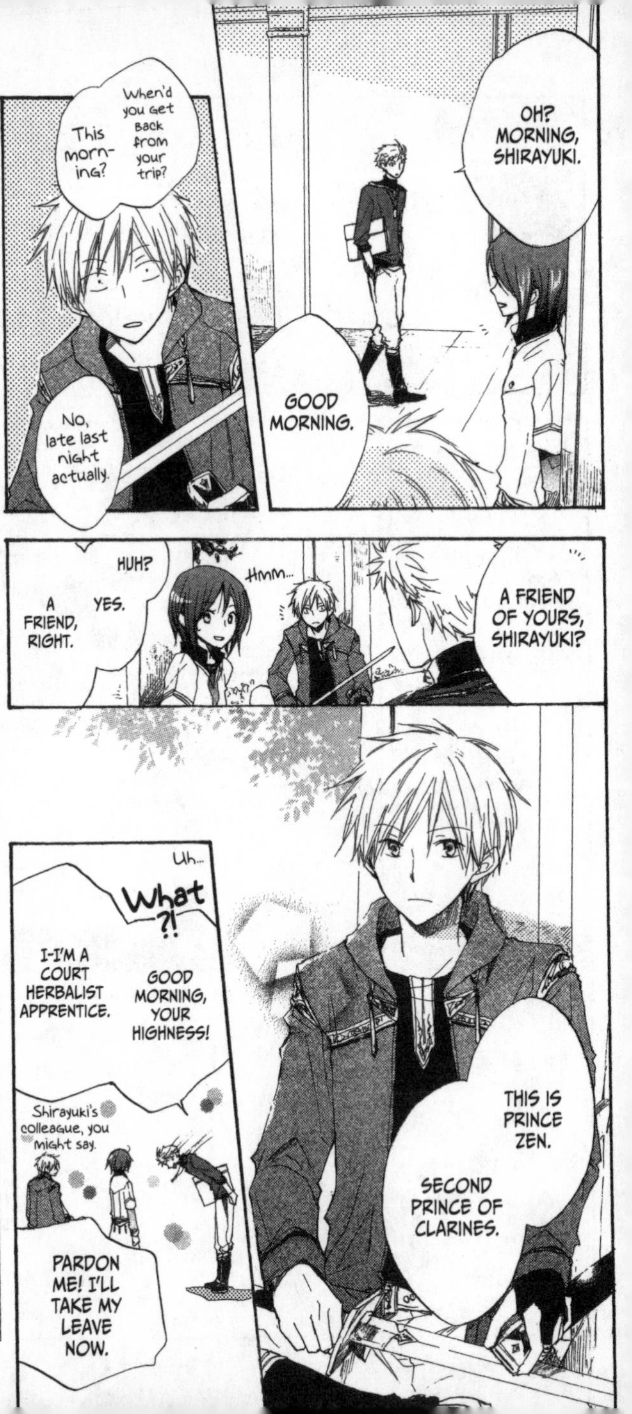
OH? MORNING, SHIRAYUKI.
GOOD MORNING.
When'd you get back from your trip?
This morn-ing?
No, late last night actually.
A FRIEND OF YOURS, SHIRAYUKI?
HUH?
YES.
A FRIEND, RIGHT.
Hmm...
THIS IS PRINCE ZEN.
SECOND PRINCE OF CLARINES.
Uh...
What?!
GOOD MORNING, YOUR HIGHNESS!
I-I'M A COURT HERBALIST APPRENTICE.
Shirayuki's colleague, you might say.
PARDON ME! I'LL TAKE MY LEAVE NOW.

Chapter 8

When this chapter ran in the magazine, they asked me to do my first-ever color-page opening.

It made me... unbelievably happy.

And I couldn't have done it without support from my readers.

So thank you very much. Ahh...

Zen's big brother first shows his face in chapter 8.

We barely even knew his name before this point, but now he's suddenly here, throwing his weight around. The guy is ruthless with no weaknesses.

The first thing my dad said after reading this was, "I hate that brother."

Talk about a first impression!!

6

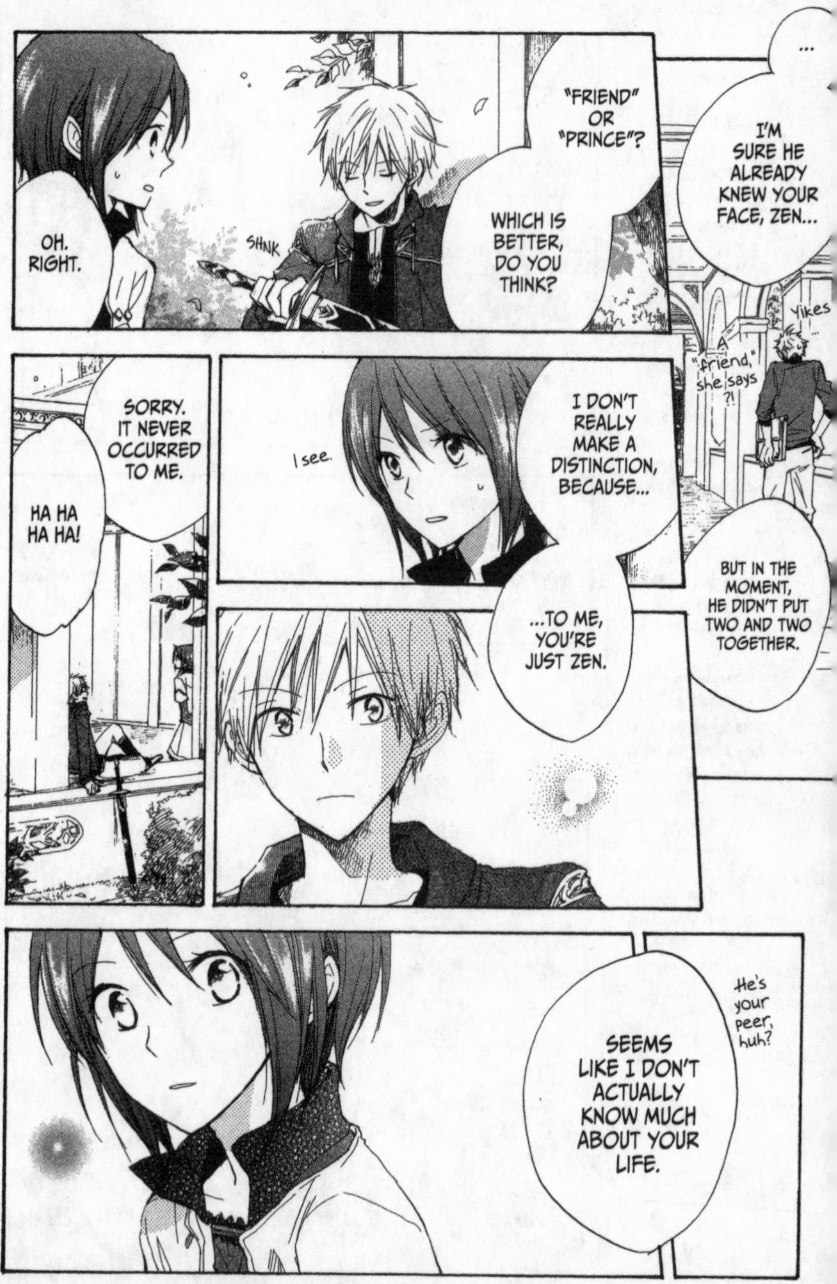
...
I'M SURE HE ALREADY KNEW YOUR FACE, ZEN...
Yikes...
A "friend," she says?!
BUT IN THE MOMENT, HE DIDN'T PUT TWO AND TWO TOGETHER.
"FRIEND" OR "PRINCE"?
WHICH IS BETTER, DO YOU THINK?
SHNK
OH. RIGHT.
I DON'T REALLY MAKE A DISTINCTION, BECAUSE...
I see.
...TO ME, YOU'RE JUST ZEN.
SORRY. IT NEVER OCCURRED TO ME.
HA HA HA HA!
He's your peer, huh?
SEEMS LIKE I DON'T ACTUALLY KNOW MUCH ABOUT YOUR LIFE.

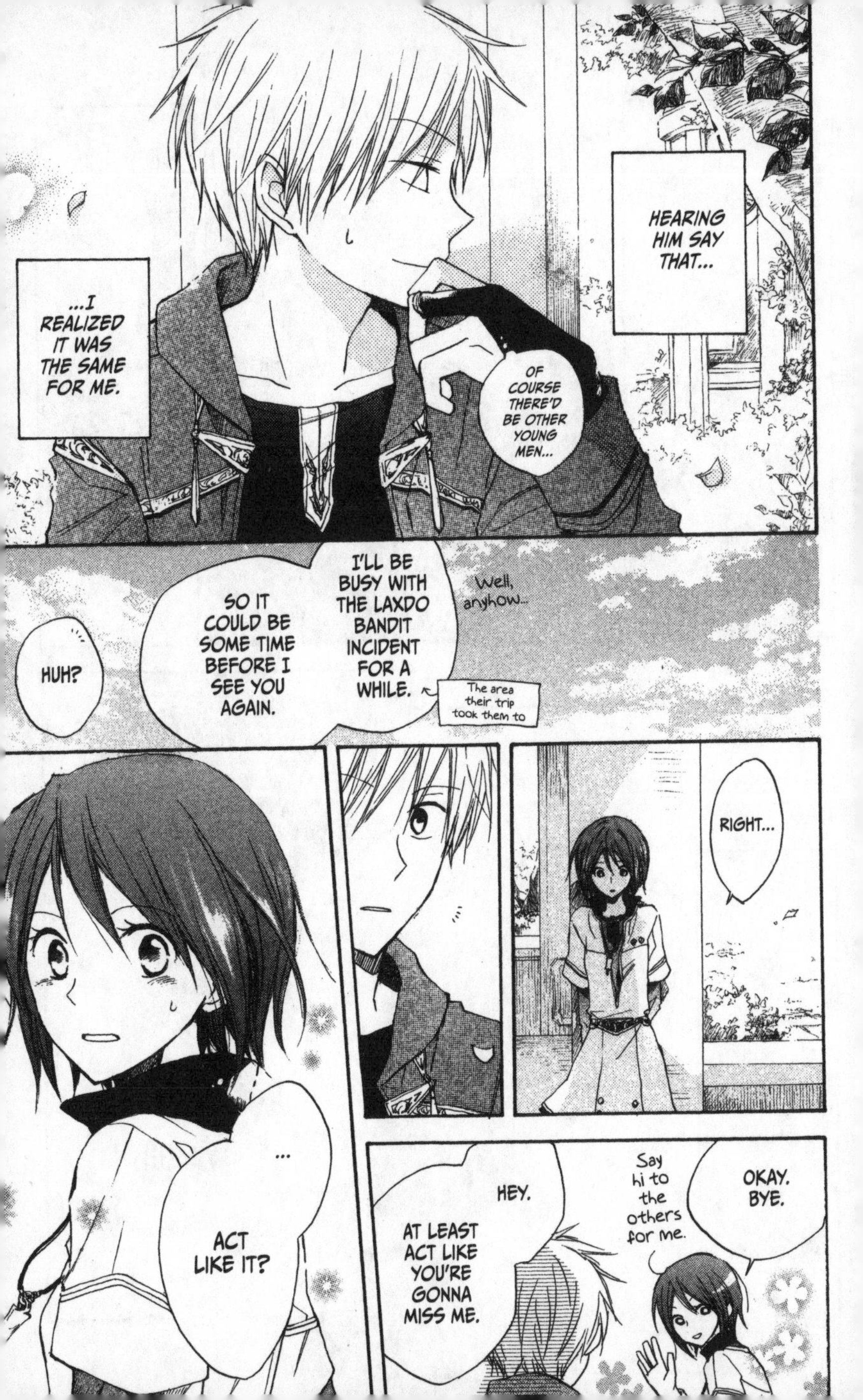
HEARING HIM SAY THAT...
OF COURSE THERE'D BE OTHER YOUNG MEN...
...I REALIZED IT WAS THE SAME FOR ME.
Well, anyhow...
I'LL BE BUSY WITH THE LAXDO BANDIT INCIDENT FOR A WHILE.
The area their trip took them to
SO IT COULD BE SOME TIME BEFORE I SEE YOU AGAIN.
HUH?
RIGHT...
OKAY. BYE.
Say hi to the others for me.
HEY.
AT LEAST ACT LIKE YOU'RE GONNA MISS ME.
...
ACT LIKE IT?

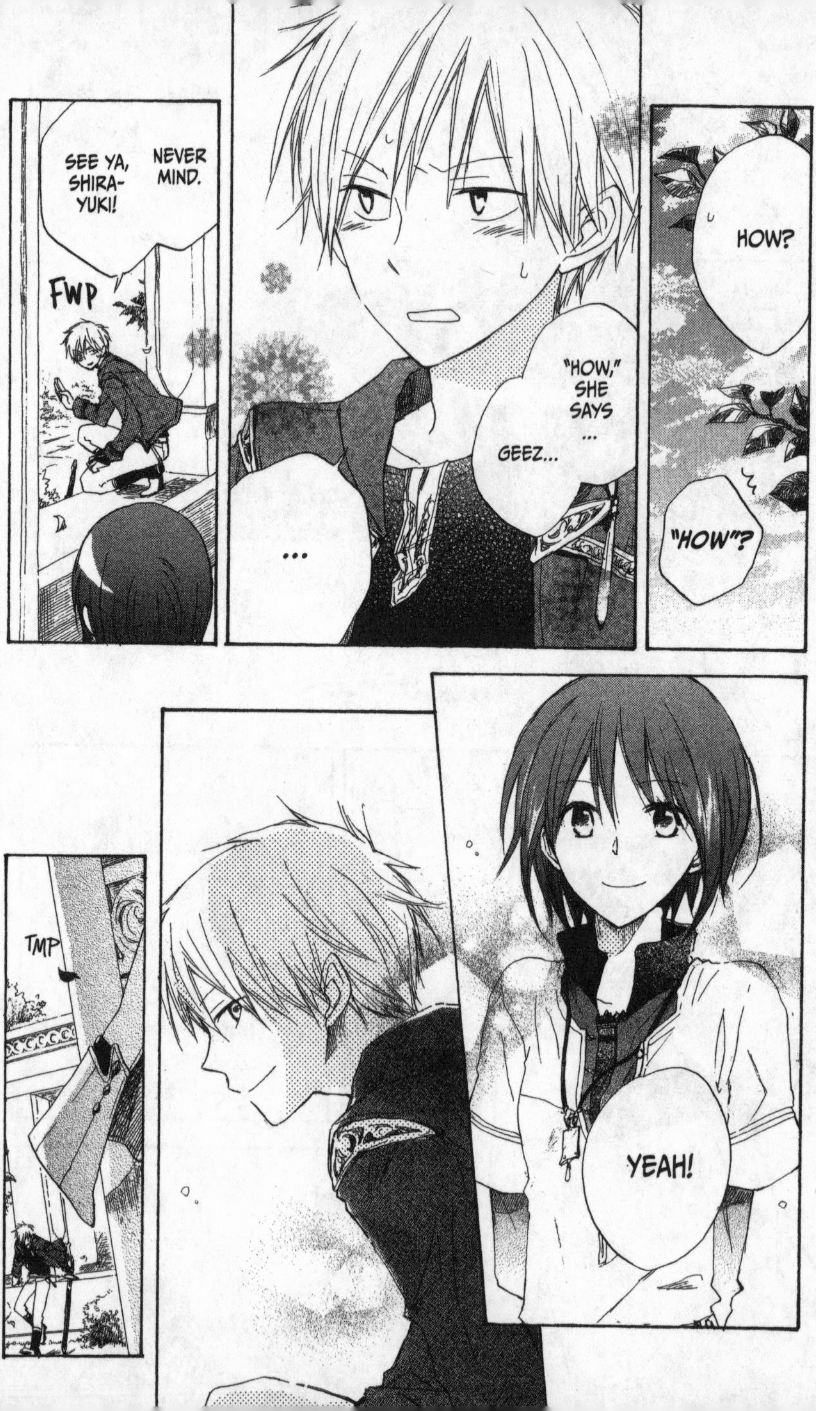
HOW?
"HOW"?
"HOW," SHE SAYS ...
GEEZ...
...
NEVER MIND.
SEE YA, SHIRA-YUKI!
FWP
YEAH!
TMP

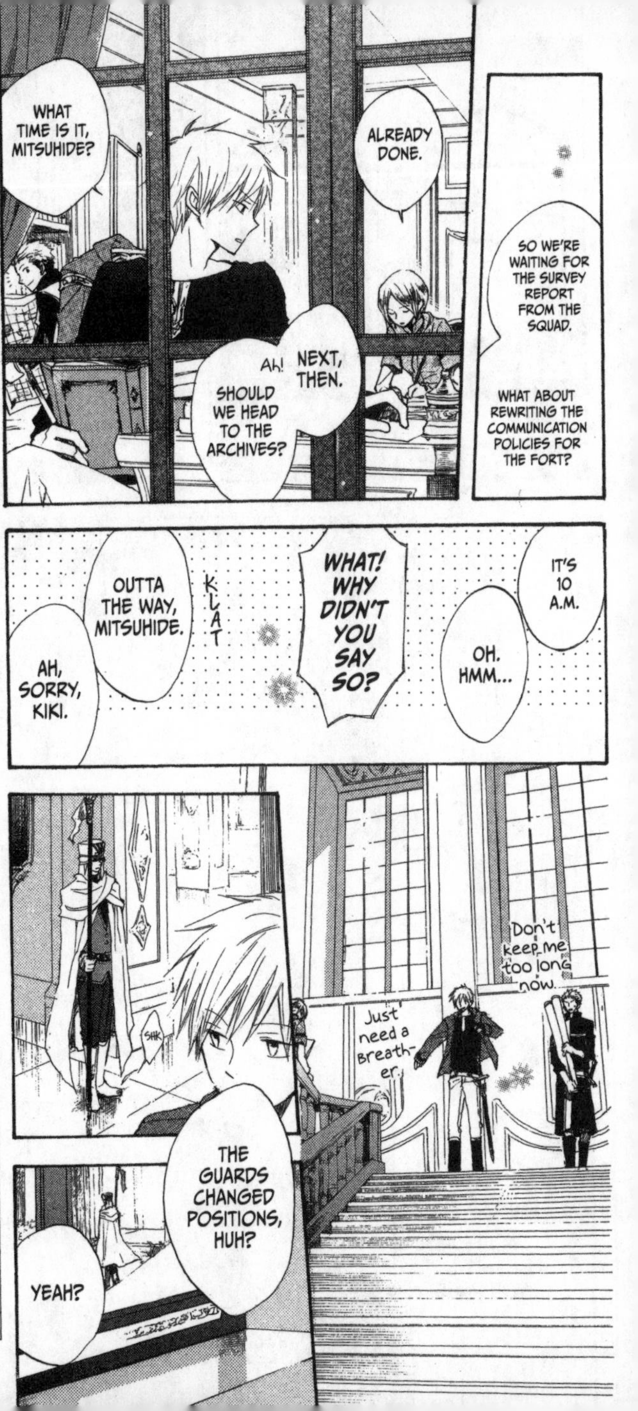
SO WE'RE WAITING FOR THE SURVEY REPORT FROM THE SQUAD.
WHAT ABOUT REWRITING THE COMMUNICATION POLICIES FOR THE FORT?
ALREADY DONE.
WHAT TIME IS IT, MITSUHIDE?
NEXT, THEN.
AH! SHOULD WE HEAD TO THE ARCHIVES?
IT'S 10 A.M.
OH. HMM...
WHAT! WHY DIDN'T YOU SAY SO?
KLAT
OUTTA THE WAY, MITSUHIDE.
AH, SORRY, KIKI.
Don't keep me too long now...
Just need a breather.
SHK
THE GUARDS CHANGED POSITIONS, HUH?
YEAH?

About Some Characters

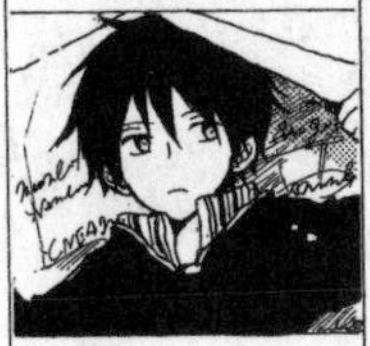

▶Ryu

When he was ten, Chief Garak recruited him to Wistal Palace.

He's got terrible posture while reading or writing, but those are some nice eyes. He loves big sheets of paper.

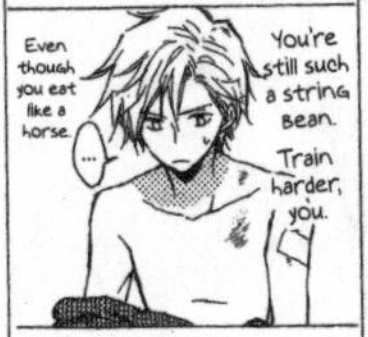
Even though you eat like a horse.
...
You're still such a string bean.
Train harder, you.

▶Trainee Kid

Works at Fort Laxdo.

At first, he was dumbfounded to see his superiors, Kiki and Mitsuhide, having ordinary conversations with Zen, and he got really emotional when Zen started talking to him too.

He's working hard to become a capable fighter for the fort.

7

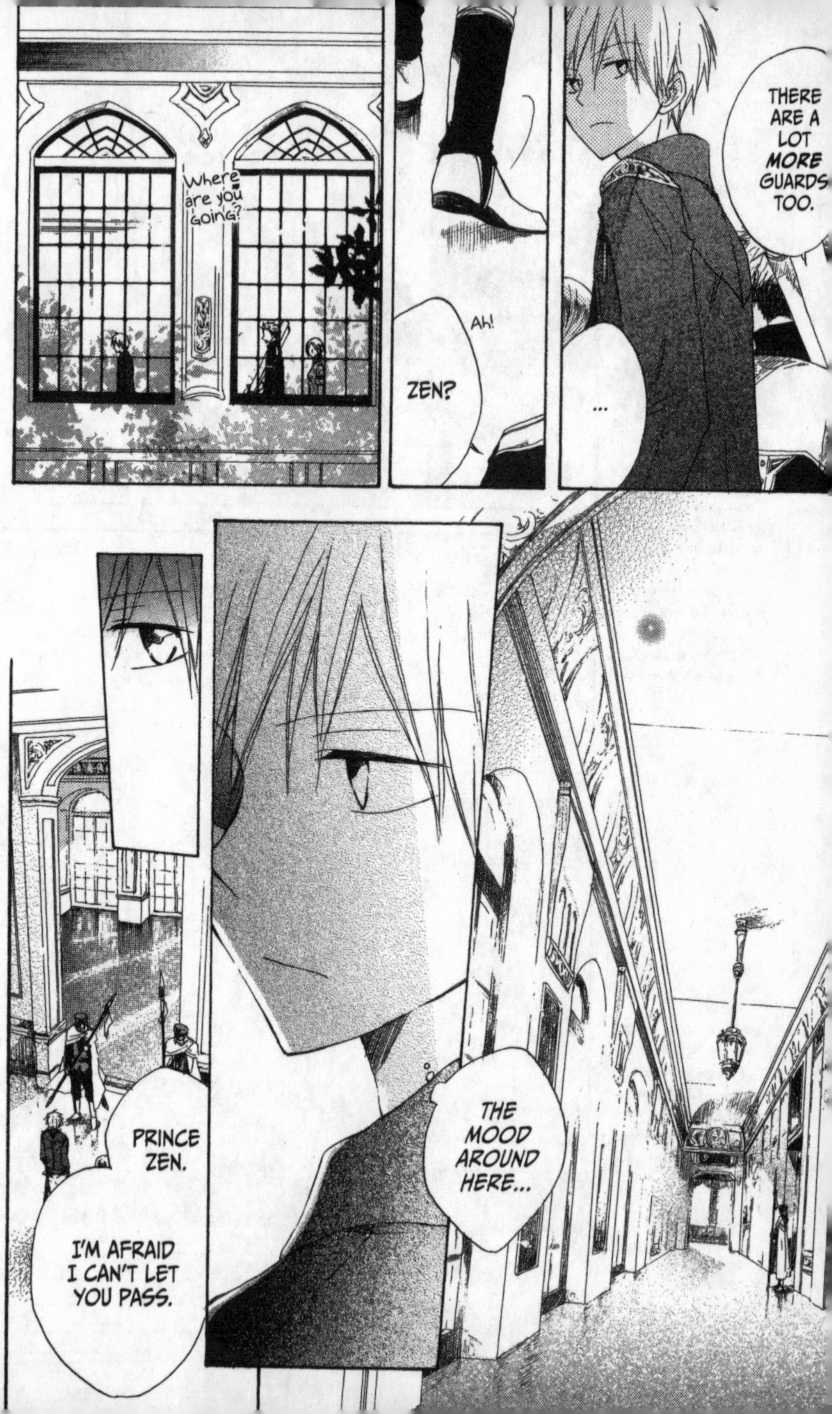
THERE ARE A LOT MORE GUARDS TOO.
...
Ah!
ZEN?
Where are you going?
THE MOOD AROUND HERE...
PRINCE ZEN.
I'M AFRAID I CAN'T LET YOU PASS.

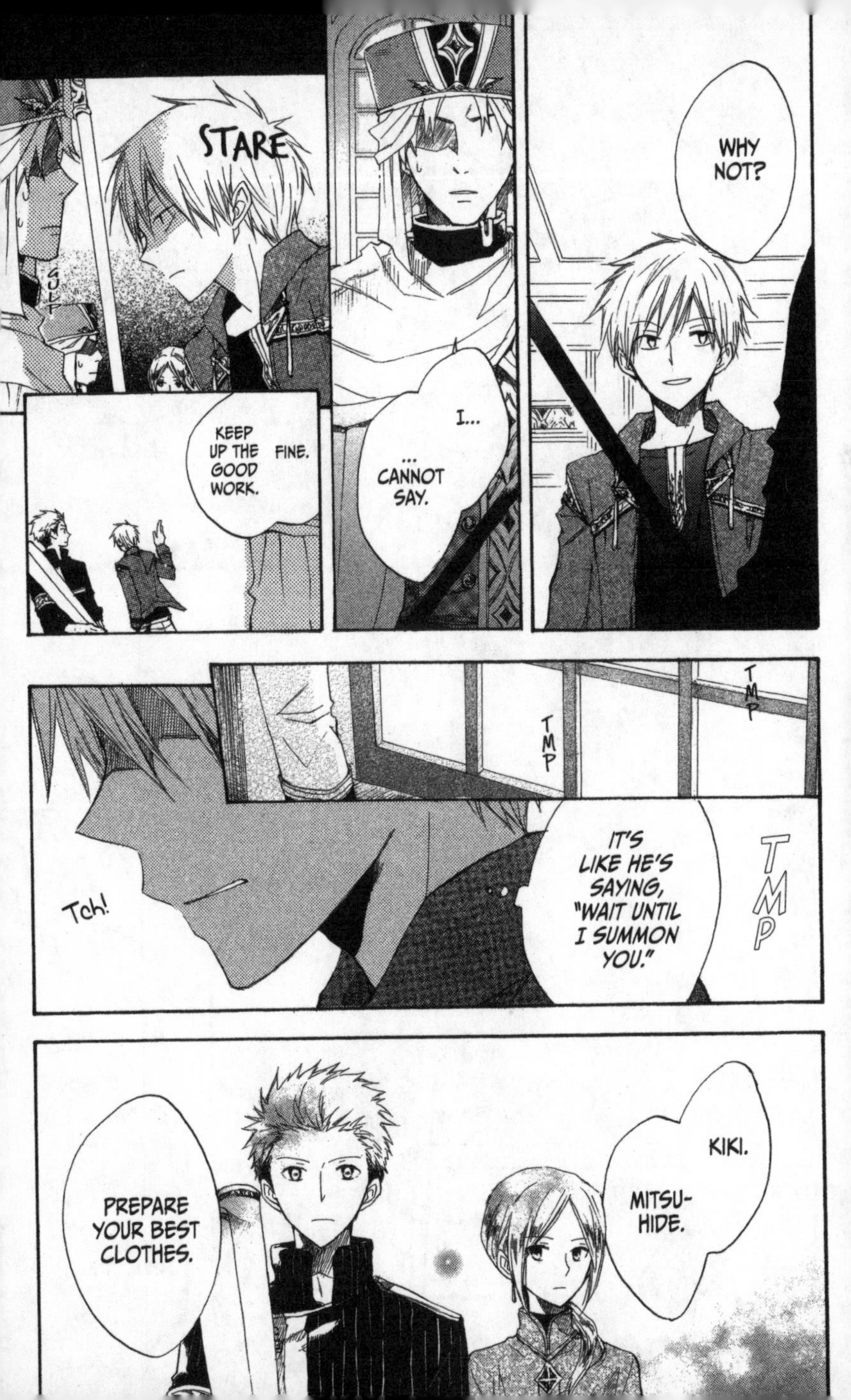
WHY NOT?
I...
...CANNOT SAY.
STARE
GULP
KEEP UP THE GOOD WORK.
FINE.
TMP
TMP
TMP
IT'S LIKE HE'S SAYING, "WAIT UNTIL I SUMMON YOU."
Tch!
KIKI.
MITSU-HIDE.
PREPARE YOUR BEST CLOTHES.

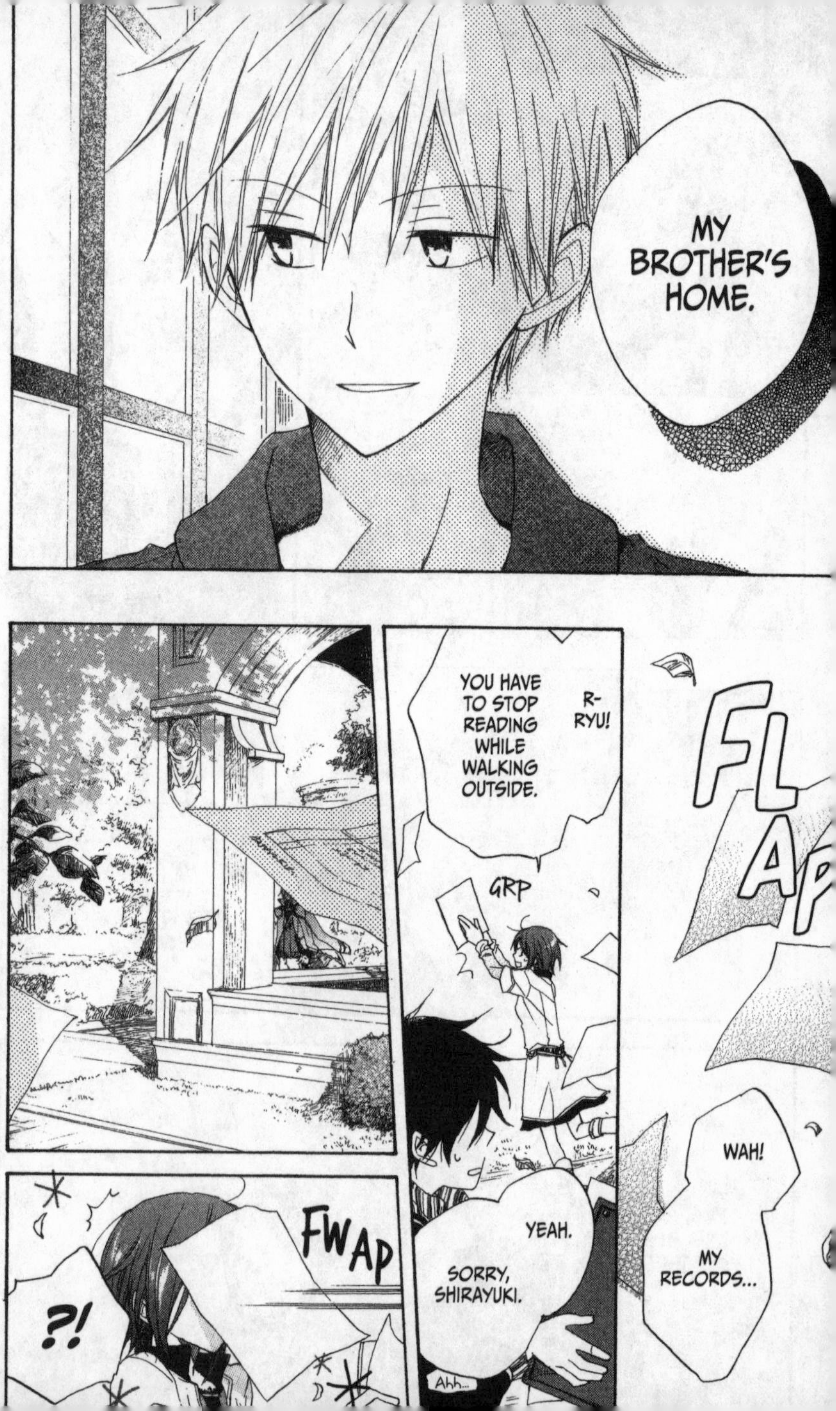
MY BROTHER'S HOME.
FLAP
WAH!
MY RECORDS...
R-RYU!
YOU HAVE TO STOP READING WHILE WALKING OUTSIDE.
GRP
YEAH.
SORRY, SHIRAYUKI.
Ahh...
FWAP
?!

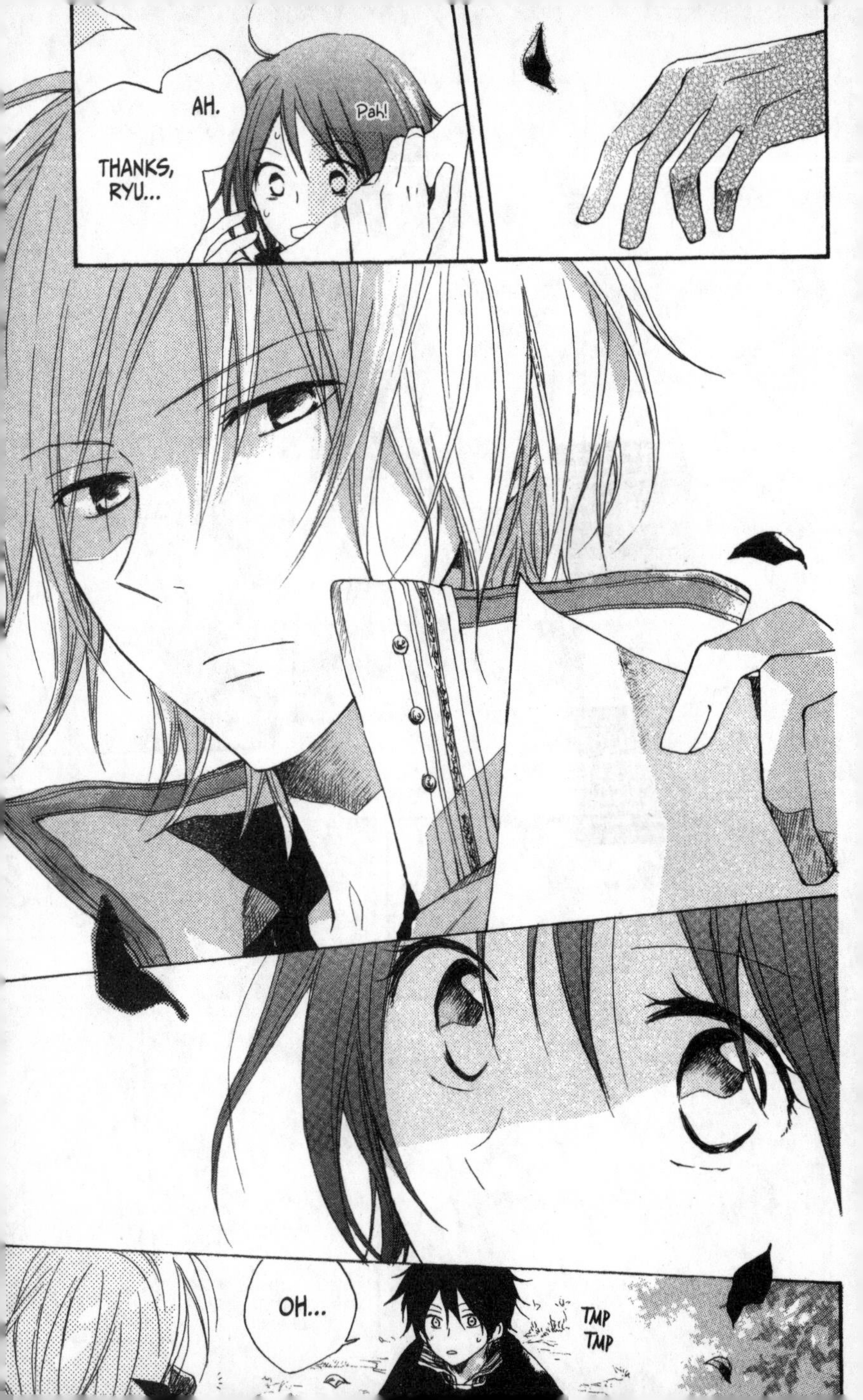
Pah!
AH.
THANKS, RYU...
TMP TMP
OH...

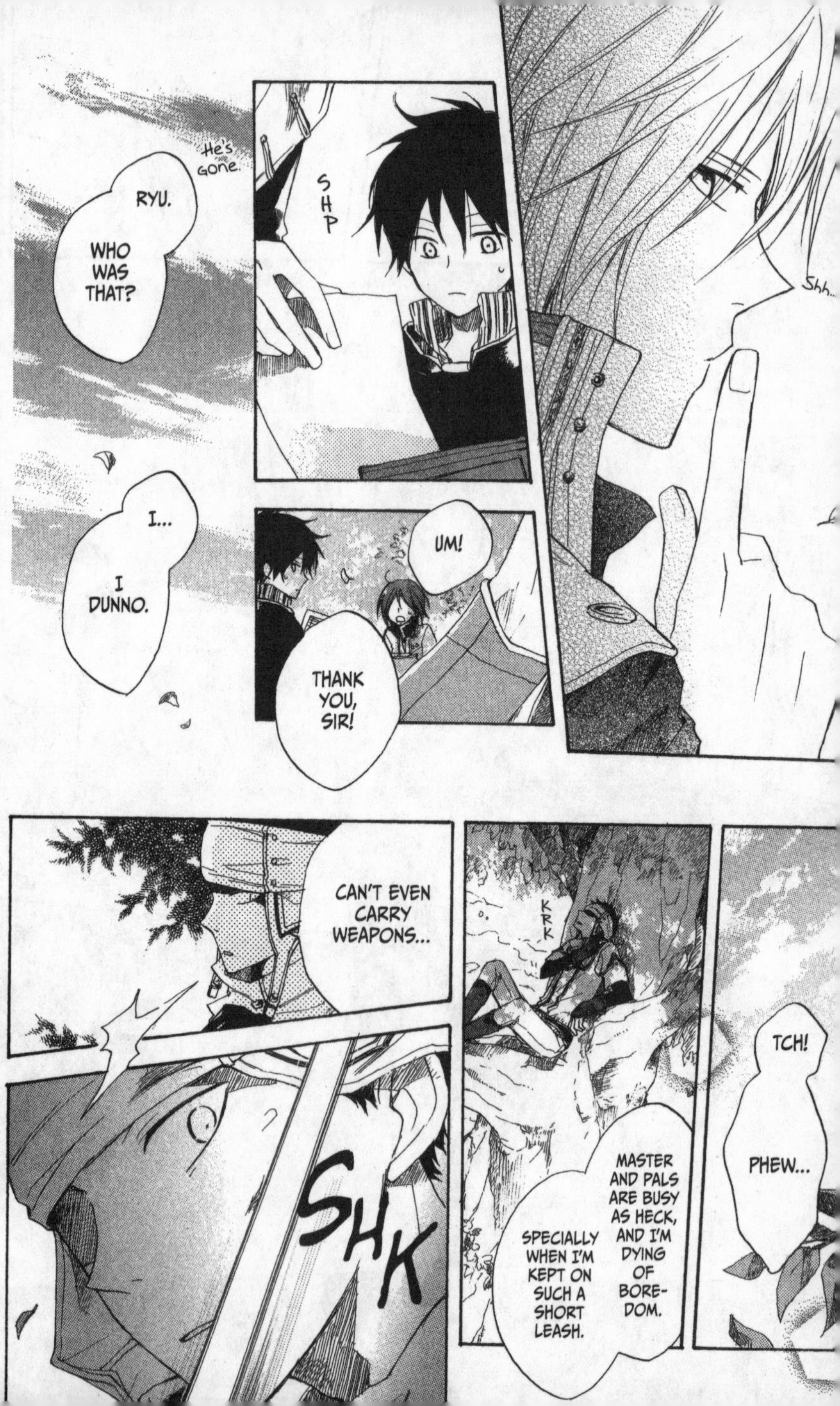
Shh...
SHP
UM!
THANK YOU, SIR!
He's gone.
RYU.
WHO WAS THAT?
I...
I DUNNO.
TCH!
PHEW...
KRK
MASTER AND PALS ARE BUSY AS HECK, AND I'M DYING OF BORE-DOM.
SPECIALLY WHEN I'M KEPT ON SUCH A SHORT LEASH.
CAN'T EVEN CARRY WEAPONS...
SHK

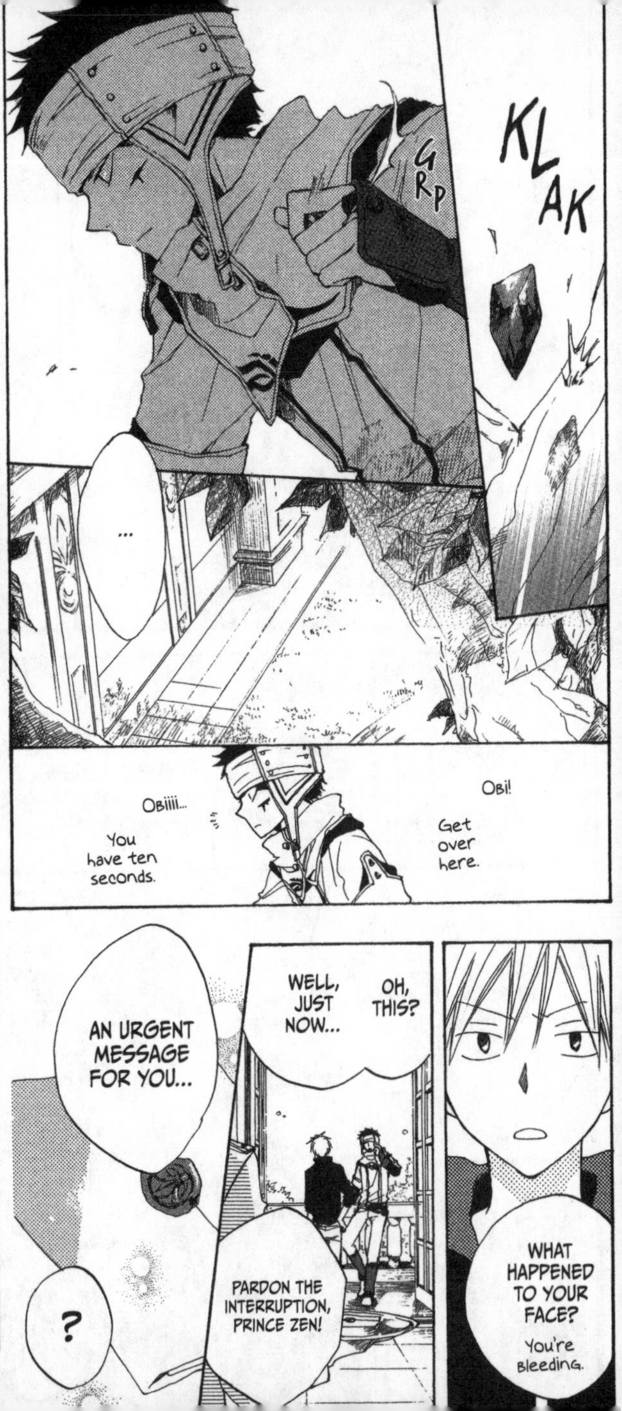
KLAK
GRP
...
Obi!
Get over here.
Obiiii...
You have ten seconds.
WHAT HAPPENED TO YOUR FACE?
You're bleeding.
OH, THIS?
WELL, JUST NOW...
PARDON THE INTERRUPTION, PRINCE ZEN!
AN URGENT MESSAGE FOR YOU...
?

This guy...
No matter
what he says,
it comes out
sounding slimy.

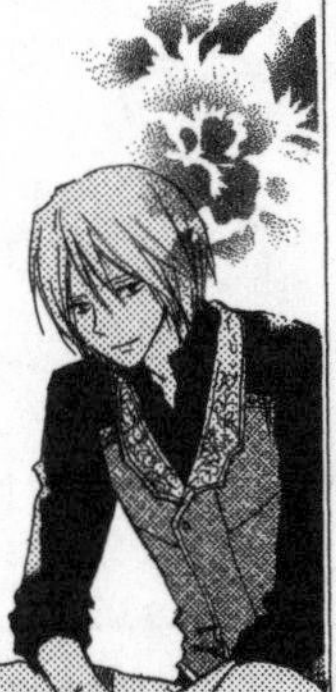

▶Izana

He has his own
palace and mansion
outside of Wistal.

Though the two
princes of Clarines
are of course related
by blood, Zen has
never called Izana by
his name. Nor has Izana
asked to be called by
his own name.

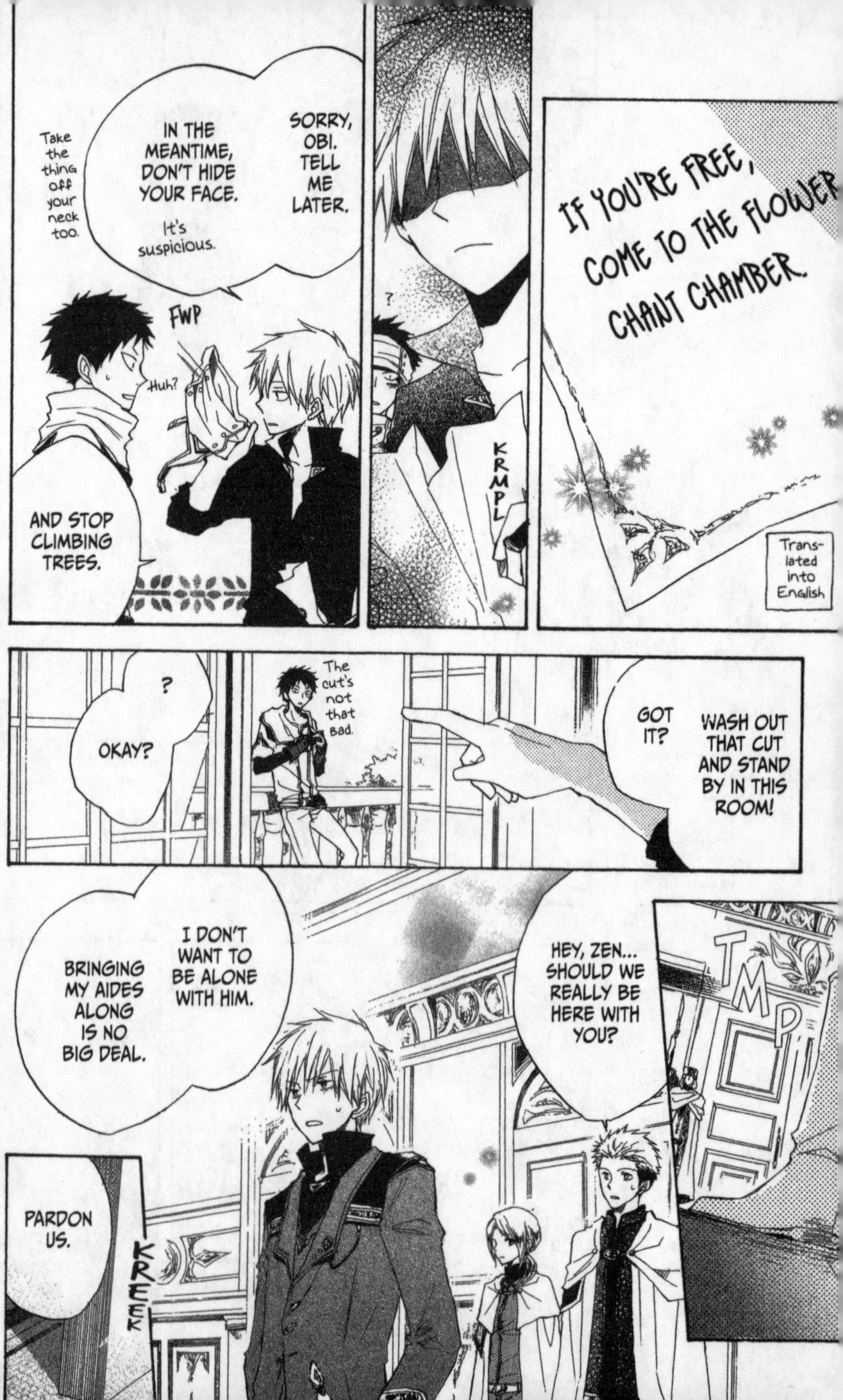
IF YOU'RE FREE, COME TO THE FLOWER CHANT CHAMBER.
Translated into English
?
KRMPL
SORRY, OBI. TELL ME LATER.
IN THE MEANTIME, DON'T HIDE YOUR FACE.
It's suspicious.
Take the thing off your neck too.
FWP
Huh?
AND STOP CLIMBING TREES.
WASH OUT THAT CUT AND STAND BY IN THIS ROOM!
GOT IT?
The cut's not that bad.
?
OKAY?
TMP
HEY, ZEN... SHOULD WE REALLY BE HERE WITH YOU?
I DON'T WANT TO BE ALONE WITH HIM.
BRINGING MY AIDES ALONG IS NO BIG DEAL.
KREEK
PARDON US.

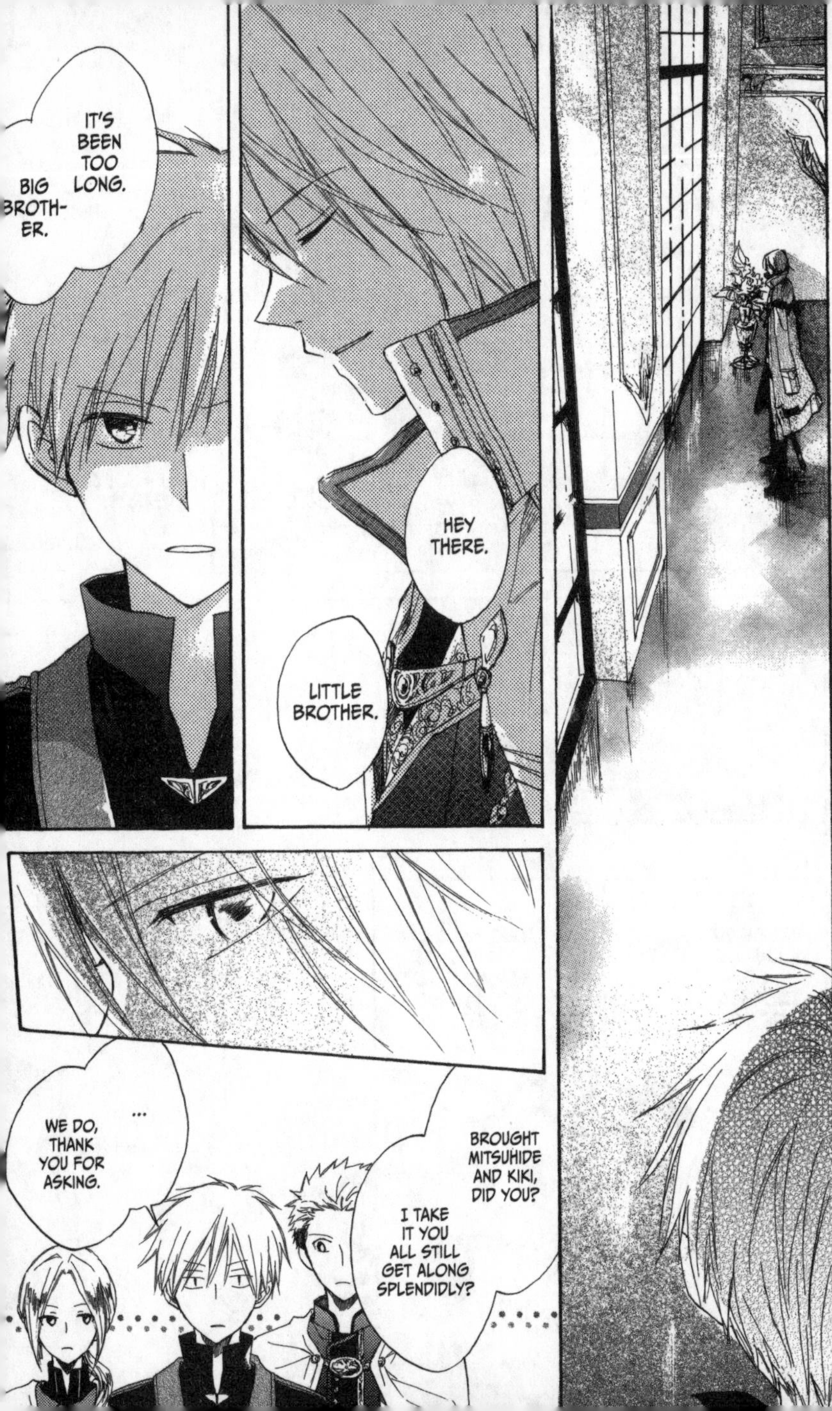
HEY THERE.
LITTLE BROTHER.
IT'S BEEN TOO LONG.
BIG BROTHER.
BROUGHT MITSUHIDE AND KIKI, DID YOU?
I TAKE IT YOU ALL STILL GET ALONG SPLENDIDLY?
...
WE DO, THANK YOU FOR ASKING.

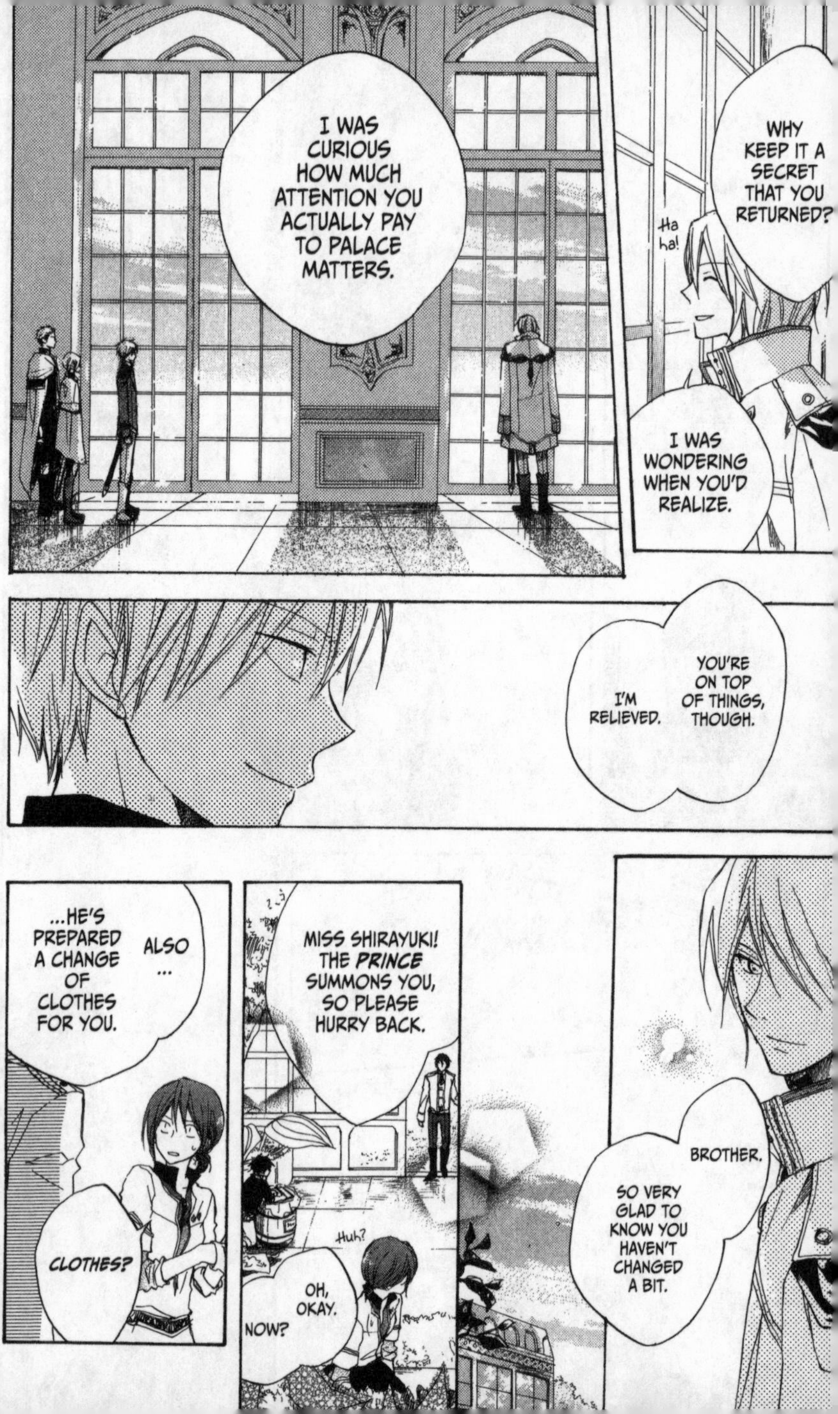
WHY KEEP IT A SECRET THAT YOU RETURNED?
Ha ha!
I WAS WONDERING WHEN YOU'D REALIZE.
I WAS CURIOUS HOW MUCH ATTENTION YOU ACTUALLY PAY TO PALACE MATTERS.
YOU'RE ON TOP OF THINGS, THOUGH.
I'M RELIEVED.
BROTHER.
SO VERY GLAD TO KNOW YOU HAVEN'T CHANGED A BIT.
MISS SHIRAYUKI! THE *PRINCE* SUMMONS YOU, SO PLEASE HURRY BACK.
Huh?
OH, OKAY.
NOW?
ALSO ...
...HE'S PREPARED A CHANGE OF CLOTHES FOR YOU.
CLOTHES?

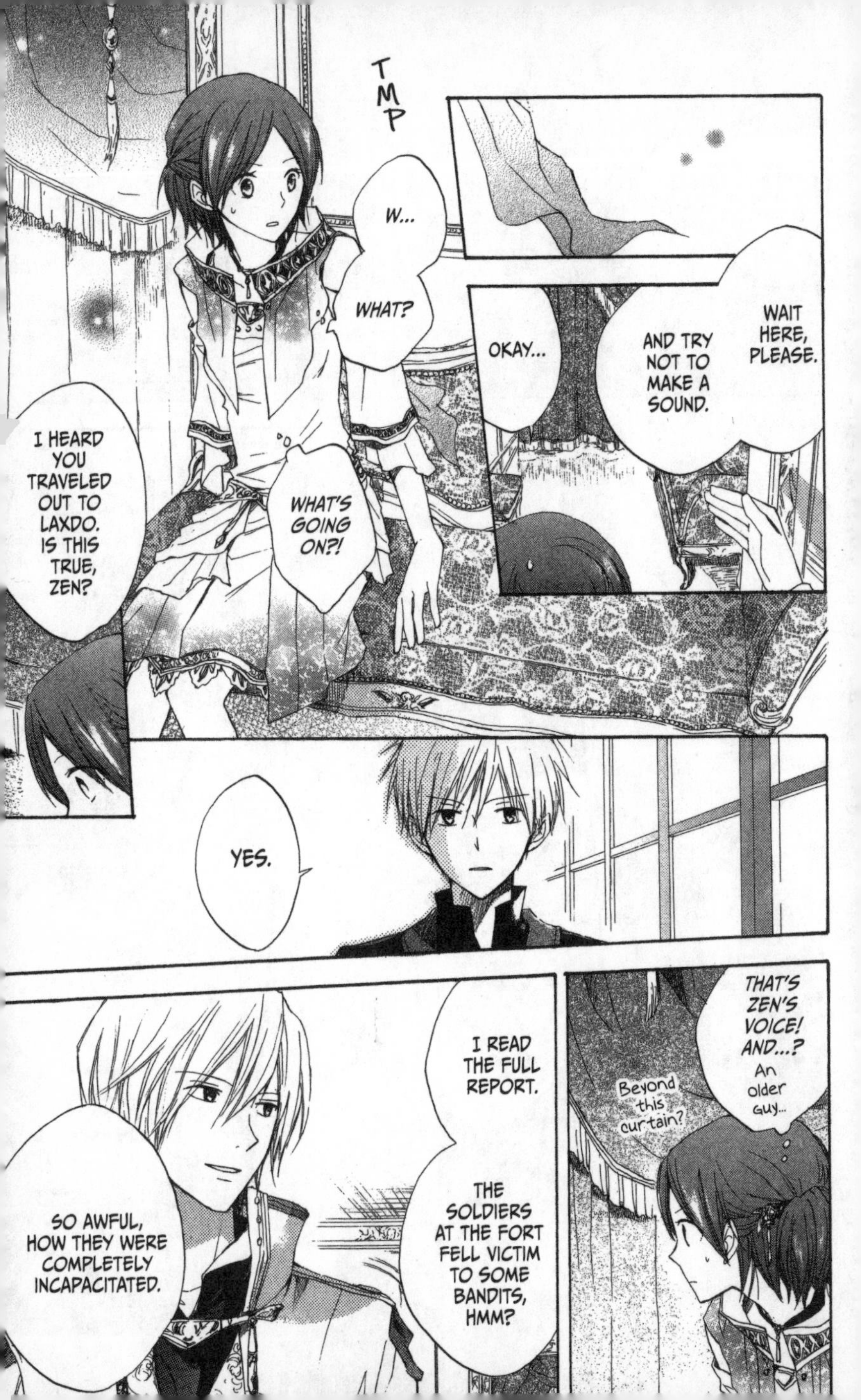
WAIT HERE, PLEASE.
AND TRY NOT TO MAKE A SOUND.
OKAY...
TMP
W...
WHAT?
WHAT'S GOING ON?!
I HEARD YOU TRAVELED OUT TO LAXDO. IS THIS TRUE, ZEN?
YES.
THAT'S ZEN'S VOICE! AND...?
An older guy...
Beyond this curtain?
I READ THE FULL REPORT.
THE SOLDIERS AT THE FORT FELL VICTIM TO SOME BANDITS, HMM?
SO AWFUL, HOW THEY WERE COMPLETELY INCAPACITATED.

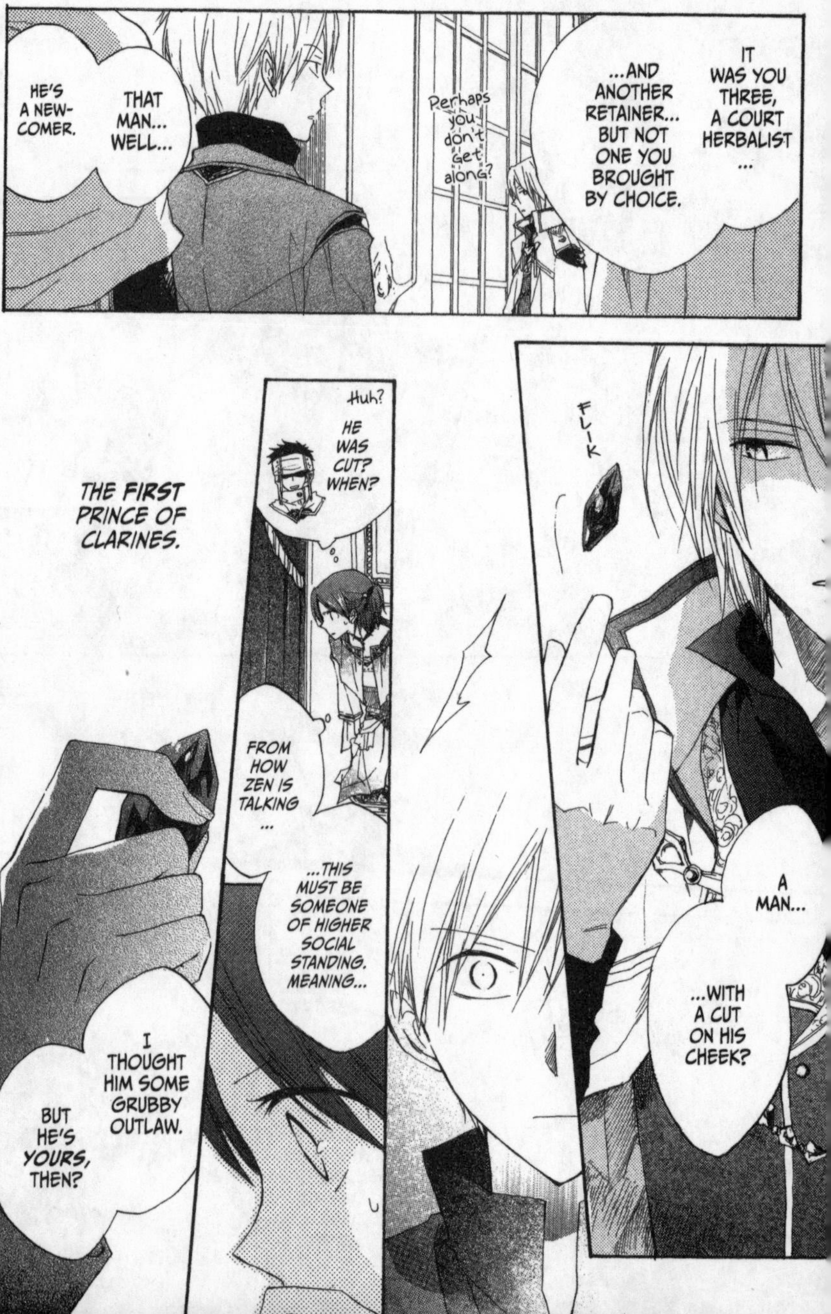
IT WAS YOU THREE, A COURT HERBALIST...
...AND ANOTHER RETAINER... BUT NOT ONE YOU BROUGHT BY CHOICE.
Perhaps you don't get along?
THAT MAN... WELL...
HE'S A NEW-COMER.
FLIK
A MAN...
...WITH A CUT ON HIS CHEEK?
Huh?
HE WAS CUT? WHEN?
FROM HOW ZEN IS TALKING...
...THIS MUST BE SOMEONE OF HIGHER SOCIAL STANDING. MEANING...
THE FIRST PRINCE OF CLARINES.
I THOUGHT HIM SOME GRUBBY OUTLAW.
BUT HE'S YOURS, THEN?

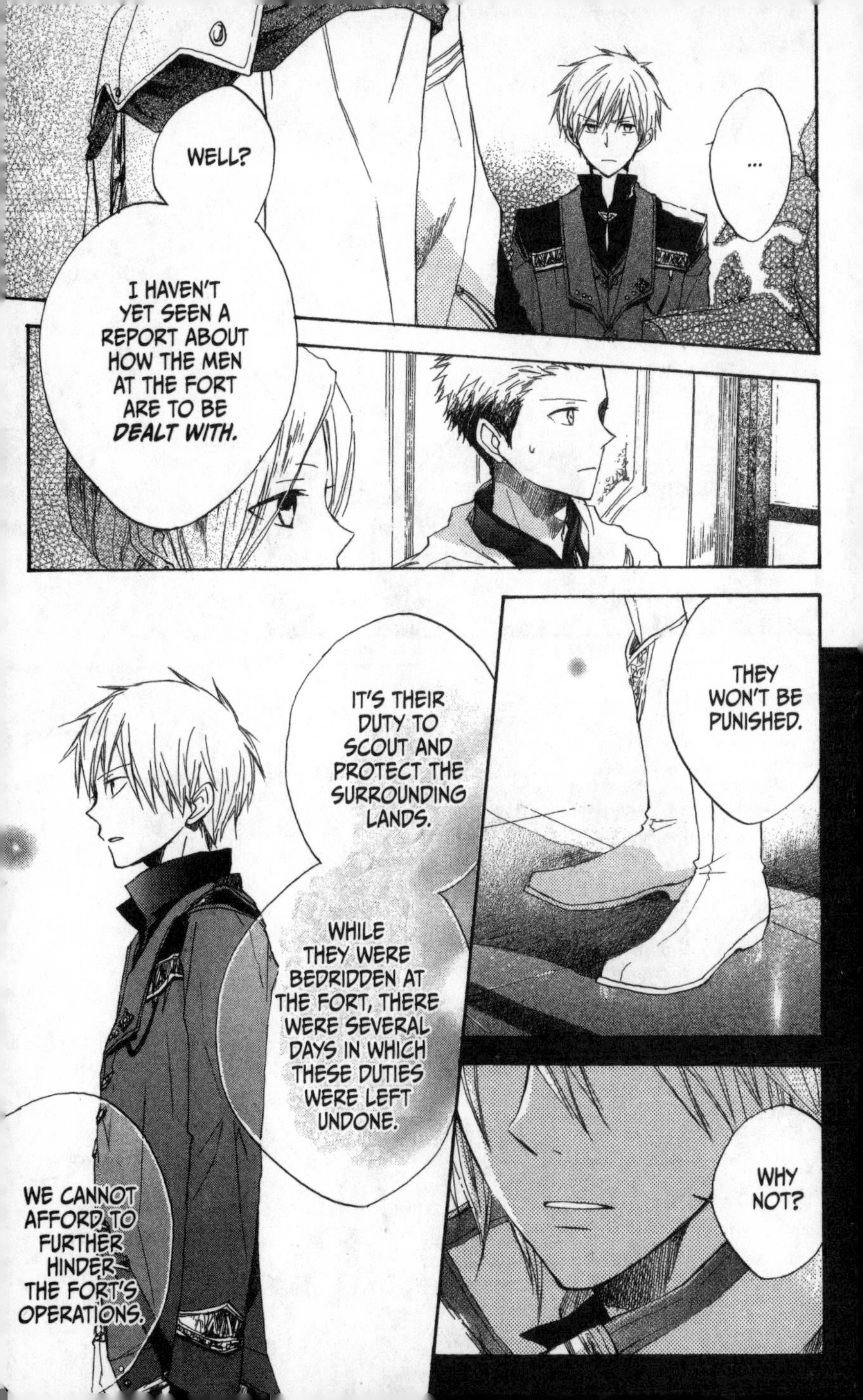
...
WELL?
I HAVEN'T YET SEEN A REPORT ABOUT HOW THE MEN AT THE FORT ARE TO BE *DEALT WITH.*
THEY WON'T BE PUNISHED.
WHY NOT?
IT'S THEIR DUTY TO SCOUT AND PROTECT THE SURROUNDING LANDS.
WHILE THEY WERE BEDRIDDEN AT THE FORT, THERE WERE SEVERAL DAYS IN WHICH THESE DUTIES WERE LEFT UNDONE.
WE CANNOT AFFORD TO FURTHER HINDER THE FORT'S OPERATIONS.

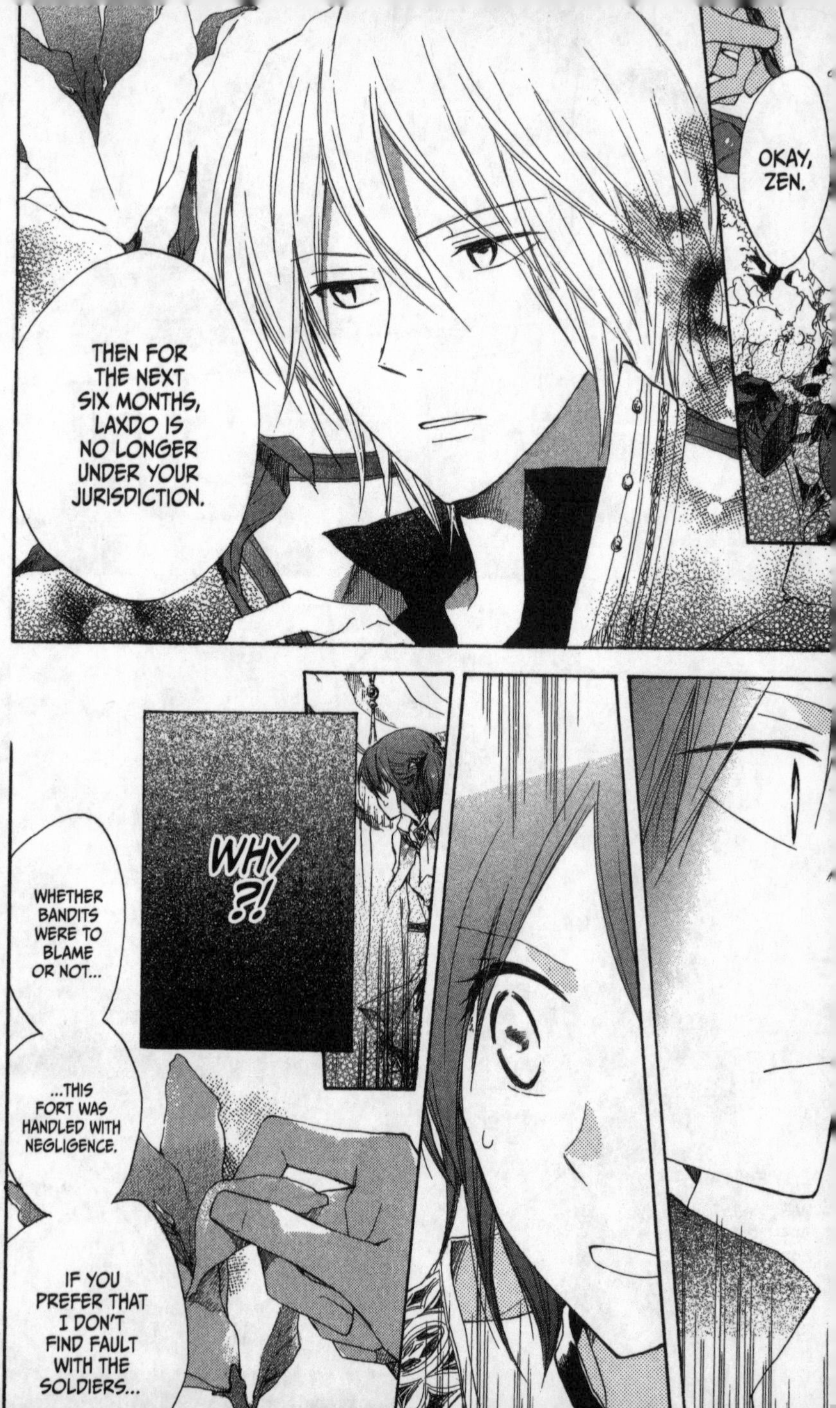
OKAY, ZEN.
THEN FOR THE NEXT SIX MONTHS, LAXDO IS NO LONGER UNDER YOUR JURISDICTION.
WHY?!
WHETHER BANDITS WERE TO BLAME OR NOT...
...THIS FORT WAS HANDLED WITH NEGLIGENCE.
IF YOU PREFER THAT I DON'T FIND FAULT WITH THE SOLDIERS...

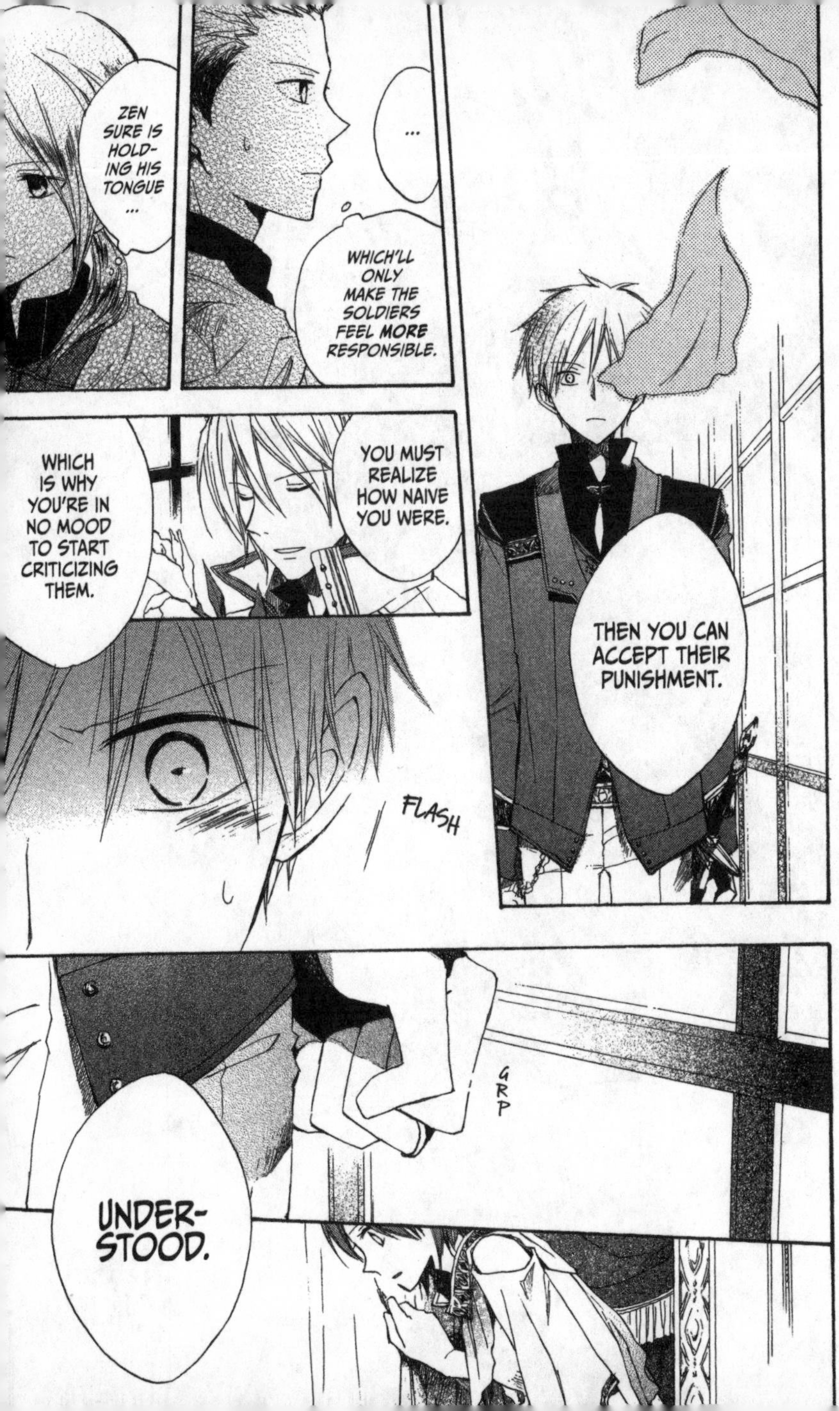

ZEN SURE IS HOLDING HIS TONGUE ...
...
WHICH'LL ONLY MAKE THE SOLDIERS FEEL MORE RESPONSIBLE.
YOU MUST REALIZE HOW NAIVE YOU WERE.
WHICH IS WHY YOU'RE IN NO MOOD TO START CRITICIZING THEM.
THEN YOU CAN ACCEPT THEIR PUNISHMENT.
FLASH
GRP
UNDER-STOOD.

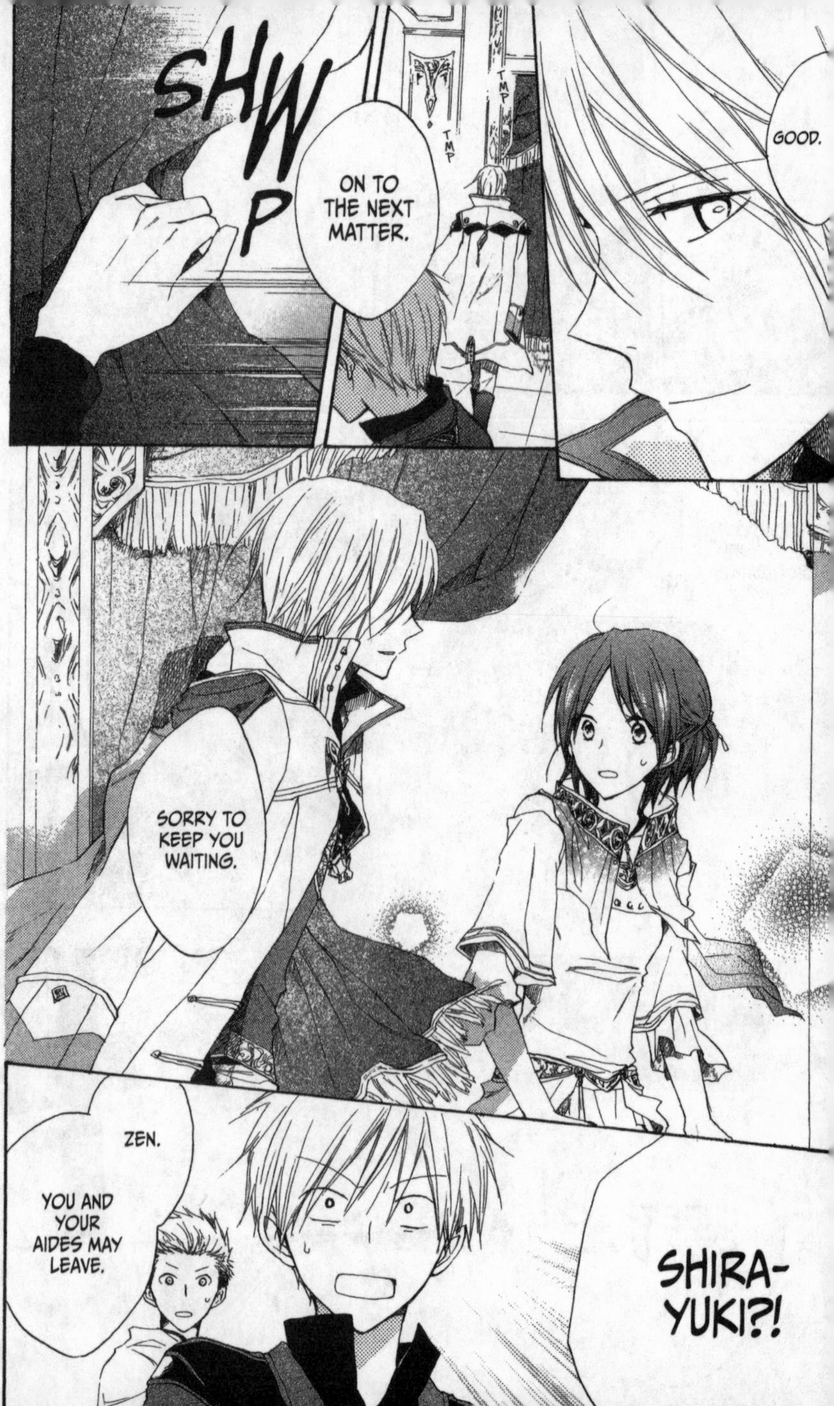
GOOD.
TMP TMP
ON TO THE NEXT MATTER.
SHWP
SORRY TO KEEP YOU WAITING.
SHIRA-YUKI?!
ZEN.
YOU AND YOUR AIDES MAY LEAVE.

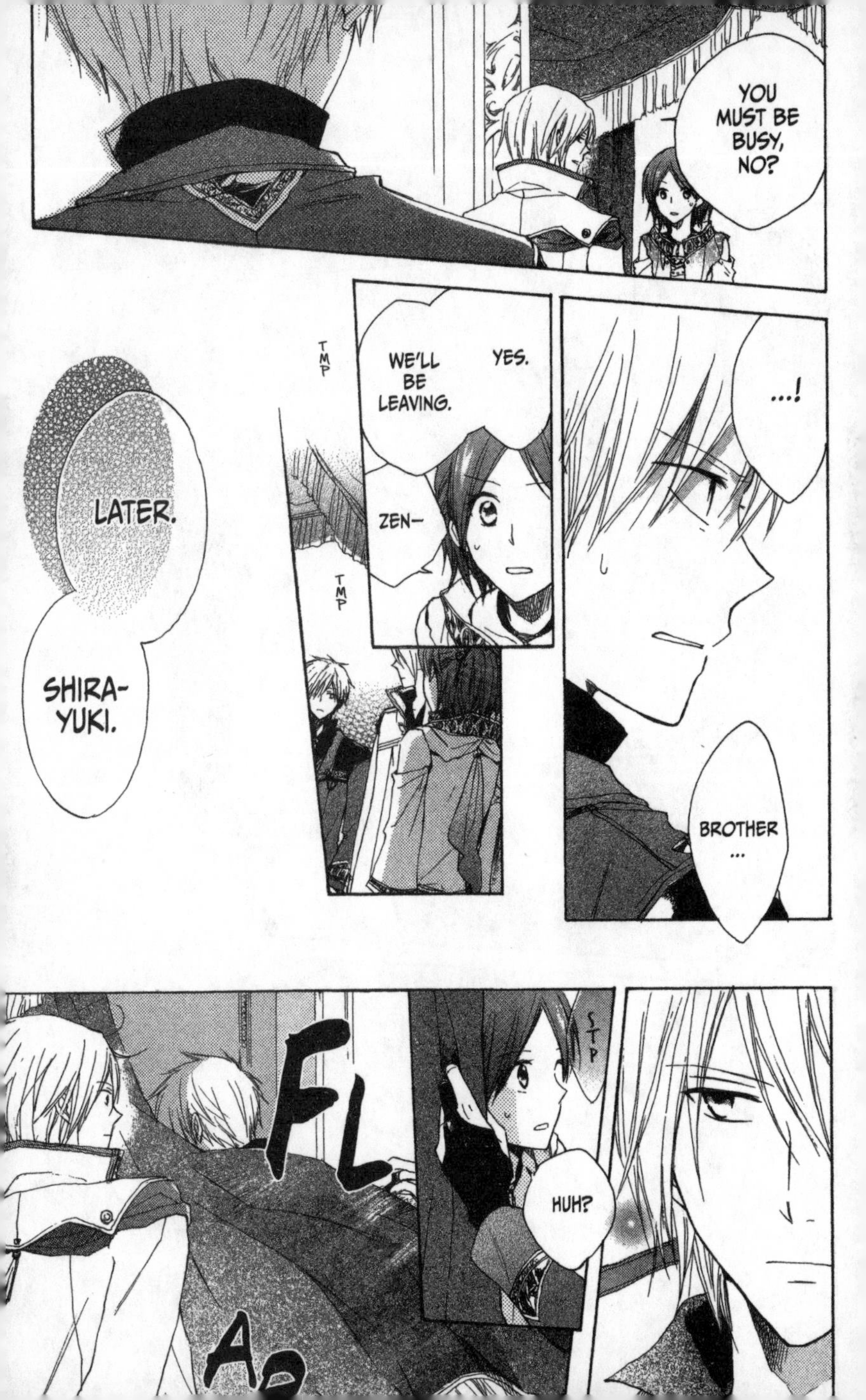
YOU MUST BE BUSY, NO?
...!
BROTHER ...
YES.
WE'LL BE LEAVING.
TMP
ZEN—
TMP
LATER.
SHIRA-YUKI.
STP
HUH?
FL
A

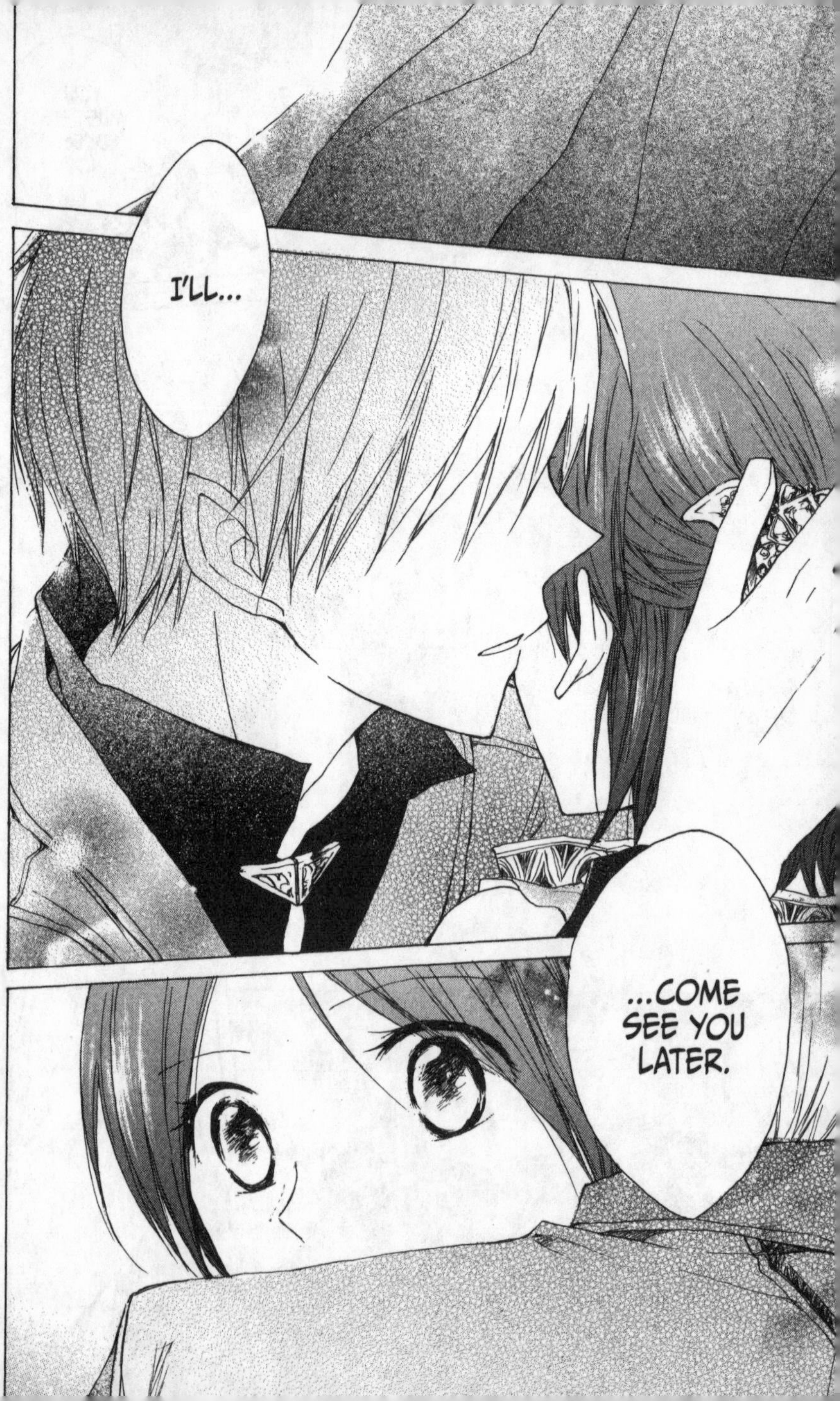
I'LL...
...COME SEE YOU LATER.

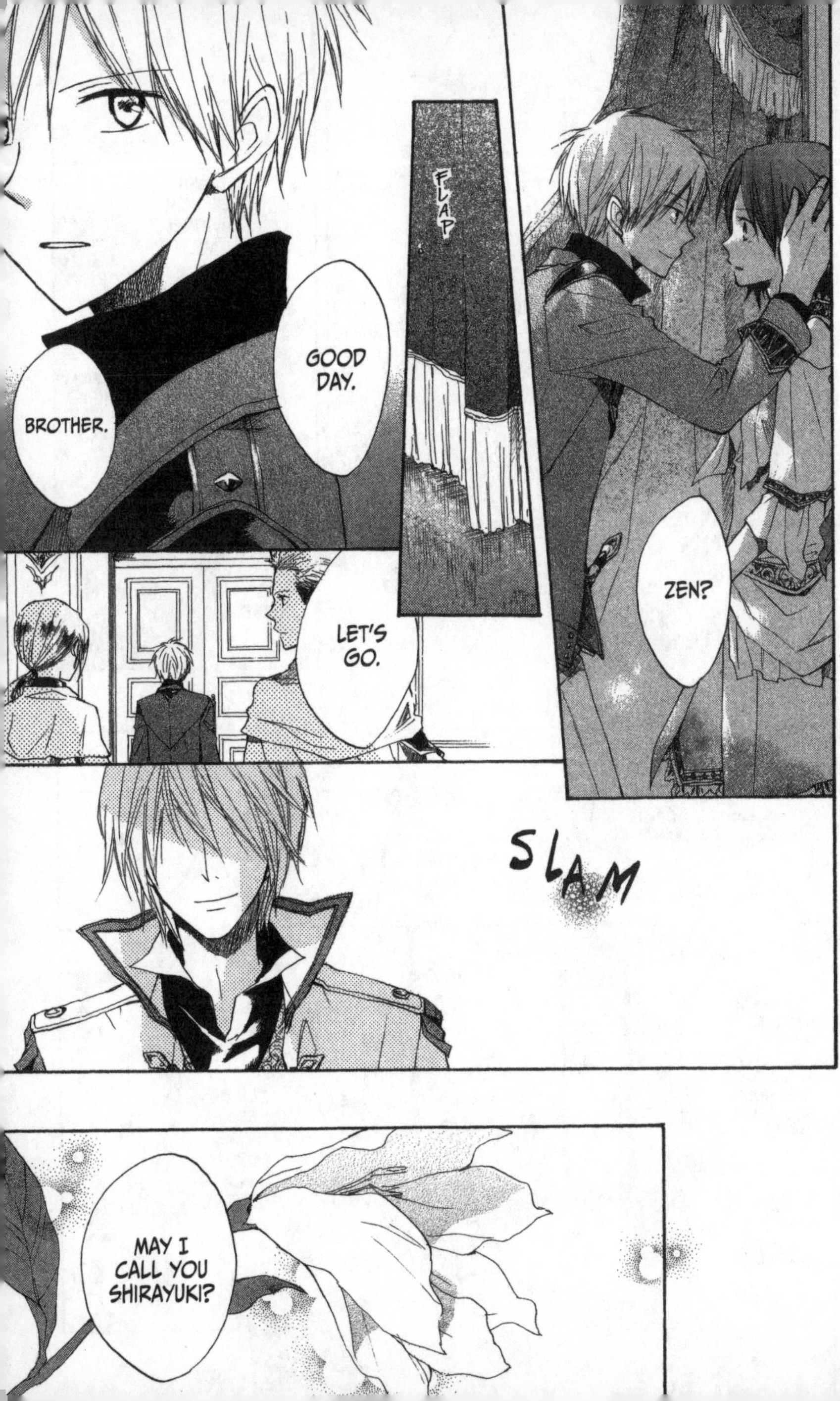
ZEN?
FLAP
GOOD DAY.
BROTHER.
LET'S GO.
SLAM
MAY I CALL YOU SHIRAYUKI?

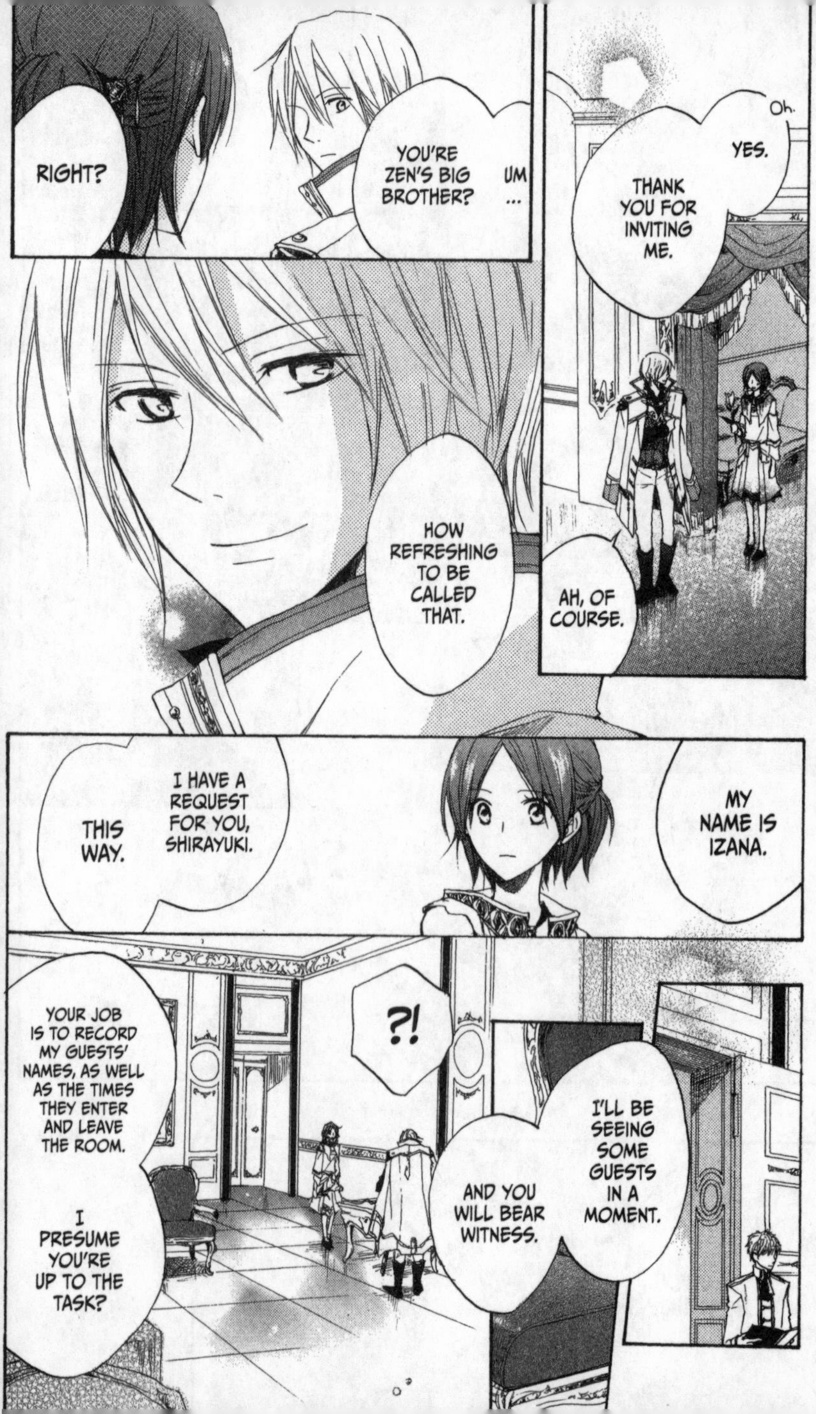
Oh.
YES.
THANK YOU FOR INVITING ME.
AH, OF COURSE.
UM ...
YOU'RE ZEN'S BIG BROTHER?
RIGHT?
HOW REFRESHING TO BE CALLED THAT.
MY NAME IS IZANA.
I HAVE A REQUEST FOR YOU, SHIRAYUKI.
THIS WAY.
I'LL BE SEEING SOME GUESTS IN A MOMENT.
AND YOU WILL BEAR WITNESS.
?!
YOUR JOB IS TO RECORD MY GUESTS' NAMES, AS WELL AS THE TIMES THEY ENTER AND LEAVE THE ROOM.
I PRESUME YOU'RE UP TO THE TASK?

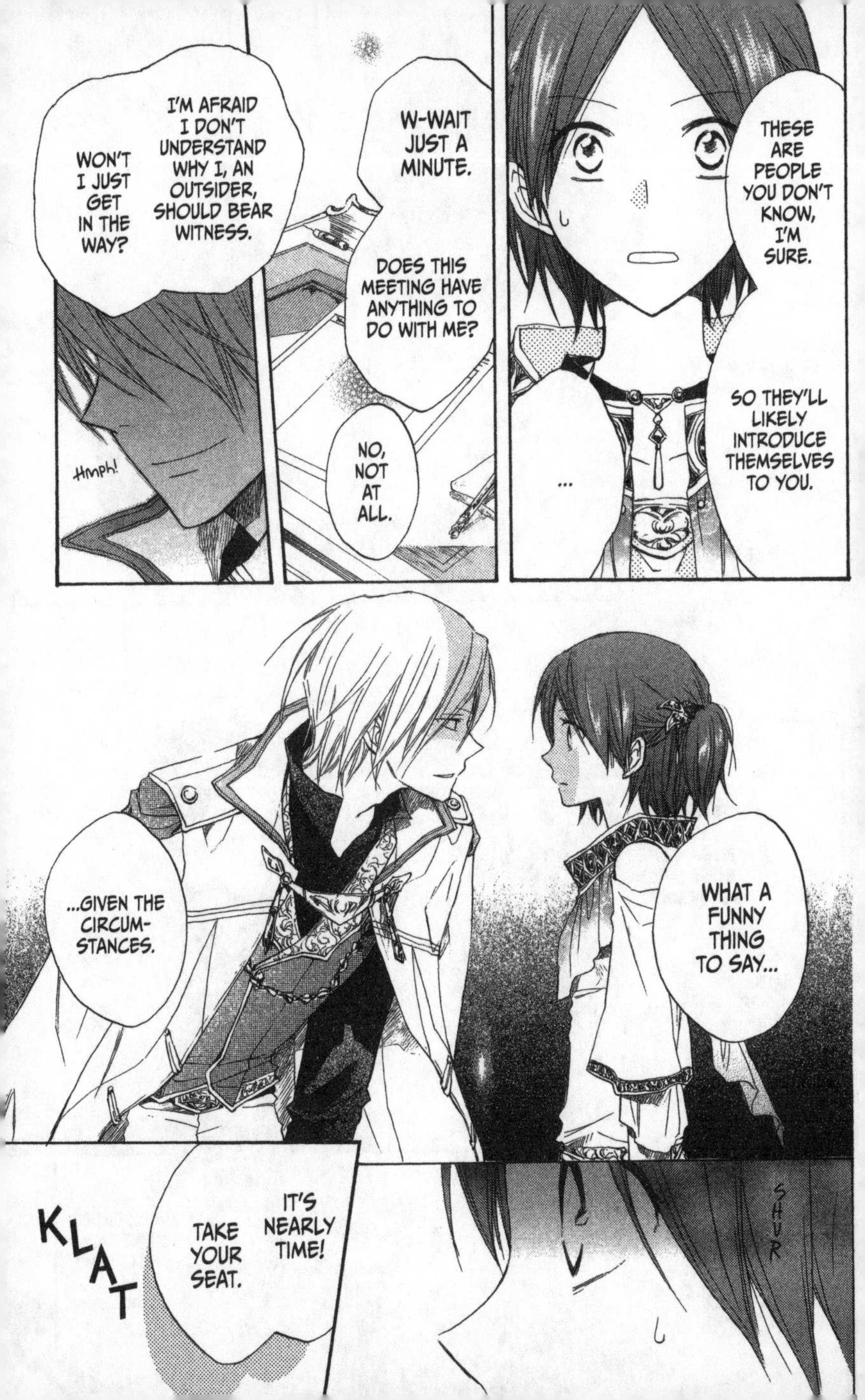
THESE ARE PEOPLE YOU DON'T KNOW, I'M SURE.
SO THEY'LL LIKELY INTRODUCE THEMSELVES TO YOU.
...
W-WAIT JUST A MINUTE.
DOES THIS MEETING HAVE ANYTHING TO DO WITH ME?
NO, NOT AT ALL.
I'M AFRAID I DON'T UNDERSTAND WHY I, AN OUTSIDER, SHOULD BEAR WITNESS.
WON'T I JUST GET IN THE WAY?
Hmph!
WHAT A FUNNY THING TO SAY...
...GIVEN THE CIRCUMSTANCES.
SHUR
IT'S NEARLY TIME!
TAKE YOUR SEAT.
KLAT

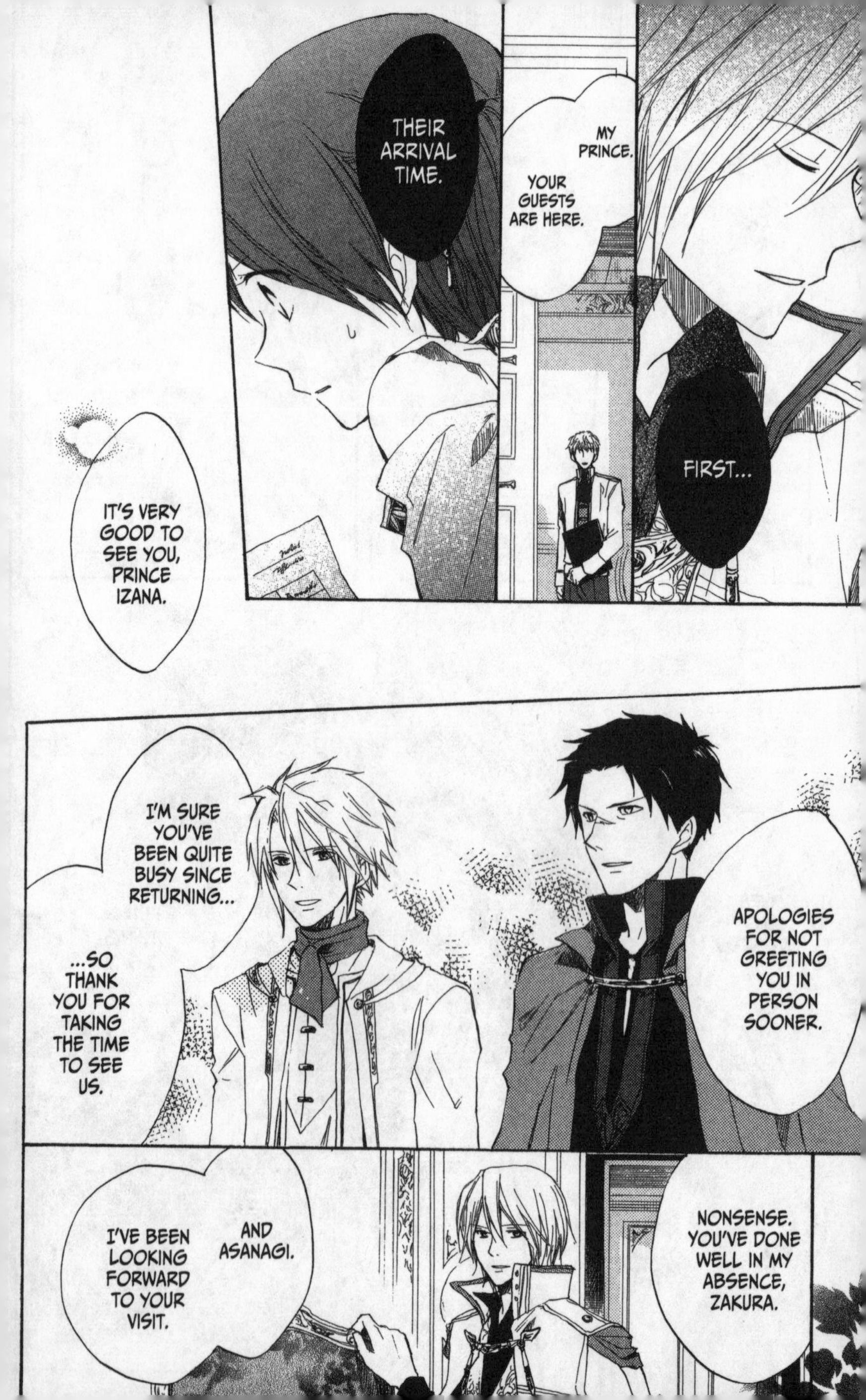
FIRST...
MY PRINCE.
YOUR GUESTS ARE HERE.
THEIR ARRIVAL TIME.
IT'S VERY GOOD TO SEE YOU, PRINCE IZANA.
APOLOGIES FOR NOT GREETING YOU IN PERSON SOONER.
I'M SURE YOU'VE BEEN QUITE BUSY SINCE RETURNING...
...SO THANK YOU FOR TAKING THE TIME TO SEE US.
NONSENSE. YOU'VE DONE WELL IN MY ABSENCE, ZAKURA.
AND ASANAGI.
I'VE BEEN LOOKING FORWARD TO YOUR VISIT.

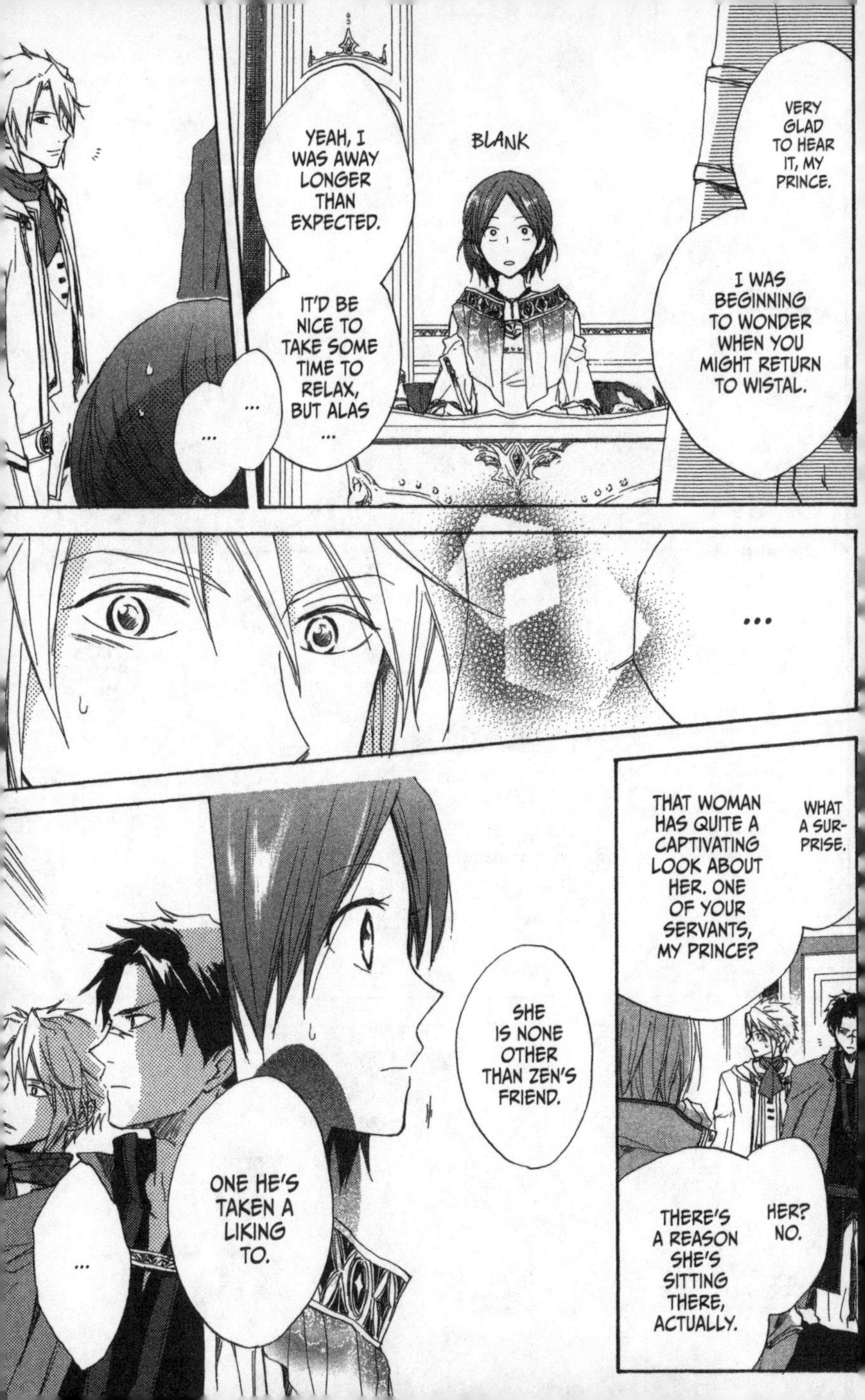
VERY GLAD TO HEAR IT, MY PRINCE.
I WAS BEGINNING TO WONDER WHEN YOU MIGHT RETURN TO WISTAL.
YEAH, I WAS AWAY LONGER THAN EXPECTED.
BLANK
IT'D BE NICE TO TAKE SOME TIME TO RELAX, BUT ALAS ...
... ...
...
WHAT A SURPRISE.
THAT WOMAN HAS QUITE A CAPTIVATING LOOK ABOUT HER. ONE OF YOUR SERVANTS, MY PRINCE?
HER? NO.
THERE'S A REASON SHE'S SITTING THERE, ACTUALLY.
SHE IS NONE OTHER THAN ZEN'S FRIEND.
ONE HE'S TAKEN A LIKING TO.
...

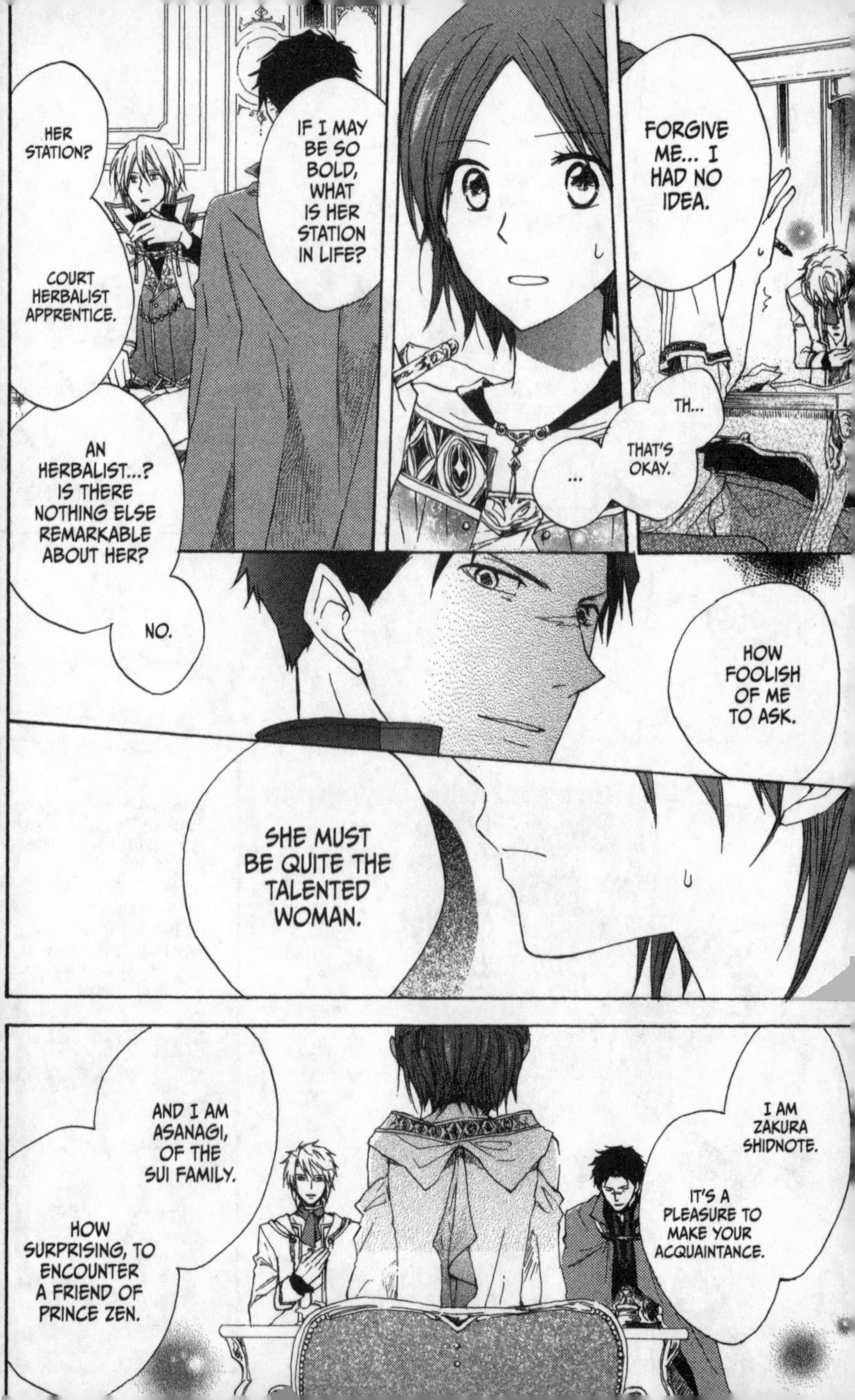
FORGIVE ME... I HAD NO IDEA.
TH...
THAT'S OKAY.
...
IF I MAY BE SO BOLD, WHAT IS HER STATION IN LIFE?
HER STATION?
COURT HERBALIST APPRENTICE.
AN HERBALIST...? IS THERE NOTHING ELSE REMARKABLE ABOUT HER?
NO.
HOW FOOLISH OF ME TO ASK.
SHE MUST BE QUITE THE TALENTED WOMAN.
I AM ZAKURA SHIDNOTE.
IT'S A PLEASURE TO MAKE YOUR ACQUAINTANCE.
AND I AM ASANAGI, OF THE SUI FAMILY.
HOW SURPRISING, TO ENCOUNTER A FRIEND OF PRINCE ZEN.

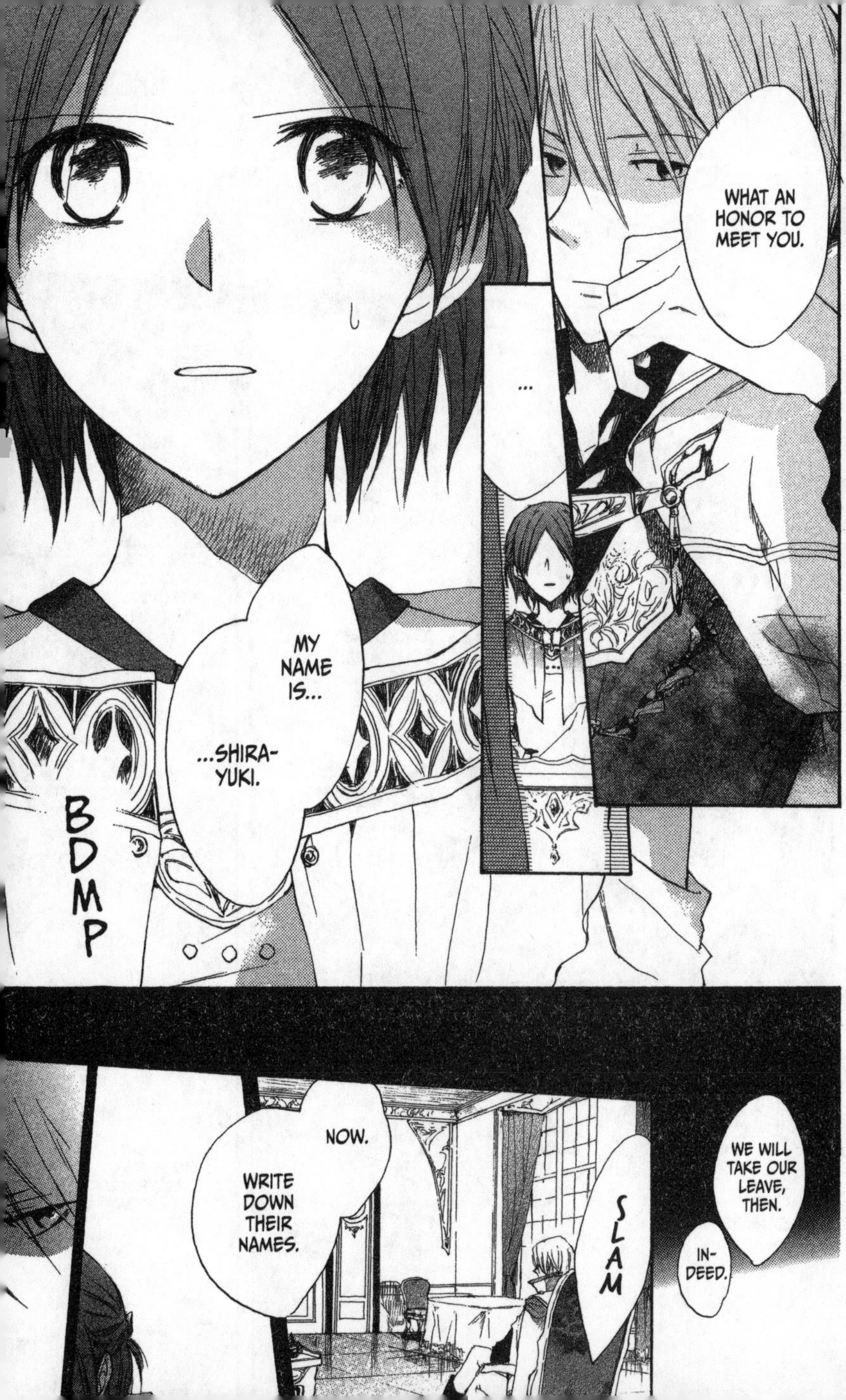
WHAT AN HONOR TO MEET YOU.
...
MY NAME IS...
...SHIRA-YUKI.
BDMP
WE WILL TAKE OUR LEAVE, THEN.
IN-DEED.
SLAM
NOW.
WRITE DOWN THEIR NAMES.

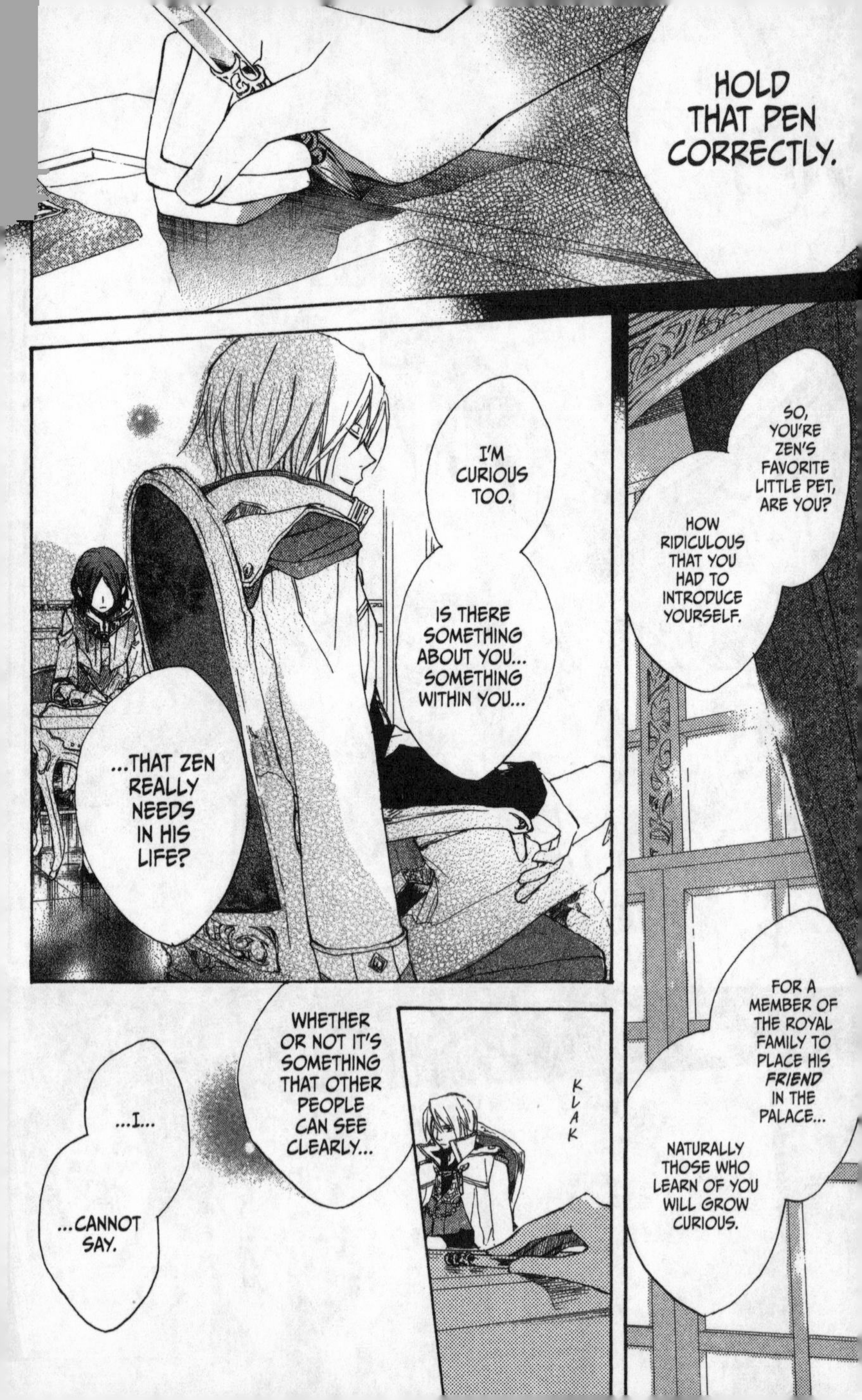
HOLD THAT PEN CORRECTLY.
SO, YOU'RE ZEN'S FAVORITE LITTLE PET, ARE YOU?
HOW RIDICULOUS THAT YOU HAD TO INTRODUCE YOURSELF.
FOR A MEMBER OF THE ROYAL FAMILY TO PLACE HIS *FRIEND* IN THE PALACE...
NATURALLY THOSE WHO LEARN OF YOU WILL GROW CURIOUS.
I'M CURIOUS TOO.
IS THERE SOMETHING ABOUT YOU... SOMETHING WITHIN YOU...
...THAT ZEN REALLY NEEDS IN HIS LIFE?
KLAK
WHETHER OR NOT IT'S SOMETHING THAT OTHER PEOPLE CAN SEE CLEARLY...
...I...
...CANNOT SAY.

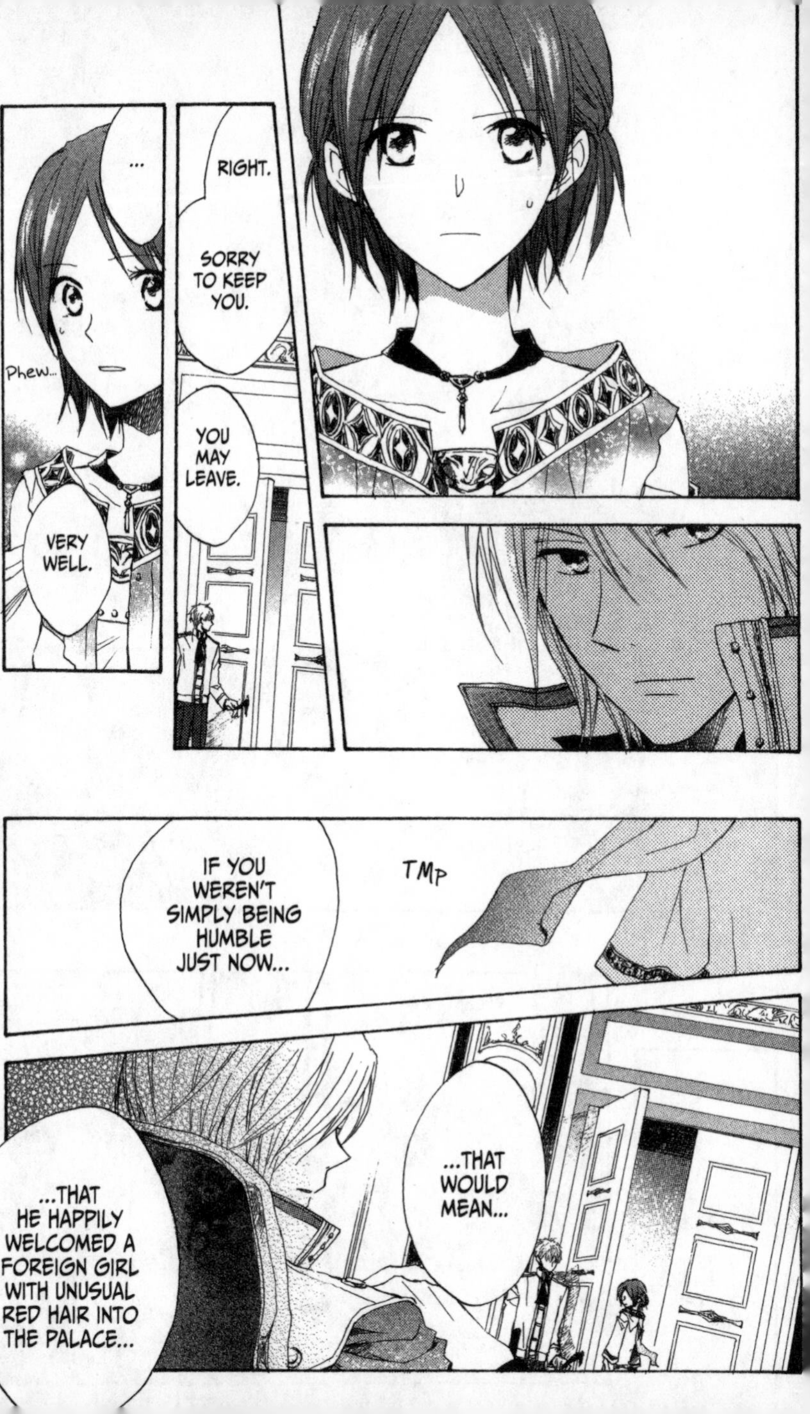
RIGHT.
SORRY TO KEEP YOU.
YOU MAY LEAVE.
...
Phew...
VERY WELL.
TMP
IF YOU WEREN'T SIMPLY BEING HUMBLE JUST NOW...
...THAT WOULD MEAN...
...THAT HE HAPPILY WELCOMED A FOREIGN GIRL WITH UNUSUAL RED HAIR INTO THE PALACE...

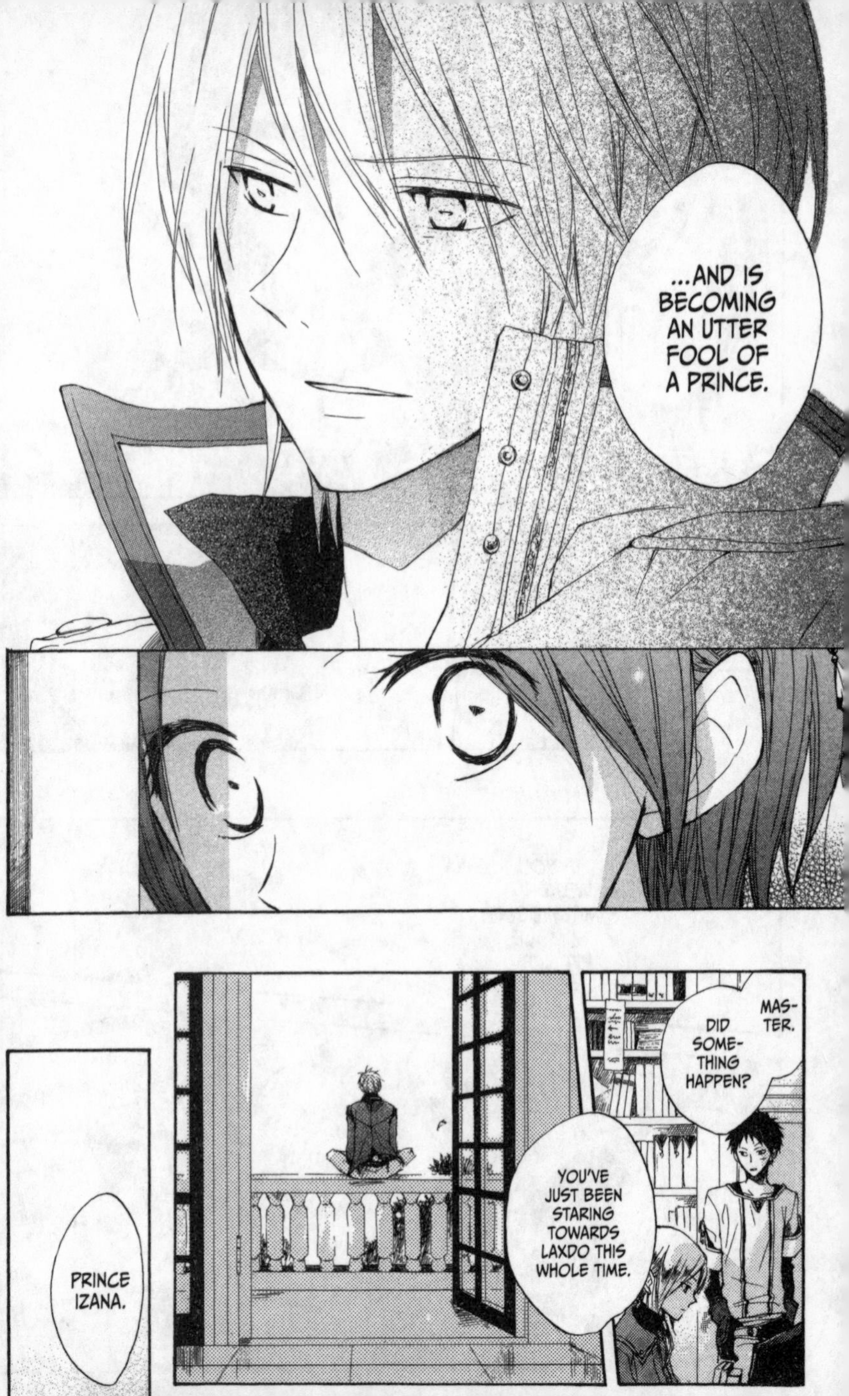
...AND IS BECOMING AN UTTER FOOL OF A PRINCE.
MAS-TER.
DID SOME-THING HAPPEN?
YOU'VE JUST BEEN STARING TOWARDS LAXDO THIS WHOLE TIME.
PRINCE IZANA.

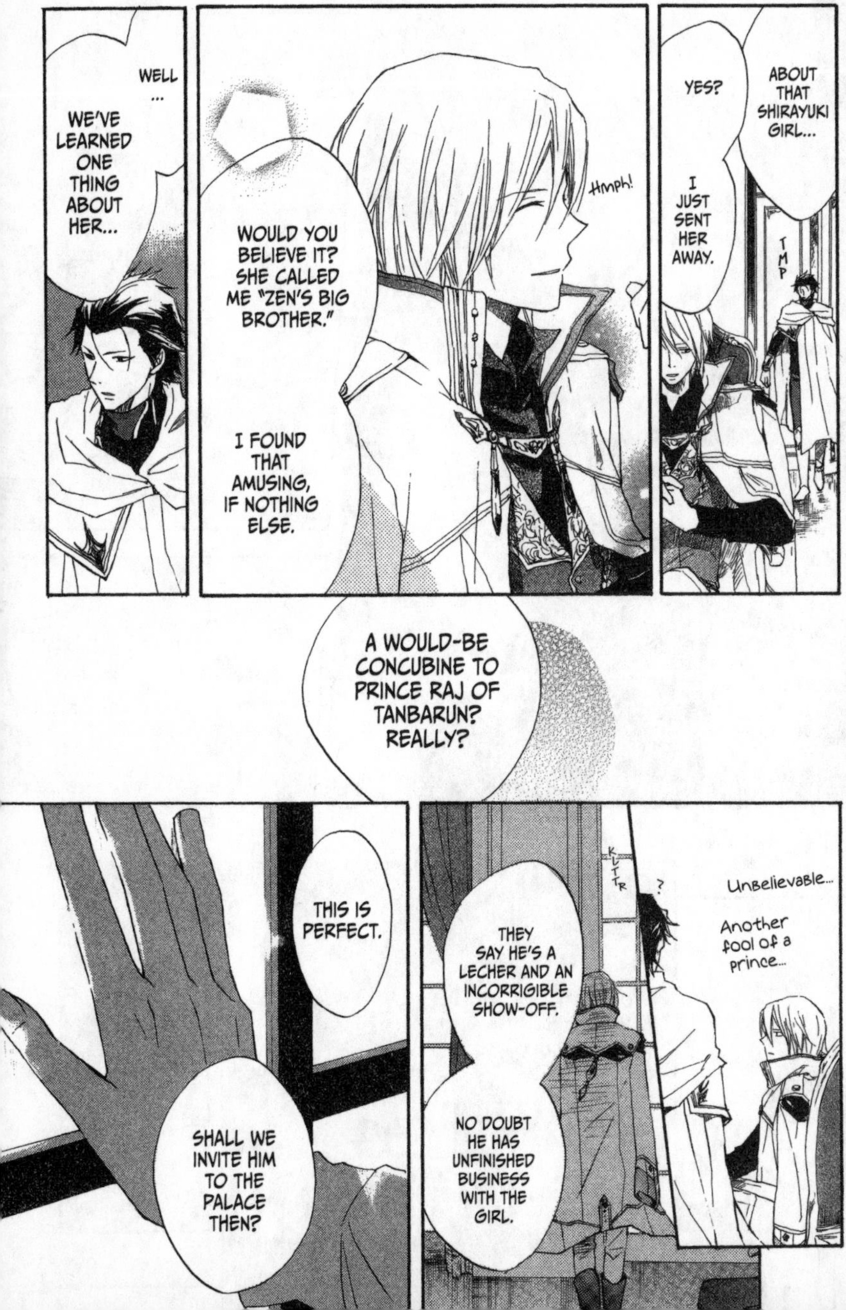
ABOUT THAT SHIRAYUKI GIRL...
YES?
I JUST SENT HER AWAY.
TMP
Hmph!
WOULD YOU BELIEVE IT? SHE CALLED ME "ZEN'S BIG BROTHER."
I FOUND THAT AMUSING, IF NOTHING ELSE.
WELL ...
WE'VE LEARNED ONE THING ABOUT HER...
A WOULD-BE CONCUBINE TO PRINCE RAJ OF TANBARUN? REALLY?
Unbelievable...
Another fool of a prince...
?
KLTTR
THEY SAY HE'S A LECHER AND AN INCORRIGIBLE SHOW-OFF.
NO DOUBT HE HAS UNFINISHED BUSINESS WITH THE GIRL.
THIS IS PERFECT.
SHALL WE INVITE HIM TO THE PALACE THEN?

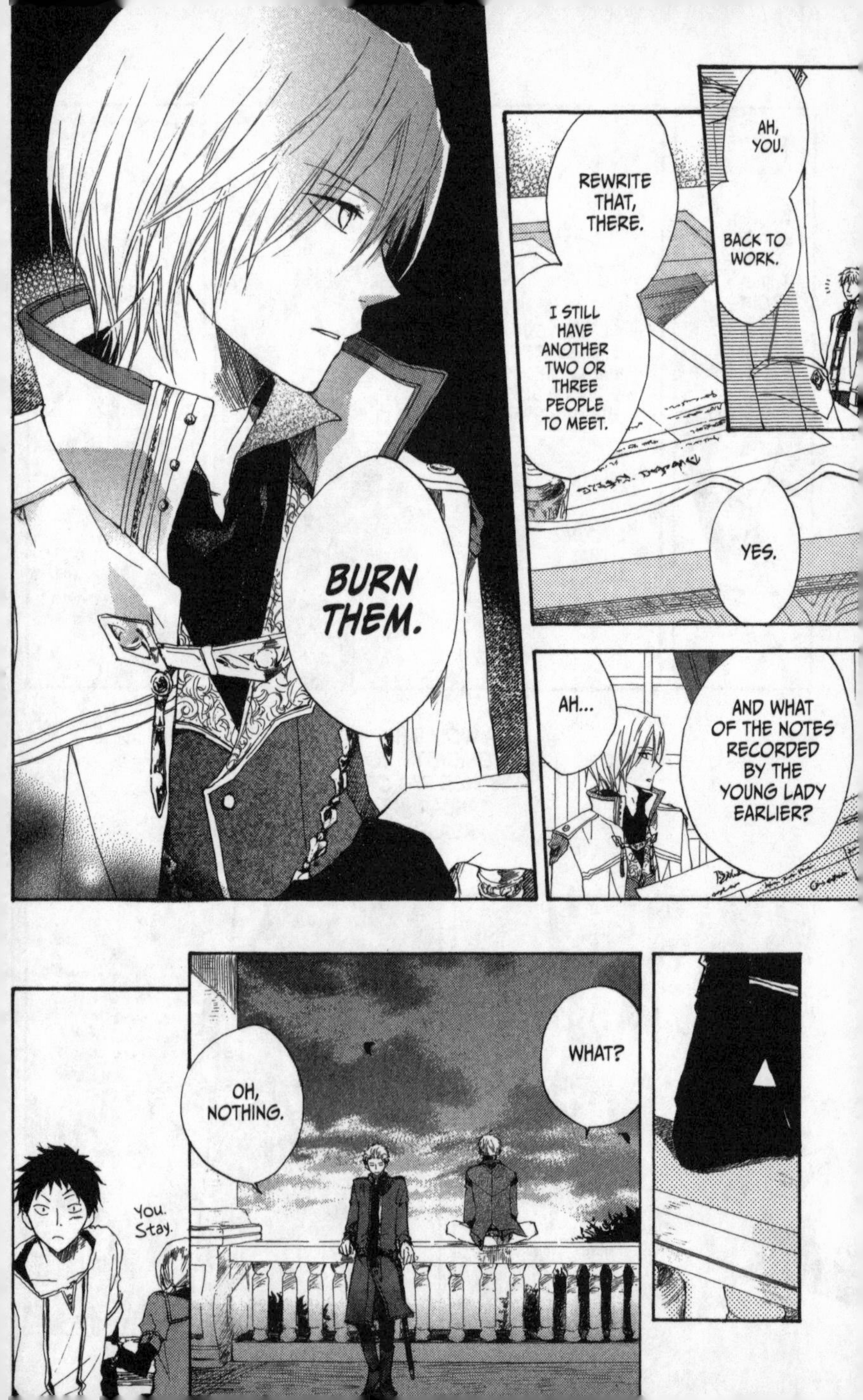
AH, YOU.
BACK TO WORK.
REWRITE THAT, THERE.
I STILL HAVE ANOTHER TWO OR THREE PEOPLE TO MEET.
YES.
AND WHAT OF THE NOTES RECORDED BY THE YOUNG LADY EARLIER?
AH...
BURN THEM.
WHAT?
OH, NOTHING.
You. Stay.

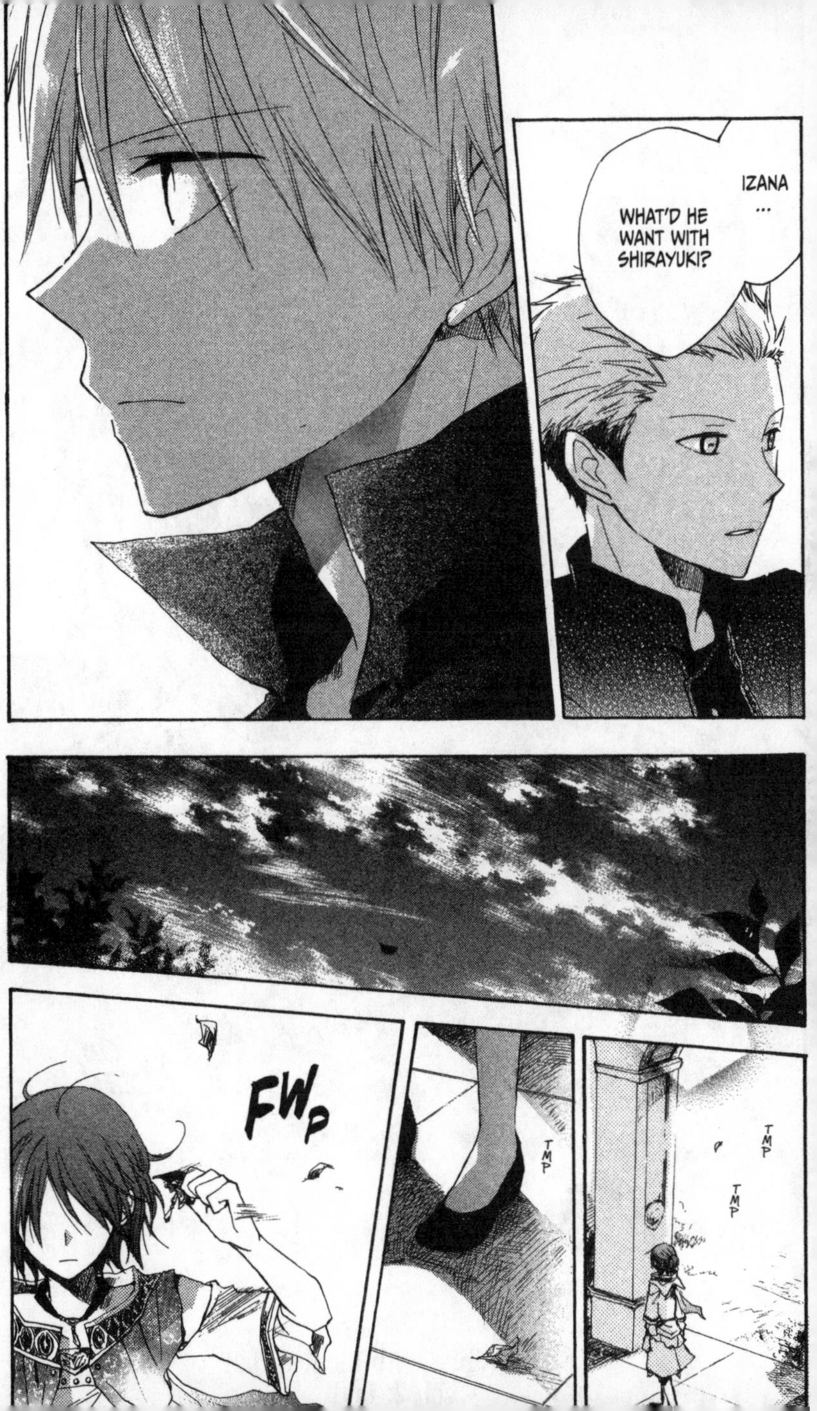
IZANA ...
WHAT'D HE WANT WITH SHIRAYUKI?
TMP
TMP
TMP
FWP

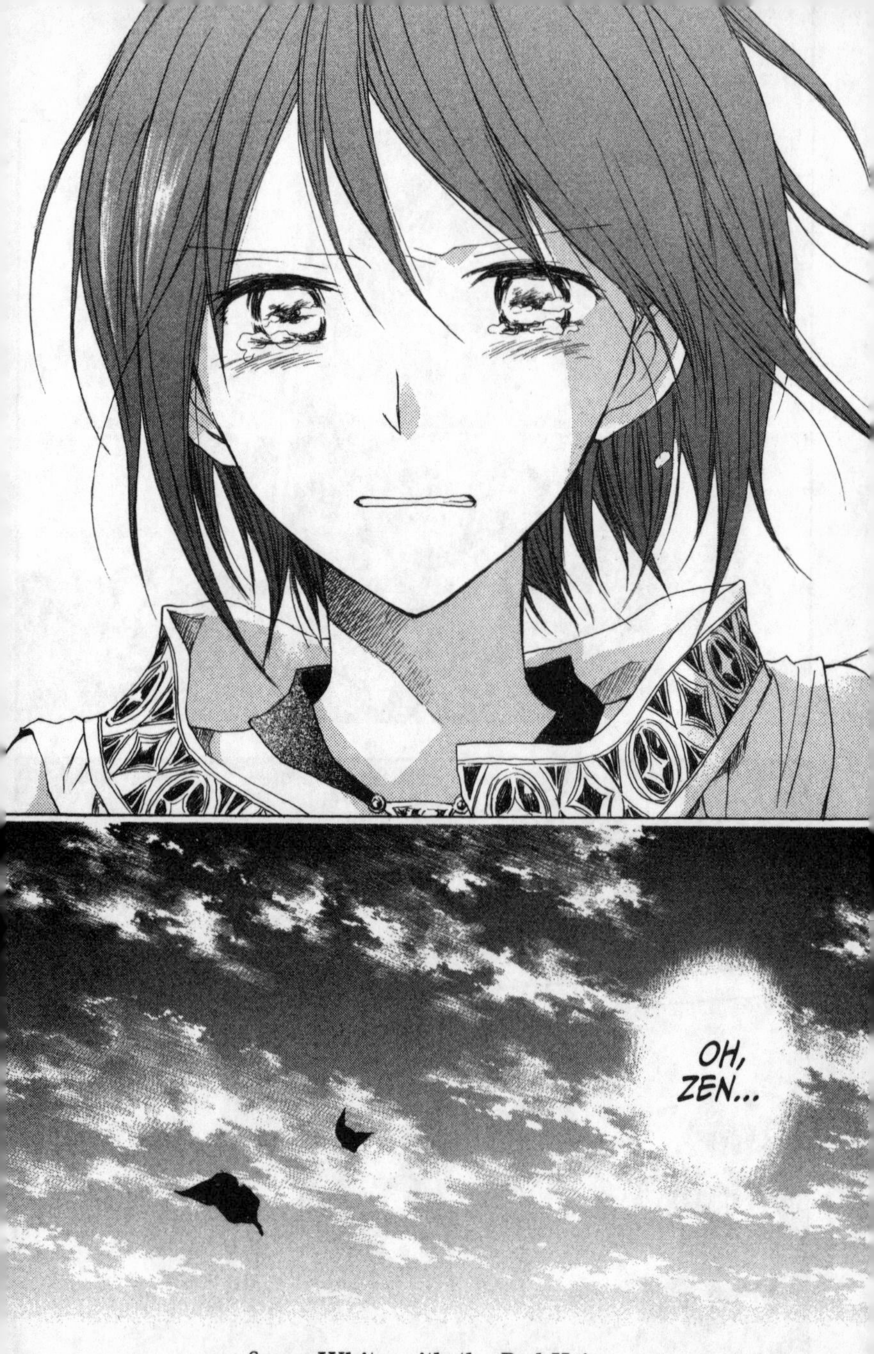
OH, ZEN...

Snow White with the Red Hair
Vol. 2: End

◆◆ Big thanks to:

-Yamashita-sama

-My editor
-The editorial department at *LaLa*
-Everyone involved in putting this book out

-My mother, big sister and father

-Fujiwara-sama (Thanks for your help!)

-Everyone who reads and supports this series

Thank you all so much!

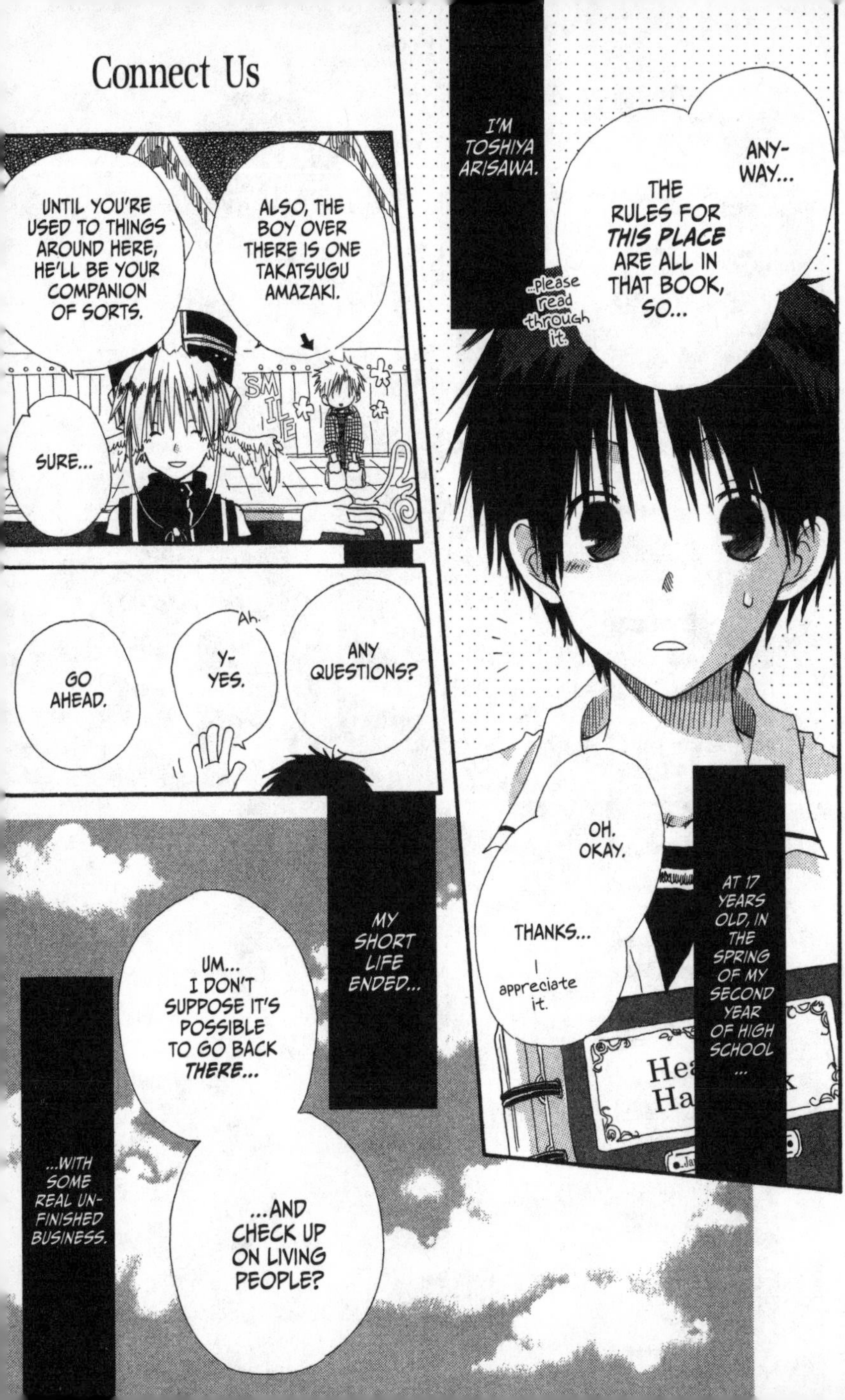
ANY-WAY... THE RULES FOR *THIS PLACE* ARE ALL IN THAT BOOK, SO...
...please read through it.
I'M TOSHIYA ARISAWA.
OH. OKAY.
THANKS... I appreciate it.
AT 17 YEARS OLD, IN THE SPRING OF MY SECOND YEAR OF HIGH SCHOOL...
ALSO, THE BOY OVER THERE IS ONE TAKATSUGU AMAZAKI.
UNTIL YOU'RE USED TO THINGS AROUND HERE, HE'LL BE YOUR COMPANION OF SORTS.
SMILE
SURE...
ANY QUESTIONS?
Ah.
Y- YES.
GO AHEAD.
MY SHORT LIFE ENDED...
UM... I DON'T SUPPOSE IT'S POSSIBLE TO GO BACK *THERE*...
...AND CHECK UP ON LIVING PEOPLE?
...WITH SOME REAL UN-FINISHED BUSINESS.

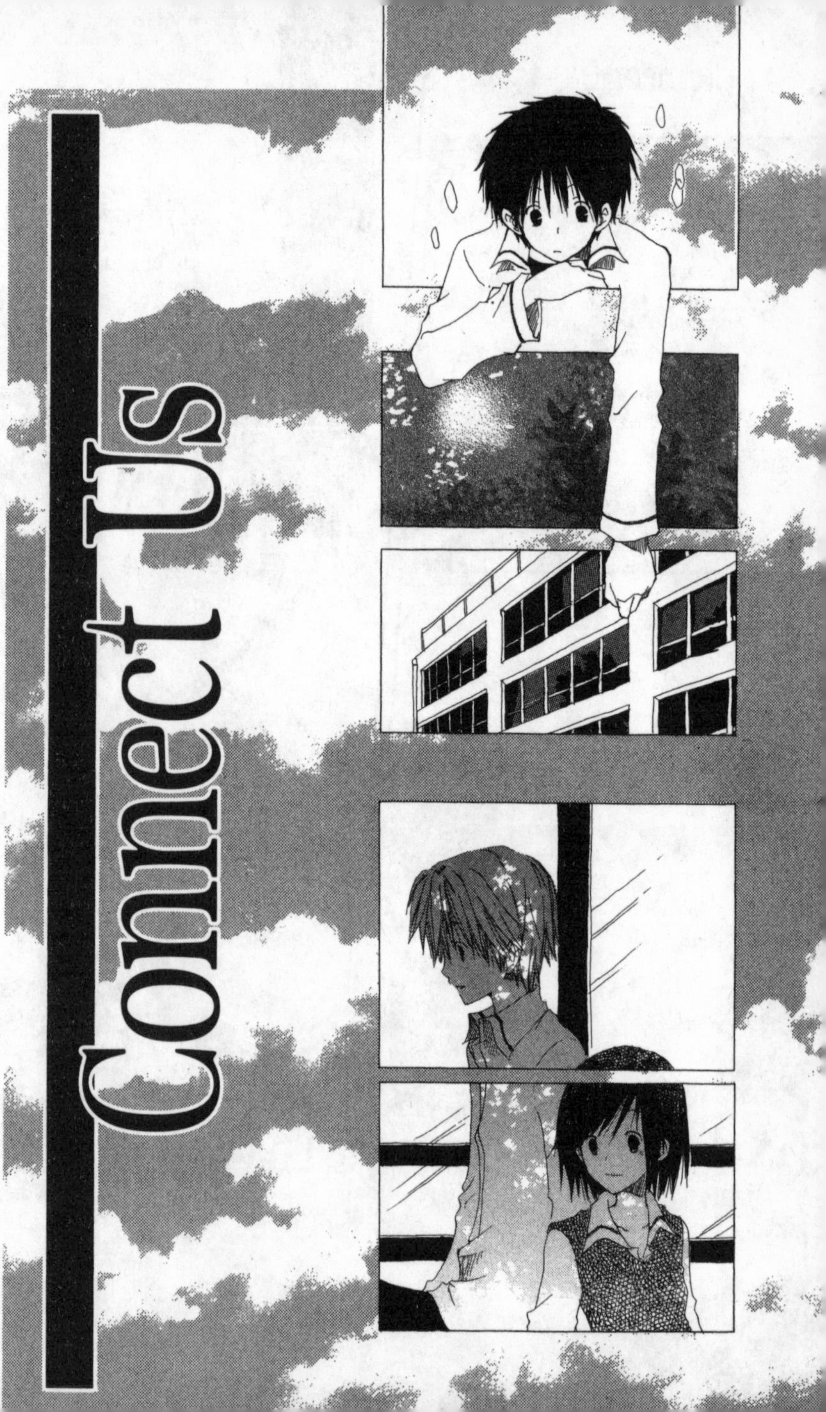
Connect Us

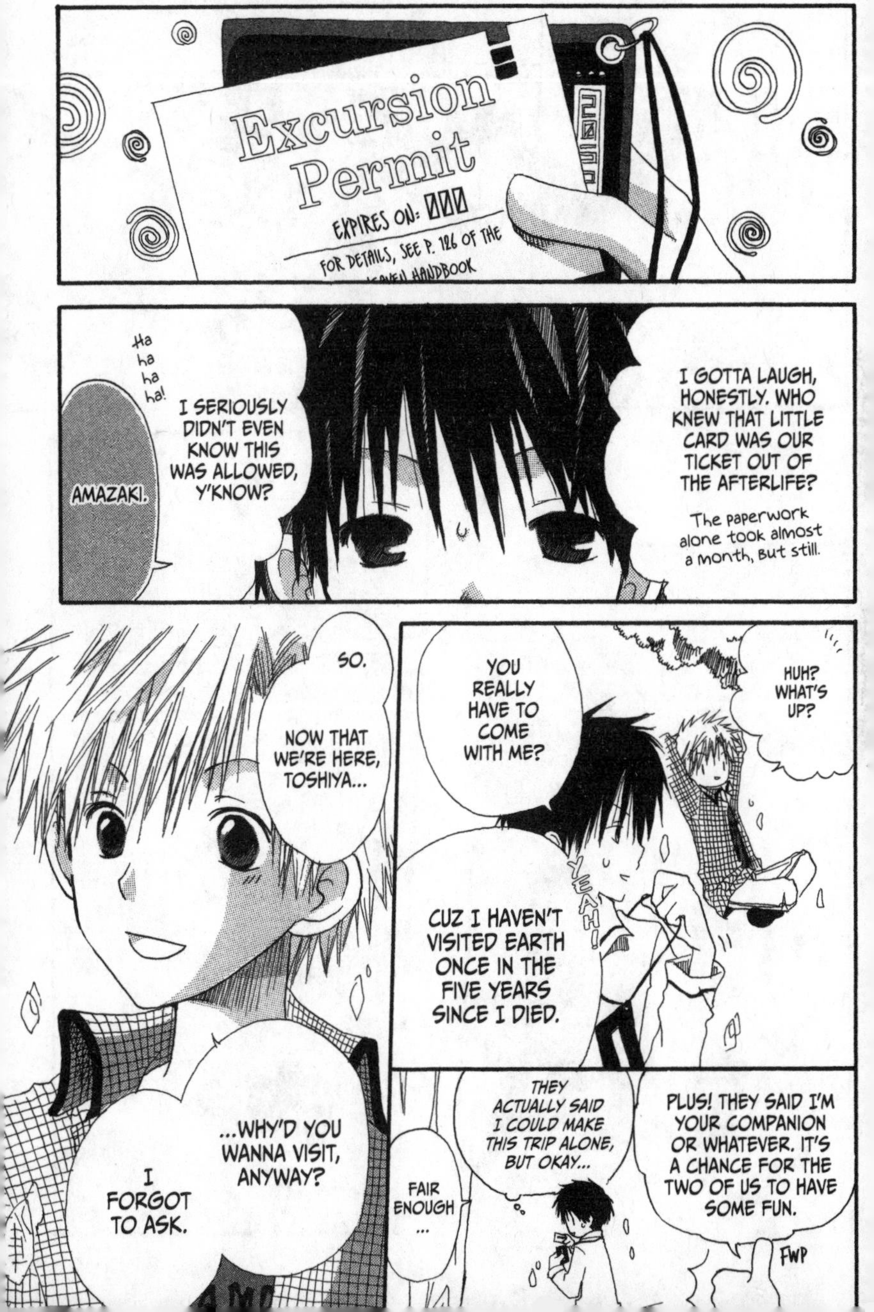
Excursion Permit
EXPIRES ON: 000
FOR DETAILS, SEE P. 126 OF THE
HANDBOOK
I GOTTA LAUGH, HONESTLY. WHO KNEW THAT LITTLE CARD WAS OUR TICKET OUT OF THE AFTERLIFE?
The paperwork alone took almost a month, but still.
I SERIOUSLY DIDN'T EVEN KNOW THIS WAS ALLOWED, Y'KNOW?
Ha ha ha ha!
AMAZAKI.
HUH? WHAT'S UP?
YOU REALLY HAVE TO COME WITH ME?
YEAH!
CUZ I HAVEN'T VISITED EARTH ONCE IN THE FIVE YEARS SINCE I DIED.
PLUS! THEY SAID I'M YOUR COMPANION OR WHATEVER. IT'S A CHANCE FOR THE TWO OF US TO HAVE SOME FUN.
FWP
THEY ACTUALLY SAID I COULD MAKE THIS TRIP ALONE, BUT OKAY...
FAIR ENOUGH...
SO.
NOW THAT WE'RE HERE, TOSHIYA...
...WHY'D YOU WANNA VISIT, ANYWAY?
I FORGOT TO ASK.

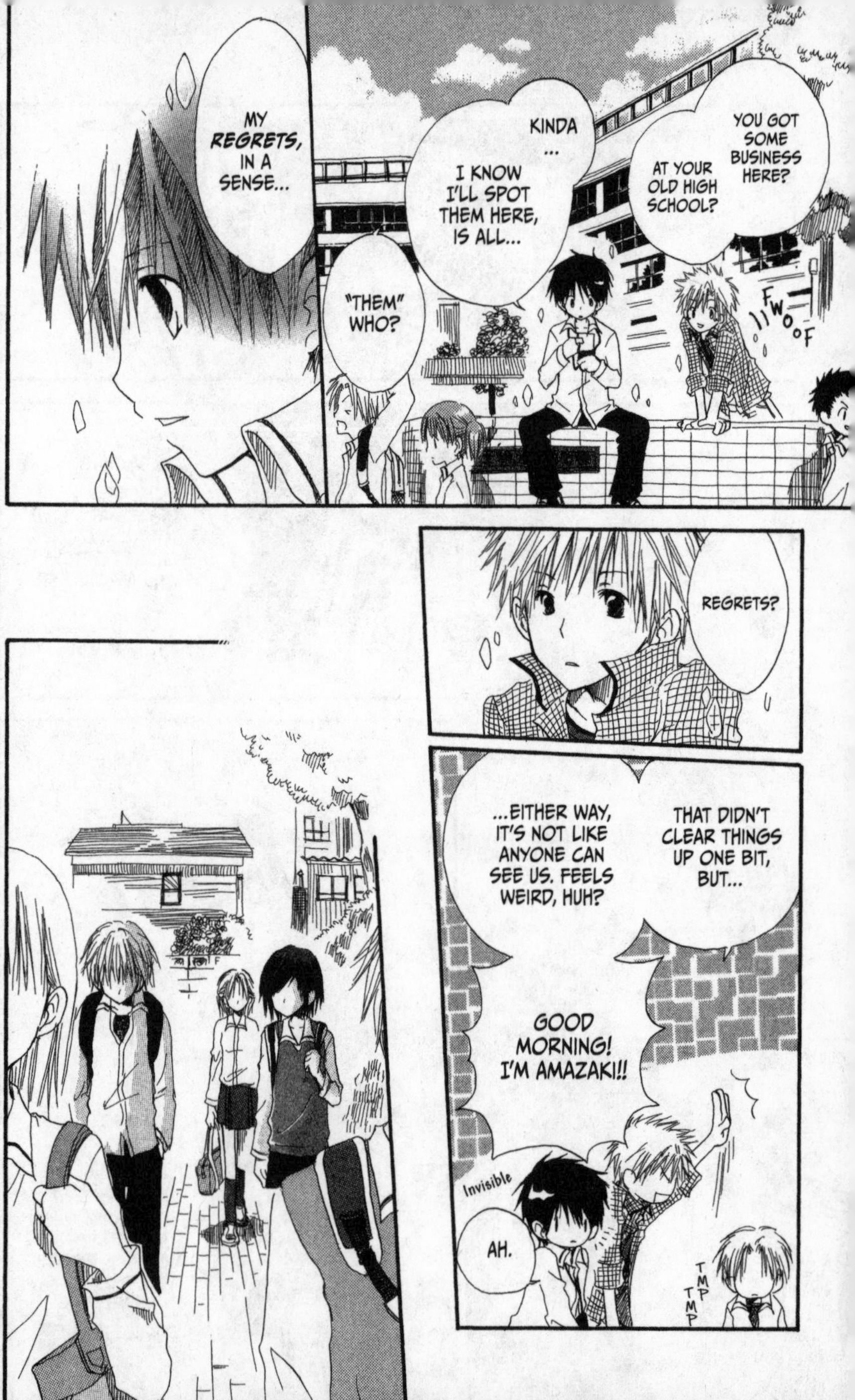
YOU GOT SOME BUSINESS HERE?
AT YOUR OLD HIGH SCHOOL?
FWOOF
KINDA ...
I KNOW I'LL SPOT THEM HERE, IS ALL...
"THEM" WHO?
MY REGRETS, IN A SENSE...
REGRETS?
THAT DIDN'T CLEAR THINGS UP ONE BIT, BUT...
...EITHER WAY, IT'S NOT LIKE ANYONE CAN SEE US. FEELS WEIRD, HUH?
GOOD MORNING! I'M AMAZAKI!!
TMP TMP
Invisible
AH.

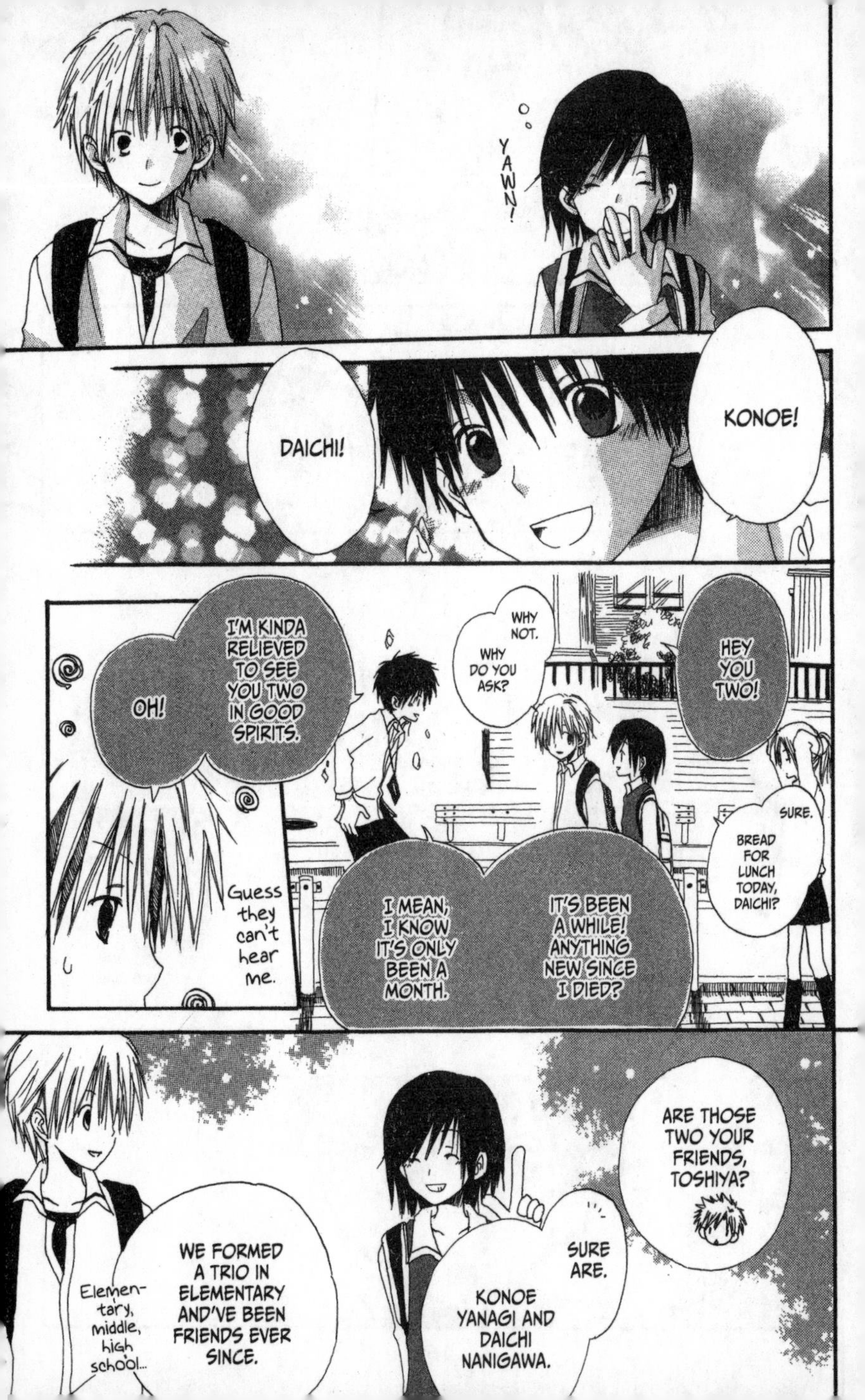
YAWN!
KONOE!
DAICHI!
HEY YOU TWO!
WHY NOT. WHY DO YOU ASK?
SURE. BREAD FOR LUNCH TODAY, DAICHI?
IT'S BEEN A WHILE! ANYTHING NEW SINCE I DIED?
I MEAN, I KNOW IT'S ONLY BEEN A MONTH.
I'M KINDA RELIEVED TO SEE YOU TWO IN GOOD SPIRITS.
OH!
Guess they can't hear me.
ARE THOSE TWO YOUR FRIENDS, TOSHIYA?
SURE ARE.
KONOE YANAGI AND DAICHI NANIGAWA.
WE FORMED A TRIO IN ELEMENTARY AND'VE BEEN FRIENDS EVER SINCE.
Elementary, middle, high school...

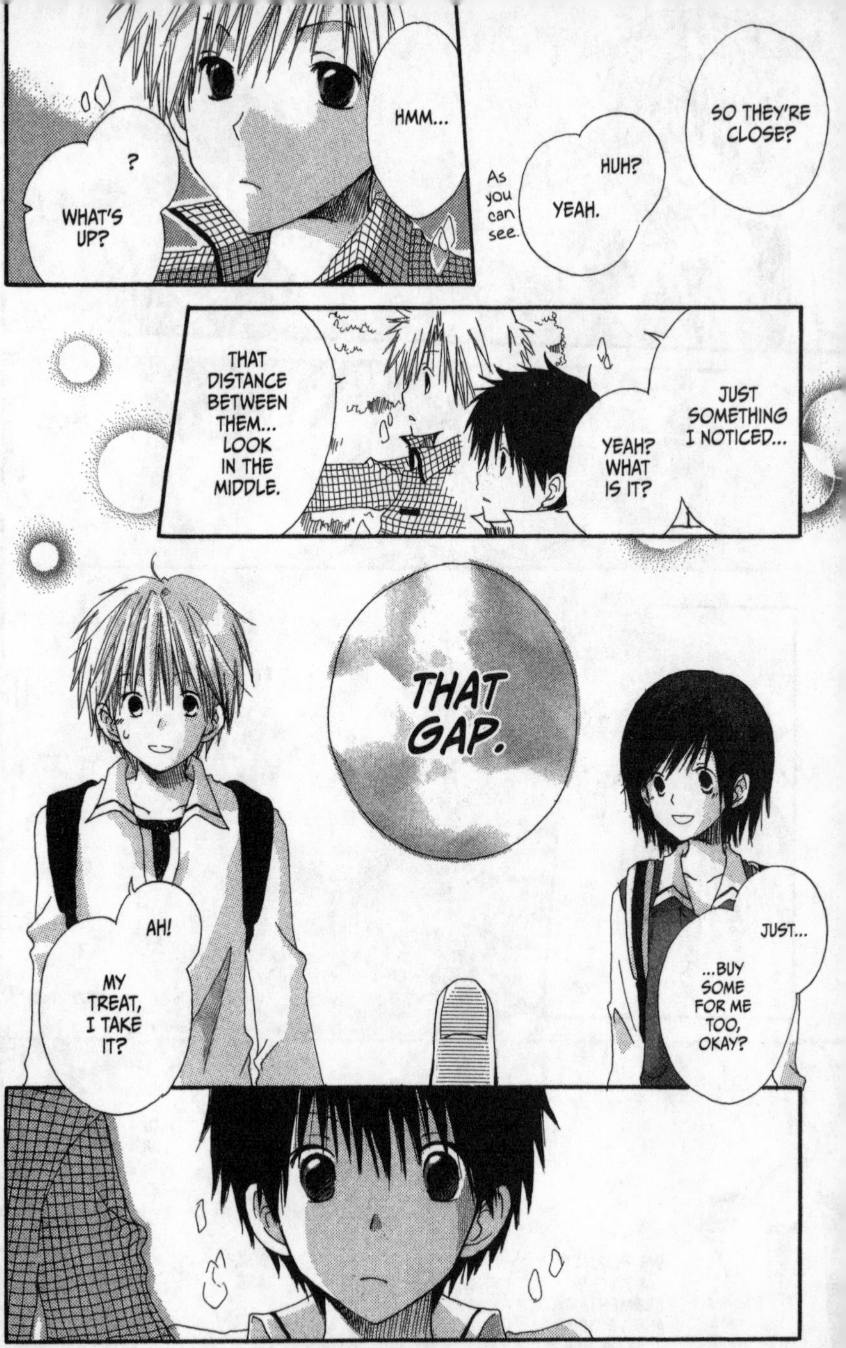
SO THEY'RE CLOSE?
HUH?
YEAH.
As you can see.
HMM...
?
WHAT'S UP?
JUST SOMETHING I NOTICED...
YEAH? WHAT IS IT?
THAT DISTANCE BETWEEN THEM... LOOK IN THE MIDDLE.
JUST...
...BUY SOME FOR ME TOO, OKAY?
THAT GAP.
AH!
MY TREAT, I TAKE IT?

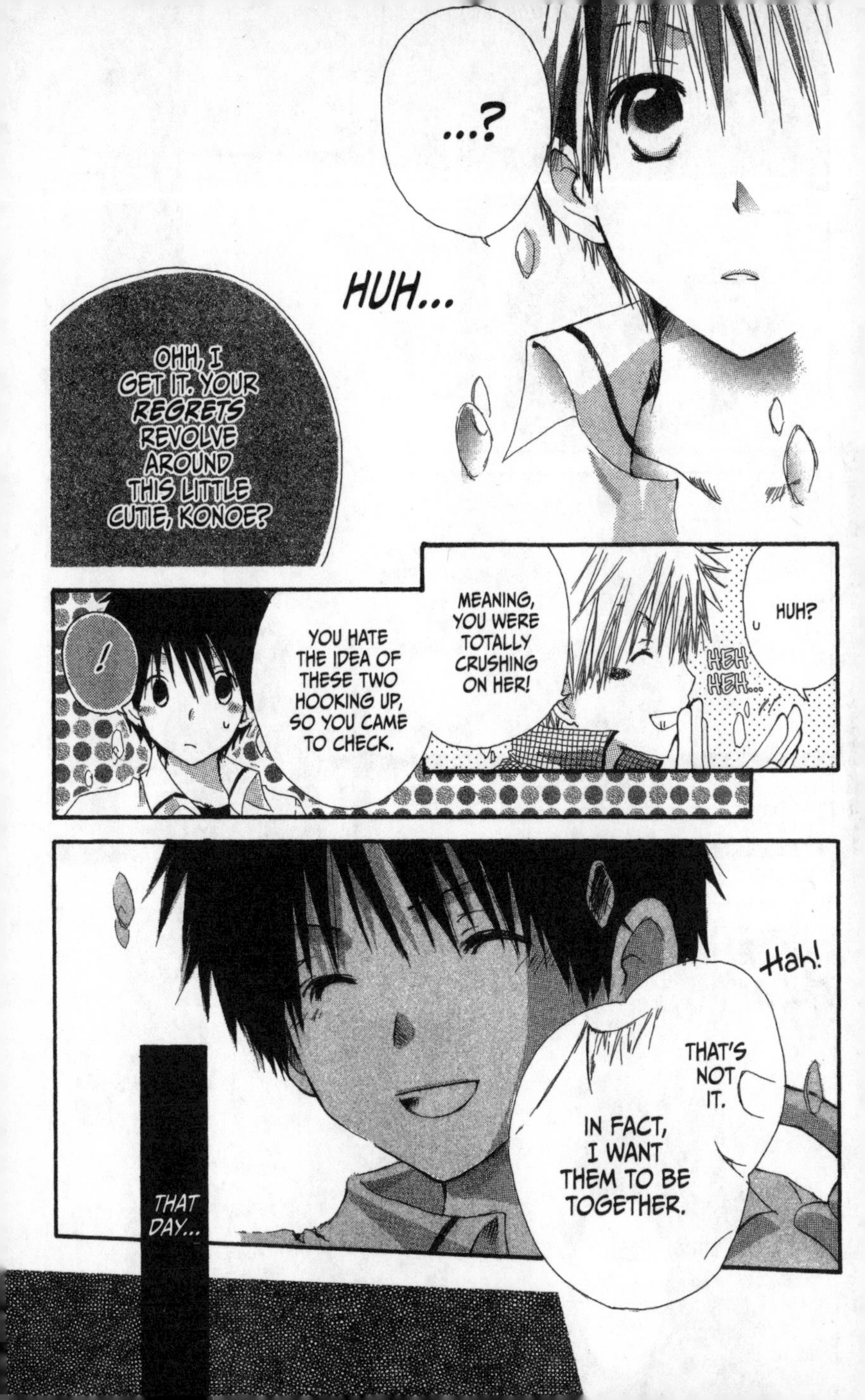
...?
HUH...
OHH, I GET IT. YOUR REGRETS REVOLVE AROUND THIS LITTLE CUTIE, KONOE?
HUH?
HEH HEH...
MEANING, YOU WERE TOTALLY CRUSHING ON HER!
YOU HATE THE IDEA OF THESE TWO HOOKING UP, SO YOU CAME TO CHECK.
!
Hah!
THAT'S NOT IT.
IN FACT, I WANT THEM TO BE TOGETHER.
THAT DAY...

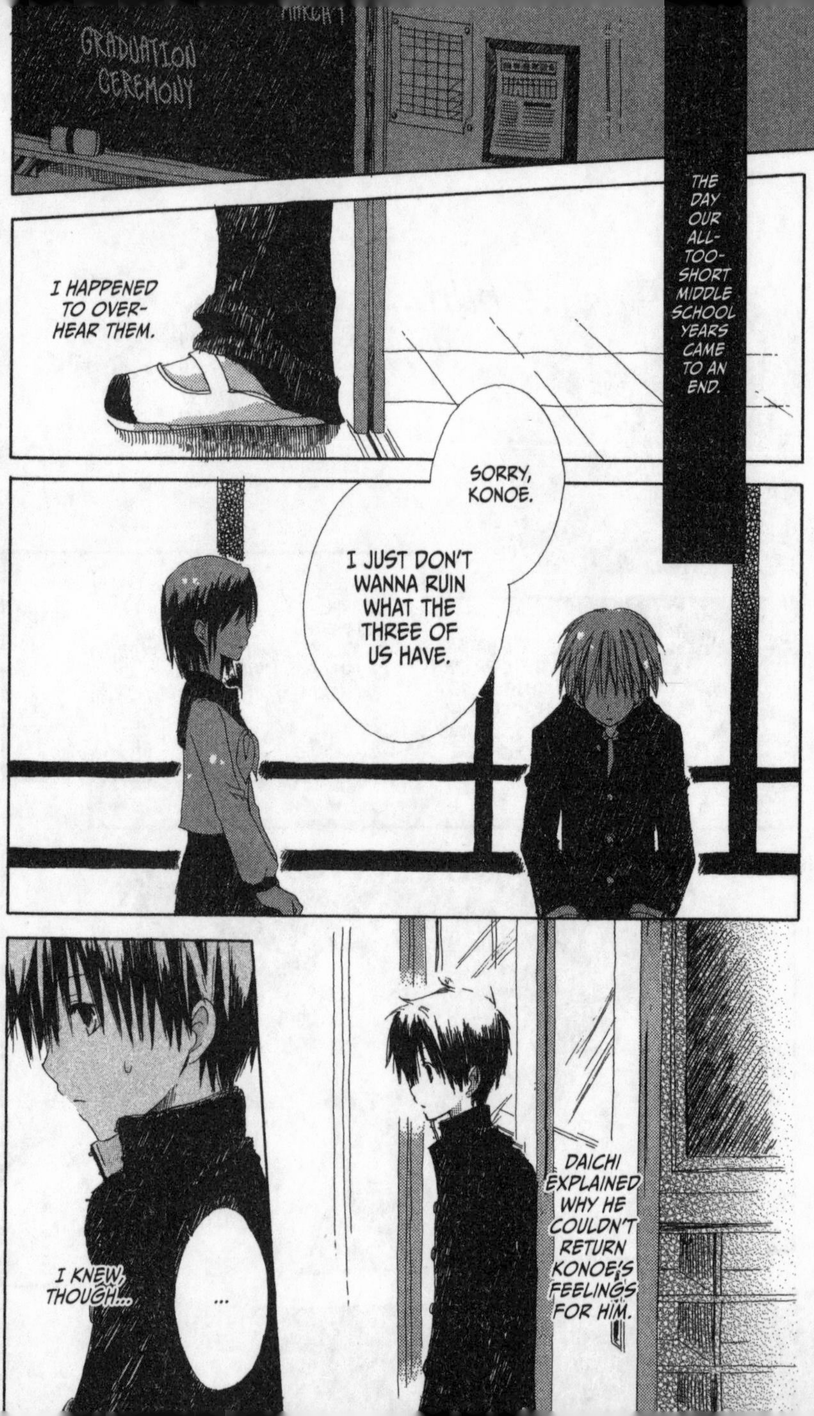

THE DAY OUR ALL-TOO-SHORT MIDDLE SCHOOL YEARS CAME TO AN END.
GRADUATION CEREMONY
I HAPPENED TO OVER-HEAR THEM.
SORRY, KONOE.
I JUST DON'T WANNA RUIN WHAT THE THREE OF US HAVE.
DAICHI EXPLAINED WHY HE COULDN'T RETURN KONOE'S FEELINGS FOR HIM.
...
I KNEW, THOUGH...

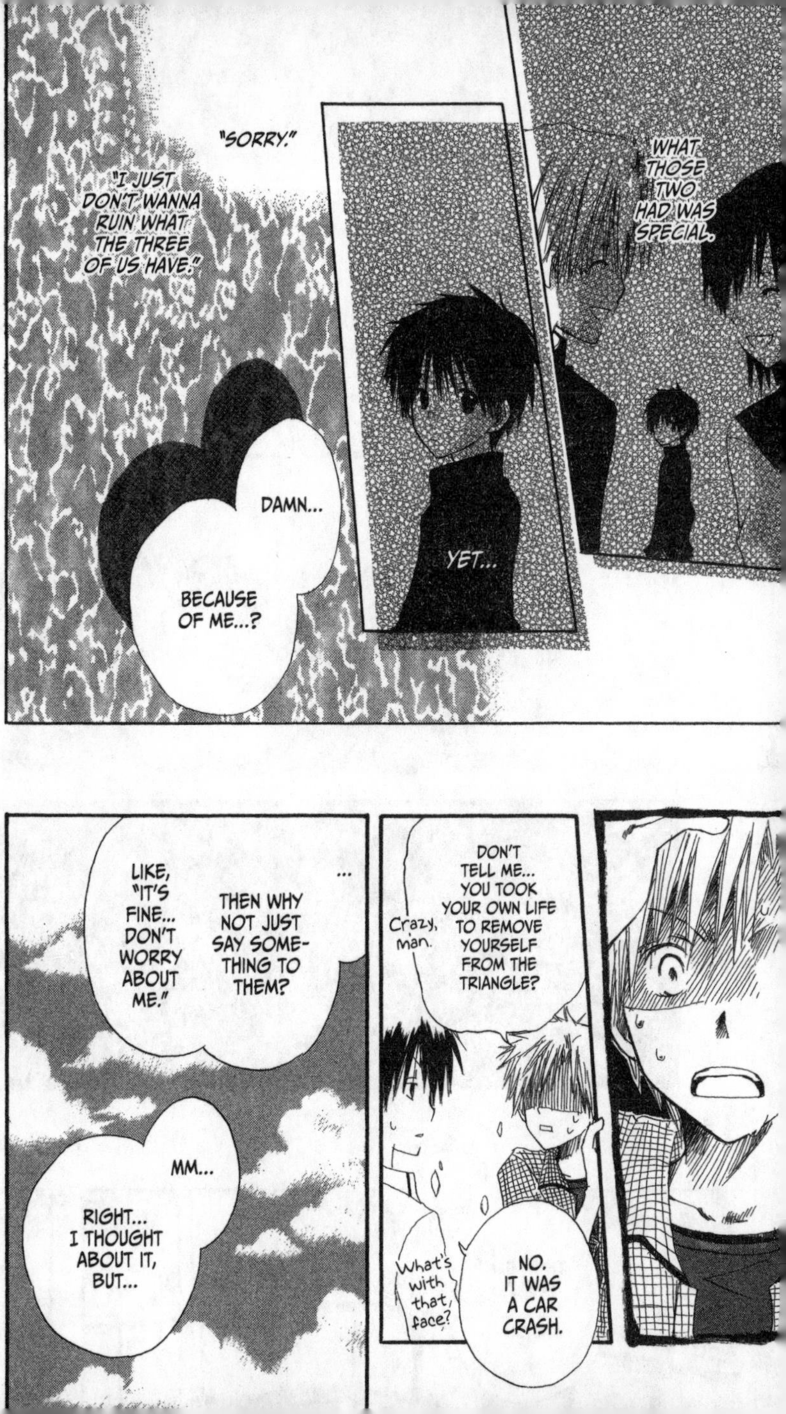
WHAT THOSE TWO HAD WAS SPECIAL.
YET...
"SORRY."
"I JUST DON'T WANNA RUIN WHAT THE THREE OF US HAVE."
DAMN...
BECAUSE OF ME...?
DON'T TELL ME... YOU TOOK YOUR OWN LIFE TO REMOVE YOURSELF FROM THE TRIANGLE?
Crazy, man.
NO. IT WAS A CAR CRASH.
What's with that face?
...
THEN WHY NOT JUST SAY SOME-THING TO THEM?
LIKE, "IT'S FINE... DON'T WORRY ABOUT ME."
MM...
RIGHT... I THOUGHT ABOUT IT, BUT...

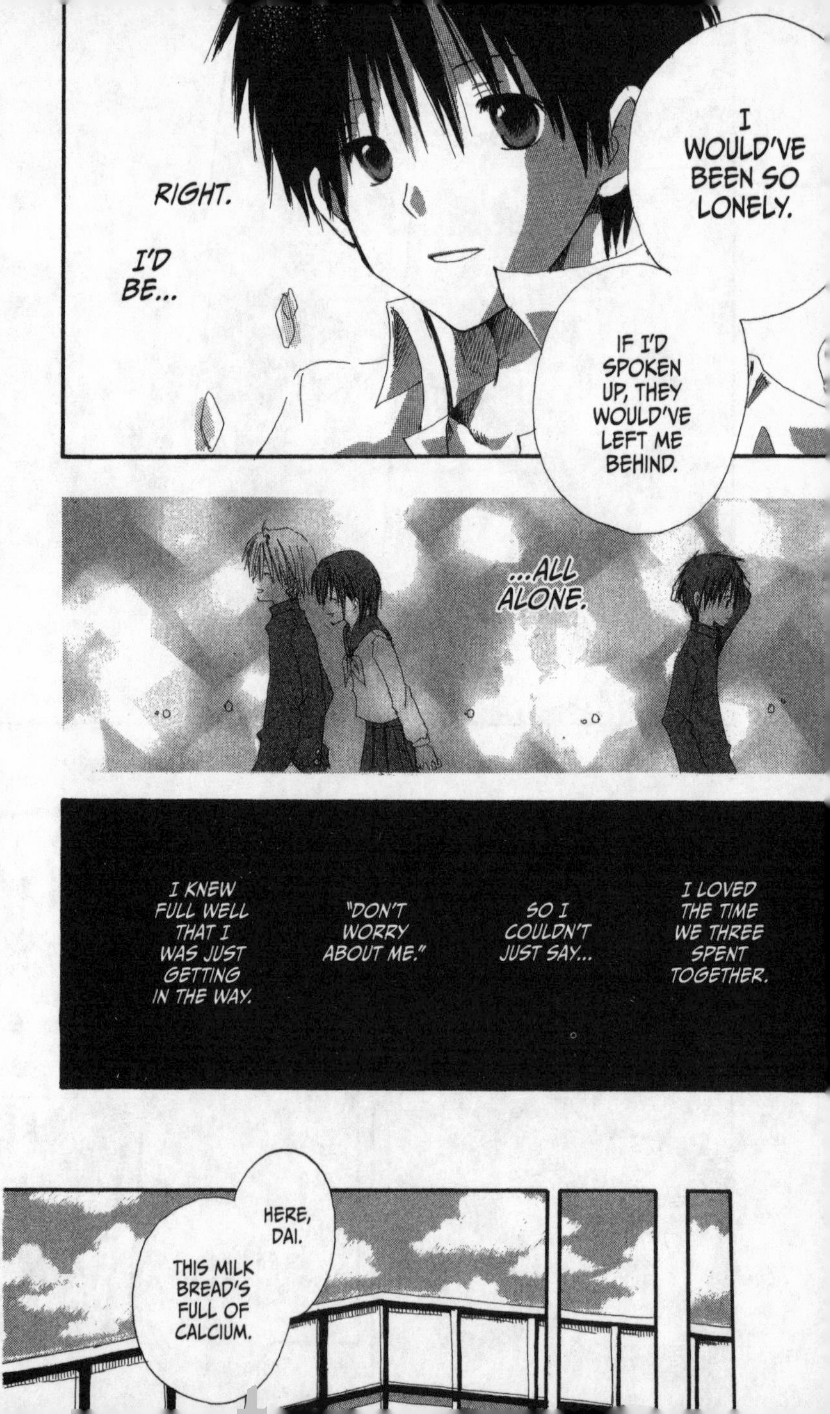
I WOULD'VE BEEN SO LONELY.
IF I'D SPOKEN UP, THEY WOULD'VE LEFT ME BEHIND.
RIGHT.
I'D BE...
...ALL ALONE.
I LOVED THE TIME WE THREE SPENT TOGETHER.
SO I COULDN'T JUST SAY...
"DON'T WORRY ABOUT ME."
I KNEW FULL WELL THAT I WAS JUST GETTING IN THE WAY.
HERE, DAI.
THIS MILK BREAD'S FULL OF CALCIUM.

CONNECT US

My first one-shot after my debut.

W-wow.

This ran in April of 2003, which doesn't sound too long ago—but to me, this story feels like a relic of my grade school days. So when they asked me about publishing it in this book, my eyes practically popped out of my head.

The art isn't great, and it's a little unsettling to look at in retrospect, but there's still something fun about this story.

This sort of nostalgia... It's no laughing matter...

Thank you for reading.

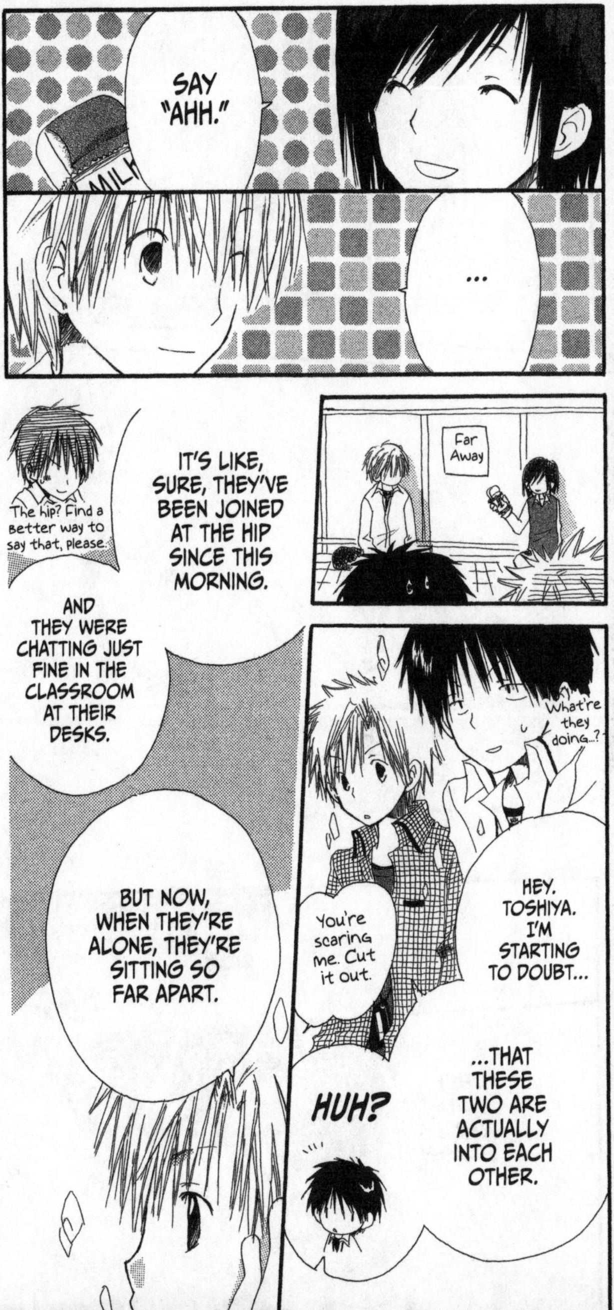
SAY "AHH."
MILK
...
Far Away
What're they doing...?
HEY. TOSHIYA. I'M STARTING TO DOUBT...
You're scaring me. Cut it out.
...THAT THESE TWO ARE ACTUALLY INTO EACH OTHER.
HUH?
IT'S LIKE, SURE, THEY'VE BEEN JOINED AT THE HIP SINCE THIS MORNING.
The hip? Find a better way to say that, please.
AND THEY WERE CHATTING JUST FINE IN THE CLASSROOM AT THEIR DESKS.
BUT NOW, WHEN THEY'RE ALONE, THEY'RE SITTING SO FAR APART.

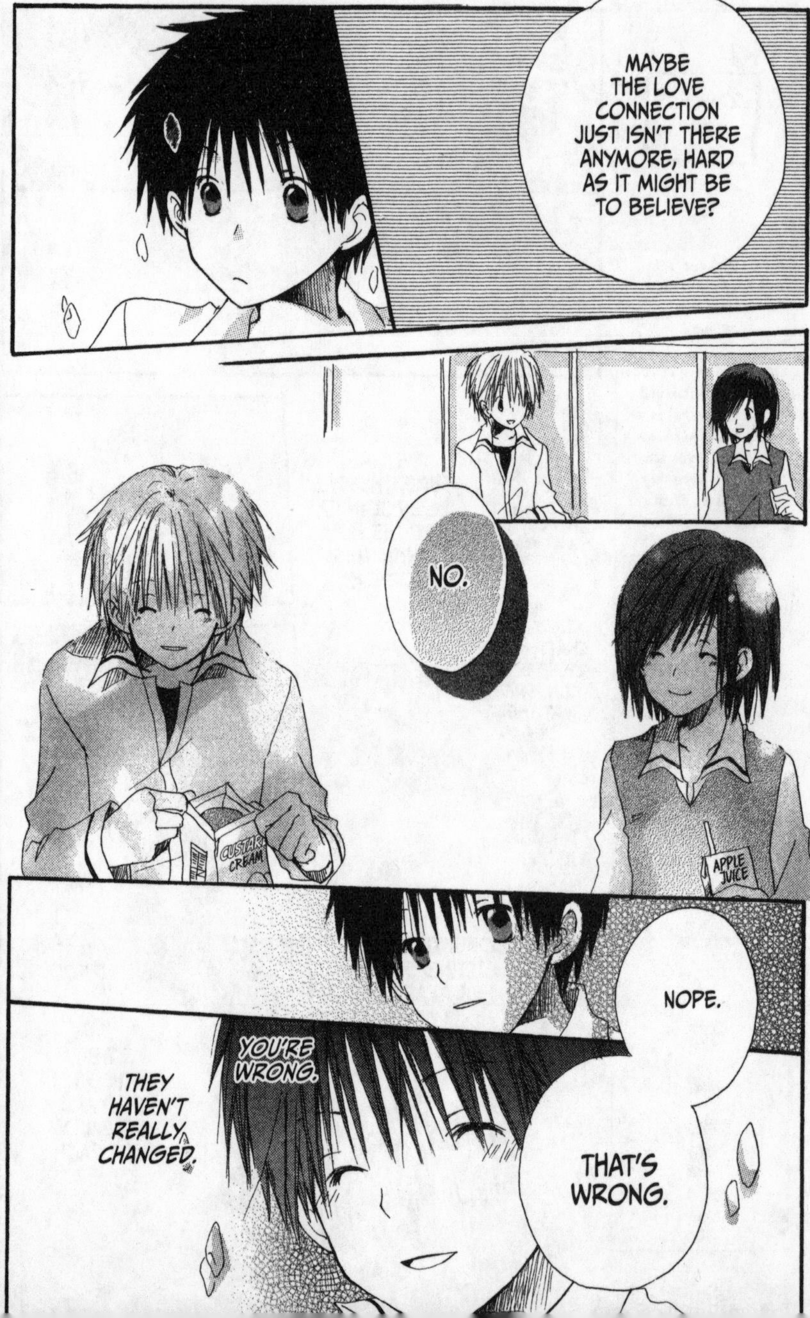
MAYBE THE LOVE CONNECTION JUST ISN'T THERE ANYMORE, HARD AS IT MIGHT BE TO BELIEVE?
NO.
APPLE JUICE
NOPE.
THAT'S WRONG.
YOU'RE WRONG.
THEY HAVEN'T REALLY CHANGED.

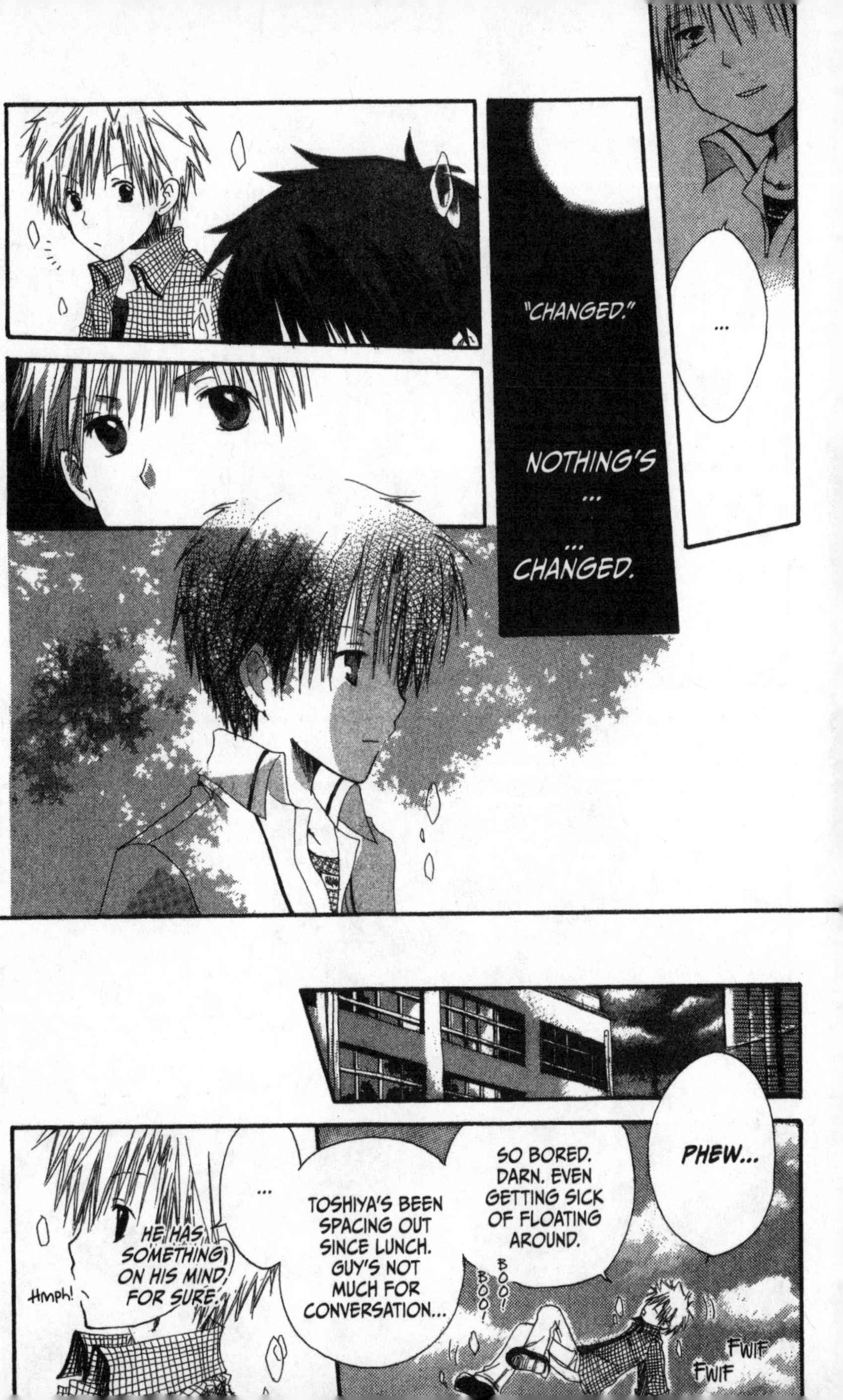

...
"CHANGED."
NOTHING'S ...
... CHANGED.
PHEW...
SO BORED. DARN. EVEN GETTING SICK OF FLOATING AROUND.
BOO! BOO!
FWIF FWIF
TOSHIYA'S BEEN SPACING OUT SINCE LUNCH. GUY'S NOT MUCH FOR CONVERSATION...
...
HE HAS SOMETHING ON HIS MIND, FOR SURE.
Hmph!

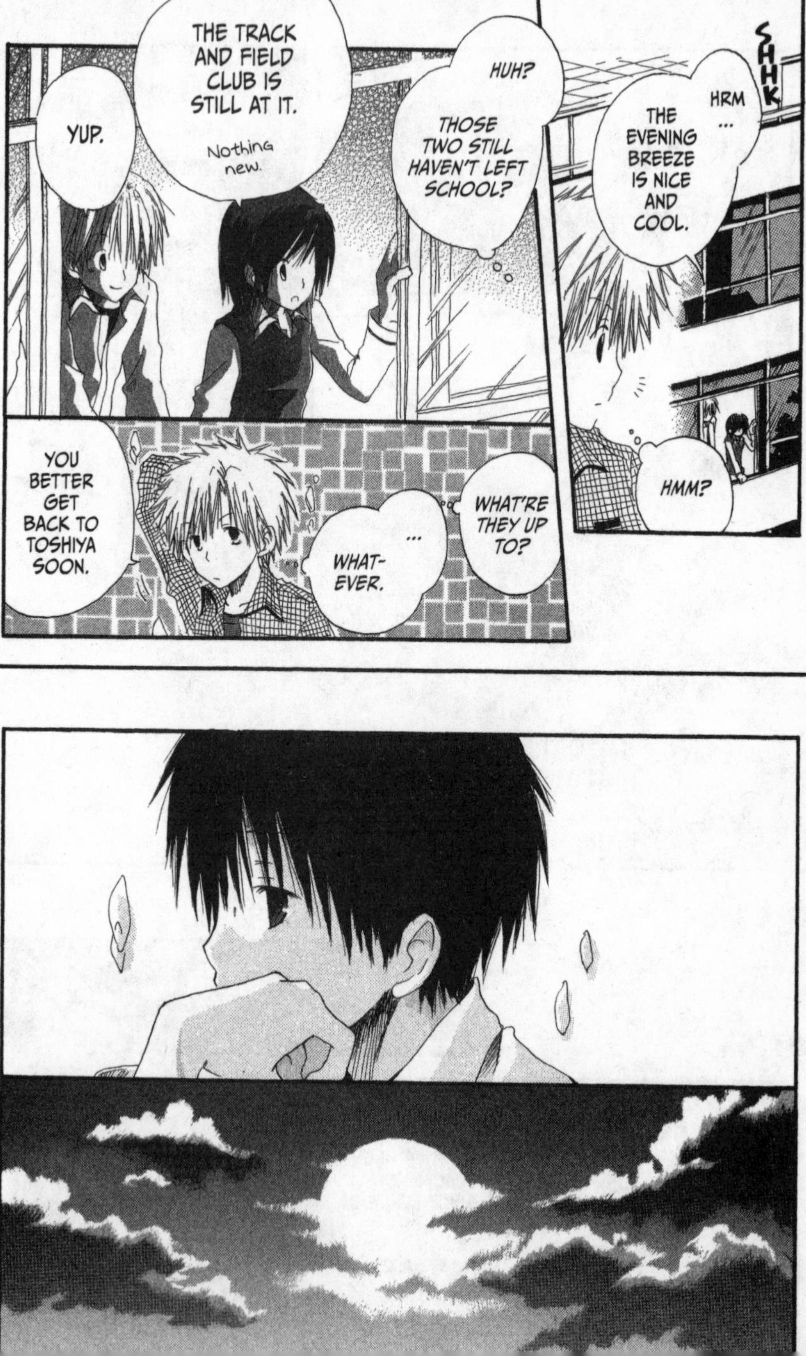
SHHK
HRM...
THE EVENING BREEZE IS NICE AND COOL.
HMM?
HUH?
THOSE TWO STILL HAVEN'T LEFT SCHOOL?
THE TRACK AND FIELD CLUB IS STILL AT IT.
Nothing new.
YUP.
WHAT'RE THEY UP TO?
...
WHAT-EVER.
YOU BETTER GET BACK TO TOSHIYA SOON.

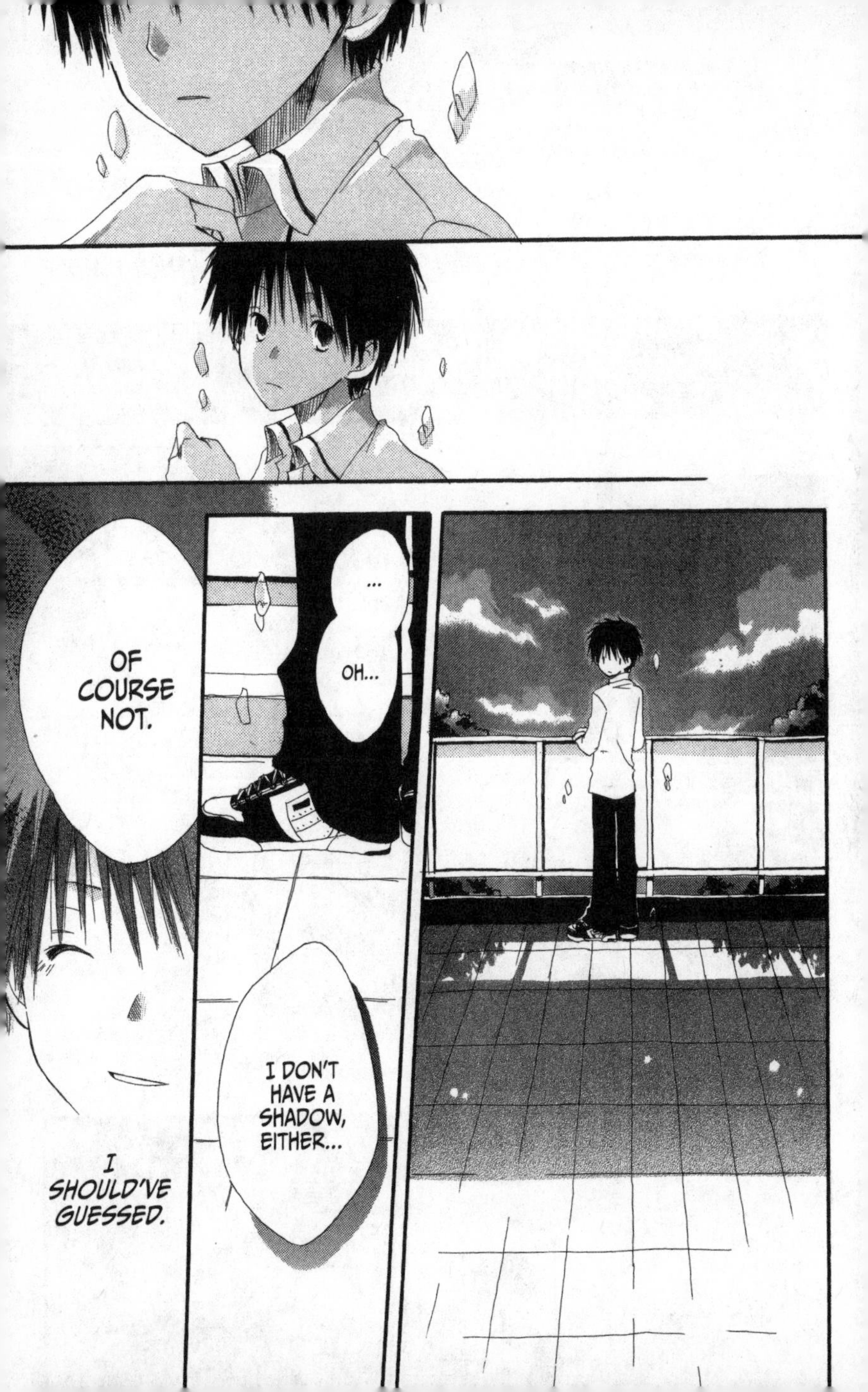
...
OH...
I DON'T HAVE A SHADOW, EITHER...
OF COURSE NOT.
I SHOULD'VE GUESSED.

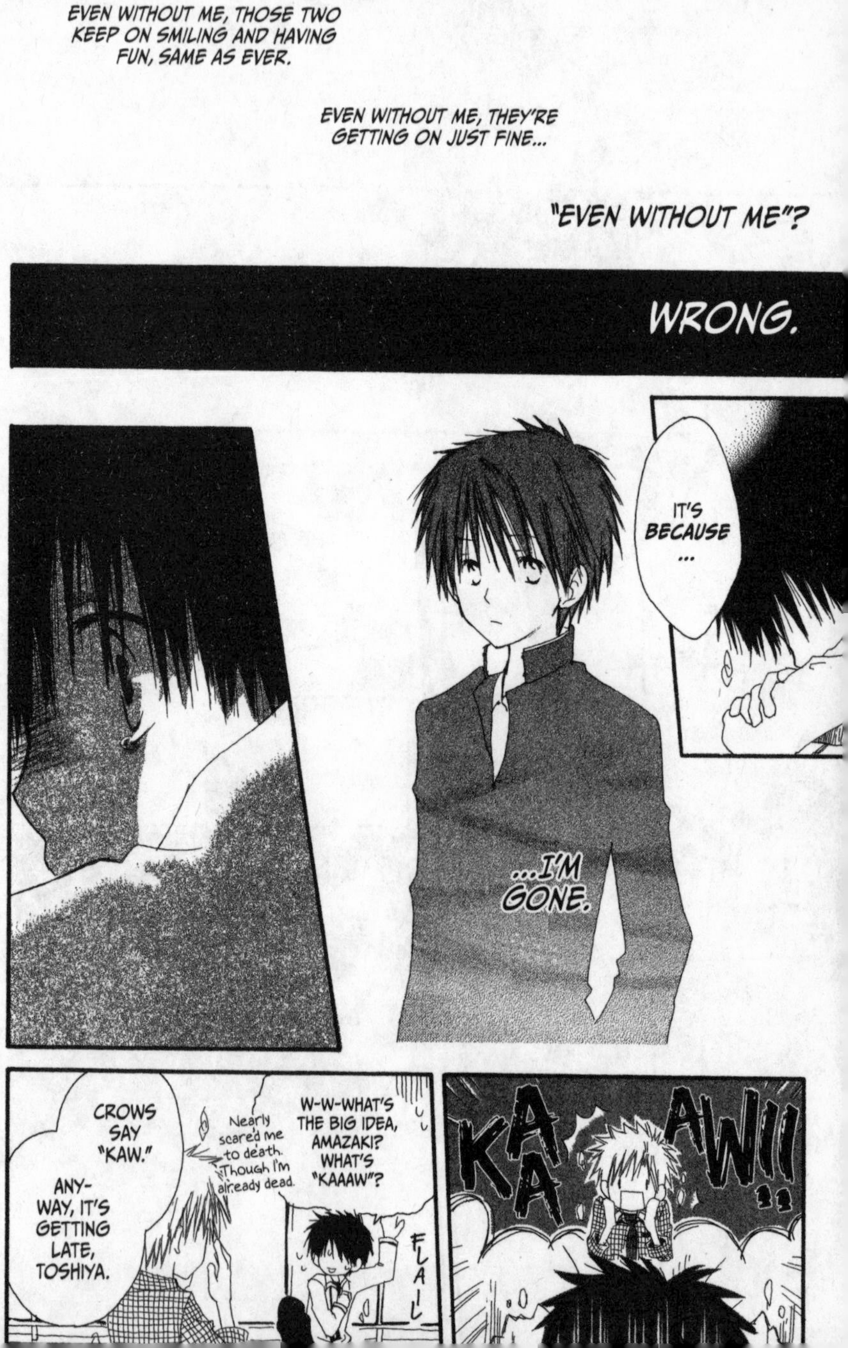
EVEN WITHOUT ME, THOSE TWO KEEP ON SMILING AND HAVING FUN, SAME AS EVER.
EVEN WITHOUT ME, THEY'RE GETTING ON JUST FINE...
"EVEN WITHOUT ME"?
WRONG.
IT'S BECAUSE ...
...I'M GONE.
KAAAW!!
W-W-WHAT'S THE BIG IDEA, AMAZAKI? WHAT'S "KAAAW"?
Nearly scared me to death. Though I'm already dead.
FLAIL
CROWS SAY "KAW."
ANY-WAY, IT'S GETTING LATE, TOSHIYA.

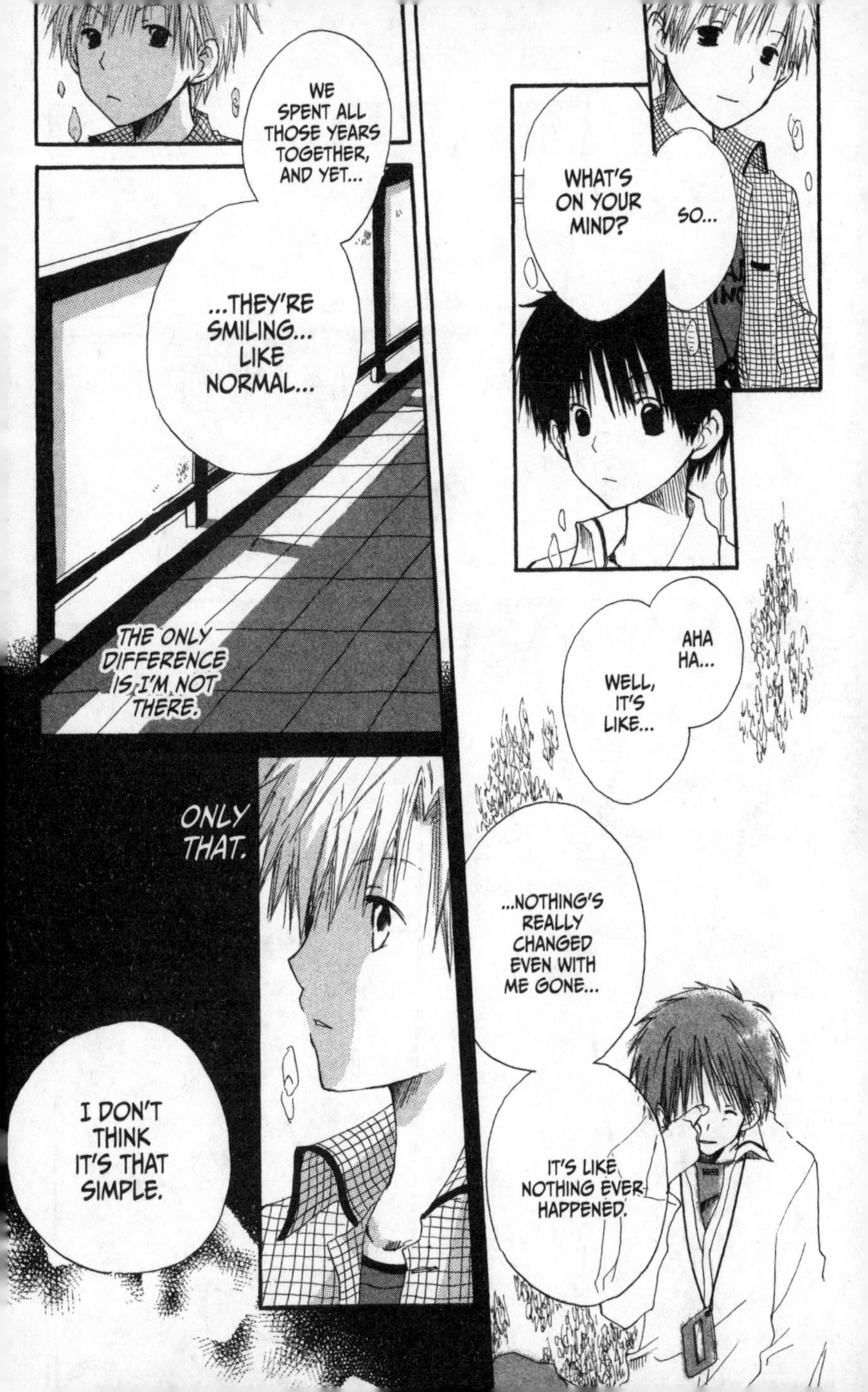
SO...
WHAT'S ON YOUR MIND?
AHA HA...
WELL, IT'S LIKE...
...NOTHING'S REALLY CHANGED EVEN WITH ME GONE...
IT'S LIKE NOTHING EVER HAPPENED.
WE SPENT ALL THOSE YEARS TOGETHER, AND YET...
...THEY'RE SMILING... LIKE NORMAL...
THE ONLY DIFFERENCE IS I'M NOT THERE.
ONLY THAT.
I DON'T THINK IT'S THAT SIMPLE.

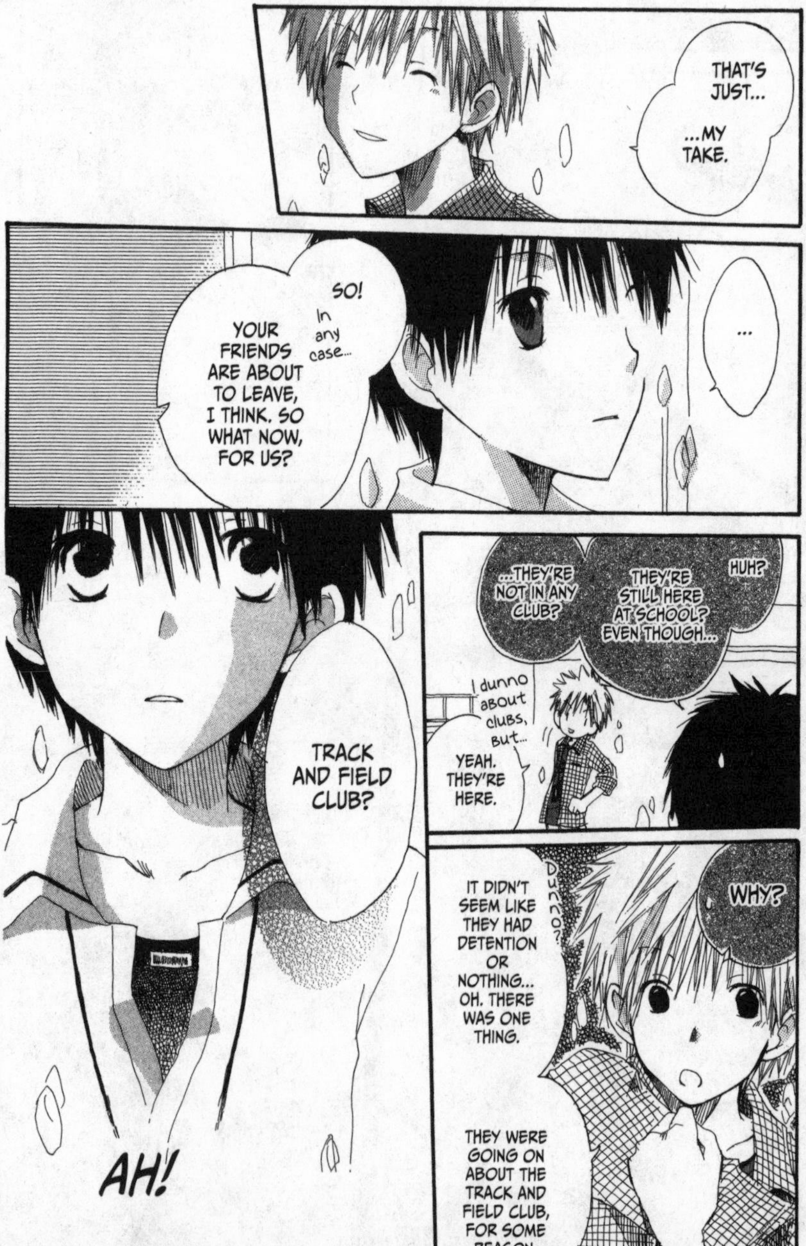
THAT'S JUST...
...MY TAKE.
...
SO!
In any case...
YOUR FRIENDS ARE ABOUT TO LEAVE, I THINK. SO WHAT NOW, FOR US?
HUH?
THEY'RE STILL HERE AT SCHOOL? EVEN THOUGH...
...THEY'RE NOT IN ANY CLUB?
I dunno about clubs, but...
YEAH. THEY'RE HERE.
WHY?
Dunno?
IT DIDN'T SEEM LIKE THEY HAD DETENTION OR NOTHING... OH. THERE WAS ONE THING.
THEY WERE GOING ON ABOUT THE TRACK AND FIELD CLUB, FOR SOME REASON.
TRACK AND FIELD CLUB?
AH!

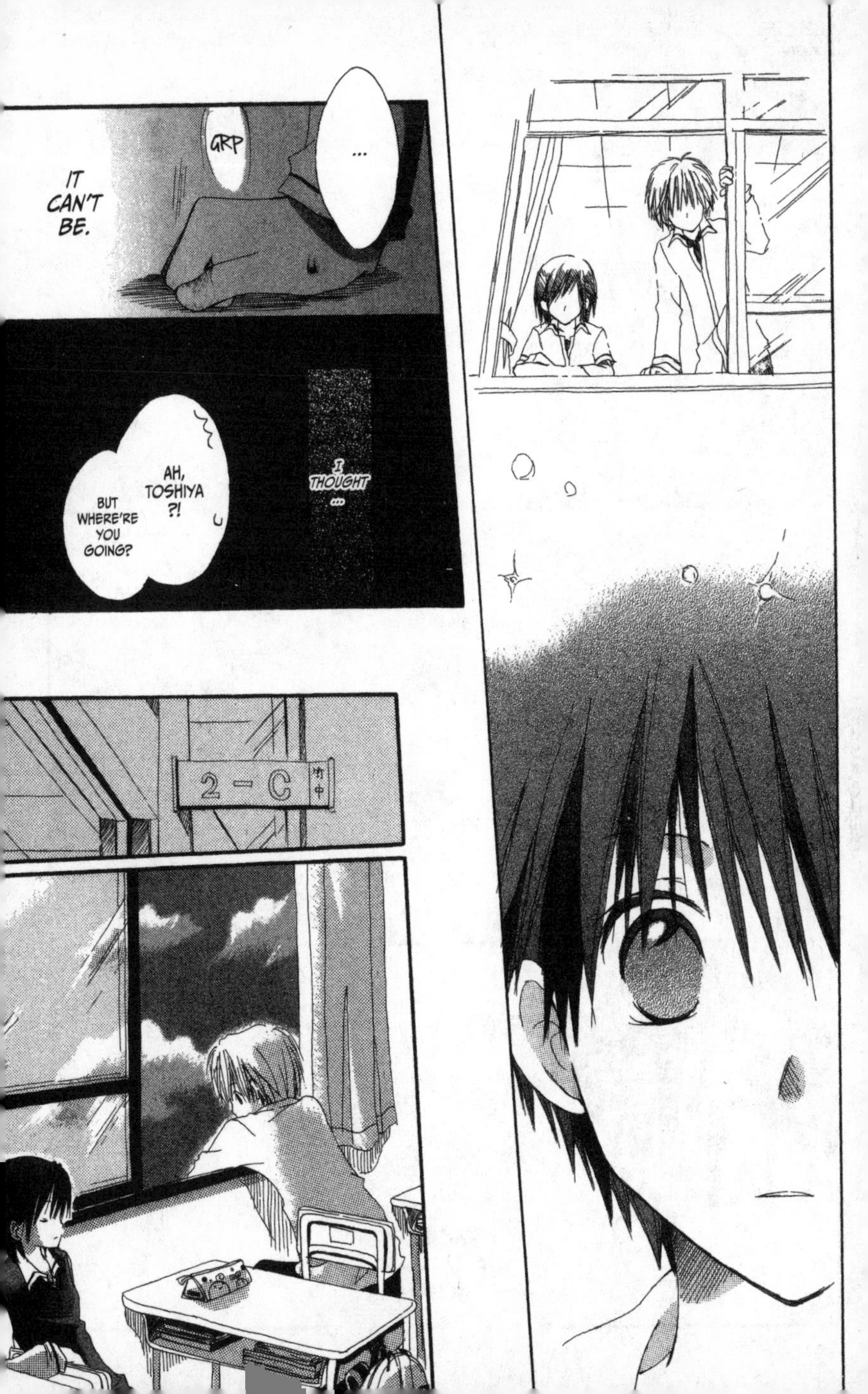
...
GRP
IT CAN'T BE.
I THOUGHT ...
AH, TOSHIYA?!
BUT WHERE'RE YOU GOING?
2 – C

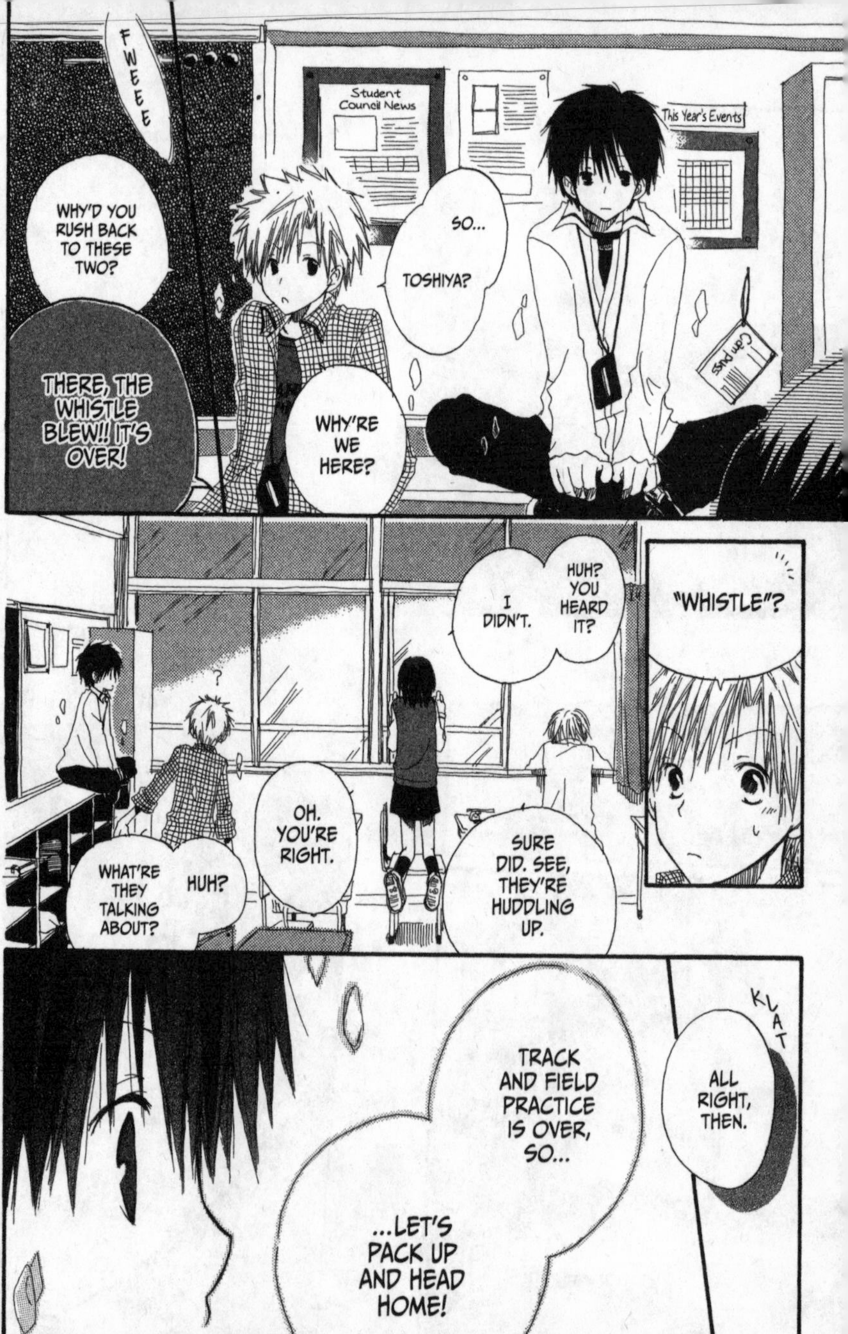
This Year's Events
Campus
SO... TOSHIYA?
Student Council News
WHY'RE WE HERE?
FWEEE
WHY'D YOU RUSH BACK TO THESE TWO?
THERE, THE WHISTLE BLEW!! IT'S OVER!
"WHISTLE"?
HUH? YOU HEARD IT?
I DIDN'T.
SURE DID. SEE, THEY'RE HUDDLING UP.
OH. YOU'RE RIGHT.
HUH?
WHAT'RE THEY TALKING ABOUT?
KVAT
ALL RIGHT, THEN.
TRACK AND FIELD PRACTICE IS OVER, SO...
...LET'S PACK UP AND HEAD HOME!

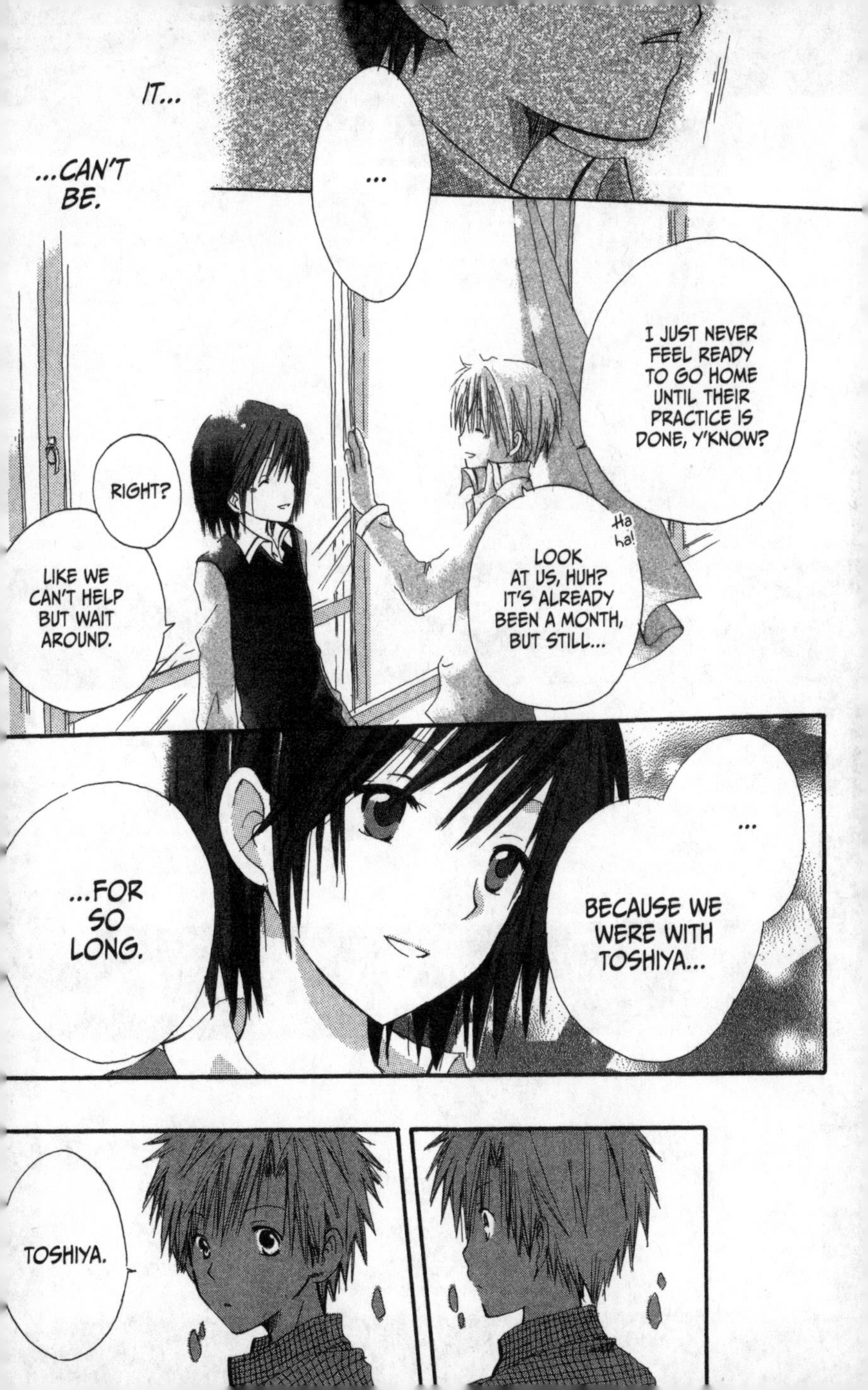
...
IT...
...CAN'T BE.
I JUST NEVER FEEL READY TO GO HOME UNTIL THEIR PRACTICE IS DONE, Y'KNOW?
Ha ha!
LOOK AT US, HUH? IT'S ALREADY BEEN A MONTH, BUT STILL...
RIGHT?
LIKE WE CAN'T HELP BUT WAIT AROUND.
...
BECAUSE WE WERE WITH TOSHIYA...
...FOR SO LONG.
TOSHIYA.

YOU WERE IN TRACK AND FIELD CLUB, I TAKE IT?
"IT CAN'T BE."
I THOUGHT, TO THEM, I WAS ALWAYS...
"I THOUGHT."
I'VE GOT MY CLUB PRACTICE, SO I GUESS WE CAN'T WALK HOME TOGETHER ANYMORE.
OH, KNOCK IT OFF.
WE'LL WAIT FOR YOU.
I WAS ALWAYS IN THE WAY.
AH, HERE HE COMES.
GOOD WORK OUT THERE!
WE GOT YOU A DRINK!

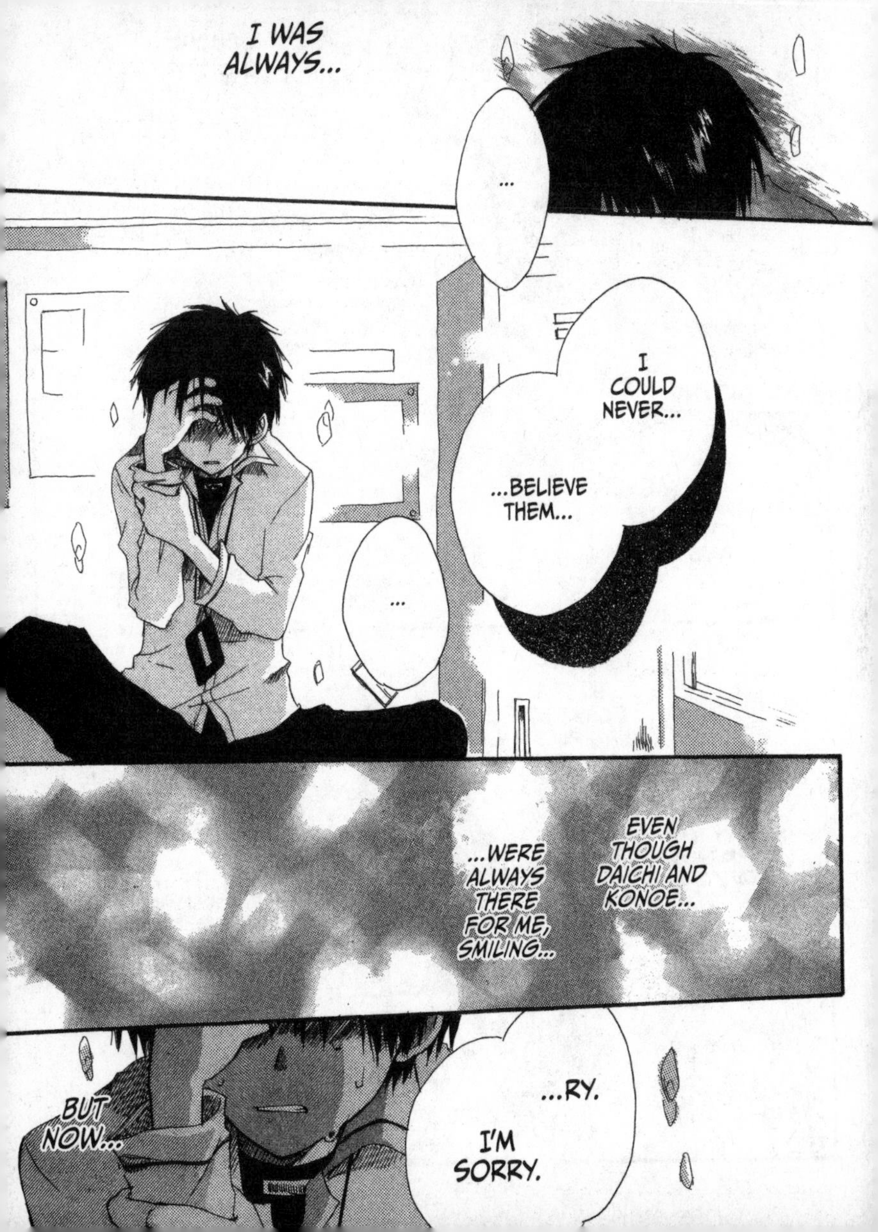
I WAS ALWAYS...
...
I COULD NEVER...
...BELIEVE THEM...
...
EVEN THOUGH DAICHI AND KONOE...
...WERE ALWAYS THERE FOR ME, SMILING...
...RY.
I'M SORRY.
BUT NOW...

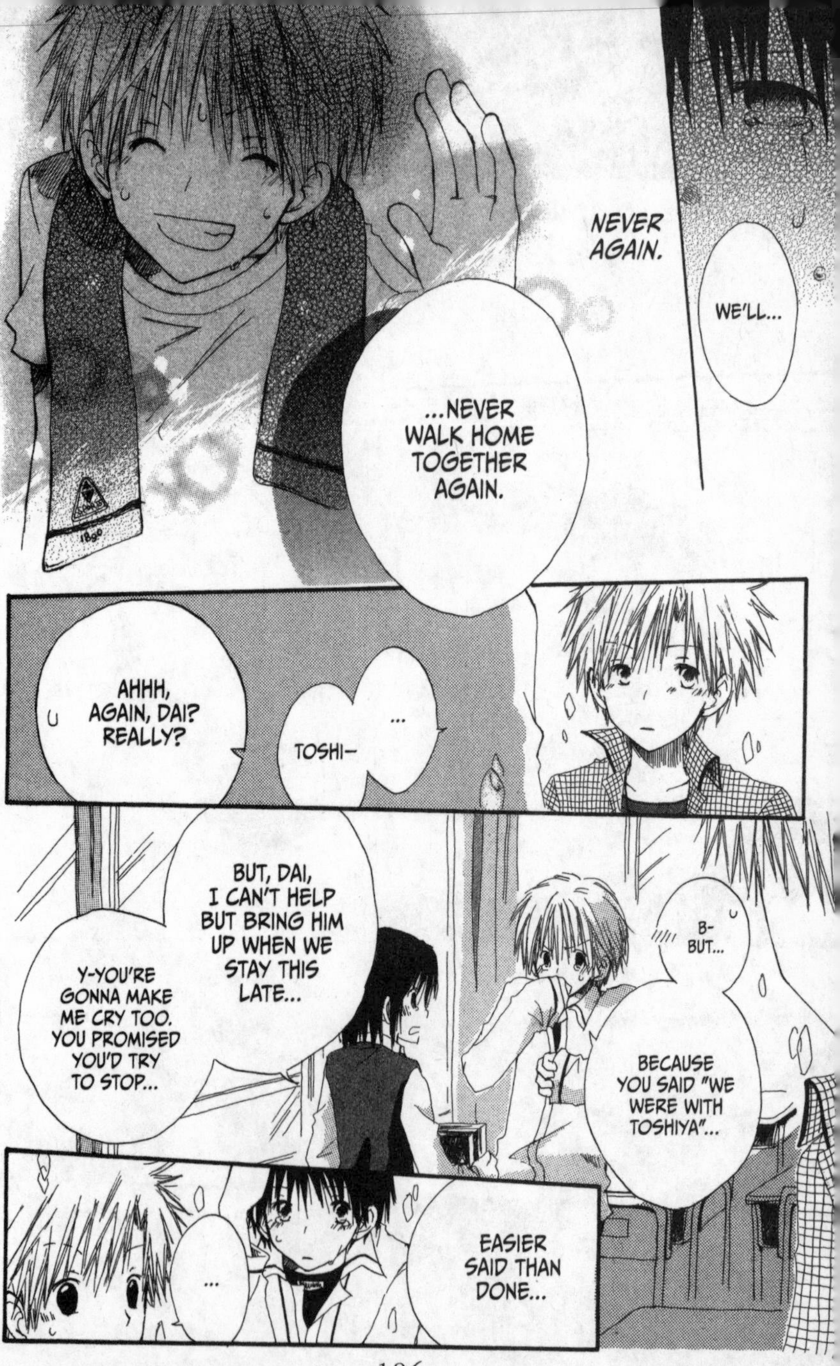
NEVER AGAIN.
WE'LL...
...NEVER WALK HOME TOGETHER AGAIN.
...
TOSHI–
AHHH, AGAIN, DAI? REALLY?
B-BUT...
BECAUSE YOU SAID "WE WERE WITH TOSHIYA"...
BUT, DAI, I CAN'T HELP BUT BRING HIM UP WHEN WE STAY THIS LATE...
Y-YOU'RE GONNA MAKE ME CRY TOO. YOU PROMISED YOU'D TRY TO STOP...
EASIER SAID THAN DONE...
...

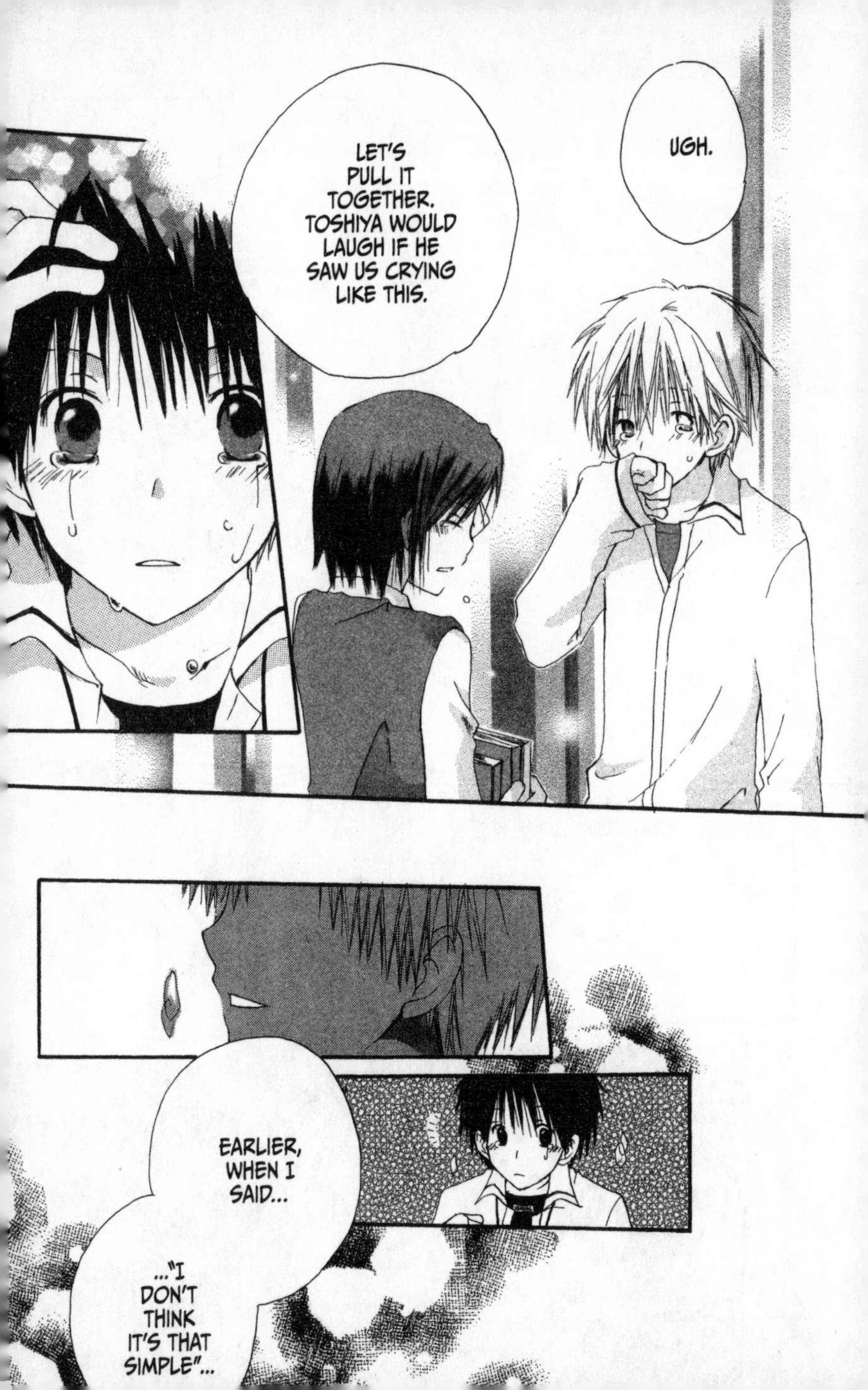
UGH.
LET'S PULL IT TOGETHER. TOSHIYA WOULD LAUGH IF HE SAW US CRYING LIKE THIS.
EARLIER, WHEN I SAID...
..."I DON'T THINK IT'S THAT SIMPLE"...

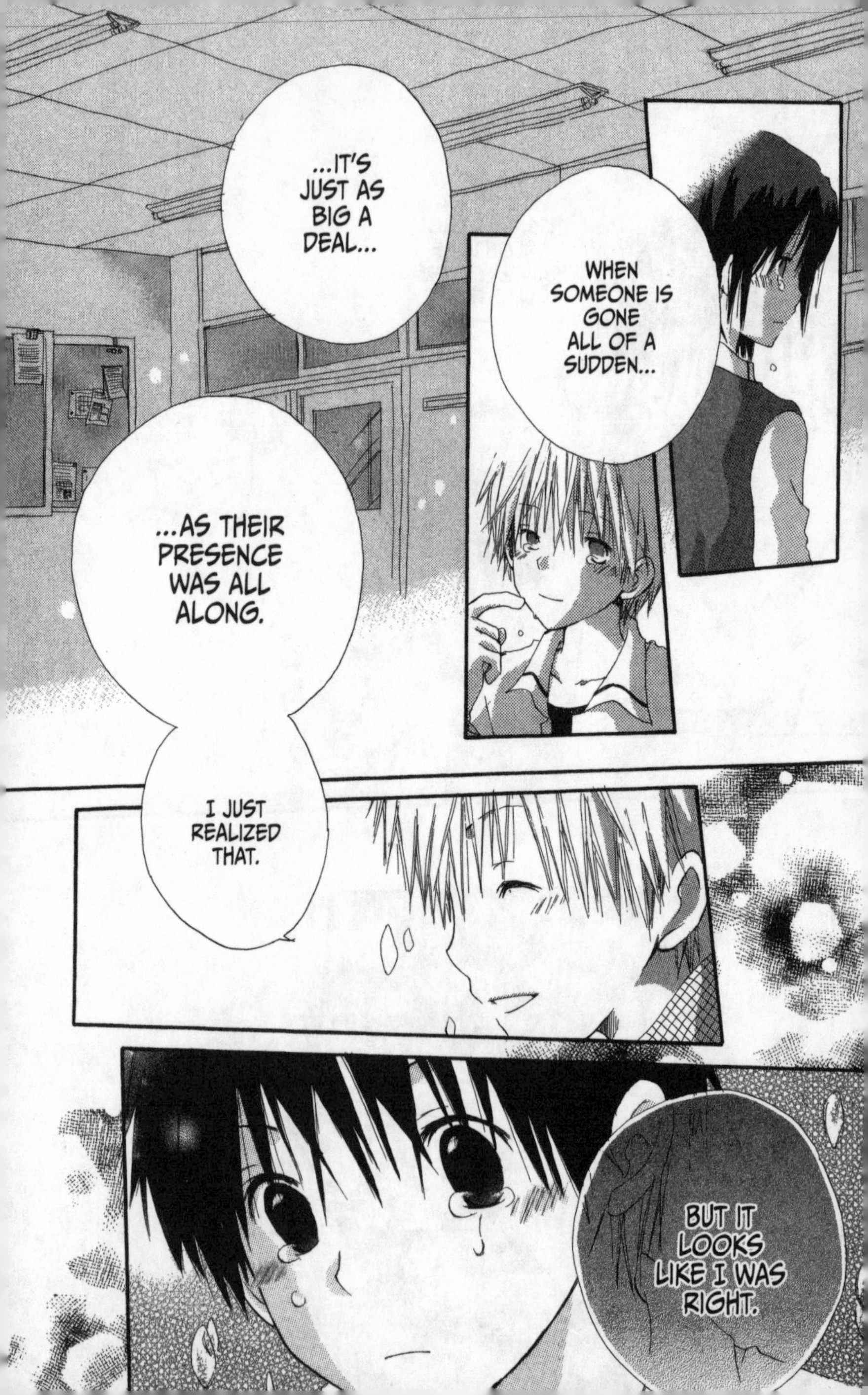
WHEN SOMEONE IS GONE ALL OF A SUDDEN...
...IT'S JUST AS BIG A DEAL...
...AS THEIR PRESENCE WAS ALL ALONG.
I JUST REALIZED THAT.
BUT IT LOOKS LIKE I WAS RIGHT.

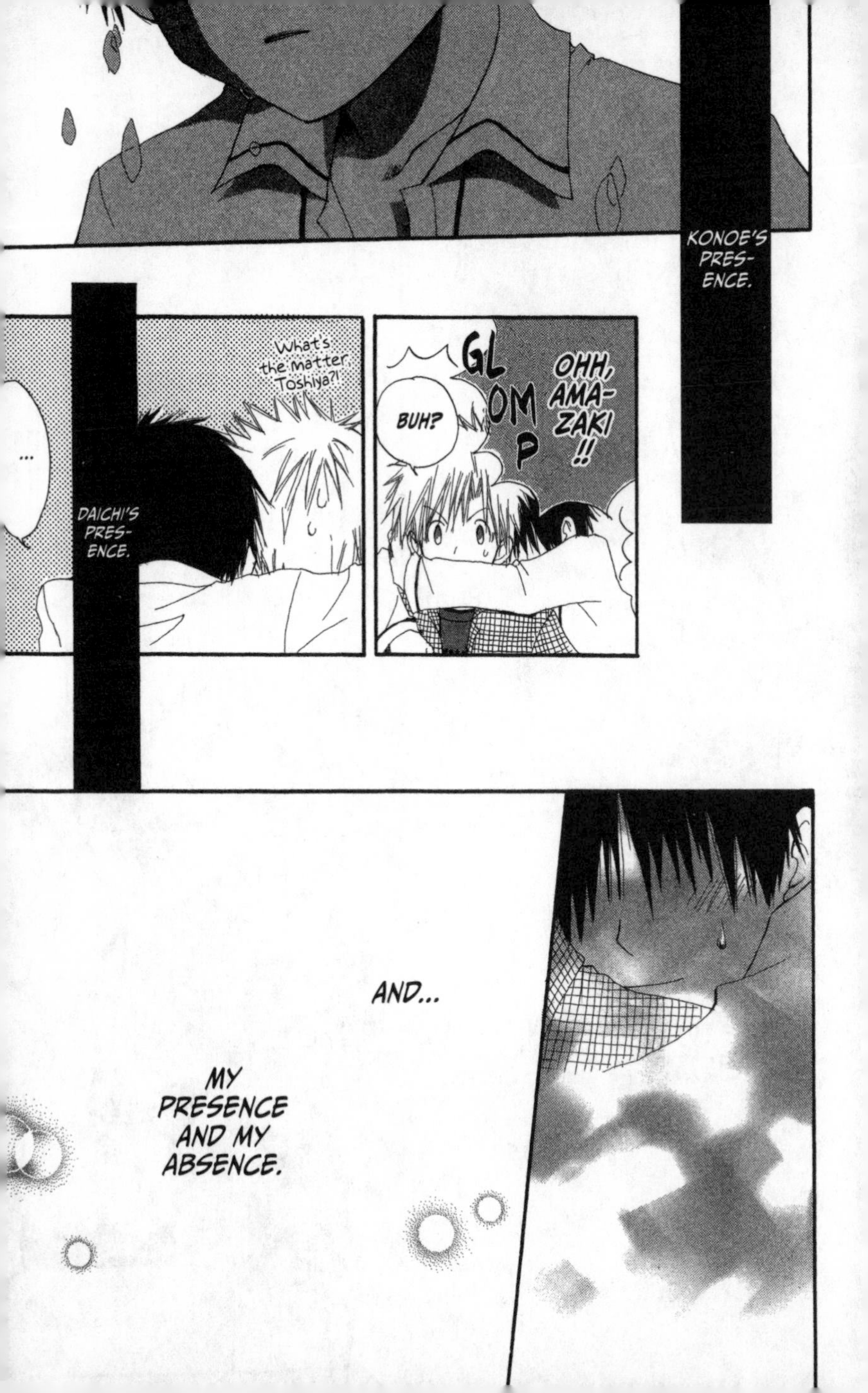
KONOE'S PRES-ENCE.
OHH, AMAZAKI!!
GLOMP
BUH?
What's the matter, Toshiya?!
DAICHI'S PRES-ENCE.
...
AND...
MY PRESENCE AND MY ABSENCE.

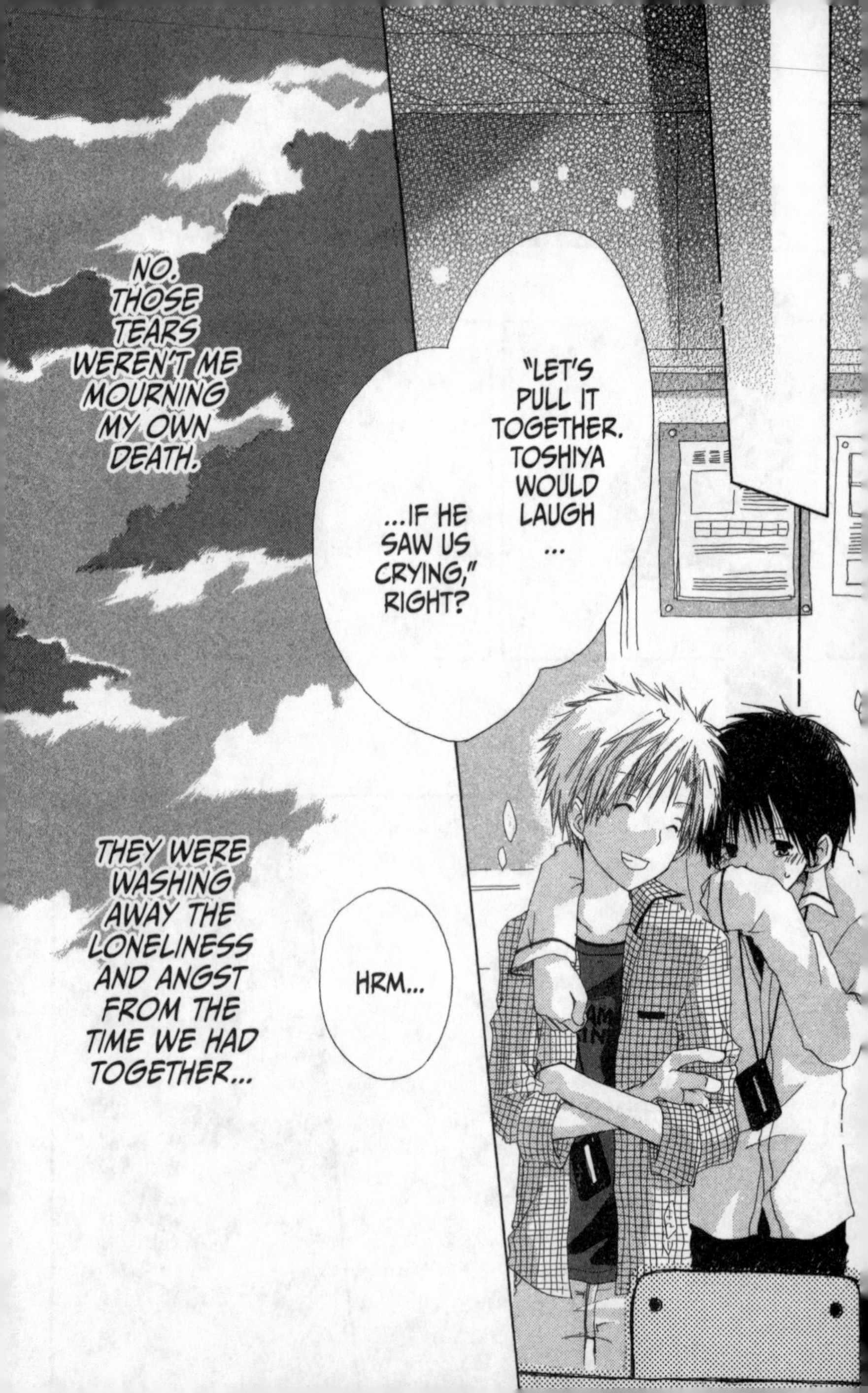
"LET'S PULL IT TOGETHER. TOSHIYA WOULD LAUGH...
...IF HE SAW US CRYING," RIGHT?
HRM...
NO. THOSE TEARS WEREN'T ME MOURNING MY OWN DEATH.
THEY WERE WASHING AWAY THE LONELINESS AND ANGST FROM THE TIME WE HAD TOGETHER...

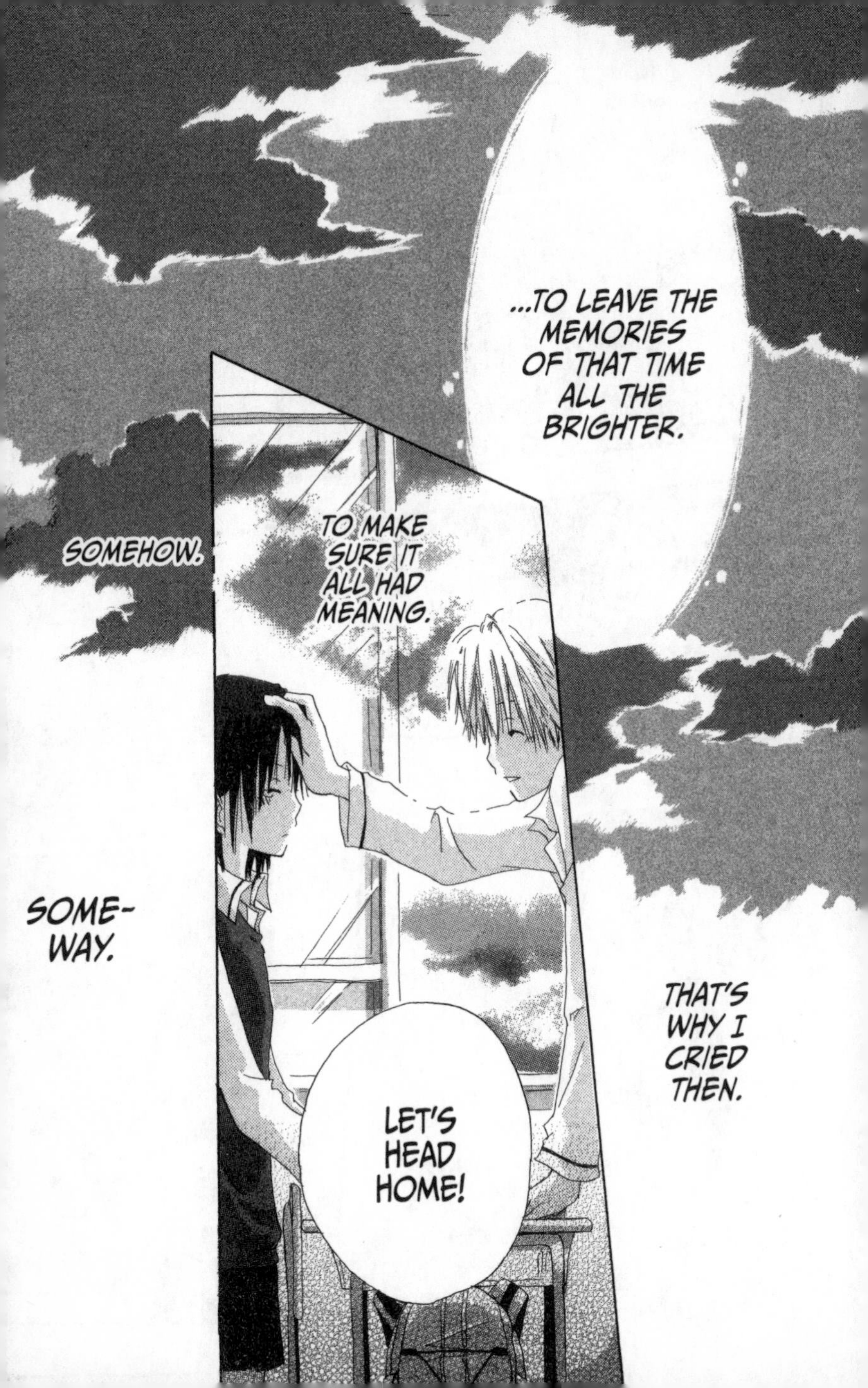
...TO LEAVE THE MEMORIES OF THAT TIME ALL THE BRIGHTER.
TO MAKE SURE IT ALL HAD MEANING.
SOMEHOW.
SOME-WAY.
THAT'S WHY I CRIED THEN.
LET'S HEAD HOME!

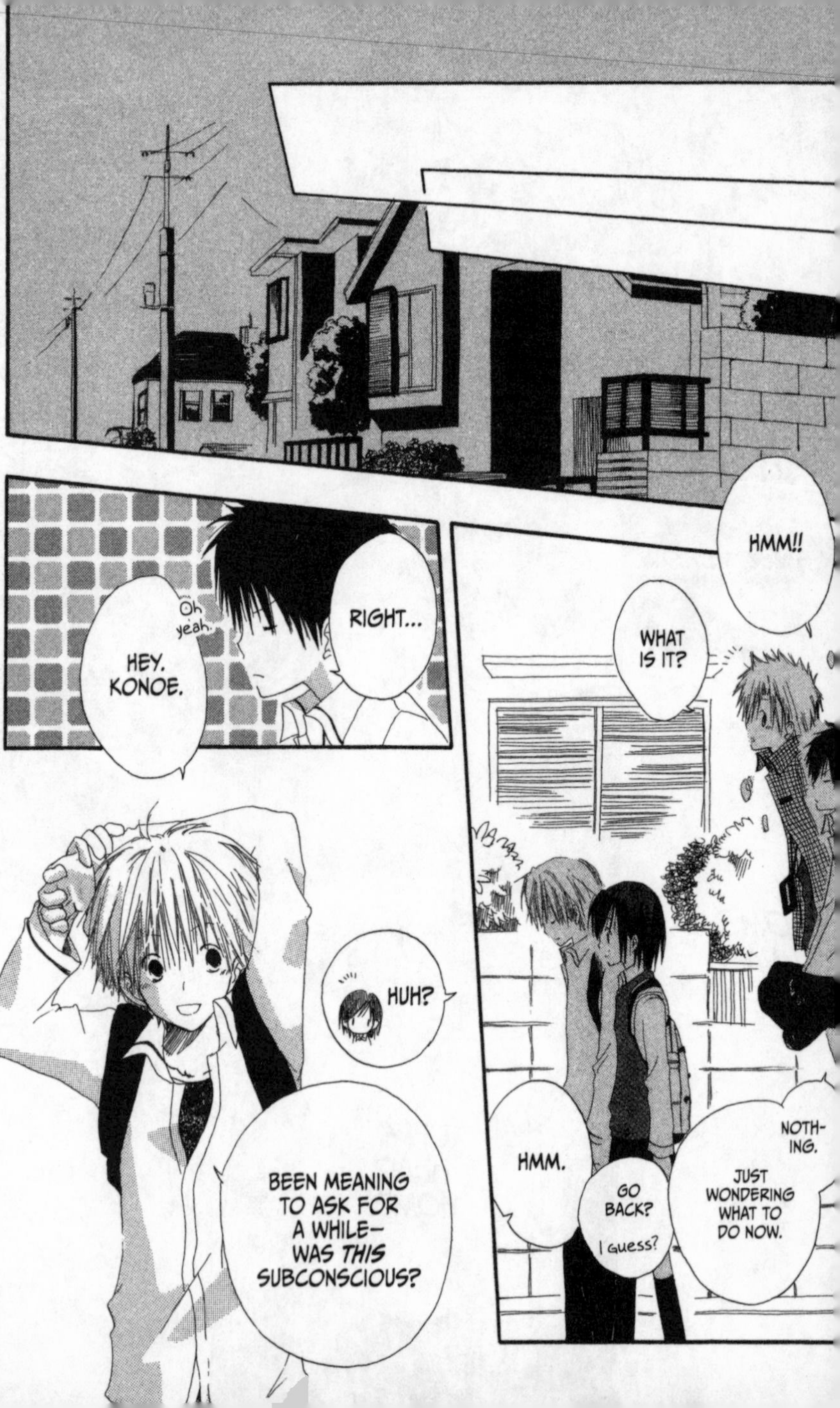
HMM!!
WHAT IS IT?
NOTHING. JUST WONDERING WHAT TO DO NOW.
GO BACK?
I guess?
HMM.
RIGHT...
Oh yeah.
HEY. KONOE.
HUH?
BEEN MEANING TO ASK FOR A WHILE—WAS *THIS* SUBCONSCIOUS?

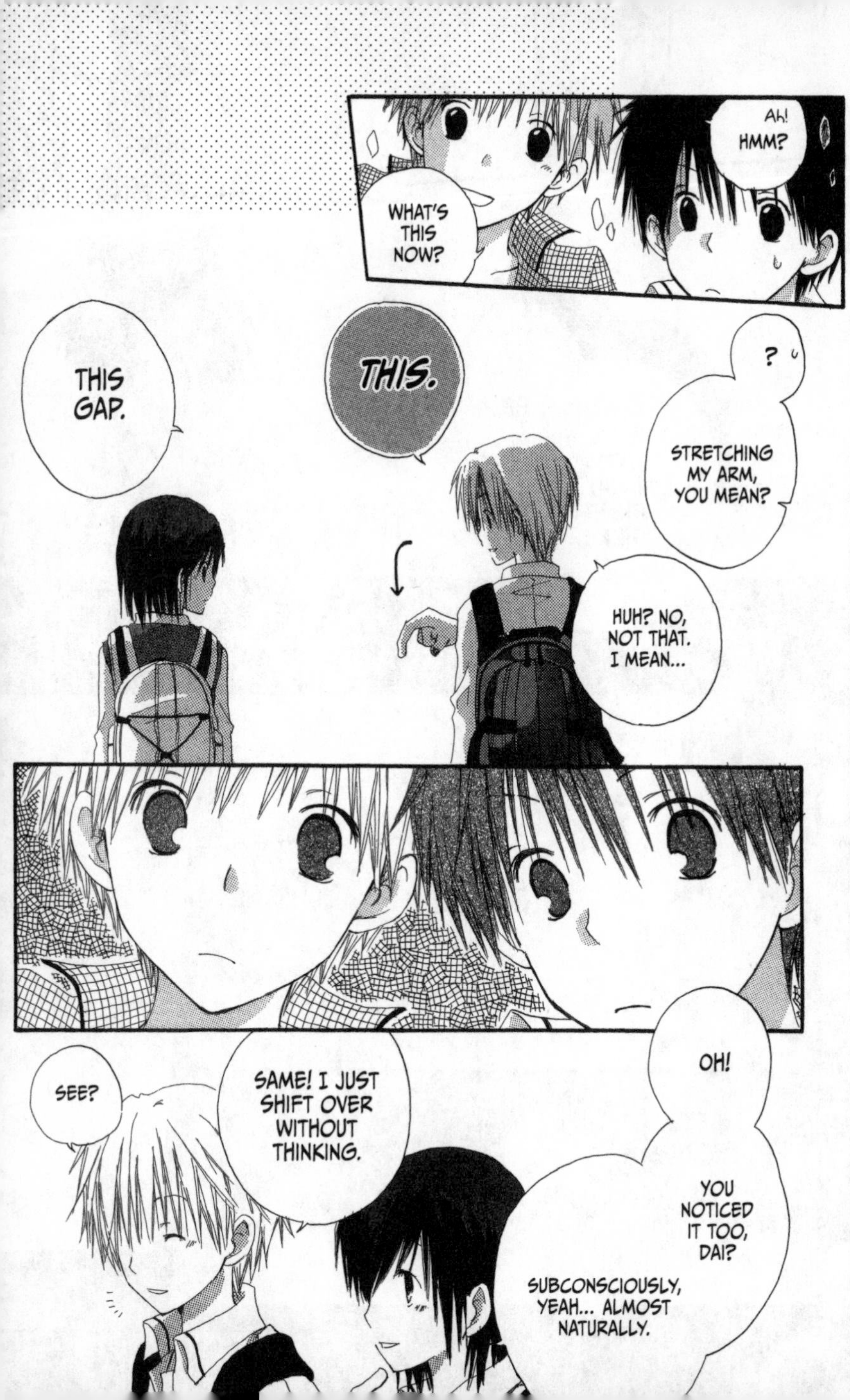
AH! HMM?
WHAT'S THIS NOW?
?
STRETCHING MY ARM, YOU MEAN?
HUH? NO, NOT THAT. I MEAN...
THIS.
THIS GAP.
OH!
YOU NOTICED IT TOO, DAI?
SUBCONSCIOUSLY, YEAH... ALMOST NATURALLY.
SAME! I JUST SHIFT OVER WITHOUT THINKING.
SEE?

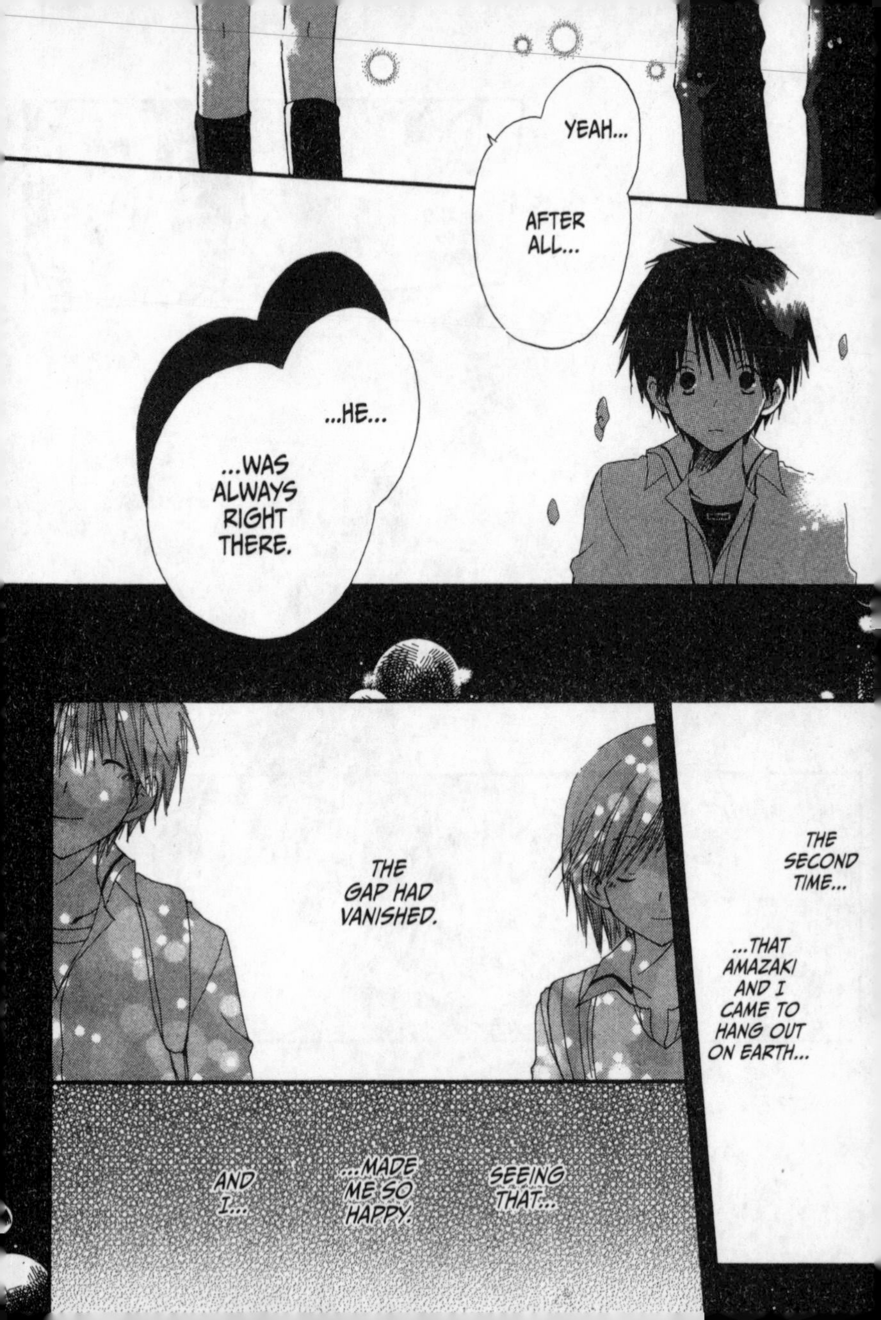
YEAH...
AFTER ALL...
...HE...
...WAS ALWAYS RIGHT THERE.
THE SECOND TIME...
...THAT AMAZAKI AND I CAME TO HANG OUT ON EARTH...
THE GAP HAD VANISHED.
SEEING THAT...
...MADE ME SO HAPPY.
AND I...

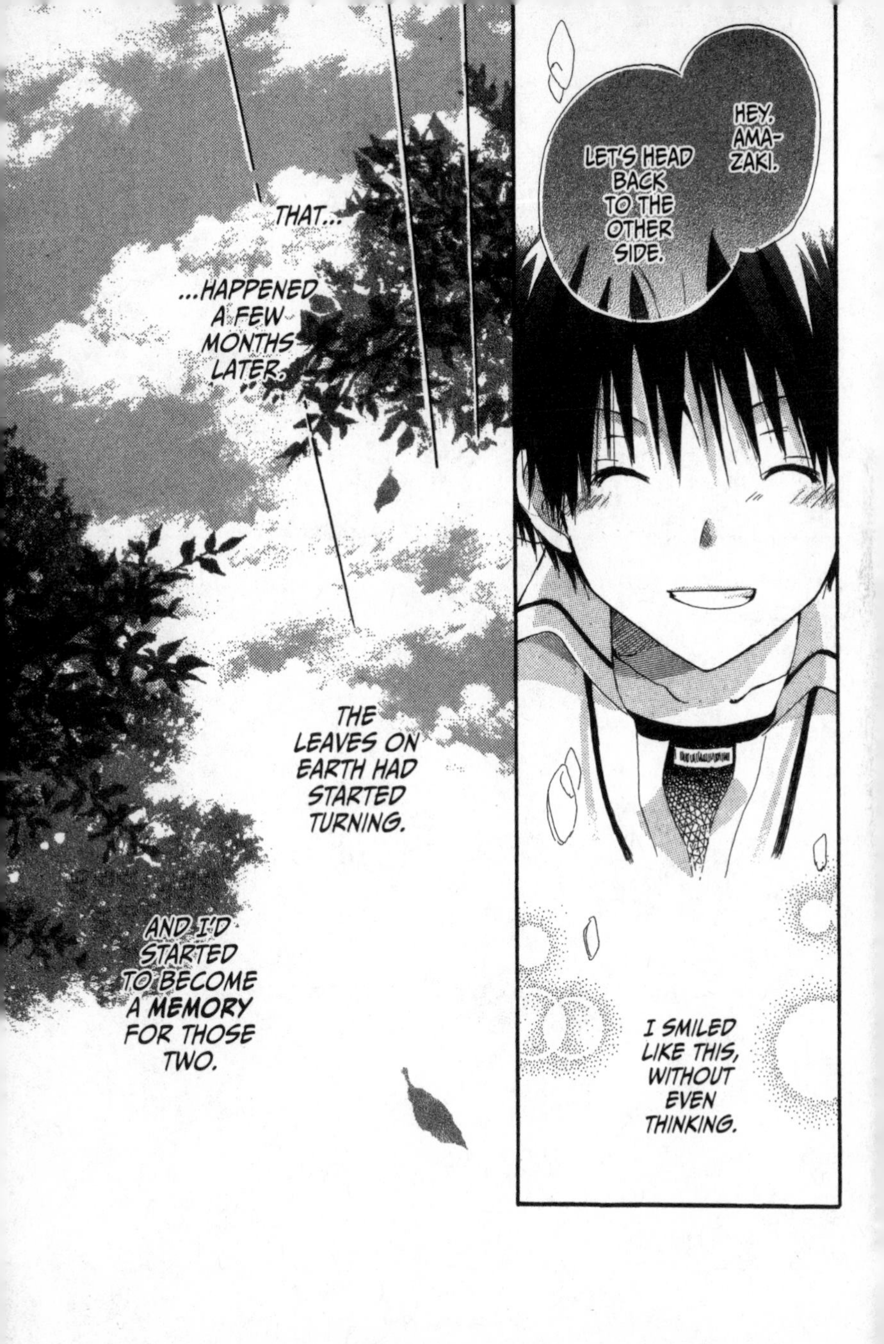
HEY. AMA-ZAKI.
LET'S HEAD BACK TO THE OTHER SIDE.
I SMILED LIKE THIS, WITHOUT EVEN THINKING.
THAT...
...HAPPENED A FEW MONTHS LATER.
THE LEAVES ON EARTH HAD STARTED TURNING.
AND I'D STARTED TO BECOME A MEMORY FOR THOSE TWO.

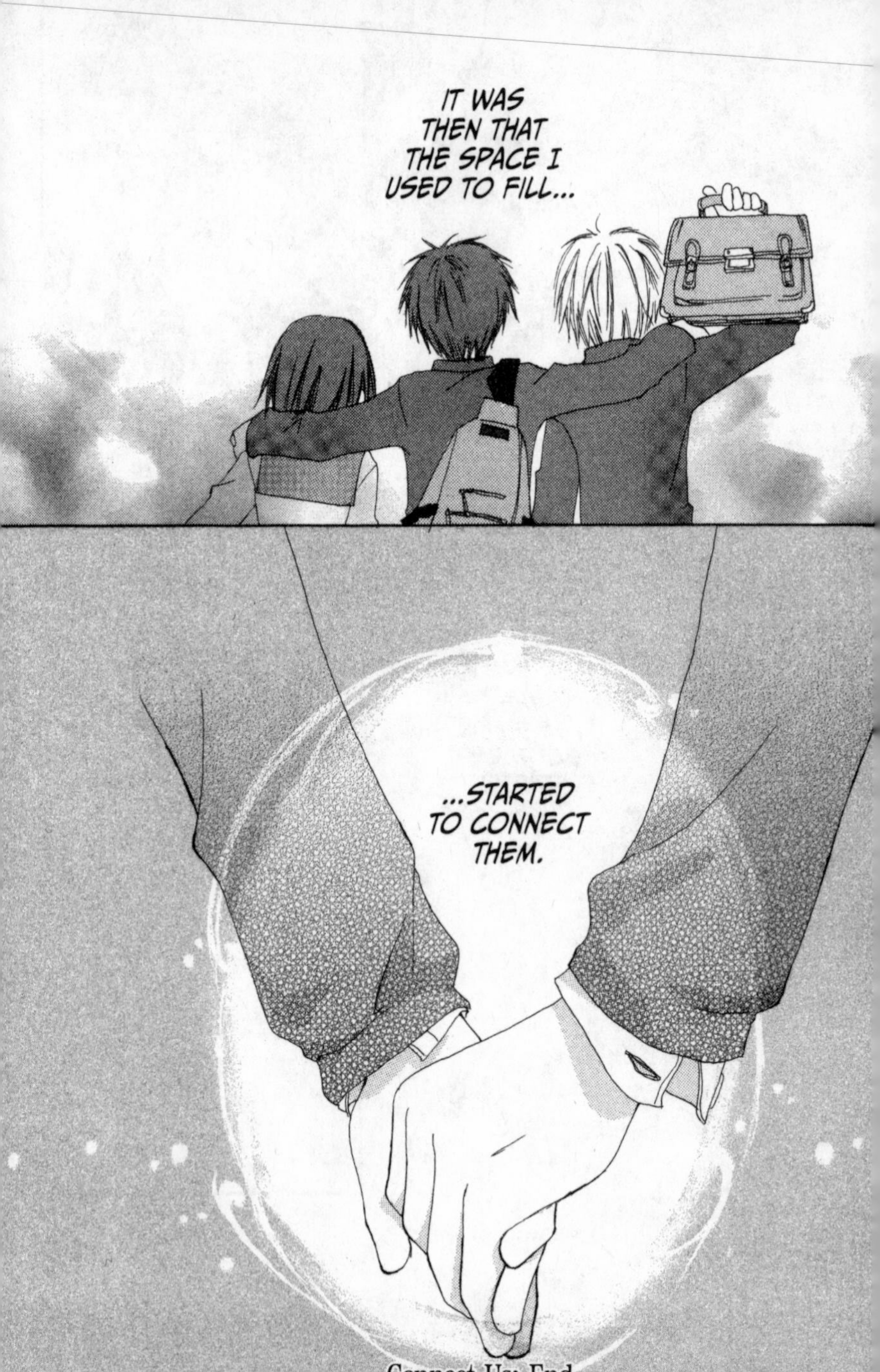
IT WAS THEN THAT THE SPACE I USED TO FILL...
...STARTED TO CONNECT THEM.

Connect Us: End

Bonus Pages

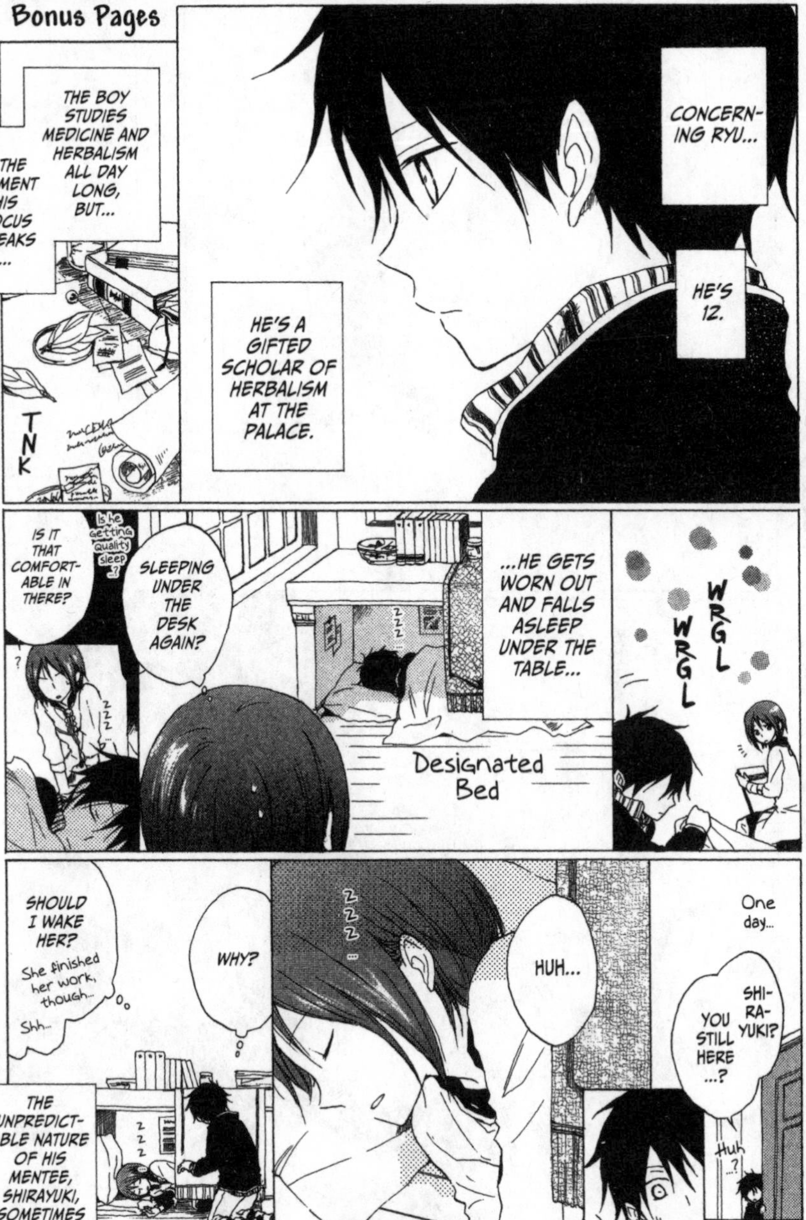
CONCERNING RYU...
HE'S 12.
HE'S A GIFTED SCHOLAR OF HERBALISM AT THE PALACE.
THE BOY STUDIES MEDICINE AND HERBALISM ALL DAY LONG, BUT...
...THE MOMENT HIS FOCUS BREAKS...
TNK
WRGL
WRGL
...HE GETS WORN OUT AND FALLS ASLEEP UNDER THE TABLE...
Designated Bed
SLEEPING UNDER THE DESK AGAIN?
Is he getting quality sleep...?
IS IT THAT COMFORTABLE IN THERE?
One day...
SHIRAYUKI?
YOU STILL HERE...?
Huh...?
HUH...
WHY?
SHOULD I WAKE HER?
She finished her work, though...
Shh...
THE UNPREDICTABLE NATURE OF HIS MENTEE, SHIRAYUKI, SOMETIMES CONFUSES HIM.
Tested it out and fell asleep

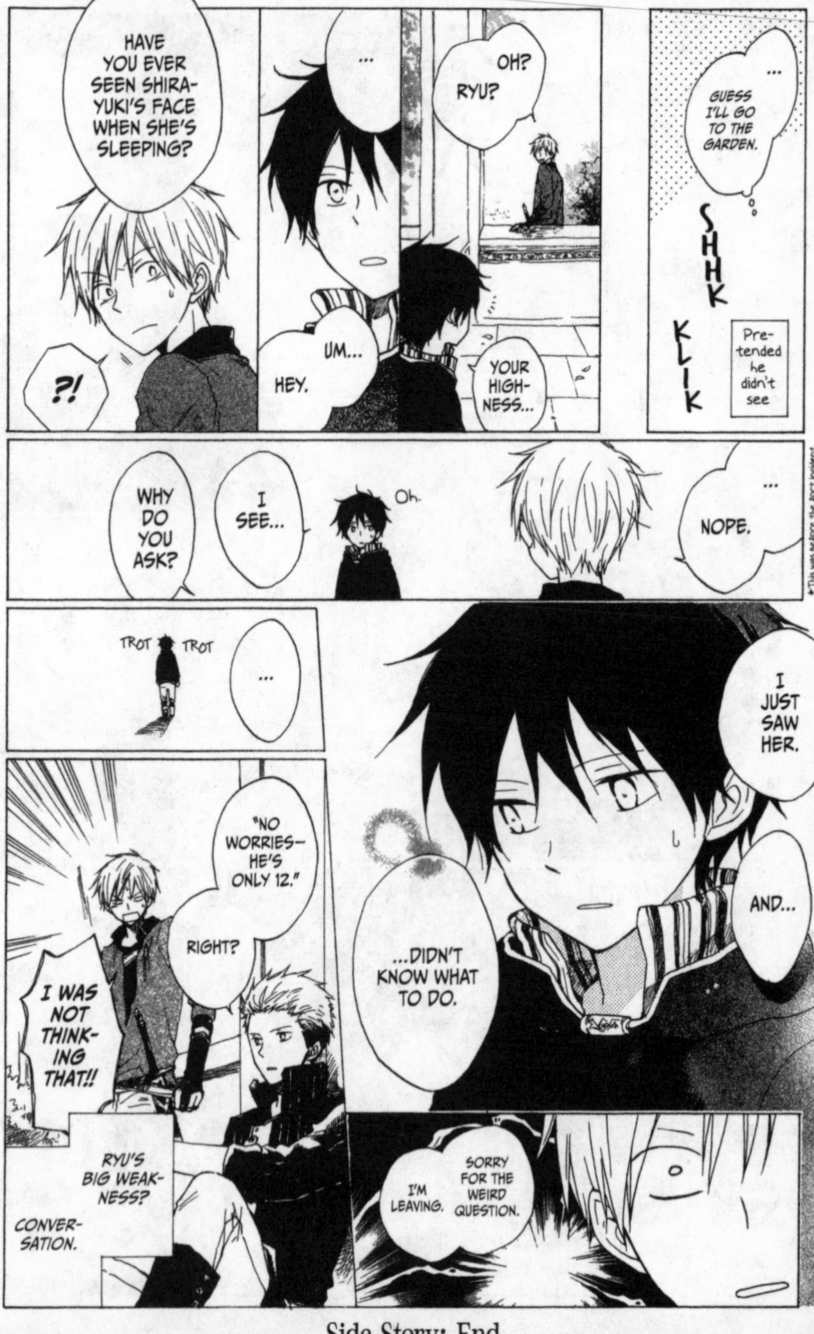
...
GUESS I'LL GO TO THE GARDEN.
SHHK
KLIK
Pre-tended he didn't see
OH?
RYU?
YOUR HIGHNESS...
...
UM...
HEY.
HAVE YOU EVER SEEN SHIRA-YUKI'S FACE WHEN SHE'S SLEEPING?
?!
*This was before the fort incident
...
NOPE.
Oh.
I SEE...
WHY DO YOU ASK?
I JUST SAW HER.
AND...
...DIDN'T KNOW WHAT TO DO.
TROT TROT
...
"NO WORRIES—HE'S ONLY 12."
RIGHT?
I WAS NOT THINKING THAT!!
SORRY FOR THE WEIRD QUESTION.
I'M LEAVING.
RYU'S BIG WEAKNESS?
CONVERSATION.

Side Story: End

Sorata Akiduki was born on March 21 and is an accomplished shojo manga author. She made her debut in January 2002 with a one-shot titled "Utopia." Her previous works include *Vahlia no Hanamuko* (Vahlia's Bridegroom), *Seishun Kouryakubon* (Youth Strategy Guide) and *Natsu Yasumi Zero Zero Nichime* (00 Days of Summer Vacation). *Snow White with the Red Hair* began serialization in August 2006 in *LaLa DX* in Japan and has since moved to *LaLa*.

Snow White
with the Red Hair

2

SHOJO BEAT EDITION

STORY AND ART BY
Sorata Akiduki

TRANSLATION **Caleb Cook**
TOUCH-UP ART & LETTERING **Brandon Bovia**
DESIGN **Alice Lewis**
EDITOR **Marlene First**

Akagami no Shirayukihime by Sorata Akiduki
© Sorata Akiduki 2008
All rights reserved.
First published in Japan in 2008 by HAKUSENSHA, Inc., Tokyo.
English language translation rights arranged with HAKUSENSHA, Inc., Tokyo.

The stories, characters and incidents mentioned
in this publication are entirely fictional.

Printed in the U.S.A.

Published by VIZ Media, LLC
P.O. Box 77010
San Francisco, CA 94107

10 9 8 7 6 5 4 3
First printing, July 2019
Third printing, October 2021

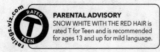

viz.com   shojobeat.com

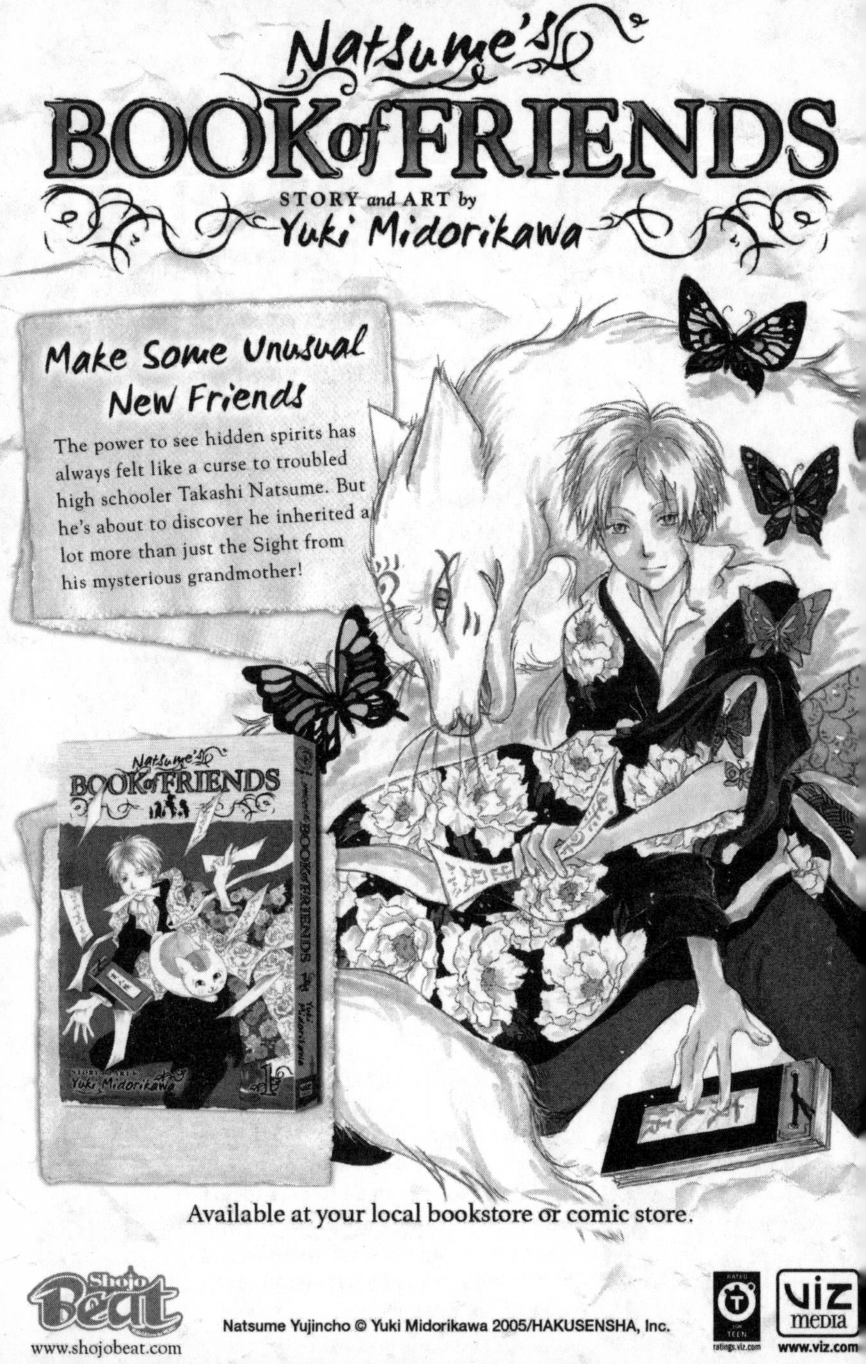
Natsume's
BOOK of FRIENDS
STORY and ART by
Yuki Midorikawa
Make Some Unusual New Friends
The power to see hidden spirits has always felt like a curse to troubled high schooler Takashi Natsume. But he's about to discover he inherited a lot more than just the Sight from his mysterious grandmother!
Natsume's BOOK of FRIENDS
Yuki Midorikawa
Available at your local bookstore or comic store.
Shojo Beat
www.shojobeat.com
Natsume Yujincho © Yuki Midorikawa 2005/HAKUSENSHA, Inc.
RATED T FOR TEEN
ratings.viz.com
viz media
www.viz.com

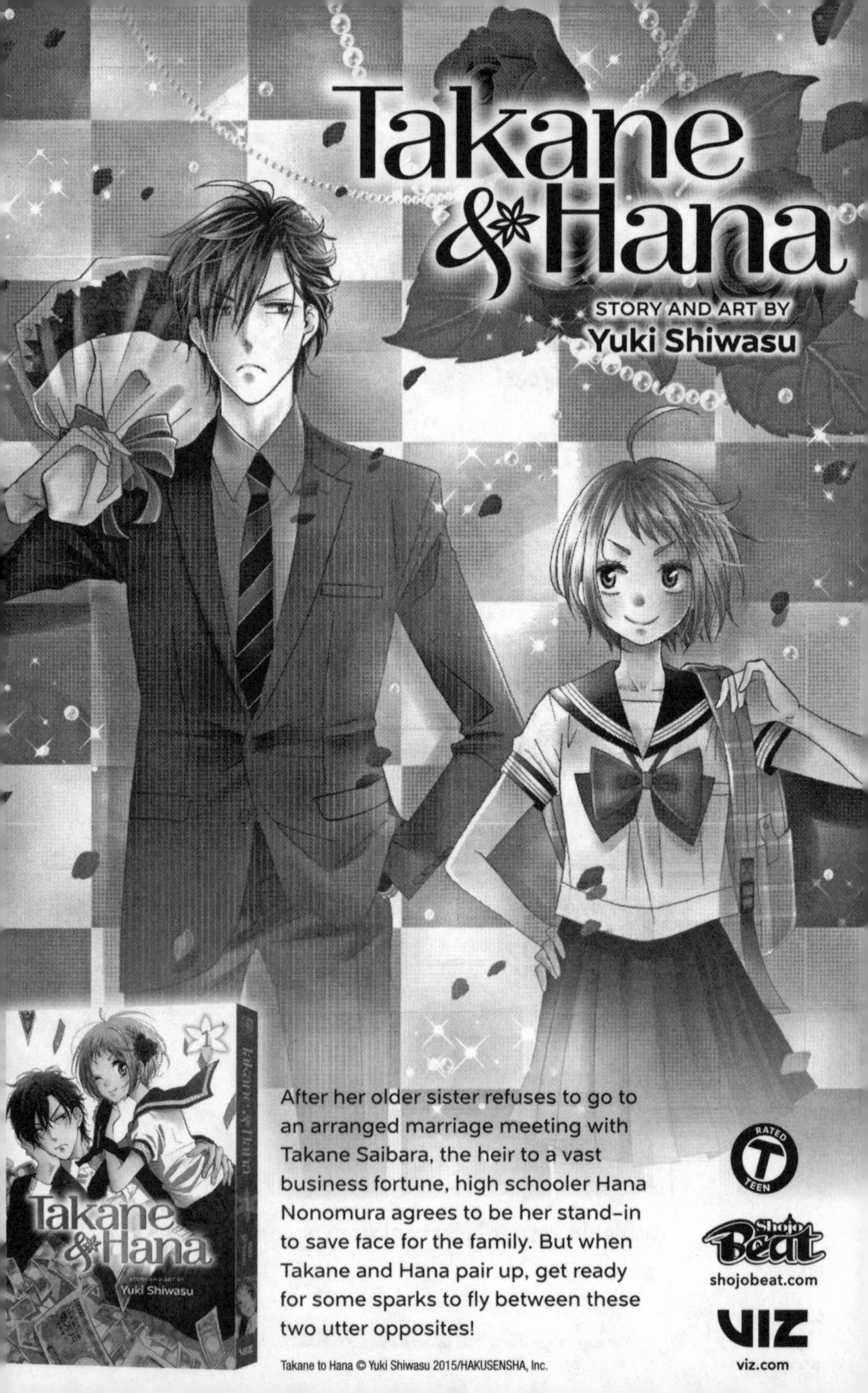
Takane & Hana
STORY AND ART BY
Yuki Shiwasu
After her older sister refuses to go to an arranged marriage meeting with Takane Saibara, the heir to a vast business fortune, high schooler Hana Nonomura agrees to be her stand-in to save face for the family. But when Takane and Hana pair up, get ready for some sparks to fly between these two utter opposites!
RATED T TEEN
Shojo Beat
shojobeat.com
VIZ
viz.com
Takane to Hana © Yuki Shiwasu 2015/HAKUSENSHA, Inc.

Behind the Scenes!!

STORY AND ART BY BISCO HATORI

From the creator of Ouran High School Host Club

Ranmaru Kurisu comes from a family of hardy, rough-and-tumble fisherfolk and he sticks out at home like a delicate, artistic sore thumb. It's given him a raging inferiority complex and a permanently pessimistic outlook. Now that he's in college, he's hoping to find a sense of belonging. But after a whole life of being left out, does he even know how to fit in?!

Beautiful boy rebels using their fists to fall in love!

KENKA BANCHO
Otome
LOVE'S BATTLE ROYALE

FERVEN

STORY & ART BY **CHIE SHIMADA**

Based on the game created by Spike Chunsoft

Hinako thought she didn't have any family, but on the day she starts high school, her twin brother Hikaru suddenly appears and tricks her into taking his place. But the new school Hinako attends in his stead is beyond unusual. Now she must fight her way to the top of Shishiku Academy, an all-boys school of delinquents!

VIZ

YOU'RE READING THE WRONG WAY!

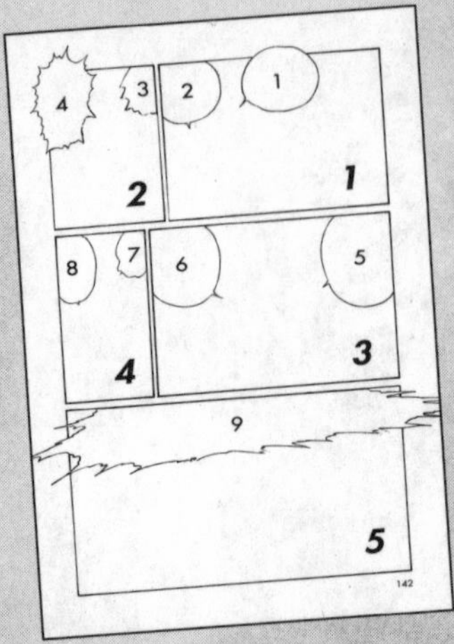
1
2
3
4
5
6
7
8
9
1
2
3
4
5
142

Snow White with the Red Hair reads from right to left, starting in the upper-right corner. Japanese is read from right to left, meaning that action, sound effects and word-balloon order are completely reversed from English order.

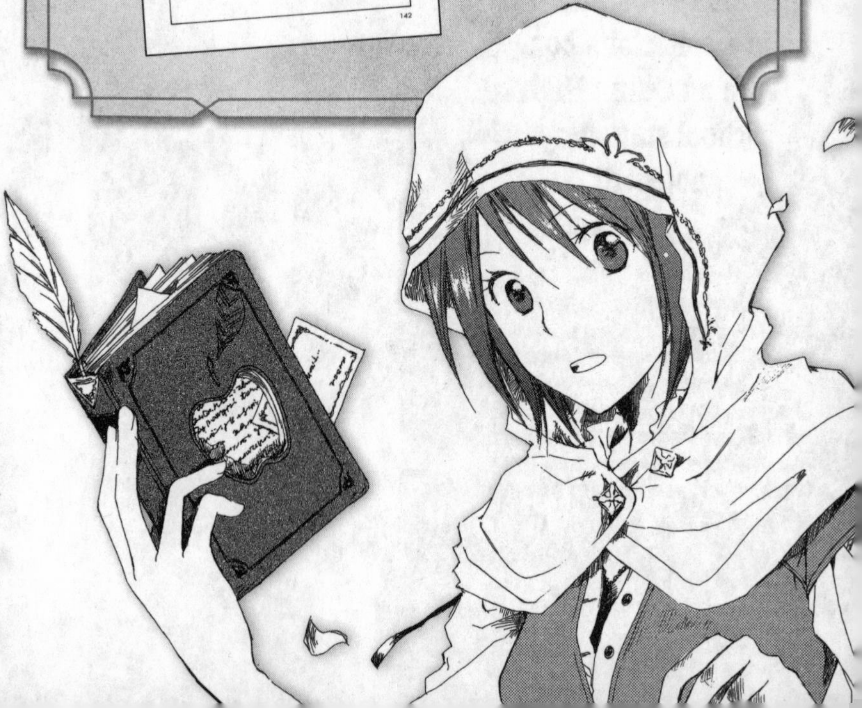